Health & Social Care

Angela Fisher • Stephen Seamons • Carol Blackmore • Marjorie Snaith

OCR
National Level 2

www.heinemann.co.uk

✓ Free online support
✓ Useful weblinks
✓ 24 hour online ordering

01865 888058

Heinemann

Inspiring generations

Heinemann Educational Publishers
Halley Court, Jordan Hill, Oxford OX2 8EJ
Part of Harcourt Education

Heinemann is the registered trademark of
Harcourt Education Limited

Text © Angela Fisher, Carol Blackmore, Marjorie Snaith, Stephen Seamons

First published 2005

10 09 08 07
10 9 8 7 6 5 4

British Library Cataloguing in Publication Data is available
from the British Library on request.

ISBN: 978 0 435 45295 7

Photo acknowledgements
Page 1: Richard Smith; **page 9:** Richard Smith; **page 18:** Richard Smith; **page 19:** Richard Smith; **page 23:** Corbis; **page 25:** Empics; **page 39:** Richard Smith; **page 42:** Getty Images/Photodisc; **page 43:** Alamy; **page 53:** Jules Selmes, Alamy; **page 55:** (both) Richard Smith; **page 60:** Corbis/Bettmann; **page 64:** Richard Smith; **page 72:** Richard Smith; **page 99:** Richard Smith; **page 107:** Richard Smith; **page 109:** Sally and Richard Greenhill; **page 112:** Richard Smith; **page 118:** Richard Smith; **page 134:** Richard Smith; **page 135:** Ginny Stroud-Lewis; **page 141:** Richard Smith; **page 146:** Alamy Images/Janine Wiedel Photolibrary; **page 154:** Science Photo Library/Kent Wood; **page 163:** Ginny Stroud-Lewis; **page 168:** Ginny Stroud-Lewis; **page 171:** Richard Smith; **page 177:** Ginny Stroud-Lewis; **page 180:** Corbis/Phil Banko; **page 183:** Sally and Richard Greenhill; **page 186:** Corbis/Ariel Skelley; **page 192:** Alamy Images/Wolfgang Pölzer; **page 194:** Mother and Baby Photograph Library; **page 202:** Mother and Baby Photograph Library; **page 212:** Getty Images/Digital Vision; **page 213:** Sally and Richard Greenhill; **page 216:** Mother and Baby Photograph Library; **page 224:** Corbis; **page 229:** Alamy Images/Elizabeth Whiting & Associates; **page 231:** Sally and Richard Greenhill; **page 233:** Bubbles; **page 235:** Getty Images/Photodisc; **page 246:** Alamy Images/Sally and Richard Greenhill; **page 256:** Richard Smith; **page 270:** Sally and Richard Greenhill; **page 275:** Corbis; **page 276:** Sally and Richard Greenhill; **page 279:** Corbis/Chuck Savage; **page 283:** Ginny Stroud-Lewis; **page 289:** Food Features; **page 290:** Richard Smith; **page 319:** Sally and Richard Greenhill; **page 325:** Richard Smith; **page 327:** Alamy; **page 336:** (both) Richard Smith; **page 340:** Richard Smith; **page 341:** Shout; **page 343:** Mediscan; **page 348:** Corbis; **page 352:** Richard Smith.

Photo Research by Ginny Stroud-Lewis

Edited by Humphrey Gudgeon
Index compiled by Diana Boatman
Typeset and illustrated by Tech Set Ltd

Original illustrations © Harcourt Education Limited 2005

Printed in Hong Kong
Cover photo: © Getty Images

Contents

Unit 8 Preparing to work with young children

Unit 9 Preparing to work with older service users

Unit 15 Work experience in health and social care settings

Index

Introduction

This book is designed to give support for students wishing to gain the *Level 2 OCR Nationals in Health and Social Care*. It aims to provide a guide for the teaching of the knowledge, understanding and skills that you will need to complete a course of study.

At *Level 2 OCR Nationals in Health and Social Care* there are **four** mandatory units:

1 Preparing to give quality care
2 Communicating with service users in care settings
3 Practical caring
4 Hygiene and safety in care settings

These are units which **must** be covered in order to achieve the award. You also need to consider which **optional** units will best help you to work towards a career of your choice. What you must remember is that you have to complete **two** optional units in order to gain full certification. The **optional units** included in this book are:

7 Development and care of young children
8 Preparing to work with young children
9 Preparing to work with older service users
15 Work experience in health and social care settings

It is very important that you complete **six** units in order to achieve the full award.

Features of the book

Throughout the book there are a number of features that relate theory to practice in health, social care and early years context. These are:

What will we learn in this unit?
A list of the knowledge that you will need to have covered.

Discussion points
Providing thoughts in the form of questions that will help you to understand how to apply the knowledge.

Activities
Examples of questions that can be used to check that you have learnt and understood the topics included in a particular section.

Case studies
Examples of 'live' situations that have been found in the world of health, social care and early years which will enable you to see how some theories are applied and, in other cases, how they are not applied.

Assessment activities
These are activities that need to be completed in order to produce the relevant material for the portfolio evidence required for assessment.

Assessment
The assessment for all portfolio units will be made by your tutor. Portfolio evidence will be graded by using the AO (Assessment Objectives) and the **grading criteria.** Whether you achieve a **Pass, Merit or Distinction** will depend on how well your work matches one of these grading criteria. An External Visiting Moderator will visit your Centre to check that the correct grades have been awarded for the work you have completed.

A range of experienced professionals have contributed their experience to this book in order to provide you with knowledge from the occupational sector that will equip you to develop your particular interest in the units.

We hope you will enjoy your *OCR Nationals in Health and Social Care* and wish you good luck and every success in achieving your qualification and in your future work or study.

Angela Fisher

Unit 1 Preparing to give quality care

All of us should have equal access to quality care

Care workers are expected to carry out their tasks to the highest possible standard when working in care settings. This is what is meant by the term **quality care**.

All care **providers** are required to implement standards set by government and regulatory bodies. Care workers have a responsibility to make sure these standards are applied in the care setting in which they work. They also have to make sure that service users' best interests are the focus of all practical help provided and that a balance is achieved between service users' rights and the requirements of the **organisation**. Providing quality care involves care workers:

- knowing how well their care setting is meeting set standards
- being aware of service users' rights and making sure that they are not **infringed**
- knowing what is expected of them when carrying out their role, and recognising that they have a **duty of care** to **empower** service users
- knowing what contributes to quality care in care settings and how this is applied in practice.

The main focus of all care workers when they are carrying out their day-to-day tasks should be the promotion of equality, diversity, rights and the maintenance of **confidentiality**. It is important that individual care workers are aware of how to overcome their own **discriminatory** attitudes and to learn tolerance. They must also know how to challenge **discrimination** if and when it is shown in care settings.

Care workers need to value those for whom they care. They need to find ways of helping service users to be as independent as possible and should try not to control other people. They need to respect different lifestyles, attitudes and beliefs, not devaluing the service user if these are different from their own.

'Quality care' requires that service users are protected, helped to be in control of their lives and supported when their rights are infringed.

If you are going to work in a care setting or if you are an informal carer at any time in your life, it will be important to know what contributes to quality practice and how quality practice is implemented in care settings with service users and with others who are involved in their care.

What will we learn in this unit?

Learning outcomes

You will learn to:

- Illustrate how to support service users to maintain their rights
- Describe how service users' rights can be infringed and the responsibilities of care workers
- Recognise the diversity of service users and how to foster equality
- Recognise how to maintain confidentiality
- Review how legislation and policies help to maintain quality care
- Conduct a survey to investigate how a care setting maintains quality care

What rights do service users have?

The rights of service users are the same as those that we all have as far as health, social care and early years provision is concerned. Just because a person lives in a residential or nursing home, or because they go into hospital to receive treatment, it does not mean that they have fewer rights than anyone else. Part of providing quality care is to make sure that service users' rights are maintained. This means that care workers should not act in a way that prevents service users from exercising their rights. Care workers who are providing quality care should do their best to empower service users, that is, to let them manage their own lives and make their own decisions. Just because a person is frail and unable to look after themselves, or has ill health, it does not mean that they cannot exercise their rights. Some service users may need help to make sure their rights are maintained, but this is part of a care worker's 'duty of care' regardless of the care setting in which they work.

All care workers should have knowledge about the rights that service users have. They should also know how to make sure that those rights are respected when carrying out their day-to-day tasks. The following table lists the key rights that service users have.

The rights of service users	Examples of how these rights can be maintained
To have their own GP (General Practitioner)	Allowing choice after having given all the options available
To choice	Giving service users the chance to make decisions about what they will wear, what to have for lunch, when to go to bed
To confidentiality	Keeping personal information safe and not sharing it with people who are **unauthorised**
To **protection**	Making sure security measures are in place both for service users and their property – so that they both feel and are safe
To equal and fair treatment	Providing the same **access** of care to all according to their needs
To **consultation**	Telling service users what the options for treatment or recreational activities are and asking for their opinions

The right to have their own GP

Just because a person lives in a residential home or nursing home it does not mean that they have to have the same GP as all the other residents. They can choose the GP that they would prefer to have. To be able to choose means that service users need to be given information about:

- which GPs are available
- how far they are from where the resident is now living
- which GPs are already visiting the residents.

Some service users will want to keep the GP that they had while living in their own home. If the service user has moved some distance from the area in which they lived, this may not be possible.

The right to choice

Service users can only make choices if they are given sufficient and **relevant** information about the topic or subject under discussion.

For example, in order to make a wise choice the service user in Figure 1.1 below needs to know:

- what the weather and temperature is like
- what activities they may be expected to participate in
- what clothes are available.

By making sure service users have information, care workers make it possible for them to make choices, to take control of their lives and to be empowered.

If service users have learning difficulties or conditions such as **dementia**, where they are unable to remember very much, they must still be allowed to make choices. An example of *not* allowing choice can be seen in Figure 1.2 on page 4.

This is taking away the service user's right to choice and is not a way to provide quality care.

Figure 1.1 *Offering the right to choice*

Don't bother asking Mavis what she wants to wear. She doesn't know what she's got on anyway

Figure 1.2 *Denying the right to choice*

Activity 1

Knowing service users' rights

1 Which of the following is a right that a service user in a residential home has?
   a To have the TV as loud as they wish.
   b To have two care workers with them at all times.
   c To choose their own bed.
   d To decide what they will wear.

2 What does maintaining confidentiality mean when talking to a service user?

3 Explain what it means to 'empower' a service user. Give an example of how a service user could be empowered.

The right to confidentiality

The Data Protection Act 1998 gives people the right to confidentiality of personal information. This applies to:

- personal information being discussed orally by care workers, e.g. discussing a service user's treatment
- written information which is personal, e.g. a **care plan**
- electronic records, e.g. a person's medical history.

Confidentiality is the ability to ensure that private and personal information is kept safe and cannot be accessed by others, except on a 'need-to-know basis', when other care workers may need to know as it will affect the care they give. Information about service users should not be **disclosed** without the service user's permission.

Case study

Breaching Miss Faulkner's confidentiality

A care worker in a nursing home received a telephone call from a person asking about the treatment given to a service user called Miss Faulkner. They asked exactly what had been done and why. The care worker gave the information to the person. The care worker:

- did not know that the caller was who they said they were
- had not checked that the caller was authorised to receive the information
- had not consulted with the line manager.

1 Discuss what actions the care worker should have taken.
2 Discuss why you think confidentiality is important.
3 Explain what is meant by the term 'disclosure'.

The correct action for the care worker in the case study to take would have been to:

- take a telephone number
- check with the line manager
- seek the service user's permission
- telephone the caller back.

If permission is not given by the supervisor to give out information the care worker could telephone to say that they could not give the information required.

Further information about confidentiality will be given later in this unit when considering Assessment Objective 3, but what should be remembered is that providing quality care involves keeping personal information safe and not sharing it with others.

The right to protection

Quality care in care settings involves providing **protection**. This applies to protection of:

- service users, e.g. by keeping them safe
- service users' property, e.g. by preventing theft
- care workers, e.g. by keeping them and their property safe.

Owners and managers of health, social care and early years settings are responsible for making sure that those within their care are protected from harm. This means that many care settings have installed security pads on all entrances and exits. To gain access to the care setting either a confidential number must be keyed in or the door bell has to be used to summon help. In this way no unwanted visitors can access the building.

Security window catches have also been fitted in care settings to make sure that **unauthorised** visitors cannot gain entry by this method.

Visitors to care settings, for example, people who are calling to maintain systems such as boilers or to do repair work, are issued with identification badges so that they can be easily recognised. The line mangers of such services telephone the care setting to give the day, time and how many workers will be attending. Such methods help both service users and care workers to feel safe and can prevent worry and stress.

Protection also means making sure that service users are not abused. Service users are often unable to protect themselves and are at the mercy of those who care for them. It would be quite easy for a care worker to become angry or **frustrated** with a service user, particularly if they had a lot to do and the service user was displaying challenging behaviour. Care workers who are not maintaining quality practice could try and **exert** power over service users through verbally abusing them. Different forms of abuse are outlined in the table on page 6.

We've come to repair the boiler

Bourneside Nursing Home

Figure 1.3 *Providing the right to protection*

Forms of abuse	Examples of abuse
Verbal	Shouting or swearing at a service user or threatening some physical harm, e.g. saying, 'I'll tie you to a chair if you ask me that again'
Physical	Actually causing harm to a service user, e.g. making a service user sit in a bath until they are cold and tired
Emotional	Causing a service user to worry or to be afraid, e.g. by saying, 'I'll remove all the light bulbs then you really won't be able to see anything'
Social	Deliberately excluding a service user from participating in a social event, e.g. by saying, 'You can't come on the outing James, you'll only want to go to the toilet all the time and we won't have time for that'
Sexual	Touching a person in personal parts of the body or having sexual intercourse with them against their will

Quality practice makes sure that procedures are in place to prevent the abuse of service users. These procedures could include having policies in place, making sure staff are trained on a regular basis, and having a named person to whom care workers can report. Care workers must always report any instance they see or hear of abuse and must not be afraid to **challenge** behaviour that does not value people.

Discussion point

Why is protecting service users part of quality practice?

Keeping service users protected also means making sure that the **environment** in which they live has had **hazards** reduced and safety

Figure 1.4 *Safety audits help service users to feel safe*

features put in place. This means that the service user's environment has been regularly checked to ensure that accidents are reduced. Safety surveys or audits should be carried out regularly. Examples of checks that could be made in a service user's bedroom, for example, are shown in the table at the bottom of the page.

Owners and managers of care settings also have a responsibility to make sure that service users' personal belongings are safe, for example, jewellery. They often do this by giving each service user a small security box which has a key. The service user can place any valuables in the box and keep the key on their person, for example on a key ring or on a necklace that they wear around their neck.

Similarly, owners must provide a safe place for care workers' personal belongings. Lockers which have a key are often made available to care staff so that they can put their personal possessions in a safe place, for example, handbags or wallets.

If service users are not protected, the effects on well-being could include:

- worry or stress with little personal energy and low **self-esteem**

- anxiousness including low self-efficiency
- headaches and other physical conditions
- fear, through insecurity with withdrawal and **learned helplessness**
- mental ill-health
- loss of motivation to achieve.

Activity 2
Key skills C 2.1a

Protecting service users

1 Discuss why it is important to protect service users.

2 List four ways in which a playgroup could make sure that the children who attend are protected. Explain how each would help.

3 How could each of the following safety features be used to protect service users:
   a Smoke alarms.
   b Thermostat controls.
   c Personal alarm systems.
   d Fire extinguishers.

4 Discuss why it is important that owners and managers provide a safe place to protect care workers' personal belongings.

Bedroom checks	How they can protect service users
Carpet not frayed or torn	Prevents tripping over and breaking a limb
Window catches are working correctly	Prevents break-in by unauthorised people, or service users from falling out
Lighting is adequate	Prevents falls as service users can see when they move around, and prevents eyesight from deteriorating
Fire instructions are in place and are clear	Promotes safety and prevents worry by instructing service users what to do in the case of an emergency
Firefighting equipment is working properly	Could be used to extinguish or contain a fire, and so save lives and prevent injury
Heating appliances and thermostat are working correctly	Enables service users to adjust heat to suit their needs, and so avoid being too cold or too hot
Alarm system working correctly, e.g. personal call system and smoke detectors	Alerts care workers to emergency situations

The right to equal and fair treatment

Service users can expect to receive care and treatment according to their individual needs. This does not mean that all service users should be treated 'the same' or receive 'the same treatment'. Services should be provided in such a way that all service users get equal benefit from them. This means that access to care and treatment should be according to the requirements that each person has. There should not be any favouritism for any reason. Service users should be treated as individuals rather than as a group. Each person should have their needs assessed and should then have a personal care plan drawn up which suits their own particular needs.

All care workers have a responsibility to make sure that service users receive equal and fair treatment. They should not act in a discriminatory way because of:

- a service user's race, e.g. the colour of their skin or their language
- a service user's beliefs and culture, e.g. their religious beliefs and customs
- a service user's ability, e.g. having a disability
- a service user's age, e.g. being over 65 years of age.

The right to consultation

Consultation involves sharing, for example giving and obtaining information, asking another person for their opinion, listening to the views of others and making decisions as a result of the opinions given.

Care plan for Sheema

Sheema, who is 80 years of age, has been admitted to a hospital for older patients after a fall. An assessment of Sheema's needs is made by a consultant, a nurse, and a hospital social worker.

When they talk with Sheema and examine her, they find that she is badly bruised, has problems with mobility and has short-term memory problems. They discuss with Sheema how best to help her.

Care workers draw up a care plan for Sheema, involving her in their discussions and decision making. The plan is for a two-day period, during which it will be **reviewed**.

> **Care plan for Sheema:**
> - turn Sheema over every three hours to prevent bedsores forming (nursing staff)
> - ask physiotherapist to visit to assess mobility problems and to suggest solutions (consultant to pass on notes)
> - investigate how relatives could help if Sheema is able to return home (social worker)
> - make sure Sheema has an increase in fluids as she is showing signs of dehydration (nursing staff)
> - give bed bath on second day (nursing staff)
> - arrange for Sheema to have an x-ray (consultant and nursing staff).

1 Discuss how Sheema's right to equal and fair treatment is being respected.

2 If the care workers were *not* providing fair and equal treatment, but were to discriminate on the basis of Sheema's old age, what would they do differently?

For a service user a consultation about treatment would involve being given information about all the options that are available and explaining what each would involve. The service user would need to know the benefits and disadvantages of all the options, so they could make decisions about which is the best treatment to suit their needs.

Quality practice in a care setting involves consulting with service users over both major and minor decisions. A major decision could be about whether to combine **traditional** medical treatment with a **complementary approach**, whereas a minor decision could be deciding what to have from the menu. In both cases the care worker must make sure that the service user is given sufficient information to make the decisions. They must be allowed to make their own decisions and not have the decisions made for them. This empowers the service user and enables them to be in control of their lives.

Case study

Brendan

Brendan, who is 87 years of age, needs a hip replacement operation. He is admitted to hospital as his operation is planned for the next day. While he is being prepared for the operation he is told that he will now have to wait for his operation as a 35-year-old motorcyclist has had an accident and needs a hip replacement.

1 Explain why Brendan is not being given fair and equal treatment.

2 Work with another person to prepare a role-play to show how staff at the hospital could consult with Brendan about the possible options he has.

3 Carry out the role-play to others in the group. Ask those observing to comment on the consultation.

4 Explain how being consulted can empower a service user. Give an example of your own of a situation where a care worker could consult with a service user.

It is important to make sure that service users are consulted

How can we support service users to maintain their rights?

Using effective communication

If service users do not understand what is being said to them they will be unable to respond or to comply with any instruction given, or the reply may be **inappropriate**. Care workers must, therefore, speak clearly and listen carefully when orally communicating with service users who may otherwise become confused or angry. Other **influencing skills** that contribute to effective oral communication are:

Influencing skill	How they can provide support when communicating
Pace	Speaking at a speed that is appropriate helps service users to follow what is being said
Tone	Variation of tone when speaking helps a conversation to be more interesting
Vocabulary	Using words that can be understood by the service users helps them to feel valued as they are able to understand what is being said
Body language	Use of positive facial expressions and smiling, for example, can encourage a service user to continue speaking
Listening	Hearing what is being said by the service user and showing that they are being heard by responding appropriately provides support and encouragement
Appearance	Dress helps a service user know to whom they are communicating, particularly if a care worker is wearing a uniform. It can identify that person as being someone who is responsible for their care

Care workers need to remember when communicating that words can mean different things to different people. A younger service user may have a different vocabulary than that used by an older service user. For example, a younger service user may use the word 'mad' as a positive term meaning 'great', forgetting that an older service user may not understand the current use of such a word.

Care workers have a responsibility not to talk down to people or **patronise** them. This applies as much when talking to children as to older service users. Support can be provided by being patient, not trying to finish a sentence for a service user and by giving warmth and encouragement.

If English is not a service user's first or preferred language, they may not understand the information they have been given. This could lead them into making a decision that does not reflect what they really want to do. It is possible that some service users, who find the language being used difficult to understand, may need the support of an interpreter in order to have effective communication.

Giving up-to-date information

If information is to be at all useful it must be up-to-date. Giving information that is not current could cause the service user to become distressed. All information should be:

- relevant, e.g. be related to what the service user wants to know
- useful, e.g. sufficient for a decision to be made
- provided in a way that the service user can understand, e.g. not too much so that they are swamped and cannot pick out the points they need
- given at an appropriate time, e.g. to allow the service user to use it in time to take any action that is needed.

Care workers should be aware that their line manager may have the information that is required and that the care setting may have a policy which must be followed relating to the collecting and giving out of information. If there is a policy in place, care workers must follow the procedures set out. It is always advisable to check any information with another care worker before giving it to service users. This prevents disappointment and incorrect information being given.

Providing quality care when giving up-to-date information means making sure the support given is appropriate to the service user's needs.

Speaking on behalf of service users who are unable to do so for themselves

There are occasions when service users need someone to speak on their behalf. Care workers need to be aware of such situations and be prepared, if required, to act on behalf of the service user. Such occasions could include for example:

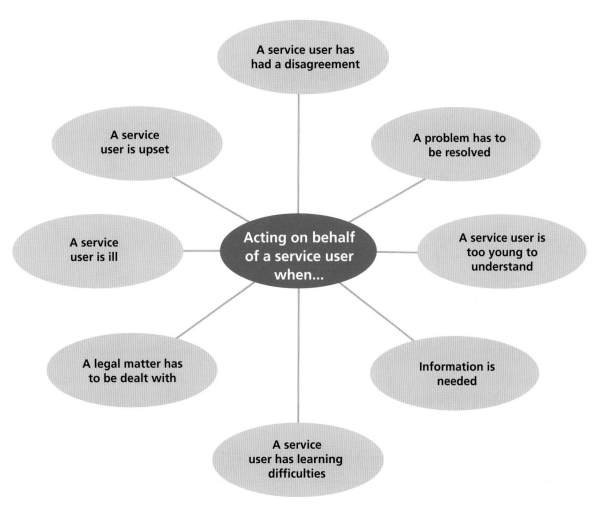

Figure 1.5 *Speaking on behalf of service users*

> ### Discussion point
>
> *Why is it important to check information with another person before passing it on to the service user?*

If a care worker thinks that an **advocate** is required they should discuss this with their line manager and with the service user, clearly explaining why an advocate may be necessary. There is more information on the role of advocates later in this unit.

Activity 3

Supporting service users

Figure 1.6 *Advocate speaking on service user's behalf*

1 Produce **four** role-plays that demonstrate influencing skills when communicating with service users. Perform the role-plays to others, asking them to guess which influencing skill the role-plays are portraying.

2 Give **two** examples of when a service user may need to have someone speak on their behalf.

3 Choose one of the situations from Question 2. Work with another person to prepare a role-play of what the care worker would say in this situation.

4 Read the situation given below:

> Malcolm has been shouted at by Tom because Malcolm was sitting in Tom's chair. Tom said that Malcolm knew that Tom always sat in that chair and he should move. Malcolm moved after arguing with Tom but now Malcolm is very upset and feels he cannot sort the problem out for himself. He has asked you as a care worker to speak on his behalf to the other resident.

Perform a role-play to others in the group asking them to comment on the appropriateness of what the care worker said to Tom on behalf of Malcolm.

Seeking support

There may be occasions when care workers need to go to others in order to obtain the support they need when supporting service users. In the first instance the care worker's supervisor should be approached. Examples of other sources of information that can be used by care workers are given in the table on page 13.

Sources of information	Type of information
Social services department	Factual information about: services available; how to arrange for an assessment of need; care in the community that is available
Voluntary organisations	Specialised information, e.g. help for older people from Help the Aged or Age Concern
NHS (National Health Service)	Information relating to medical treatment or about where to go to get medical help
NHS Direct	Information about medical conditions and their treatments through actual discussion with experts
Local library	Leaflets and directories giving information about services
The Patient's Forum	A group of service users who meet to put forward concerns about the way procedures are carried out
The Internet	Information about a variety of topics that can be downloaded

Providing information on complaints procedures

Service users must be aware that there is a **complaints procedure** and how to access it. Care workers must be willing to provide this information. Often the procedures for making a complaint are included in the 'Information Pack' provided by the care setting, but service users may need to be told exactly what to do if they want to make a complaint. If complaints are dealt with quickly and are taken seriously, trusting relationships are likely to be maintained. A complaint may seem insignificant to the care worker but it may appear to be a major incident to the service user. If left undealt with it could cause poor relationships between the care worker and service user as well as physical and emotional effects on the service user such as anxiety, withdrawal symptoms, low **self-esteem**, headaches and feeling unwell.

How do I make a complaint?

Figure 1.7 *Making a complaint*

Mavis and her TV programme

Mavis does not have a TV in her own room so she watches programmes on the TV in the residents lounge. She has told everyone that she must see the second part of a detective story which is on at 9.00 p.m.

Mavis settles herself ready for the programme at 8.30 p.m., but when her programme starts at 9.00 p.m. two other residents bustle into the room and switch the programme over to another channel. Mavis is very upset and complains to the care

worker, particularly as the two other residents both have a TV in their own room. The care worker tells Mavis to stop complaining as it's only a programme and nothing to get upset about'.

1 Discuss what the care worker should have done in this situation.

2 Discuss what Mavis could do about the care worker's attitude.

3 Explain the likely affect on Mavis of the care worker's attitude.

Further details about complaints procedures and how they contribute to quality practice are given later in this unit.

Challenging discriminatory behaviour

Discriminatory behaviour is behaviour that results from having attitudes that are biased and which cause a person to treat another person differently because of something about them, for example, because of their race or gender or because they have a disability.

Challenging discriminatory behaviour means not letting such behaviour happen without taking some form of action. Knowing what to do and how to challenge people who act in a discriminatory way is important for care workers. This is particularly difficult if the person who is discriminating is older, more experienced, or has more responsibility than the care worker who has noticed the behaviour.

Figure 1.8 *Challenging discriminatory behaviour*

Discriminatory behaviour can be challenged by:

- speaking out immediately when witnessing discriminatory behaviour, e.g. taking the person to one side where the conversation cannot be overheard and pointing out to them that their behaviour is unacceptable
- reporting the behaviour to a supervisor, e.g. making it known to another person who has some responsibility in the care setting
- intervening if there is an immediate risk to the service user.

Quality practice in care settings to prevent discriminatory behaviour from occurring involves making sure that the points shown in the table alongside are followed.

Quality practice	Example of effect
Regular staff training	Raises staff awareness of the causes, forms and effects of discrimination
Encouraging new staff to examine their own attitudes and prejudices	Shows staff how their attitudes and prejudices can affect their practice
Encouraging service users to speak out if they experience discrimination	Raises awareness of managers and informs staff training
Having policies in place	Sets standards and guidelines for staff to follow
Monitoring staff	Observation of staff practice will inform **appraisals** and staff training
Having a resident(s) on management committees	Aids direct reporting of issues relating to discrimination

Assessment activity 1.1

Key skills [C] 2.1a, [ICT] 2.3

Note: This assessment activity is best completed with Assessment Activity 1.2 because the collection of primary and secondary evidence is required for both activities.

Supporting service users' rights

Bourneside Residential Home has 25 residents with learning difficulties. The residents are aged between 25 and 65 years.

OR

Bowleaze Playgroup has 25 children, aged between 2 and 4 years, who attend for morning and afternoon sessions.

Choose one of the above care settings then:

1 Work in pairs to prepare questions that could be used when visiting a care setting or when a visiting care worker speaks to the group, to find out about quality practice. The questions should focus on:
   - what rights service users have
   - how the rights of service users are maintained
   - how care workers can provide support for service users to make sure their rights are maintained
   - how service users' rights could be infringed (Unit 1.2)

   - what the responsibilities of care workers are (Unit 1.2).

2 Share the questions with another pair in the group. Rework any questions as a result of the discussion you have had.

3 Share the questions with the whole group. Produce a set of questions that can be used during the visit to the care setting of your choice or during the talk.

4 Arrange to visit a care setting (with your tutor's permission) to find out the information required.

5 Produce a 'Guide to Service Users' Rights' which explains **three** rights service users have. Use the case studies above and/or any other information collected from the visit to provide examples.

6 Using the case studies and/or the primary evidence collected from the visit as examples, explain how these rights are maintained in care settings. Make sure you include information about how support is provided by care workers. This information is to be included in the 'Guide to Service Users' Rights'. (Remember to keep the primary evidence collected during the visit for Assessment Activity 1.2.)

How can service users' rights be infringed?

Infringements of personal rights

> **Infringements** of rights are what take place when care workers have not made sure that service user rights are maintained, either deliberately or unintentionally.

Direct infringement

Direct infringement of a service user's rights means that a service user has been deliberately treated less favourably than others on such grounds as their sexuality, religion, disability or marital status. The discrimination is open and obvious, disadvantaging a person or group. Examples of direct infringement of service users' rights are:

- talking about someone disrespectfully, e.g. name calling
- giving challenging looks at service users, e.g. frowning hard or being aggressive
- singling out a person for **ridicule**, e.g name calling
- preventing a person from doing something they really wanted to do, e.g. watching a programme on TV
- removing the service user's right to choice, e.g. making decisions for them
- breaking confidentiality, e.g. by gossiping about a service user in a place where others can hear and can identify the person
- not allowing privacy.

From a care worker's perspective direct infringement of rights would include paying two people who are doing exactly the same job different rates.

Indirect infringement

Indirect infringements of a service user's rights means that the infringement could be accidental. Examples of actions that could occur in care settings are:

- creating rules which apply to everyone, but the result of the rules is that some groups are particularly disadvantaged, e.g. insisting that men are clean shaven would be an infringement of rights for a Sikh service user
- only printing information in one language which could exclude a number of people from accessing the information
- ignoring service users when they complain about a minor incident.

Infringement of rights can make service users feel powerless or worthless and could cause them to feel they had no control over their lives.

Infringements of physical rights

Infringements of physical rights can be deliberate or unintentional. The affect of both could lead to serious consequences such as injury or death. Examples of infringements of physical rights are shown in the table below.

Infringements of physical rights	Consequence of the infringement
Lack of medical attention	Worsening of the service user's condition, increased pain and/or discomfort and increased anxiety
Lack of safety in the environment of the care setting	An increase in accidents and personal injury
Limited or no provision of mobility or sensory aids	Decreased mobility, lack of quality of life, increased isolation
Poor hygiene	Social isolation, low self-esteem
Poor diet	Development of conditions such as irritable bowel syndrome, anaemia and ill-health
Physical abuse, e.g. slapping, sexual	Bruising, fear, low self-esteem, depression

Care workers should be provided with training to make sure that they are aware of the physical rights of service users. Having knowledge of the subject will often prevent infringement from occurring.

Activity 4

Personal and physical rights of service users

1 For **each** of the following examples of infringement, state which rights are being infringed.

  a Anita has not been given a Zimmer frame to help her walk.

  b Adrian is laughed at because he has a stutter.

  c A flex from a portable electric fire has been left trailing across Barabara's bedroom floor.

  d Margaret is only given a bath once each month.

2 Explain the difference between direct and indirect infringements of service users' rights, giving an example of each.

3 Which is an example of a physical infringement of rights?

  a Making fun of a person.

  b Breaking confidentiality.

  c Poor diet.

  d Removing choice.

Infringements of financial rights

Service users should, if they have the ability, be allowed to control their own financial affairs. Children should be allowed to manage their pocket money and should be able to decide how and what they spend their money on. That is not to say that parents and main carers will not offer advice and guidance about how the money should be spent, and they should **intervene** if the money is being spent on harmful goods. Empowering a child in this context means allowing them to make the decision on what to spend after they have received advice.

Similarly, service users who are in residential or nursing care should also be able to decide for themselves how they spend or save their money. Just because they are being cared for it does not mean that they give up their right to manage their own financial affairs. Service users have the right to managers, solicitors, financial advisors etc. at their request.

Theft of money from a service user should be taken very seriously and is a crime. Theft could involve a care worker or another service user deliberately taking money from a service user. In other words, trying to cheat a person from what

Figure 1.10 *Infringing on financial rights*

is rightfully theirs. It could also take the form of a care worker or relative or another resident doing some shopping on behalf of a service user and not giving them the right amount of change, or any change. When carrying out any financial transactions on behalf of a service user it is important to **account** for how the money has been spent and on what. Not to do so is infringing on the service user's rights and can lead to poor relationships with them.

Case study

Key skills [C] 2.1a

Joan

Joan, who is 81 years old, is a resident in Brooks Residential Home. Her niece collects her pension each week and pays most of it into an account to pay for her residential care. The remaining £15 is given to Joan for her personal spending. Each week a care worker does some shopping for Joan. She buys personal items such as toothpaste, soap, talcum powder, writing pads and stamps. Sometimes she buys small items of clothing. Joan hands over all of her money. The care worker does the shopping but rarely hands over any change. After a few months, Joan complains about this to her niece when she visits.

---

1 Discuss how the care worker is infringing Joan's rights.

2 Explain what the care worker should be doing when she has purchased the items for Joan.

3 Explain what likely effects the care worker's actions might be having on Joan.

All service users have the right not to be financially abused

A service user's financial rights are also infringed when:

- relatives and care workers try to influence or put pressure on older service users about to whom they should leave their property or money (they may wish to have property or money made over to themselves)
- information about welfare benefits that could be obtained is not provided, again preventing service users from having what they are legally entitled to.

The attitude of a care worker or relative towards a service user could be 'they've got plenty of money anyway, they don't need any more'. This could lead to attempts to control a service user's money and the service user themselves. It is exerting power, not empowering the service user. Service users must be protected from such abuse and infringement of their rights.

Who do care workers have a responsibility to seek advice and guidance from?

All care workers have a responsibility to make sure that service users' rights are not infringed. Some care workers also have a 'duty of care'. This is a legal and a professional duty. In law, the courts could find a registered practitioner (e.g. a nurse or midwife) negligent if a person suffers harm because he or she has failed to care for them properly. Even if the service user has not suffered harm, a nurse or a midwife could be 'struck off' from the official register of care workers if they are found not to have given appropriate care.

The Care Standards Act 2000 has also made training compulsory for all care workers in residential and nursing homes. New staff must

When you need advice ask your line manager

Using line managers and supervisors

Asking questions, seeking clarification and obtaining knowledge from line managers and supervisors is a major aspect of care workers' responsibilities. A care worker cannot know or have answers to everything that is asked of them. Line managers and supervisors are usually people who are very experienced and will certainly know who to put care workers in touch with if they are unable to give the information required. A line manager or supervisor should be the first person to approach for support and guidance.

complete Foundation or Induction training within six weeks of starting their employment. The intention of training staff as soon as they start their employment and in having a duty of care, is to improve the standards of care provided within care settings and to be sure that service users receive the quality of care to which they are entitled.

Care workers have a responsibility to seek advice and guidance from:

- line managers and/or supervisors
- policies and procedures
- professional organisations.

If an incident occurs that causes a care worker to be concerned about the treatment of a service user, it is not sufficient just to pass the information on verbally. A written report should be made. The information given in the report should include:

- the service user for whom you are concerned
- the situation that caused concern
- if there have been any previous incidents
- the time the incident occurred, the date and the care worker's signature.

Figure 1.11 *Reporting an incident that infringes a service users rights*

However small the concern appears to be, the care worker should always seek guidance from their line manager or supervisor. It is better to report something, rather than ignoring it and it becoming a bigger problem later.

Using policies and procedures

All care settings have policies and procedures in place to ensure that quality practice is implemented. They set standards and give guidelines about what actions to take when certain situations arise. They also make sure that there is **consistency** of approach by all care workers when incidents arise.

A care setting's policies and procedures should cover a wide range of situations. Examples of policies and procedures are shown in the table below.

Care workers should either be given copies of policies and procedures when they start working at a care setting, or they should be shown where they are kept and how they can be accessed. Knowing what is in the policies is a responsibility of all care workers. If a care worker is unsure about a procedure they can read the appropriate policy and find out how to deal with the situation and what actions they should take.

Policies and procedures	Examples of purpose
Health and Safety	• To name the person who is responsible for first aid • To set out guidelines about procedures in the event of fire or emergencies • To set out procedures for the safety of staff and service users
Complaints procedure	• To inform service users how to make a complaint and how that complaint will be dealt with • To provide guidelines to staff about what to do if a complaint is made
Equal opportunities policy	• To set out how the home intends to implement equal opportunities in its day-to-day organisation. • Enables service users to know the standards that they can expect • Provides guidance to staff about how to ensure that service users are treated fairly
Training policy	• To inform care workers of the systems that are in place for training and the expectation of managers and owners • Provides information about how care workers can keep abreast of current training needs and how training will be provided

Case study

Hebbi

Hebbi attends Hope playgroup. She is playing on the large equipment when suddenly she falls off the slide and is found by Jonathan, the nursery nurse, lying unconscious on the floor. Jonathan does not know what he should do. He runs to look for another nursery nurse to find out, but cannot find one near at hand. Eventually he approaches the playgroup leader and tells her what has happened, but by this time six minutes have passed since the incident.

1 Discuss what Jonathan should have known before the accident happened.

2 Describe where he could have found the information he needed.

3 Explain why policies are important.

4 What could be the result of Jonathan's inappropriate behaviour?

Using professional organisations

Which organisations can provide support for care workers?

Figure 1.12 *Organisations supporting care workers*

The Commission For Racial Equality

Funded by the Home Office, its main purpose is to:

- give advice to people who believe they have suffered racial discrimination
- provide legal representation for such people in a court or an industrial **tribunal**
- take action of its own if it thinks something is discriminatory, e.g. advertisements
- investigate organisations where it has evidence of racial bias
- advise employers, health and local authorities about how to prevent and deal with racial discrimination
- issue codes of practice on how to promote equality of opportunity.

The Equal Opportunities Commission

Set up in 1976, its main purpose is to:

- investigate cases where there is the likelihood of an organisation breaching equal opportunities

- issue non-discriminatory notices which advise employers to stop any discriminatory practice
- take employers to court if warnings about discriminatory practices are ignored
- carry out reviews of the Sex Discrimination Act 1975 to see if its content is still current.

Help the Aged, Age Concern and the Citizen's Advice Bureau

All of these organisations provide facts and advice about specific topics and can be accessed by service users and care workers who make an appointment. They provide confidential advice and give information about other organisations that can help with particular issues.

The Data Protection Commissioner

This organisation investigates claims of breach of confidentiality and provides advice about what to do in the event of such a breach.

Infringement of rights

Bourneside Residential Home recently had an inspection by the local authority inspection team. The report stated that some service users' rights had been **breached**.

- Staff swore at service users while they were on duty but it was not reported.
- A service user who was a Muslim was made to eat pork and was prevented from following his religious activities.
- Staff did not knock before entering service users' bedrooms.
- Some experienced staff were heard to tell trainees that they need not ask Ben what he wanted to eat but were just to give him what was easiest as he did not know what he was eating anyway.
- Staff gossiped about service users and their personal affairs by name.

OR

Bowleaze Playgroup had an OFSTED inspection. The inspection stated that some service users' rights had been breached.

- Staff shouted at children and made them sit in a room on their own for at least half an hour if they misbehaved.
- A service user who was a Muslim was made to eat pork and was prevented from following his religious activities.
- Staff did not give some children a choice of activity but made them do what the staff had chosen.

- Some experienced staff were heard to say to a trainee and in front of all the other children, 'Just give David colouring to do, he's a bit backward and that will keep him happy, he'll have to miss out on the painting'.
- The staff talked about children by name, gossiping about their abilities and home life.

You have been asked to collect primary and secondary information to illustrate how service users' rights can be infringed. Use one of the case studies given above and the information collected from visiting a care setting (see Assessment Activity 1.1).

1 Prepare information to put in the 'Guide To Service Users' Rights' to help care workers understand how service users' rights can be infringed. Use the case studies given for Bourneside Residential Home OR Bowleaze Playgroup, together with evidence collected from the visit as examples, to illustrate the points you make.

2 Produce information for the 'Guide To Service Users' Rights' to show what would be good practice in a care setting to prevent the infringement of service users' rights.

3 Produce a detailed leaflet or a series of detailed handouts that could be given to care workers to inform them of their responsibilities in seeking advice from line managers/supervisors, policies, procedures and organisations. Make sure you include specific information to show how each would help.

What is diversity?

We are not all the same. Society is made up of many different types of people. Figure 1.13 outlines some types of the diversity affecting service users.

Some people consider their own race or culture to be **superior** or better than others. They have a very narrow view and think that the beliefs and values they hold are the only correct ones to have. They are not prepared to be open to the beliefs and values of people from other cultures or new ways of looking and thinking about things. They often try to influence others to their way of thinking. By valuing diversity people have the opportunity to have new experiences and their lives are enriched.

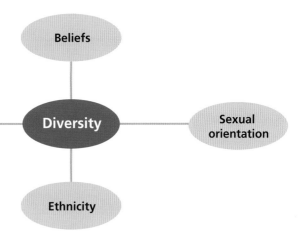

Figure 1.13 *What is diversity?*

Each year the Notting Hill Carnival celebrates diversity

Diversity of beliefs

In care settings, care workers are certain to meet people from a wide range of cultural backgrounds. Some of these service users are likely to have different beliefs from the care workers' own, for example, they may believe in Islam, Judaism or Christianity. Being aware of the differences and the day-to day requirements of service users who have other beliefs is an essential part of a care worker's role. For example, a person who is a Muslim will not want to eat pork, and a person who follows Judaism will celebrate their holy day on a Friday, while a Christian will want to celebrate their religion on a Sunday. Some service users may want to pray at particular times during a day and this should be incorporated into the arrangements made for them. Care settings can show that they value all world faiths by arranging specific activities and by not behaving as though one religion is more important than another. Respecting the beliefs of others is to value diversity.

> ## Discussion point
>
> *Nadir, a Muslim, has been admitted to your residential home. He was recently discharged from hospital after treatment for a stomach complaint which caused him to lose a lot of weight. He needs a healthy diet but it is Ramadan and he refuses to eat between sunrise and sunset. What would you do?*

Diversity of values

Values are those things that we count as being important. For example, being truthful and honest, showing good manners, being on time for an appointment and allowing others to express their opinions even if we do not agree with them. Because we have different values we have different **priorities**. For example, a nurse may see being healthy as a top priority, but a service user may put the care of a pet dog or cat before anything else. Actions often reflect the values that people have.

> ## Discussion point
>
> *What actions reflect your own values?*

Care workers must not allow the different perspectives of service users to lower the quality of care they provide. They need to be aware of their own values but allow others the right to have their own and not undermine them when they do not agree. This is part of empowering service users, helping them to make their own choices and decisions whether the care worker agrees with the outcome or not.

Diversity of sexual orientation

Sexual orientation is the preference that people have for sexual partners. Males who prefer same sex partners are often referred to as 'gay'. Women who prefer same sex partners are called 'lesbian'. People who have both male and female partners are known as 'bi-sexual'.

When caring for service users, a care worker must not allow themselves to be influenced by the sexual preferences of those for whom they care. Service users can make their own choices about sexual orientation, whether they are able-bodied, disabled, young, older people or from different cultures. Care workers must ensure that they do not discriminate against service users whose sexual orientation is different from their own, by ignoring or neglecting them or by verbally harassing or ridiculing them. Quality practice in this context means that all service users, whatever their sexual orientation, should be given equality of access to the care they need.

> ## Case study   Key skills C 2.3
>
> ### Jules and Sandy
>
> Jules and Sandy, same sex partners, have been living together in a stable relationship for 25 years. They are now both in their seventies and are finding it difficult to cope.
>
> After visiting the Swallows Residential Home with their social worker, Jules and Sandy decide to move in. They have requested that they have a double bedroom, just like any other married couple.
>
> Some of the care workers at Swallows Residential Home and a few of the residents are not happy about the arrangement.
>
> 1 Explain what is meant by the term 'diversity', giving examples to illustrate the points made.
> 2 What could be influencing the attitude of the care workers and service users who have objections to Jules and Sandy having a double bedroom?
> 3 Describe the quality practice procedures that could be used by managers to make sure that Jules and Sandy are not discriminated against.

Diversity of ethnicity

Ethnicity refers to a national culture or identity. Everyone has their own source of ethnicity or ethnic origins. This means that people of Gaelic origin are an ethnic group just as much as people of Asian origin.

Ethnic diversity in Britain goes back a long way in history. For example, signs of previous black populations can be traced in the West Country surname 'Blackmore', which is thought to be a reference to North African Moors, seafarers who visited these isles. Present day society is often shaped by what has happened in the past.

Today in Britain, people from many different cultures live side-by-side and there is an acceptance of different beliefs, values and cultural diversity. Where there is not acceptance discrimination occurs which is recognised by offensive remarks, physical violence and open rejection of those who do not **conform** to the traditions of the majority of the population of an area.

How can we foster equality?
Anti-discrimination

> **Anti-discrimination** is making sure that people are treated equally, and promoting procedures and policies that support this.

Treating people equally does not mean treating everyone the same. It means treating service users in such a way as to give them equal access to all services, and ensuring that service users get equal benefit from the services.

The aim of anti-discrimination policy is to make sure that all the population feel that they are valued regardless of their colour, beliefs, sexual orientation or disability. Care workers in all health, social care and early years settings, have a responsibility to promote equality. Each care setting has policies in place that care workers

The Dalai Lama speaking at the World Religions Conference

Case study Key skills C 2.1a

Highgrove Playgroup

Highgrove Playgroup has various activities for the children to do when they attend. There is a dressing-up corner where clothing from different cultures is made available for the children to use. They also have a Wendy House with dolls that are Chinese, Asian, Afro-Caribbean and White European. Throughout the year the playgroup celebrates events from different world faiths.

1 Explain how the playgroup is valuing the beliefs of individual service users.

2 List three points of advice that could be given to the playgroup to make sure that service users' beliefs and values are respected

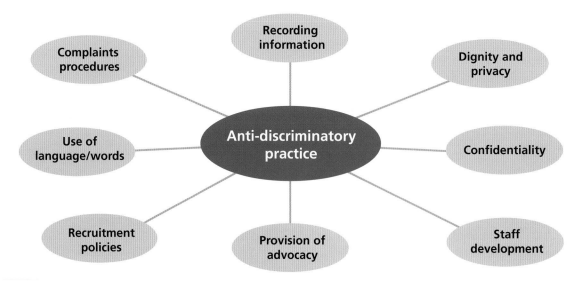

Figure 1.14 *Anti-discriminatory practice*

should follow to ensure that the best interests of each service user are upheld and that they are not mistreated. Policies that ensure anti-discriminatory work practice can include, for example, those shown in Figure 1.14.

Quality practice requires not denying one service user or a group of service users the same quality of opportunity or service that a different group receives. Anti-discriminatory policies ensure that one person or group is not favoured over another. For example, only printing a menu in English when for many patients in a hospital English is not their first or preferred language would not be acceptable, as it favours one group above another.

Bases of discrimination

Discrimination is centred around peoples attitudes and beliefs. These attitudes and beliefs can influence the behaviour of individuals and groups and form the basis of discrimination. The culture in which we live can be an influencing factor, as can family, friends, the media and education, for example.

Attitudes such as those given as examples in the table below, demonstrate prejudice and affect working practice. Anti-discriminatory practice seeks to actively discourage such attitudes and challenges behaviour where discrimination is shown. Discriminatory attitudes are learned from others. Care workers should act as good role models and should not fail to respect diversity.

Bases of discrimination	Example
Thinking of older people as being a burden	Treating older people in a patronising way and considering it is not worth spending money on services for them
Not placing any value on people who have disabilities	Ignoring a person in a wheelchair and talking as though they were not there
Thinking that all people with mental illness will harm someone	Considering that people with mental illness should be hidden away in remote institutions
Being of the opinion that people who have HIV/Aids only have themselves to blame for their condition	Not wanting a child with HIV/Aids to be admitted to a playgroup where they will mix with children who do not have the condition, as it is thought they could 'catch it'

Effects of discrimination

Service users are affected in different ways by discrimination and this may mean that there are several effects and not just one. Discrimination takes away most of a service users rights and their voice 'to be heard', for example, it prevents them from voicing their opinions and often **belittles** them in front of others. Discrimination devalues, making people feel uncomfortable and vulnerable.

Activity 5

Key skills  ICT 2.1, C 2.2

Fostering equality

1 Carry out research to find out how a complaints procedure would be implemented in a health, social care or early years setting.
2 Explain how a care worker could make sure that language was used in an anti-discriminatory way.
3 Find a short newspaper article that shows a basis for discrimination. Read the article to others in the group asking them to state the basis of discrimination.
4 Explain the term 'basis of discrimination'.

Assessment activity 1.3

Key skills 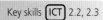 ICT 2.2, 2.3

Diversity and equality

Bourneside Nursing Home OR Bowleaze Playgroup has asked you to prepare a variety of training materials that can be put into a resource pack to be used with trainees. Whenever possible use primary and secondary sources of information.

1 Prepare handouts or other materials to help trainees understand how to recognise the diversity of service users. Try to link theory with practice when completing this task.
2 Write case studies to show how diversity can be fostered in care settings.
3 Produce a detailed 'Guide' that could be put into the resource pack to explain how to foster equality at Bourneside Nursing Home OR Bowleaze Playgroup.

Make sure you link theory with practice, giving reasons and opinions within the evidence produced. You must include detailed information on:

- anti-discriminatory practice
- the basis of discrimination
- types of discrimination
- the different effects discrimination can have on service users.

Use workplace practice and theory to give examples to illustrate the points you are making.

What legislation exists to maintain confidentiality?

Figure 1.15 *Everyone working with service users should be familiar with legislation relating to confidentiality*

Legislation refers to decisions made by Parliament which have been passed by law and which must be applied by care settings. There are three main pieces of legislation that relate to the procedures that must be followed in care settings relating to confidentiality. These are the:

- Data Protection Act 1998
- Access to Personal Files Act 1987
- Access to Medical Records Act 1990.

The word 'confidentiality' comes from the word 'confide' which means to tell someone secret information that you trust they will not pass on. Confidential information must be handled sensitively and with great care.

However, there are occasions within care settings when it is necessary to share 'confidential' information. For example, if a social worker is told that a father is abusing his children, the social worker must share the information with the Child Protection Department in order to protect the child.

As another example, if a service user moves from a residential home into hospital, it is necessary to share the information held by the residential home with the appropriate staff at the hospital so that the best possible care can be provided. This is known as information given on a 'need-to-know' basis, but the service user's permission must be asked first.

The information service users give is protected by law.

Data Protection Act 1998

There are eight main principles to this act which apply to paper and computer records. These principles guide the way that health, social care and early years services deal with information they hold about service users. Staff in all care settings therefore need to be aware of the responsibilities that the act places upon them.

Principle of the Data Protection Act 1998	How legislation is applied in care settings
Personal data must be obtained and processed fairly and lawfully	• Service users should know about all records kept and be told why they are being kept • Service users must be told with whom this information will be shared and why, and asked to give their permission • Service users must be told of their rights to access this information
Personal data must be held only for one specified and lawful purpose	• There must be a lawful purpose to hold the data on individuals, e.g. to provide, monitor and review services
Personal data must be relevant, adequate and not excessive	• Organisations should only keep information they need to provide services, nothing more, nothing less
Personal data must be accurate and kept up-to-date	• Before recording the facts they should be checked • Service users' records should be reviewed regularly to make sure all the information is correct • Changes to service users' circumstances must be recorded
Personal data must not be kept for longer than is necessary	• There must be a disposal date for records. The setting must destroy the records when that date is due • Note: adoption records and records of those who have committed offences may be kept for 100 years
Personal data must be processed in accordance with the rights of data subjects	• All individuals have the right to access their data and rights as to whom and when data can be passed on. They have control over their data
Personal data must be kept secure from unauthorised access, alteration or disclosure, loss or destruction	• Paper records must be stored safely • A system for the removal and return of files must be in place • Records kept on computer must only be accessed by those authorised to do so using a password • Computerised records should be backed up regularly
Personal data should not be transferred to a country outside the European Economic Area	• Only if the country agrees to use an adequate protection system can records be transferred. This could apply when the NHS arranges with another country (e.g. France) to provide operations for UK residents

The legislation makes it necessary for every care setting to have a nominated member of staff who will act as 'controller of data'. It is important that all care staff follow the principles of the Data Protection Act 1998.

Activity 6
Key skills ICT 2.1, C 2.2

Data protection

1 Carry out secondary research to find out when a person would not have control of their data.

2 Invite a care manager or supervisor of a care setting to the centre (with your tutor's permission) to find out how confidential information is managed.

3 For each of the eight main principles of the Data Protection Act 1998, state what would happen in a specific care setting, e.g. Bowleaze Playgroup.

Access to Personal Files Act 1987

The Access to Personal Files Act 1987 and the Access to Personal Files (Social Services) Regulations 1989 give people the right to access material recorded about them after 1st April 1989 that an authority holds.

The act states that the Social Work Department should let service users see information about themselves unless there is good reason for not doing so. This is similar to the Data Protection Act 1998, which allows service users to have access to any personal details. However, information about other people must be removed before a service user has access to the records.

Access to Medical Records Act 1990

This act gives service users the right to have access to health information written about themselves since 1 November 1991. This covers all written records but not computer records, which are already accessible as a result of the modifications made under Section 21 of the Data Protection Act 1998.

A service user must make a direct request to a service provider, for example, at an outpatient consultation, otherwise requests should be made in writing. Written requests are usually dealt with by an administrator who will have to get permission from the service provider before any information can be released. A charge can be made for giving this information to the service user.

Information held in medical records is only available to other people if the service user gives their consent. This is usually done with a signed consent form.

What are the organisational requirements to maintain confidentiality?

Policies in organisations

Policies arise out of legislation. They provide a framework which ensures that care workers within a health, social care or early years **organisation** or setting, or across a number of settings, all have the same approach to a task or procedure. The content of a policy will give guidelines on how a task should be done or to whom staff should report in the case of a particular occurrence. An organisation could have a number of polices, all of which are intended to maintain standards of care, to give guidance to staff and to promote the best interests of service users.

Policies are usually kept in a folder and placed in the staff rest area or lounge. A copy should be kept in the manager's office. Service users are usually given a copy when they use or are admitted to a setting, in the form of a 'mission statement'.

Case study

Key skills 2.1a

Liz

Liz, who is 25 years of age, has moderate learning difficulties and lives in a small residential home in the community.

While being helped to get ready for bed, Liz tells a night worker that some of her ornaments have been stolen. Liz appears to be very concerned about this and repeats her concerns several times.

The care worker tells her, 'not to worry, I expect you are mistaken. Just settle down and forget all about it'.

Liz then hands a file over to the care worker. The file contains all the personal records for Jack Hart, whose room is next door. Liz told the care worker that the file had been left on her bed.

1 Name a piece of legislation that requires the care worker to take action about the complaint Liz has made.

2 What should the care worker have done when Liz told them about her missing ornaments?

3 Explain which pieces of legislation apply to security of paper-based personal records?

4 Explain what should happen to maintain security of paper-based records at the care setting.

Confidentiality policy
- The controller of all confidential information is Mrs Jxxx...
- Two care workers, AF and BH, will hold the password to computer data...

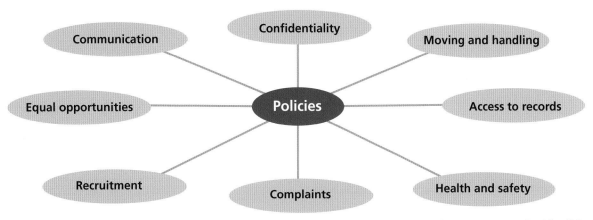

Figure 1.16 *Examples of policies*

Procedures in organisations

A procedure sets out exactly what a care worker must do in a particular situation or task. For example, if a person makes a complaint what must a care worker do? The procedure will give instructions as to exactly what steps to take, for example:

Complaints procedure

If you have a complaint please immediately tell the supervisor on duty or if you prefer, the Manager.

The supervisor/manager will record the complaint and log the time, date and details.

If you prefer to put the complaint in writing...

Recording information in an organisation

Information should only be recorded when it is needed for the organisation to carry out its duties and responsibilities. A care worker must decide which is fact and which is opinion, and only the facts should be recorded about service users. The Data Protection Act 1998 gives very clear instructions about what can be recorded, how it should be recorded and what should be recorded relating to a particular individual. All information must be:

- **legible**
- accurate
- up-to-date.

There are four stages involved when recording information, all of which are shown in Figure 1.17 below.

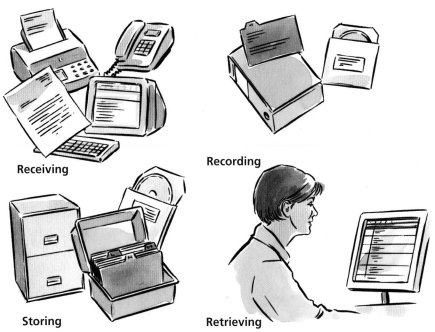

Receiving

Recording

Storing

Retrieving

Figure 1.17 *Confidentiality must relate to each of these different forms of communication*

It is important to make sure that information is correct, as incorrect information could lead to a person receiving the wrong treatment. Also, records can be used as evidence in a court of law, a **tribunal** or a formal enquiry. Being able to communicate effectively through accurate record keeping is a basic part of good practice that all care workers should maintain. Records can include:

Records	Examples
Written	Written letters, memos, assessments, reports, messages, policies, procedures, review documents
Electronic	Email, Internet information, networking, databases

Care workers need to be clear about the purpose of records. They need to think about:

- who will be reading the records
- what they are to be used for
- what the care worker hopes they will achieve.

Care must be taken not to include:

- too much information, e.g. do not include padding
- too little information, e.g. the end result could put a service user at risk.

When completing records it should always be remembered that service users can access them and ill-feeling can arise if there are inaccuracies or points have been made that are insensitive or judgemental.

Storage and security in organisations

Storage of information can be:

- **manual**, e.g. using a filing system/ cabinet
- electronic, e.g. using the computer.

All records of service users must be protected. Access to information must be controlled to prevent unauthorised people from accessing it. Records that are kept manually should be placed in a locked room, with access limited to certain nominated people. The records themselves should be stored in locked filing cabinets within the rooms to make doubly sure that they are protected. Many large organisations set a time when records can be accessed, after which the protected area is locked and access is only available if an emergency arises. Most care settings have a clear policy relating to the storage of records. Below is part of a 'Control of records policy' for a residential home:

Control of records

1 Each set of records will be maintained in a secure location within the home's administration offices, and in such a manner as to prevent deterioration or spoilage. Records will be collated and filed in an orderly fashion and indexed so as to be easily retrievable.

2 A Quality Records Log will be maintained which will identify the following for each set of records, taking into account statutory requirements as applicable:
2.1 Location of storage
2.2 Disk references, where records are stored on computer
2.3 Length of time records are kept
2.4 Responsibilities for maintenance and control
2.5 Staff who are authorised to have access to individual sets of records

3 Records will be kept in accordance with the data protection legislation.

Records held on computer should require each person who wishes to access information to have an identified number (ID) and/or password to enable them to do so. This prevents unauthorised people from gaining entry to personal information. Some care workers could be **restricted** or limited to particular information on the computer. For example, care workers involved in providing personal care do not need to have access to financial aspects of the care setting and vice versa.

A large organisation such as a Trust hospital may have a system known as 'ownership' of information or data. All information coming into the organisation is given an 'owner' or person who is responsible for the storage and security of the information they hold. In the NHS they are known as the Caldicott

Guardians. People who have such responsibility have to:

- keep a record of all the information they hold
- explain to others how the information can be used
- agree, with the person responsible, who can access the information
- agree what type of access is permitted for each user.

Activity 7

Organisational requirements

1 What is a policy? How does a policy help to maintain quality practice?

2 What is meant by the term 'manual storage'? Give two examples of records that could be stored by manual storage in a playgroup.

3 How can data kept electronically on computer be protected in a hospital?

4 Why must service user's personal information be kept confidential?

5 Work in pairs. Make a list of the different sources of confidential information that are likely to be received by:
   - a nursing home (person A)
   - a playgroup (person B).

Compare your lists. What are the differences?

What are care workers' responsibilities when handling confidential information?

Who might see or overhear the information

It is visiting time at Bloxwich Hospital. A group of three nurses are standing at one end of the ward, near the nurses station, talking loudly together:

Nurse 1 I was very surprised to find out that Kate Prescott had a thrombosis in her leg.

Nurse 2 Does she? On top of all her other problems! She is taking three different lots of pills already for the ulcer she has.

Nurse 3 Did you know that John Masters has come in for a foot amputation? His records show that he left it a long time before he went to his GP. If he'd gone sooner it might only have been his toes that had to come off.

Nurse 2 Who is his GP?

Nurse 3 James Bacon at the Hayloft practice. His records about John show that he's always been a heavy drinker.

In this situation anyone who is near has overheard what should be private and confidential information. The patients could have heard, visitors could have heard and any maintenance or domestic assistants could all have accessed confidential and personal information.

Such conversations are a major breech of confidential information and should be reported immediately to a line manager. The inappropriate use of confidential information is likely to lead to serious consequences.

Care workers have a responsibility:

- not to talk about service users in a way that can identify them, either outside of work, in a public place or in their own homes
- to move to a room where a door can be closed if they wish to share information about service users
- not to leave service users' written records where other people can read them. A service users file should be returned immediately to the secure area as soon as it has been finished with.

Who might have access to the information

Even though every service user's information has to be kept confidential, there is no such thing as 'complete' confidentiality. This is because information about service users has to be shared among other care workers within a setting, or with other care workers if the service user is using more than one service. Service users' relatives must not be given information unless the service user has given permission.

Care workers must follow the policy and procedures of the care setting to insure that service users' information is kept confidential. Care workers can also provide support by making sure that:

- if service users know and understand how confidentiality will be maintained
- service users know that their permission will be required before information can be passed on
- all policies and procedures relating to confidentiality are followed
- the requirements of legislation (e.g. the Data Protection Act 1998) and its effect on what happens in a care setting are known by care workers.

Look back at the section in this chapter on legislation to remind yourself of the requirements for care settings.

Disclosure of information

> **Disclosure** is passing on personal information that has been given by a service user in confidence and which was considered to be a secret between the service user and the care worker.

Care workers should never make a promise not to pass on personal information. They should explain to the service user that they will not pass on personal information unless there is a very good reason for doing so.

Disclosure of information can be necessary in special circumstances. For example:

- if a service user intends to harm themselves
- if a service user intends to harm others
- if a service user is involved in a criminal activity.

> **Discussion point**
>
> *A good friend of a patient who has been admitted to a psychiatric clinic demands to know why her friend has been admitted. What would you do and why?*

What support is available to maintain confidentiality?

Support from colleagues

It often helps to 'talk things over' with colleagues when in doubt as to the best course of action to take. This does not mean talking about the actual problem or issue if it is confidential, but to explore all the possibilities available. Talking and sharing often helps to find a solution. A colleague may have had experience of a similar problem or issue and would be able to explain what happened as a result. This does not mean that the same solution would be the right one for the current **dilemma,** but hearing what other people's experience and views are can help.

Support from line managers

A line manager should be familiar with legislation, policies and procedures within the care setting. If a care worker has a concern they should share that concern with the line manager as soon as possible. The line manager will provide advice and guidance, but if the issue is major they may prefer to deal with it themselves.

Maintaining confidentiality

The inspection report for Bourneside Nursing Home and Bowleaze Playgroup stated that staff needed to have their awareness raised about two pieces of legislation and two policies that help to maintain confidentiality.

You have been asked to prepare training materials to be used with all staff on the next training day for ONE of the care settings in the case studies.

1 Carry out research and then prepare materials to be used for training care workers to demonstrate the key principles of **two** pieces of legislation relating to confidentiality, showing how care settings would have to apply these principles in practice. Confidentiality relating to oral, written and electronic information should be included.

2 Prepare a quiz with answers, to test the knowledge of the trainees after the session on legislation.

3 Visit a care setting or invite a speaker to your centre to find out about **two** policies that relate to confidentiality and how these help to maintain confidentiality in the care setting.

4 Use the information gathered about the two policies relating to confidentiality to produce training materials for a presentation for the care workers. Make sure you link theory to practice and support your information by giving reasoned and informed judgements when discussing:

- the responsibilities of care workers
- when disclosure should be made
- the importance of obtaining support from colleagues and line managers.

What are the key features of legislation?

Human Rights Act 2000

The Human Rights Act came into force on 2 October 2000 and incorporates into UK law certain rights and freedoms set out in the European Convention on Human Rights such as:

- the right to life (article 2)
- protection from torture and inhuman or degrading treatment or punishment (article 3)
- protection from slavery and forced or compulsory labour (article 4)
- the right to liberty and security of person (article 5)
- the right to a fair trial (article 6)
- protection from retrospective criminal offences (article 7)
- the protection of private and family life (article 8)
- freedom of thought, conscience and religion (article 9)
- freedom of expression (article 10)
- freedom of association and assembly (article 11)
- the right to marry and found a family (article 12)
- freedom from discrimination (article 13)
- the right to property (article 1 of the first protocol)
- the right to education (article 2 of the first protocol)
- the right to free and fair elections (article 3 of the first protocol)
- the abolition of the death penalty in peacetime (sixth protocol).

Countries who have signed up to the Convention must secure the above rights for everyone in their jurisdiction and individuals must also have an effective remedy to protect those rights in the country's courts without the need to go to the European Court of Human Rights. The role of the European Court of Human Rights is to determine whether the domestic courts have been true to the Convention.

All national courts and tribunals must take into account the case law of the European Court of Human Rights. The Human Rights Act 2000 covers England, Wales, Scotland and Northern Ireland.

The act does not create any new criminal offences, but does apply to the criminal courts. The act does not take away or restrict any existing human rights recognised in a country.

The Children Act 1989

Local authority social services departments were required by the Children Act 1989 to act together to provide services and support for children and young people and their families, including disabled children. The act covers children and young people under 18. Key features of this piece of legislation are:

- the aim is to protect children who are at risk – the **paramountcy principle**
- children have the right to be heard
- children's wishes have to be taken into consideration
- support must be provided to keep families together where this is possible.

The services provided under the Children Act 1989 can include:

- social work
- help with housing and support
- equipment and adaptations
- occupational therapists or other specialists
- short-term breaks
- counselling
- interpreters
- an advocate or representative for individuals or families
- benefits advice.

Under this act a county court has the ability to protect a child by making it a ward of court and placing it under the protection of the court and the official solicitor. It also has the ability to make orders that can remove a child to safety or take other protective action.

The Children (Scotland) Act 199, and the Children (Northern Ireland) Order 1995, have similar provisions for children's services in Scotland and Northern Ireland.

Activity 8

Legislation

1 Work in pairs to produce a quiz which checks the knowledge of others in the group about the Human Rights Act 2000 and the Children Act 1989.

Here is an example of a question that could be asked:

'Which act has as a key focus the 'paramountcy principle'?' (A: the Children Act 1989.)

2 a What would be done as a result of the Children Act 1989 to help families stay together?

b What have to be taken into consideration for children?

c What are the rights given under the Human Rights Act 2000 known as?

d What does article 13 of the Human Rights Act state?

3 Explain how the Human Rights Act 2000 and the Children Act 1989 promote equality of opportunity.

Race Relations Act 1976

This act makes racial discrimination illegal in public life. It states that people can take action if they feel they have been discriminated because of their race in situations involving employment, housing, education, or provision of goods and services.

The act describes direct discrimination as treating a person less favourably because of their race and indirect discrimination as applying criteria that works to the disadvantage of one group of people over another.

Victimisation is also illegal under this act – it is illegal to treat somebody differently because they have made a complaint about discrimination.

Sex Discrimination Act 1975 (revised 1986)

This act applies equally to men and women. It makes it illegal to discriminate according to gender in areas of recruitment, selection, promotion and training. It is also unlawful to discriminate because a person is married. The act covers:

- direct discrimination – where one person is treated differently because of their sex
- indirect discrimination – where conditions are applied to a situation which favours one sex more than the other
- victimisation – where a person is treated less favourably because they have complained about sex discrimination in the past.

Case study

How could legislation help?

Claudia is a social worker who specialises in working with children. She is asked to visit Portway Playgroup to discuss some concerns that the named person has about James.

James has recently moved to the area with his mother and sister. His mother has recently separated from James' father.

James has arrived at playgroup on several occasions with bruises on his face, legs and arms.

His mother has said that he keeps falling of his bicycle but the staff are not convinced this is what is happening. His sister also attends the play group but she never arrives with bruises.

1 Which piece of legislation would help the social worker?

2 How could this act help?

When talking with James' mother, Claudia is told that she had been asked to remove her children from a previous playgroup as the other parents objected because they were black.

3 Which act makes this discrimination illegal?

4 Explain how this act helps to prevent discrimination.

5 Is asking the children to leave the playgroup direct or indirect discrimination? Explain why.

The Sex Discrimination Act set up the Equal Opportunities Commission to promote equal opportunities for men and women.

Discussion point

You are a female nurse in a large Trust hospital. Your supervisor, who is a married man, has started to sexually harass you. You have politely asked him to stop, but he says he's only joking and continues to tell embarrassing jokes. The harassment continues. What would you do and why?

How do policies maintain quality care?

Earlier in this unit there is a section about policies (see pages 30–31). Look back and re-read the section relating to 'policies' before going on.

Policies for individual care settings could be those that are specifically for that setting or could **originate** from those of an overarching organisation. For example, the NHS has a great many policies which settings, such as hospitals, GP practices, Health Centres and clinics, use as a basis for their own individual policies. For care workers it is important that they are aware of national organisational policies, but they should recognise that it is the policies of the setting in which they work that must be implemented.

The role of any policy is to ensure that service users' rights are upheld and that staff have guidelines to follow so that the best possible care can be provided. Service users' rights are written into policies as are equal opportunities principles in order to promote anti-discriminatory practice.

Complaints procedures

If a service user does not have the right to complain they have no way of standing up for

themselves. The complaints system is a part of any organisational policy and should be written in such a way that it is easily understood.

The NHS (an organisation), has a complaints policy. Part of that policy is shown below:

How to make a complaint about the NHS

If you are unhappy with the treatment or service you have received from the NHS you are entitled to make a complaint, have it considered and receive a response from the NHS organisation or primary care practitioner concerned. The NHS...

A complaint can be made by a patient or person affected by...

In every health, social care or early years setting there is a policy that sets out what is to happen if a **formal** complaint is made. Procedures vary slightly from setting to setting but they all follow the same pattern. For example:

- Immediately upon receiving a formal complaint the manager will meet with the service user or relative/advocate to discuss the matter fully.
- A full investigation will be carried out and a report made available to the service user or relative/advocate.
- If the service user or the relative/advocate wish to pursue the matter further they should be given the information about whom to contact, e.g. in the case of a nursing home it would be 'The Nursing Homes Inspectorate' or the NHS.

Care workers should make sure that service users know how to complain, and should support them by providing advice and guidance or arranging for an advocate to complain on their behalf.

Health and safety policies

All care settings must have a health and safety policy, the purpose of which is to provide protection for all who are connected with the setting. The aim of a health and safety policy is to provide an environment which will ensure, as far as is practical, safety of service users, staff, visitors and maintenance visitors, such as decorators, gardeners and repair personnel. The policy should comply with, and reflect the legislation that applies for health and safety.

Health and safety policies usually give information about:

- *the duties* of employers and employees
- *the organisation*, e.g. senior management, line management team, care and ancillary staff
- *general issues*, e.g. maintenance, health and safety inspections, fire drills
- *first aid and accident* reporting systems, e.g. accident reports
- *evacuation and fire* procedures, e.g. including named personnel and assembly points
- *moving and handling* procedures, e.g. using hoists.

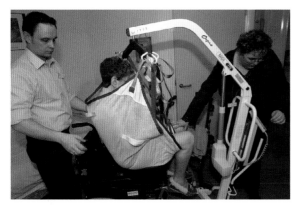
You must follow procedure when using a hoist to lift people

What else is included in the policy depends on the type of care being provided by the setting. For example, for some settings the removal of body waste will be included, while for others, sending specimens to the laboratory will need to be addressed.

Equal opportunities policies

The Equal Opportunities Commission (1986) outlined ten aspects that should be written into organisational policies if the organisation wishes to become an equal opportunities employer. The policy has to include:

- a definition of direct and indirect sex and marriage discrimination, victimisation and sexual harassment
- a statement of the organisation's commitment to equal opportunities
- the name of the officer(s) responsible for ensuring the policy is carried out
- details of how the policy is to be carried out
- an obligation upon employees to respect and act within the policy
- procedures for dealing with complaints of discrimination
- examples of unlawful practices
- details of monitoring and reviewing procedures
- commitment to remove barriers to equal opportunities
- provision of equal opportunities training for staff.

In order to provide quality care all these points must be implemented within a health, social care or early years setting.

All organisations are committed to monitoring their equal opportunities policy in order to obtain a discrimination profile. This is often based on the ethnicity and disabilities of service users and staff and is based upon a person's **self-declaration** against the categories shown in the table below, as recorded in the original Service Users' Plan of Care (for service users), job application forms (for staff) and registered disabilities.

White UK	White (Other European)	White (Other)	Irish	Black Afro-Caribbean
Black African	Black (Other)	Indian	Pakistani	Bangladeshi
Asian (East African origin)	Asian (Other)	Chinese	Mixed parentage	Other

Ethnic groups

Policies

1 Think of three questions that you would need to ask to find out about a care setting's complaints policy and procedures. Try the questions on others in the group to see if they think they are appropriate.

2 Explain how having a health and safety policy contributes to providing quality care.

3 An equal opportunities policy requires an organisation to 'monitor and review'. As a whole group, 'mind-map' ideas of what the setting should be monitoring and discuss how this would contribute to quality care.

4 Role-play with another person how you, as a service user, would make a formal complaint. Reverse the roles.

5 Try to put yourself in the place of a service user who is wanting to make a complaint. What advice would you offer?

Mission statements

A mission statement sets out the aims and objectives of a care setting and the standard of care that service users can expect. Mission statements are often placed in the reception area of the setting or given to service users when they use the service, for example, when an older person applies to live in a residential or nursing home. Below is part of a mission statement for a residential home:

Policy 207: Mission statement

It is the objective of Rochester Court to provide care for all service users to a standard of excellence which embraces fundamental principles of good care practice, and this may be witnessed and evaluated though the practice, conduct and control of quality care in the home. It is a fundamental ethos that those service users who live in the home should be able to do so in accordance with the home's 'Statement of Values', reference Policy 207.

It is the objective of the home that service users should live in a clean, comfortable and safe environment, and be treated with respect and sensitivity to their individual needs and abilities. Staff will be responsive to the individual needs of service users and will provide the appropriate degree of care to assure the highest possible equality of life within the home.

To meet these client's needs the care home...

From this mission statement it can be seen that the residential home refers to:

- principles of good practice which can be evaluated (measured)

- conduct and control of quality care which means practice will be monitored

- treating service users with respect and sensitivity which indicates that service users' beliefs, values and sexual orientation will be respected

- meeting the individual needs of service users, which demonstrates a person-centred approach and awareness of equal opportunities.

The mission statement goes on to mention:

- a formal programme of staff training, selection and recruitment

- making best use of resources so that service users get value for money

- making sure that all service users receive written information on the home's procedures for handling complaints.

When visiting a care setting or when on work experience look for the mission statement and see if it addresses all the quality care requirements. It is possible that the care setting would be prepared to let you have a copy.

How do legislation and policies apply to care settings?

For service users

If service users are aware of existing legislation they will know of their entitlements.

Legislation is a means of making sure that service users are protected from receiving a poor quality service. Legislation often sets 'targets' which providers of services must meet. For example, targets to reduce the waiting time between a service user's request and the response.

For care workers

All care settings must apply legislation. Inspection teams check that legislation has been put into practice where it is applicable. For early years settings OFSTED are the inspectorate team.

For social care services the local authority inspectorate teams are responsible for checking that standards of care are maintained. For NHS providers there is a complex inspection system which ensures that standards of quality practice are maintained.

Policies, as previously discussed, are a way of turning theory into practice. Legislation is, therefore, applied through the existence of policies which staff must follow and implement.

Assessment activity 1.5

Key skills C 2.3, ICT 2.1

Applying legislation and policies

Choose either Bourneside Nursing Home OR Bowleaze Playgroup.

Bourneside and Bowleaze want to produce training materials to help raise staff awareness of legislation that helps to maintain quality care. They have asked you to carry out research and to produce materials, either a written report, handouts or a guide, for example, that can be used for training. The materials should be in a form which can be used by staff for reference at any time when they may need to use it.

1 Review, in depth, using secondary sources, **three** pieces of legislation which apply to the care setting chosen, explaining how each helps to establish and maintain quality practice.

2 Arrange to visit a nursing home or a playgroup, or invite a speaker from a care setting to your centre (with permission), to find out how the legislation you have researched has been turned into policy and how policies are applied in the care setting. Make notes to help you produce information for the training that is required.

3 Use a range of both the primary and secondary research to produce a comprehensive, accurate and detailed account of how the legislation and policies should be applied in the care setting chosen. Make sure you draw connections to show this from both the service users' and the care workers perspective. This could be achieved by discussing examples.

What are the different kinds of care settings?

A provider of services

Organisations that provide health, social care and early years care are known as '**providers**'. Think about the services you may have used. You may have used many of those from the following list.

Services can be broadly divided into those that provide:

- for health needs, e.g. hospitals, dentists, GPs
- personal care and support, e.g. day care centres, home care assistants, independent living centres
- early years care and education, e.g. childminders, playgroups, nurseries
- *voluntary* care, e.g. hospices
- *private* care, e.g. nursing homes, residential homes, private hospitals.

Health care is usually in the **statutory** care sector and includes services that are provided by the NHS and local authorities. These include both health and personal care and support services and early years care and education.

The private sector charges for the services it provides. It is not provided by law and consists of

profit-making organisations, which means they charge for the services they provide. The private sector can include such services as hospitals, dentists, complementary therapies, residential homes, nursing homes, playgroups, childminders and nurseries.

The voluntary care sector provides services and advice, and often 'plugs the gap' where statutory services are not making any provision. Sometimes it works with statutory providers, for example, the Women's Royal Voluntary Service (WRVS) works with the local authority to provide meals for older people who live in their own homes, but who might find it difficult to cook for themselves. Voluntary organisations include, for example, charities, day care centres, support groups, hospices and parent and toddler groups. Voluntary groups are 'not-for-profit' organisations. Sometimes a voluntary service charges a small fee for the service that it provides, but this money is often used to pay the cost of overheads, for example, petrol if delivering Meals on Wheels.

All service providers must provide quality care for those who are using the services. To make sure that the services are doing this by applying legislation, policies and maintaining service users' rights, regular inspections are made by people who are trained to check that standards are being maintained. For example, for early years care and education OFSTED is the organisation who does the checking.

What is quality care?

The care values that underpin social care are based on ideas about human rights. These are the rights to which all people are entitled. A care worker must aim to 'act in the best interest of the service user'. This means valuing them as individuals and treating them in a way that the care worker would want to be treated themselves. A care worker will, therefore, show that they 'value' each individual by applying the care

Activity 10

Meet the Bishop family

Martin is in his late thirties. He is married to Pauline who is 34 years old. They have two children, Donna who is four years old and Jonathan who is nine years old.

Pauline's mother, Sue, lives next door to the family, but she has mobility problems and finds it difficult to do the daily living tasks.

1 For **each** of the following scenarios, decide whether the services visited by each member of the family is a health, social care or early years provider.

  a Jonathan has an ear infection so Pauline takes him to the GP.

  b Donna goes to a childminder twice each week.

  c Sue has a local authority home care assistant to help with daily living tasks.

  d Martin takes Jonathan for dental treatment for which he pays.

  e Pauline helps to deliver Meals on Wheels to people living in their own homes.

  f Martin works in an independent living centre.

2 Explain the difference between a private and a voluntary organisation.

3 Carry out research to find out about:
- independent living centres
- NHS Direct.

- freedom from discrimination, e.g. not to be singled out and treated differently
- confidentiality, e.g. to have all personal information kept private
- choice, e.g. to be able to make own decisions and to be consulted
- dignity, e.g. to be treated with respect
- effective communication, e.g. to have things explained and to be listened to
- safety and security, e.g. to be protected from harm
- privacy, e.g. having own space which is not invaded by others without consent

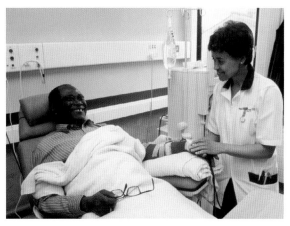

How are the care values being applied in this situation?

---

values in the day-to-day tasks that they do. Part of providing quality care means applying the care values when working with service users.

What are the care values?

In health and social care settings the three care values that underpin the work of care workers are:

- fostering service users' rights
- maintaining confidentiality
- fostering equality and diversity.

Each of these care values can be broken into further components or parts.

Fostering service users' rights

These rights include:

- the right to be different, e.g. sexual orientation, beliefs

Maintaining confidentiality

This involves:

- keeping personal information from unauthorised people
- not leaving files containing personal information where others can access them
- having passwords that must be used for accessing electronic records
- not gossiping about service users.

Fostering equality and diversity

This includes:

- understanding and not showing prejudice, stereotyping and labelling
- understanding and valuing the benefits of diversity

- understanding the bases of discrimination, such as gender, race, age, sexuality, disability or social class
- understanding own beliefs, assumptions and prejudices.

Remember: the care values are a statement of the values which underpin practical caring.

Early years care values

Care workers who work in early years care and education settings need to be aware that there are other 'values' or ' principles' that also need to be applied in their day-to-day tasks.

Early years care values	How they are applied in the settings
Upholding the welfare of the child	The child's best interests are paramount. They should be listened to and their views taken into account
Keeping children safe	Quality work practices must exist to keep children safe and healthy, e.g. access to children by unauthorised people must be prevented
Working in partnership with parents and families	Sharing openly information about children's development and progress. Respect must be shown for family traditions
Encouraging children's learning and development	Children should be offered a range of experiences and activities that support all aspects of development: physical, intellectual, emotional and social. Activities should be stimulating
Valuing diversity	Information relating to traditions should be presented in a positive manner. Events from a range of cultures should be celebrated
Providing equal opportunities	Each child should be offered equality of access to opportunities to learn and develop, and so work towards their potential, e.g. equal access to all play activities
Fostering anti-discrimination	Expressions of prejudice by children or adults should be challenged. Leaflets should be produced in more than one language
Maintaining confidentiality	Information about children and adults should never be shared with others without consent. Secure storage of records is legally required
Working with other professionals	Care workers should be willing to work with others. Liaison with other care professionals should only take place with prior permission
Being reflective practitioners	Early years workers need to reflect on their attitudes and practices, to accept feedback and to plan for developing and extending practice

Activity 11

Applying the care values to achieve quality care

Ahmed is working as a nursery nurse in a local playgroup.

Stuart is working as a care assistant in a day care centre.

1 Compare how Ahmed and Stuart will apply the care values in the workplace. You should consider similarities and differences.

2 Stuart is going to take an older person to the toilet. How will he:

- maintain dignity
- use effective communication
- provide choice.

3 Ahmed is responsible for providing a healthy and safe working environment for the children who attend the playgroup. What will this involve? Think about organisational policies and legislation when answering this question.

4 How can the 'care values' and 'principles' of care contribute to quality practice?

How is a survey conducted?

Conducting a survey is a way of gathering information about a certain subject.

In this unit you will conduct a survey to find out how quality practice is achieved and maintained in care settings.

Before starting to collect information, the person who is conducting the survey has to decide which data collecting tool or research method would be best to get the information that is needed. There are advantages and disadvantages to all data collection tools.

There are a range of methods that can be used for the collection of information, for example:

- interviewing people
- using questionnaires
- observing people or situations
- carrying out experiments.

Sometimes more than one method can be used to gather information for a survey, depending on what you are trying to get information about. For this survey, which is based on 'how quality practice is achieved in care settings', the focus of information gathering will be:

- through interviews
AND/OR
- by using questionnaires.

Such methods produce both *quantitative* data and *qualitative* data. Quantitative data is numerical and can be analysed using statistical methods. An example of a question that produces quantitative data would be, 'how many complaints are received during a six-month period?'. Quantitative data can be displayed using graphs, charts and tables.

Qualitative data concerns attitudes and opinions and often cannot be produced in numerical form. The participants might talk about their feelings, for example, a service user may say 'I feel quite safe because I know that the security measures are really good, so I do not need to worry'. Qualitative data is expressed in words and not in numbers.

Both qualitative and quantitative data can produce useful and meaningful results.

Using interviews

An interview involves asking a person questions in a 'face-to-face' situation. The person being interviewed has probably consented to take part beforehand. The interviewer prepares questions for the interview that will give the information that is needed. Interviews can be *structured* or *in-depth*.

Structured interviews

A structured interview is when the researcher (the person gathering the information) meets with the participant(s) and then asks a prepared list of questions, with little **intervention**. The data (information) collected from this type of interview is likely to be quantitative, but a limited amount of qualitative data could also be gained.

The advantage of using a structured interview is that response rates are usually quite good, the researcher knows who is answering the questions, and **prompts** and **probes** can be used to encourage responses (see Unit 2.2). A disadvantage of using the structured system of interviewing is that it is time consuming, so that only a small sample can be used.

In-depth interviews

This is where the researcher meets with the participant and allows the participant to talk freely about the chosen topic, using questions as prompts and probes. As the aim of this type of interview is to encourage the participant to get their true feelings across, only qualitative data is collected. The advantage of using in-depth interviews is that participants are able to open up on sensitive issues, as there is little structure and the researcher can explore any interesting areas that arise. The disadvantage is that the interviewer can influence the answers given.

Using questionnaires for a survey

A self-completed questionnaire is one where the researcher hands out questionnaire forms to the participants, who then answer the questions by filling in the answers in the spaces provided. The forms are then collected by the researcher when they are completed. This is a way of collecting qualitative data. The advantage of using questionnaires is that they are cheap, quick, anonymous and a way to collect information without interviewer bias. Participants can also take their time to answer the questions. The disadvantage is that there may be a poor response rate. For a survey that is investigating how quality care is maintained in care settings, a questionnaire may not be the best option on its own.

How do you plan a survey?

Methods to be used

Ideas for the methods to be used for a survey could come from secondary research into the topic (in this case, quality practice) from the work of others who have already completed similar research topics. Secondary sources can provide data that would be difficult to collect for oneself. Examples for this survey are: government papers, research papers and statistics completed after inspection reports.

It is always a good idea to produce a plan for a survey which provides a framework within which to work. Decisions will need to be made about:

- the aim of the survey, e.g. what is its overall purpose?
- the objectives, e.g. what are the steps within the aim to achieve the outcome?
- the timescales for the survey, e.g. start and completion times
- which care setting, e.g. residential home, day care centre, playgroup – remember to choose a setting where you know you will be able to obtain all the information you need
- who is to be involved in the research, e.g. care worker or manager?
- the method(s) to be used, e.g. self-completed questionnaire, structured interview or both?
- the type of questions, e.g. open and/or closed, follow on questions?
- how the results are to be presented, e.g. graphs, charts, tables.

Planning helps with the organisation of thoughts and the putting of things into the correct sequence or order. A plan, for example, could look like the one given at the bottom of this page.

Date	Action	Reason for action
1st November $\frac{1}{2}$ hour	Research three secondary sources of information about quality practice. Make notes	• To find out what research has been done previously and the methods used
3rd November $\frac{1}{2}$ hour	Make decisions on aims, objectives, methods to be used, timescales, care setting, who to gather information from	• To help inform the process, e.g. what do I want to find out?
4th November $\frac{1}{2}$ hour	Letter to care provider to explain what I would like to do, to whom I wish to speak, topic that is being researched, and examples of questions	• To get permission to use the setting and care worker • To give advanced notice of the questions that will be asked
6th November 1 hour	Plan structured interview questions for care worker and service users and group together in an organised sequence	• To make sure that there is full coverage of all the topics • To make sure the questions are appropriate and not ambiguous • To make sure all the questions on one particular topic are grouped together
7th November 1 hour	Visit care setting Ask questions	• To obtain the information needed
Etc…		

Knowing service users' rights

Choosing the research tool

You have been asked to collect information about how a care setting ensures quality practice.

1 Work in pairs to produce **five** research questions based on quality practice issues that could be used if you were producing a self-completing questionnaire.

2 Share your questions with another pair within the group and ask them to try answering the questions. Did you get the type of answers you were looking for? Rewrite any questions that were ambiguous or were not successful.

3 As a whole group discuss some of the issues that have arisen when producing the questions.

4 Work in a small group to think about qualitative data that you might want to collect about quality practice. Work out the main topics.

5 Write five questions that could be used in an in-depth interview with a care worker or manager to find out about quality practice.

Sequence of questions to be used

We have decided to do a survey through an in-depth interview.

The sequence of the questions cannot be decided until the questions themselves are written. Before even that is done the topics that are to be included in the survey must be established. For example: What are the topics and what information about each topic is needed?

For this survey there are three main topics:

- how the rights of service users are maintained
- how diversity and equality are fostered
- how confidentiality is maintained.

Each of these main topics need to be broken down into smaller parts or components. For example:

Once all the topics and the component parts have been listed, the questions can be correctly formed. It must be remembered that the focus of this survey is quality care practice and provision, so questions must be focused on this topic. Some questions should be 'open', that is they should allow the person being interviewed to give a longer and less structured answer, other questions should be 'closed', that is focusing on specific facts. (See Unit 2.2 for more detail on how to form open and closed questions.)

Once you have written the questions, you can organise them into a sequence that will form the basis of the interview. Some sound rules to follow when doing this are:

- start simple, i.e give your name and state the purpose of the interview – this will provide an introduction to the questions
- keep 'groups' of questions together
- questions can become 'harder' as the interview progresses
- always finish with 'thank you'.

Rights	What do we need to find out? (Draft)
What rights do service users have?	• How do care workers make sure the service users' rights are maintained? • How can care workers support service users to make sure their rights are maintained? • Is this dealt with in staff training? • How often does staff training take place? • Can you talk me through the type of topics that would be covered? • How does staff training help to maintain clients' rights? • Have there been any occasions when clients rights have not been maintained?
Advice and guidance	From whom can you seek advice if…

Questions	Answers
1 What type of information is considered confidential in the setting?	
2 What systems are in place to prevent access to confidential written documents?	
3 Do you have a policy relating to confidentiality?	
4 Can you give me some ideas as to what is in the policy? OR If you had a policy what would you want to see included?	
5 How is confidential information stored electronically kept safe?	
6 How are new staff made aware of the setting's policies on confidentiality?	
7 How are staff prevented from gossiping about service users both in the setting and in public places?	
8 What would happen if confidentiality was broken?	
9 Who has access to any form of confidential information?	

Collection of information

When conducting a survey, the researcher needs to prepare a document for recording the questions and a space to be able to write the answers given. For example, one of the topics to be included in this survey is 'how confidentiality is maintained in the care setting'.

To address this topic, your recording document for a structured interview may look like the table at the top of this page.

An example of an open question in this recording document is:

'What would happen if confidentiality was broken?' (Q8). This question allows the person being interviewed to give their thoughts and feelings on the subject as well as being able to talk about the facts.

An example of a closed question in this recording document is:

'Do you have a policy relating to confidentiality?' (Q3) The person being asked can answer 'yes' or 'no' to this question.

Sometimes 'follow-on' questions are required in order to collect all the information needed and to obtain the whole picture of what is happening. For example, in question 3, if the care worker says 'yes', the follow-on question would be 'what

is in the policy?' (Q4). If the care worker says 'no' the follow-on question would be the second part of question 4, or 'why you do not have a policy relating to confidentiality?'

Before going to an interview with questions and recording documents, it is always a good idea to 'trial' the questions. This means trying them on another person to see if they are **unambiguous** and that they produce the type of answers that are needed. Questions could be trialed by giving them to other people in the group, to relatives or friends. This is known as a 'pilot'. Being able to trial questions provides the opportunity to alter any questions that are not clear.

Conduct the survey

By this stage you will have prepared the questions and recording documents and will have arranged a date and time for the visit.

Remember:
- allow sufficient time to reach the care setting, i.e. don't be late!
- dress appropriately for a care setting, i.e. smart or smart-casual, with a clean, fresh and tidy appearance
- go to the front entrance and ring the doorbell, i.e. do not just wander around 'looking for someone'.

An assessor once arrived at a care setting and just wandered in. She could not find anybody until she reached the lounge. To her surprise she found a black pig sitting in an armchair in front of the fire! The pig promptly chased her from the room, snuffling at her ankles and making terrible squealing noises that did not sound at all friendly! The visit went downhill from there as the care workers and the residents were upset that the pet pig had been annoyed! Since then she has always rung the doorbell!

Figure 1.19 *An unfortunate surprise!*

Present and analyse the results of the survey

When all the data has been collected, the person who has conducted the survey needs to examine it. As the survey will have probably been conducted through in-depth interviews it is more than probable that the data will be qualitative and will need to be considered question by question.

Examining the responses will help you to analyse and interpret the information collected. Analysis of qualitative data may seem a little like writing a report. You need to sum up the comments that have been made, trying to give an accurate account of what they have said. You should not write the answers word for word. Quotes can be given to clarify and confirm what the care worker or service user has said. The answers should be grouped under separate overarching headings.

It is important to keep referring back to the questions that were asked so that a meaningful picture is given. For example:

> When asked, how information stored electronically was stored safely, Mr S said that 'only three people are given access to such records'. Each person had a password and it was only by using the password that the records could be accessed. Also, Mrs D had been given responsibility to make sure that there was compliance with the Data Protection Act 1998 and that records were not kept beyond the permitted time.

In this example the analysis makes reference to:

- the question asked
- a quote from the answer actually given by Mr S (care worker)
- other information that confirms quality practice and awareness of legislation.

Each question asked in the in-depth interview should be analysed in this way.

Draw conclusions from the survey

The purpose of analysing the results of a survey is to draw conclusions about the topics being researched. For example, having conducted a survey to find out how a care setting maintains quality care, your conclusions might be organised under these headings:

- How are rights maintained?
- How are diversity and equality fostered?
- How is confidentiality maintained?

It is very important to make sure that your conclusions are supported by the data (information) collected. For example, it would not be appropriate to conclude that service users' rights were being maintained if the data indicated that the service users were not allowed to choose their own GP or the clothes they wear, or that there was no consideration given to confidentiality.

However, the information collected may show that some rights were being maintained, for example, confidentiality, but that other rights to which service users are entitled were not. Whether rights were being partially met or fully met the conclusions drawn must be supported by evidence from the data collected.

An example of drawing a conclusion supported by evidence from the data:

At H R residential home I asked how service users' rights were promoted. I was told that this was done by providing the service users with choice. Two examples were given to illustrate the point made. One was giving the residents the option to choose which foods they would like at meal times. I was shown a menu with a wide range of dishes and was asked to sit and observe how care workers supported the service users in choosing their meal. I did note that they gave them plenty of time to choose their meals and also explained any dishes that they were unfamiliar with.

The care worker also stated that H R supported service users' rights by providing safety and security. Doors had electronic locks and only care workers knew the four digit code. Fire plans were also located around the building, and the health and safety policy, which I was given, clearly stated 'in the event of a fire the care workers on duty will make sure the service users are helped from the building to the assembly point. The supervisor in charge will...'

I was also encouraged to talk to some of the service users about rights. Mabel told me that she had been asked which GP she would like and she had said she wanted to stay with the one she already had. It was agreed that she could. I asked her whether she could choose which clothes to wear. Mabel said that she was taken out to do shopping once a month and could buy what she wanted. She also said that the care workers always asked her each morning what she would like to wear and reminded her what was in her wardrobe.

From the interviews with the care worker and Mabel, and the observation of care workers helping service users to choose their meals, the evidence showed that service users' right to choice was being met.

From this statement it is possible:

- to know the question that was asked
- to recognise that a conclusion has been drawn
- to see that conclusion drawn is supported by evidence, e.g. observation, written policies, answers to questions.

When drawing conclusions remember that they must be clearly directed to the questions asked.

Conducting the survey

You have been asked to plan and conduct a survey by visiting a care setting, for example a residential home, nursing home or early years setting, to find out how they are maintaining quality care.

Following the visit you have been asked to write a report about the setting which gives details about the following topics:

- how the service users' rights are maintained
- how equality and diversity are fostered
- how confidentiality is maintained.

You must plan the survey, conduct the survey and draw conclusions.

1 Decide which care setting you would like to visit (in consultation with your tutor). Draw up a detailed plan of how you will prepare for the visit and how you will conduct the visit itself, showing the actions you propose to take in order to collect the information, giving reasons for each action.

2 Prepare a detailed questionnaire that will help you collect the information required.

Trial the questionnaire with others to make sure the questions are clear and unambiguous.

3 Draw up an appropriate recording document which groups the questions in order within the topic and which gives a space to record the answers given.

4 Write a letter to the care setting asking if it is possible to conduct the survey. Give information about the topics that you will need to find out about during the visit and the methods you propose to use for collecting the information. You may wish to enclose a copy of the questions so that the care worker(s) can prepare for the visit.

5 Conduct the survey at the care setting.

6 Analyse the results of the survey and present them in the form of a report. Remember to focus on the questions asked and the responses given. You must also draw conclusions from your findings. You must cover the three topics mentioned above.

Glossary

Access: to get into something, or a way in

Account for: be responsible for explaining

Advocate: a person who speaks on behalf of another when they are unable to represent or speak on their own behalf

Anti-discrimination: making sure everyone is included; being against discrimination

Appraisals: a system of working out how well staff are doing

Belittle: make someone look small or silly in front of others

Breached: broken, when the law is not observed

Care plan: the recommended programme of care for a service user; a plan of action relating to the care to be provided

Challenge: to question

Complaints procedure: a way of allowing a person to let those responsible know that they are not satisfied

Complementary approach: an alternative method of doing something, e.g. treatment that involves herbs or therapies rather than traditional use of pills or surgery

Conform: to come into line with; to follow the set or expected way

Consistency: the ability to do the same thing or to act in the same way, without varying

Confidentiality: keeping private information safe

Consultation: meeting to seek information or advice from a professional

Dilemma: a problem where one point of view has to be balanced against another

Dementia: a loss of mental ability (most of which usually affects memory)

Discriminate: to make an unjust distinction on the basis of race, colour or sex etc.

Disclosed/disclosure: when confidential information is revealed to others

Duty of care: something that a carer has a responsibility to do

Empower: to enable a service user to be in control of their lives and to make their own decisions

Environment: the area that surrounds us, that we live or work in

Exert: to exercise or bring to bear (power, pressure etc.)

Formal: when something is used, done or held in accordance with rules

Frustrated: not able to see the way forward

Hazards: things that can cause harm; a risk

Inappropriate: not acceptable for the situation or occasion

Influencing skills: skills that have an effect on the outcome of a conversation

Infringed/infringement: when something that should not be taken away is taken away, e.g. a service user's rights

Intervene/intervention: interrupt or interfere/an act of interruption

Learned helplessness: becoming dependent on others through repeatedly not doing something for yourself

Legible: readable, clear

Legislation: Law passed by government

Manual: an action done by hand

Organisation: a large group which provides a service, usually more than one service

Originate: to start, or begin, or create something

Paramountcy principle: in law, when the child's best interests are to be regarded as paramount

Paramount: of top importance; first

Patronise: to talk down to someone

Priorities: things that we hold to be important, that we must deal with first

Prompts/probes: comments that encourage a listener to say more or to explore a subject more

Protection: being kept from harm

Providers: people or organisations who give a service or make a service available

Quality care/quality practice: to provide a level of care that is of a high standard and which is in the best interest of the service user

Relevant: appropriate for the purpose

Restricted: stopped from doing or having something

Reviewed: reflected upon, thought about

Ridicule: to make a person look silly

Self-esteem: how we see and think about ourselves

Self-declaration: a form that states something which someone fills in for themselves

Statutory: something that exists by law

Superior: in a higher position or rank

Traditional: based on the usual way of doing things

Tribunal: a group of people who have been appointed to hear disagreements relating to work practices

Unambiguous: clear or definite in meaning

Unauthorised: having no authority or permission

Victimisation: to be picked on

Unit 2 Communicating with service users in care settings

Effective communication can help to make service users feel valued

Oral communication is an important part of all of our lives as we use it every day for a variety of reasons. Oral conversations are such common, everyday events that we often think they do not require any special skills. Think about the number of conversations you have had already today. Some were informal, such as when you spoke with friends or family members. Other conversations were more formal, for example, you may have had a conversation with a care worker such as a GP (General Practitioner) or a teacher or employer. In all these conversations specific skills will have been used, such as words, body language, gestures and active listening.

A major part of a care worker's day-to-day task is to make sure their communication is effective. People who use health, social care and early years services, are often dependent on care workers for obtaining and giving information, and they may also want to express their feelings and emotions to them. Service users want to know that they can rely on care workers to value them as people, and that information shared will be kept confidential.

Effective communication is at the heart of any relationship. This means that care workers need

to be aware of the skills required to communicate effectively with service users. When communicating with service users and others care workers should remember that those with whom they are communicating need to understand what is being said. The ability to understand others and to make ourselves understood as care workers, is a skill often taken for granted. If, for example, an older person in a residential home or a day care centre does not understand what a care worker has said, then their reply could be inappropriate. Older people can become frustrated, angry or aggressive if they think they have not been understood. Similarly, a child in a playgroup may misunderstand something that has been said by the nursery nurse and may be upset and cry as a result. Inappropriate communication can have the effect of lowering a service user's self-esteem and could in extreme cases cause the service user to become emotionally agitated.

If a person is going to work in a care setting or if they are an informal carer at any time in their life, it is important that they know how to communicate effectively with service users and with others who are involved in their care.

What will we learn in this unit?

Learning outcomes

You will learn to:

- Recognise how to encourage oral communication
- Investigate the range of skills used when communicating effectively
- Review how to communicate through effective listening
- Recognise how to apply the care values that underpin communicating with others
- Communicate effectively with service users
- Evaluate the range of communication skills used and plan for improvements

Why do service users and carers need to communicate orally?

People communicate in order to:

- obtain information, e.g. about jobs or to learn
- give information to others, e.g. when providing support
- exchange ideas and opinions with people with whom we form relationships
- meet our physical, intellectual, emotional and social needs, e.g. the need to feel valued.

To give and obtain formation

What is communication?

Communication is the **interaction** between two or more people. That is, two or more people talking with or having a conversation with one another. Oral communication is only one method of interaction among many.

In a typical care setting, a care worker uses all these methods of communication. For example:

- written communication – letters, menus, care plans

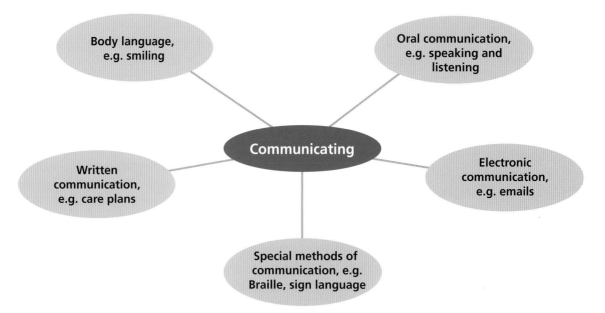

Figure 2.1 *Different ways of communication*

- electronic communication – prescriptions can be sent from a GP surgery directly to a pharmacy, or information from a GP about a service user can be sent directly by email to a specialist at a hospital
- body language – when talking to people, we often send out and pick up non-verbal messages as well as speech. These messages can be conveyed by body posture, gestures, expressions or even just a look in the eyes (more information on this in Unit 2.2)
- special methods of communication – this depends on the needs of specific service users (later in this unit).

The purpose of most of these types of communication is often to give information or to obtain information.

> ### Discussion point
> *Why is positioning important when interacting with service users?*

What are the skills of effective communication?

At some time in their lives, most people experience difficulty when talking to others. It may be that this happens when they fail to get a word in edgeways when talking, or when they feel that they don't know what to say next, or they worry that when they speak, others may consider them to be boring. Effective and meaningful communication is dependent on the use of appropriate skills and social **co-ordination**. It involves:

- showing an interest
- being interesting
- having the ability to start conversations and end them.

It also involves using skills such as listening, clarifying, summarising and knowing how to be **assertive**. In this situation being assertive means you will not let the other person take the interaction in a direction that is meaningless. It means focusing the interaction on the points that need to be explored.

Communication is not just about talking

Professional care workers must know how to use skills when communicating, and when to use them. The work that is done in care settings depends very much on using effective communication. Effective communication requires care workers to:

- **analyse** their own thoughts and think about what they are going to say
- use skills to **interpret** the language and non-verbal behaviour of service users
- understand and draw conclusions
- present the next ideas for continuing the conversation.

Communication means understanding what has been said

What happens when we communicate orally?

When we communicate with one another we are sending messages and **disclosing** information. When communicating orally, messages are encoded by a sender and decoded by a receiver. Figure 2.2 at the top of page 56 shows this process.

Encodes   Decodes

| Sender | → | Message | → | Receiver |

Figure 2.2 *Sending and receiving messages*

Here is an example of how this would apply to messages given and received in a care setting:

A care worker (sender) puts words together (**encodes**) to say 'Joan, are you joining the computer class today?' (message).

The service user (receiver) listens, the brain interprets the signal (**decodes**) and then the message is received.

However, effective communication means more than just passing on information. It means involving or engaging the other person. Communication in health, social care and early years settings is of a complex nature. Care workers need to be aware that each individual has their own way of interpreting messages.

The process of communicating involves various stages within a cycle:

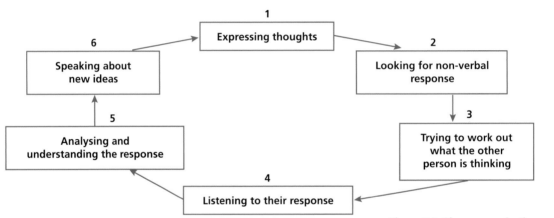

Figure 2.3 *The communication cycle*

Here is an example of how this works in practice:

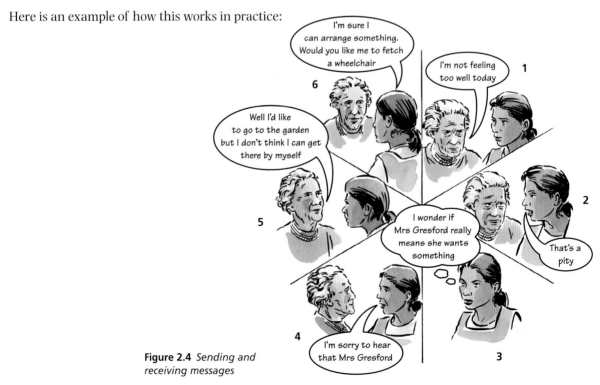

Figure 2.4 *Sending and receiving messages*

Communicating has to be a two-way process where each person is trying to understand, interpret or make sense of what the other person is saying. Often it is easier to understand people who are similar to ourselves, for example a person who has the same accent, or a person who is in a similar situation to ourselves. Our decoding equipment in the brain tunes in, breaks down the message, analyses the message, understands it and interprets its meaning and then creates a response or answer. This is all helped by the body language or signals, such as smiles or gestures, that have been given by the person who is giving the message. When a care worker is speaking with a service user he or she is forming a mental picture about what they are being told.

Activity 1

Giving and obtaining information

Aub is 72 years old and is living in a residential home. He has only been living in the home for one day and finds everything a little confusing. A care assistant sits down with Aub and talks to him about his choice of meal for midday, and gives him information about the menu.

Figure 2.5 *Communicating and advising about a meal*

1 Use Figure 2.5 as a model.
   a Give the first line of the conversation for the sender of the message.
   b Give a response that could be given by the receiver of the message.

2 Suggest two different ways that the care assistant could 'engage' Aub during the conversation.

3 Role-play the case study with another member of the group, taking the part of the care assistant. How difficult did you find this? What was your message? Was it decoded correctly?

4 Change roles and do the role-play again. How did it feel to be the service user? Did you understand the message?

The different purposes of oral communication

In a care setting, service users may want to communicate to share their problems. A child in a playgroup may want to know 'Why didn't mummy stay?', or an older service user at a day centre may want to know 'Why did I have to attend'? If the answers given are not understood, the service user could become unhappy or unco-operative. Service users in a hospital may want to know what choices they have about proposed treatments, while older service users in residential homes may want to share their views on different topics with care workers.

Communication with service users has different purposes. Care workers need to recognise the differences between these purposes if communication is to be effective. Some interactions have more than one purpose and decoding the message is more complex, requiring the use of more skills.

The needs of human beings are complex and care workers often work with service users who may be afraid or who may not understand what is going to happen to them. They may feel threatened by the situation that they find themselves in.

At each stage of development communication plays a major part in meeting these needs.

The importance of clarity and accuracy in oral communication

A care worker should use words that are **unambiguous** so that the meaning is clear and cannot be misinterpreted. The message should not use unnecessary **technical terminology** which could be better explained by using simpler vocabulary.

When giving information accuracy is important. The person with whom a care worker is talking will probably want to use the information that has been given. If that information proves to be incorrect, the service user is likely not to place any trust in future information given by that particular care worker. Information is given by care workers so that service users can make informed choices and decisions.

Figure 2.6 *Is this a new language?*

Obtaining information is a very important aspect of the relationship between a care worker and a service user. The care worker may need to find out about the service user's personal health and care needs, about their **medical history**, about the medication they are taking, or about who to contact in the event of an emergency. Listening to the service user very carefully and using the appropriate skills will enable them to access this information. If the information gathered is not accurate the service user could be given incorrect treatment or medication, or the wrong relatives could be contacted in an emergency.

> **Discussion point**
>
> *How can a care worker know that their message has been understood?*

> **Discussion point**
>
> *Why is accuracy important when interacting with service users?*

Case study

Maxine – giving information

Maxine is in her seventies. She lives in her own home but feels isolated as she cannot get out to meet her friends. She has agreed to visit the local day care centre for one day of each week. When she arrives for her first visit she is anxious because she does not know what to do or what is expected of her.

Work with another person if possible to do the following activities.

1 What information should the care assistant give to Maxine?

2 Plan a role-play to show others how this information should be given to Maxine by the care assistant.

3 Demonstrate the role-play to others.

4 What is important when giving information verbally to service users?

Case study

Brendan

Brendan is five years old and is starting school. His parents are going with him to visit the school and to meet his teacher. When they received the invitation to go with Brendan they were told that they would be spending a short time with the teacher as she would need some information about the family.

Work in pairs for this activity:

You are the teacher of the reception class.

1 Write down four pieces of information that you would need to obtain from Brendan's parents.

2 List three points to remember when obtaining information from a service user.

3 Role-play talking to Brendan's parents to obtain information.

Figure 2.7 *Obtaining information*

To exchange ideas

Informal communication allows care workers and service users to explore their ideas. A care worker could, for example, ask a service user what they think about an item that has been in the news or about their ideas for an outing or event. A service user could make enquiries of a care worker about what they think it would be best to do in a given situation or about how best to manage their day-to-day situation. This sort of communication is a part of meeting our various needs.

To meet physical, intellectual, emotional and social needs

Abraham Maslow's theory was that human life could be understood in terms of an individual's development of their ability and **potential.** Maslow suggested that we all have levels of need which have to be met.

Abraham Maslow

When we are communicating with others our physical, intellectual, emotional and social needs are being met:

- physical needs – these are met because we are actively sitting or standing with others, as well as using communication to make requests for physical needs
- intellectual needs – we have to think before we can communicate in order to sort out the words we will use. We also have to understand what the other person is saying so we are using our intellectual abilities, that is, thinking about what is being said
- emotional needs – talking to people can be a very satisfying experience, giving a sense of achievement. Sometimes we can be made very angry by something that others say to us. Our emotions can be influenced in a good way or in a negative way. If the influence is negative, our self-esteem may be reduced, making us feel bad about ourselves
- social needs – these are met when we are in the company of others. Interacting takes more than one person, so when we communicate, whether on a one-to-one basis or with a group of people we are meeting our social needs.

Care workers need to find out about service users' physical, intellectual, emotional and social needs (P.I.E.S). Whether a service user trusts a care worker not to do anything that harms them depends on the care worker's attitudes and on the interactions that the service user has had with the care worker. A lack of clear communication could result in a service user's physical,

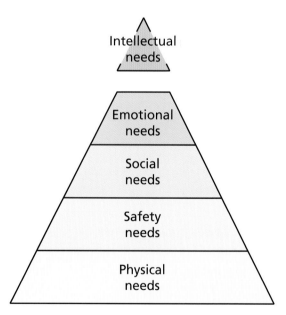

Figure 2.8 *Maslow's pyramid of needs*

intellectual, emotional and social needs not being met.

For example, a person who is confined to bed because of their physical condition could become **withdrawn** and may not feel valued if they are left alone for long periods of time. This could lead to the service user becoming **clinically depressed.**

Figure 2.9 *The service user in this room wouldn't be able to see out of the window from their bed*

Key skills 2.1a

Case study

Meet Sunil and his family

Sunil has recently moved to the town of Portway with his wife and two children. He visits a local Health Centre to find out what services are available for himself and his family.

Sunil's wife, Miriam, needs a counselling service as she has mental health needs. His son, Ali, has asthma attacks. Sunil needs regular prescriptions for high blood pressure.

Work with others when doing the following activities.

1 Plan and carry out a role-play to show how to communicate effectively with Sunil to gather information about his family and himself so that he can be registered with the Health Centre.

2 The Health Centre offers medical care, physiotherapy, counselling services, home visits by a psychiatric nurse as well as medical care. Plan and carry out a role-play to exchange ideas with Sunil about what the Health Centre has to offer and what Sunil thinks he would like.

Professional care workers and volunteers who work in care settings must be able to change the way in which they communicate to suit the service user that they are working with. For example, they may need to speak at a slower pace, or they may need to write some points down. Some service users may have specific needs, for example, they may have had a stroke which prevents them from speaking, or they may be visually impaired. Sign language and **Makaton** are methods that care workers use to communicate with service users who have hearing difficulties. Braille could be used with service users who cannot see. Makaton is a simple form of sign language and is usually taught to children at a young age when it is discovered that they have a hearing impairment. Braille is used to help those people who have a severe sight impairment.

What factors influence communication?

Have you ever been talking to someone and not been able to hear what they say because the music is too loud or because of some other noise? If you have, you know how difficult it can be to try and understand or make sense of what is being said in those circumstances. Perhaps you stopped listening because it was too hard to follow the conversation.

Factors such as noise, heating, lighting, seating, ventilation and proximity can have a positive or negative effect on service users, and can affect the way in which they interact with care workers and with other service users. These are known as 'environmental' factors.

> ### Discussion point
> *How can Makaton and Braille help service users with a sensory impairment to communicate?*

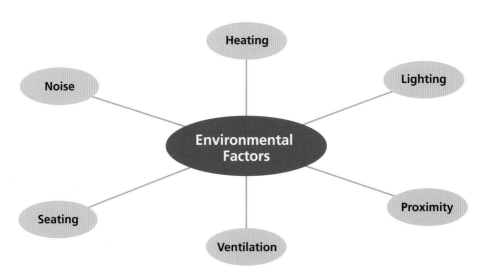

Figure 2.10 *Environmental factors influencing communication*

Noise

For example, if it is noisy when a care worker is giving information, the service user may not hear exactly what is being said and may receive incorrect information. This could lead to the service user making the wrong decision. It is important, therefore, that noise is kept to a minimum when having conversations. On the other hand if it is very quiet in the room, a service user may be reluctant to exchange ideas with a care worker or volunteer, because they may be afraid that everyone in the room will be listening to what they have to say.

> **Discussion point**
>
> *How can noise affect a service user who is attending a day centre for the first time and who is listening to a care worker explain what happens at the day centre?*

Lighting

Lighting needs to be appropriate for the occasion. If a service user is having a counselling session, shining a bright light directly on them is not going to help them to talk about their needs and the things that are worrying them! If a service user is trying to obtain some information from a care worker, being able to see them as they speak and the body language that they are using could help to convey meaning.

> **Discussion point**
>
> *How can poor lighting affect communication with a service user who is being shown information in a leaflet about the treatment that is being proposed?*

Figure 2.11 *Could you hear what was being said in this situation?*

Ventilation and heating

Trying to have a meaningful conversation with someone if you or the other person is too hot or too cold, or in a room that is not well ventilated, can also lead to ineffective communication. Too much heat or a room that is too cold can cause lack of concentration and loss of interest. Lack of ventilation could cause the person to become drowsy and they may even fall sleep!

Discussion point

When communicating how can too much heat and little ventilation affect a service user in a residential home?

Space

The amount of space required depends on the type of interaction. A dietician who is exchanging ideas with a service user may want to be seated side-by-side with a small table nearby to spread leaflets and information on. In this way the dietician is at the same level as the service user and the service user will feel equal in the conversation. Similarly, if an interaction is to take place in a nursery with a child, it is best for the adult to be at the same level as the child. To stand over a child who is sitting on a low chair is very threatening. At a nursery, joining in the activity that they are doing is a very good way to share ideas and exchange information.

Discussion point

Why is it important for people to feel 'equal' when having an interaction?

Seating arrangements

When a consultant is sharing the results of a diagnostic test it may be appropriate to have a table with the consultant seated on one side and the service user on the other. Such a formal situation reduces the likelihood of an emotional reaction and helps the service user to stay in control.

On another occasion when a care worker wishes to provide comfort and support, sitting side-by-side may be appropriate.

Discussion point

Think of other situations where formal positioning would be more appropriate. Why is this so?

Proximity

Proximity is how close a person is to another. If a service user is placed in a room that is too small they may feel **inhibited** and uncomfortable. Each of us likes to feel that we have our own space. We do not like it when someone pushes their face or body close to our own, because we feel threatened.

Relationships

In care settings, effective relationships need to be established between:

- care workers and service users
- service users and other service users
- care workers and other professionals
- care workers and service users' families.

Thank you, I really feel less frightened now

If good relationships are achieved, then communication will be more effective, but effective communication itself can contribute to the forming of good relationships. Components that contribute to building relationships can be seen in Figure 2.12.

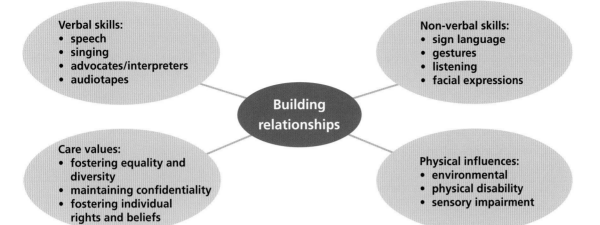

Figure 2.12 *Building relationships*

Forming good relationships with others involves:

- showing respect, e.g. listening carefully
- trust, e.g. not gossiping about personal information relating to others
- using appropriate vocabulary, e.g. not using verbal abuse or technical terms which the service user may not understand
- making sure service users with physical disabilities and sensory impairment are not prevented from participating, e.g. providing hearing aids, Braille or an advocate.

Whatever the occasion for communicating, it is important that the service user and the care worker can have direct eye contact. This must be a priority when arranging seating. Not to have eye contact could cause barriers to form during the conversation, preventing the service user from openly sharing their ideas. Good eye contact at appropriate times can encourage a service user to talk. It also conveys interest and can convey **empathy**. By using eye contact appropriately, the care worker is showing that they understand the service user's situation. They are able to put themselves in the service users position and can see things from their perspective.

Whenever a care worker is thinking of having a conversation with a service user they should at least have a mental plan of the desired layout of the seating, even if they do not have a written plan. A **socio-gram** can be used to show the seating arrangements and to check after the conversation whether eye contact was maintained and the frequency of such eye contact.

Activity 2

Making seating arrangements

A room is arranged for discussion like the one shown in Figure 2.13.

1 Who did not communicate with whom?

2 Could all the participants see each other?

3 Could each person easily make eye contact with others in the group?

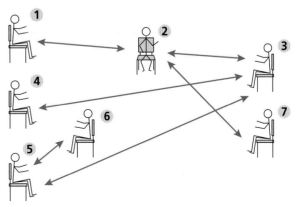

Figure 2.13 *Is this the most effective arrangement?*

Having a long and serious conversation with a service user who is tired or who may be in pain should be avoided. A service user who is in pain is unable to concentrate and may become aggressive. Their energy will be taken up with managing the pain rather than with the conversation. Similarly, a person who is emotionally upset will also be influenced in a conversation by their problem. If a service user has suffered a **bereavement** for example, they are not likely to be able to focus on a topic and their decisions will be influenced by their recent loss. Similarly, if a service user has recently had an argument with their friend or with a relative, this could influence the way they speak and the decisions they make.

> ### Discussion point
>
> *How could being worried affect the conversation between a service user and a care worker?*

Communication is influenced by the relationship that exists between the sender and receiver of a message. If a service user has a good relationship with the person with whom they are talking, this will be reflected in their tone of voice, body language and eye contact.

Their tone is likely to be warm and sincere, and their body language will show interest by a slight leaning towards the other and smiling. Eye contact will reflect friendliness and will be at appropriate intervals. If the two people who are interacting do not have a friendly relationship, the opposite behaviour will be demonstrated. If this happens the conversation is more likely to be negative and both will go away from the interaction with feelings that the exchange was unsatisfactory.

What are the barriers that can inhibit oral communication?

It is important that care workers find out as much as possible about the way the service user likes to be addressed and about their views and opinions relating to issues that will be raised at any meeting.

This can be achieved by:

- outlining to the service user the topics that the care worker hopes to cover during the meeting
- asking the service user what they would like added to the list
- finding out how the person prefers to be addressed, e.g. by their first name or by their title and name. This can often be established at the very beginning of the interaction when the care worker introduces themselves.

Case study

Arranging a meeting with a service user

An occupational therapist is meeting with Christine to discuss how Christine's home could be adapted after she has had her leg amputated, to make daily living activities easier.

Environmental factors that the occupational therapist should take into consideration when arranging the room for the meeting are:

- the skills that will be used
- how well the room is ventilated

- the way notes will be taken
- the time the meeting will take.

1 Draw a plan to show the arrangement of the seating for the meeting. Explain why you would arrange the room in this way.

2 Carry out research to find out what a 'socio-gram' is and explain how one could be used to find out whether the conditions enhanced or inhibited communication.

The opening conversation between a service user and a physiotherapist in a hospital could be as follows:

> **Care worker** Hello, I'm Anita, your physiotherapist. I hope we can get that arm moving more easily and free you from pain
>
> **Service user** Hello, I'm Donna Morgan.
>
> **Care worker** How would you like me to address you in this meeting? Shall I call you Mrs Morgan or would you prefer Donna?
>
> **Service user** Oh! Please do call me Donna, it sounds less formal.
>
> **Care worker** I've drawn up an outline plan for our six sessions. I would just like to go through the plan so you know what to expect, and I will answer any questions you have. Is that OK?

The care worker is less likely to raise barriers between themselves and the service user by this approach. The physiotherapist is recognising that the service user needs to feel comfortable, so asks the preferred name that the service user wants used. Also any distress or anxiety has been reduced by informing the service user what has been planned for the session. The service user knows what to expect.

Barriers can affect the results of a conversation and care workers should do their best to reduce these barriers. Examples of barriers and how they can influence communication are given in the table below.

Barrier	How barriers can influence communication
Distress	If a service user is worried or upset they will not be able to concentrate on the topic of a conversation. The care worker will need to deal with the emotional condition first
Patronising language	Care workers can be **dismissive** in the way they speak to a service user by 'talking down', or speaking to them as though they were much younger than they are. This often happens when talking to older people or to children. A service user does not feel valued if this approach is used and is less likely to be co-operative
Invasion of personal space	We all like to have our own personal space. Care workers must take care not to intrude on this
Having a negative attitude	Examples of negative attitudes are: being in too much of a hurry; making **assumptions** about people because of their appearance or age; being emotionally stressed by the needs of service users
Tiredness or boredom	A service user can soon tell if a care worker is bored, as this will be shown through their body language and through tone of voice. A tired service user lacks concentration and is unlikely to **retain** the information given
Off-loading own experiences	Care workers' own poor experiences should not be reflected in the workplace. For example, a service user should not be shown lack of empathy because of a breakdown in a personal relationship at home
Inappropriate body language	The way a care worker sits can convey positive or negative messages. Sitting with arms crossed and low in a chair can indicate disinterest
Inappropriate use of language	Examples of this are: using technical terminology where simpler vocabulary would be more appropriate; verbally abusing a service user just because they have dementia or a similar condition. A care worker was heard to shout at a service user who had dementia: 'Gwen, I'll wash your mouth out with soap if you ask me that question again. That's the fifth time in the last ten minutes that you've asked the same thing'. This is not the attitude care workers should take with service users, however annoying they may be by asking repetitive questions. A care worker must learn to control their emotions.

Case study

Barriers in a residential home

Baljit wanted to talk to her care assistant about her dental and hospital appointments. The care worker told Blajit:

'I can't stop to talk to you about that. You've been before so you know what to expect. Go and sit in the lounge with the others, I've got enough trouble of my own without dealing with yours.'

1 Identify the barriers that are likely to occur as a result of this conversation.

2 Draw up a conversation between a care worker and a service user to show the correct way the conversation should have been managed.

3 Role-play the conversation to show others how the interaction should be handled, explaining the reasons.

How do stereotyping and labelling affect communication?

Stereotyping is thinking that all people in the same group are the same. For example, thinking that all people over the age of 80 need mobility aids and do not have any intellectual ability, or that all children below the age of four are unable to make any decisions for themselves.

Stereotyping often occurs because it is an easy way of grouping people together. For example, service users may be stereotyped because of their language. It could be wrongly assumed, because of the colour of their skin, that all people who are not white cannot speak English. This is demonstrated when care workers speak in 'broken English' to a service user without first finding out if they can speak English or if English is their preferred or first language.

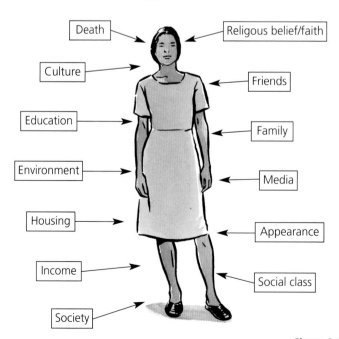

Death
Religous belief/faith
Culture
Friends
Education
Family
Environment
Media
Housing
Appearance
Income
Social class
Society

Figure 2.14 *What has influenced me?*

Care workers sometimes impose their own views and opinions on situations at work. These are often views and opinions learnt while growing up or which have been assumed because they have friends who hold such opinions. A good care worker makes sure that they are informed and knowledgeable so that they avoid stereotyping and labelling. They should also have examined their own attitudes and values to make sure that they know themselves and are not unjustly judging others.

> **Discussion point**
>
> *How can a care worker's own views and opinions influence the care they provide?*

> **Labelling** is thinking that a particular person belongs to a certain category just because of the way that they look or what their needs are. That category will then be viewed with all the assumptions of stereotyping. For example, a care worker could label all service users who are dirty as 'being lazy' when it could be that a few are dirty because they are lazy, whereas most who are dirty may not have had care workers who kept them clean or the ability to keep themselves clean.

Care workers must remember that each individual is **unique**. They are to be valued for themselves, and care workers must have **non-judgemental** attitudes as an important part of their caring role.

Stereotyping and labelling undermines relationships and communications in a care setting because:

- it gives an inaccurate picture of an individual, leading to assumptions that might lead to poor care provision
- it is hurtful to people on the receiving end, harming their self-esteem, meaning that care workers are not doing their job in meeting the needs of service users.

> **Activity 3** Key skills ICT 2.3
>
> **Anti-discrimination**
>
> 1 What is the difference between stereotyping and labelling?
>
> 2 Give one example of stereotyping that could occur in a children's nursery.
>
> 3 Prepare materials that could be used to explain to new care workers how stereotyping and labelling could be avoided when working in care settings.

How can culture and belief affect oral communication?

If service users are from other cultures or have different beliefs from those of service users, these should be acknowledged. For example, when communicating, having direct eye contact in Western European culture is considered to be desirable and acceptable, while in many African cultures it can be considered rude and totally unacceptable. Some gestures can also be acceptable in some cultures and not in others. Body language too can have different meanings in different cultures. Care workers need to know about the different cultures that they are most likely to meet in the course of their work. This would help to prevent some misunderstandings, for example, you might need to know that:

- in some cultures, young women in a family can only receive medical attention if they are accompanied by an older family member
- many women from many cultures would prefer to have a female doctor or care worker.

These considerations may not at first seem to be directly linked to communicating with service users, but they do have an impact on the way in which we communicate and with whom. For example, consider a conversation with a service user in a day care centre:

> *Care worker: Hello love, how are you today? Sit yourself over there, I'll be with you in about ten minutes.*

Such a way of addressing a service user does not necessarily show respect and does not show that the care worker values the service user. The care worker has not taken the trouble to find out how the service user would like to be addressed or given them sufficient time. The service user is unlikely to respond positively, if at all! Whereas if the care worker said:

> **Care worker:** Hello, I'm Kate. I am going to be looking after you today. I know this is the first time you have been to the day care centre. Tell me, how would you like to be addressed?

In this example the care worker has:

- given her name
- made the service user aware that she is expected by showing that she knows it is the service users first time at the day care centre
- asked how the service user would like to be addressed
- engaged the service user by asking a question which requires a response.

How can lack of awareness of difficulties and disabilities inhibit oral communication?

Not all disabilities are at first obvious. If a person is walking with the use of a mobility aid this is very apparent. However, if someone has a disability that affects the digestive system, such as irritable bowel syndrome or an ulcer, or that is the result of a stroke such as loss of short-term memory, it will not be so obvious. The service user could look quite well at a first glance.

Care workers should be aware that service users with whom they are dealing may have a 'hidden' disability and may be in pain. The disability and/or the pain could affect any communication between care worker and service user. Managing pain can take a lot of energy and can cause service users to be worried and emotionally upset. Care workers need to observe and ask appropriate questions if they suspect that a service user does have a disability.

If, for example, a person has difficulty hearing from one ear, the care worker should be careful to sit on the side of the ear which does not have impairment. If a service user has difficulty in looking or turning their head in a particular direction, the care worker needs to sit so that a strain is not put on the service user in this way. If the service user is in pain they may:

- not be able to concentrate
- lack interest
- not retain the information
- become withdrawn and non-communicative.

Activity 4

Culture and belief

1 What is culture? Choose from the following:
   - the type of education we have had
   - the different types of illness we have experienced
   - the attitudes and beliefs we have from the society in which we live
   - the influence of our friends when we socialise.

2 Explain how a playgroup could make sure that the religious beliefs of the children that attend are promoted.

3 How can having a physical or sensory impairment affect communication?

4 How might care workers support each of the following service users with impairment, through oral communication?
   a Harry, who is deaf in his left ear.
   b Aub, who is confined to a wheelchair and gets tired easily.
   c Darren, who has learning difficulties.

What is empowerment, and how can communication skills achieve it?

Empowerment in a care setting means allowing service users to take control of their own lives. This means presenting them with all the relevant information and allowing them to make choices and decisions. Service users who feel that their views and decisions are valued respond positively when communicating. Service users need to feel that they are equal to others and not people for whom things are done or arranged. The target for effective communication is to form a good working relationship or partnership where each contributor is valued. This means:

- respecting service users' rights
- maintaining confidentiality
- respecting individual people's beliefs and cultural views and opinions
- allowing service users to express their views and opinions
- tolerating **diversity** when service users do not have the same opinions or ways of doing things as us.

Effective communication and empowerment enables service users to retain their own identity and does not involve care workers imposing their identity on them.

> ### Discussion point
> *What can care workers actually do in their day-to-day tasks to empower service users?*

Assessment activity 2.1

Key skills C 2.2, ICT 2.1

Communicating with service users

You have been asked to prepare a resource pack that could be used when training care workers in a care setting. The resource pack is to be titled 'How To Communicate Effectively with Service Users'. Use a variety of methods to present the information within the resource pack, for example, posters, displays, handouts and written information.

Complete the following tasks and include them in your resource pack.

1 a Arrange (through your tutor) to visit a care setting to carry out research to find out how and why care workers and service users communicate and what the factors are that can influence communication. Prepare some questions to help you find out the information you need.

  b Prepare materials that could be used to show the trainee care workers the reasons people communicate. You should give examples to illustrate the points you discuss. Give as much detail as you can.

2 Include general information for the trainees about the factors that can influence communication between care workers and service users. Use at least **three** different case studies or scenarios in this section.

3 Provide information to explain to the trainees possible barriers that can inhibit communication between care workers and service users, linking these to the factors that you have already researched. Use at least **three** examples in this section.

4 Write a definition of stereotyping and labelling for the trainees, illustrating the points you make with examples from care settings to show how they affect communications between care workers and service users.

5 Find some examples of cultural variation within a care setting. Prepare materials that will explain to the trainees how culture can influence communications between care workers and service users.

6 Prepare materials for the trainees to explain, using examples, how disabilities can affect communication between care workers and service users. Make suggestions as to how barriers to communication, caused by disabilities, can be overcome.

7 Produce **three** case studies to show how care workers can empower service users when communicating, and explain to the trainees the reasons why the service users were empowered.

Recognise how to encourage oral communication 71

What skills are used when communicating orally with service users and care workers?

Effective communication involves a care worker giving undivided attention and conveying acceptance to the service user. Skills can be used to help send and receive messages. These can include:

- the use of appropriate questioning and other oral techniques
- using body language that is acceptable, e.g. eye contact, expression
- active listening
- exchanging information
- building a relationship with the service user, in other words establishing **rapport**.

Gerald Egan in his book *The Skilled Helper* recommended using an **acronym** to help build all the **components** of communication with others. The acronym he used was SOLAR. More information is given about this in Figure 2.15.

Effective communication involves eye contact

> **Discussion point**
>
> *Imagine that a consultant at a hospital has to give a service user the news that she has breast cancer. How could SOLAR be applied within the conversation?*

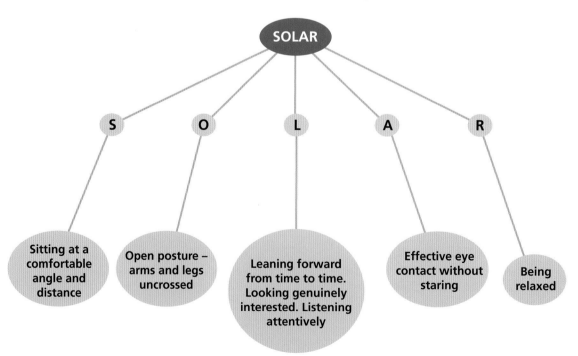

SOLAR

- **S** — Sitting at a comfortable angle and distance
- **O** — Open posture – arms and legs uncrossed
- **L** — Leaning forward from time to time. Looking genuinely interested. Listening attentively
- **A** — Effective eye contact without staring
- **R** — Being relaxed

Figure 2.15 *Components of communication*

Questioning skills

Asking the right questions and phrasing them in just the right way is very important. Questions should be kept short, and the language or vocabulary used should be easy to understand. Long and multiple questions should be avoided. For example, a care worker should avoid a question like the one below:

So when did you first have this problem with the pains in your legs and how and when did you notice it, and what were you doing at the time?

A service user would have lost track of the question after the first line!

There are two types of questioning technique that can used when communicating with service users. These are:

- closed questions
- open questions.

Closed questions

Closed questions are those that require specific answers. For example, a care worker might say to a service user:

How many days are you attending the day care centre?

Or, to a child in a playgroup:

Do you like playing with the dressing up things?

Closed questions are a way of gaining factual answers. They do not provide the opportunity for service users to express their opinions or to discuss issues. They are an important part of a conversation, however, as sometimes care workers need to know about specific points, for example, a service user's date of birth, or about any illnesses they may have had.

Open questions

Open questions provide service users with the opportunity to give longer answers and the care worker can, as a result, gain an **insight** into how the client is feeling or about their views and opinions. Successful open questions are more likely to begin with the words 'what' or 'how'. Examples of open questions are:

How do you feel about the treatment that has been proposed?

Or

What activities have you already tried?

Both questioning techniques can be used successfully when communicating with service users, depending on the type of response and information the care worker is seeking.

Practising open and closed questions is essential before working with actual care workers.

Case study

Communicating with Meena

Meena, who is three, is being very difficult at playgroup. She is falling out with her friends and running away into corners and crying.

1 What are each of the following questions – open or closed?
   a How do you feel about the situation?
   b How much do you weigh?
   c How often do you attend the clinic?
   d What you would like to see happening as far as your treatment is concerned?

2 Write **three** open and **three** closed questions that you, as a nursery nurse, could use when talking to Meena to find out why she is acting this way and what she would like to do while at the playgroup.

3 Put the questions together and write out the transcript of a three to five-minute conversation that you might have with Meena.

4 Role-play the conversation.

5 Evaluate how effective your questions were and show any improvements you would make. How would the improvements help?

Other communication skills

Communication is not just about the questions that are used. There are other skills that can determine the outcome of a conversation. These include:

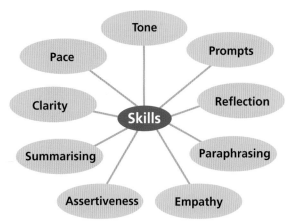

Figure 2.16 *Further skills that can influence communication*

Pace

This is the speed at which we speak. We often tend to speak much too fast, particularly when we are nervous. Some people speak at the same rate throughout a conversation. This can cause the conversation to be boring. In any conversation we need to alter the pace at which we speak, sometimes speaking more quickly and at other times slowing down, so that **emphasis** can be added to what is said.

Tone

The tone used indicates whether a speaker is being friendly or aggressive. For example, a warm friendly tone helps a service user know that the care worker they are speaking to is genuinely interested in the conversation, and is more likely to help build a trusting relationship. A tone of voice that indicates that a care worker is almost too busy to speak, sends the message that the person to whom they are speaking is not valued.

Clarity

In order to achieve clarity it is necessary to organise our thoughts before we speak. A 'cluttered mind' often results in a 'muddled conversation', so that neither person knows what

points are being made. If we are clear about the purpose of a conversation, the communication is more likely to be successful. The vocabulary used should also be appropriate for the person to whom we are speaking. Short sentences help the receiver of a message to understand more easily.

Prompts

A prompt can be used to encourage a person to go on with what they are saying or to be more specific. For example, a service user who is attending a day care centre for the first time may say 'This is the worst thing that has ever happened to me'. A prompt would be, 'Worse, in what way?'

Reflection

To reflect is to look back during a conversation and to recap the most important points of the conversation. Where did the conversation start? Where has it led? Has anything been left out?

For example, a care worker may say:

> *We have talked about what activities you don't want to do and you have explained why. Can you just talk me through how you feel about trying something completely new?*

By using **reflection**, the care worker has drawn the service user back to think about what has been said, but has also moved them on to a new **focus**.

Activity 5

Understanding skills

1 Why should care workers change the pace at which they speak during a conversation with a service user?

2 Explain why clarity of thought is important when communicating with service users.

3 Explain when and how prompts could be used when communicating with service users. Give **two** examples.

Assertiveness

To be assertive is to be focused. Sometimes a service user will want to tell their life history but there may not be time for this. The care worker may need to firmly draw the service user back to the purpose of the conversation. For example, the care worker may say:

> *I am really interested in hearing about your childhood, being one of six children was certainly different, but can we now think about the menu for lunch so that you can decide what you would like?*

In this situation the care worker has acknowledged what the service user has been talking about but has gently but assertively refocused the conversation on the menu.

Empathy

To empathise is to see a person's world as they see it: to be able to step into their shoes and to see things through their eyes. It is accepting the person 'warts and all' and valuing them as an individual. It does not mean liking the individual or the things they do, but being able to see things from that person's **perspective.**

Paraphrasing

Paraphrasing is to reword what a person has said to show what you have understood by it, and to check that you have got it right. It is a brief response that captures the main points of the content of what the other person has said. It **condenses** or **expands** what the other person has just said. A care worker might say for example:

> *So, you think you would like to join either the art, computers or drama activities?*

By paraphrasing, a care worker can clarify the thoughts and feeling of the service user, and make sure both parties are speaking on the same wavelength – understanding the same things by what has been said.

Summarising

The aim of summarising is to:

- outline the relevant facts
- prompt further exploration of ideas
- close a particular part of a discussion and to move the conversation forward.

Summarising is the process of tying together all the points or facts that may have been scattered throughout the conversation. It is drawing together all the threads of what has been discussed. It can include a mixture of what was said and what was **implied**. When summarising, a care worker needs to be very clear in what they say, should not use **jargon** or technical terminology unnecessarily, and should make sure that they include the essential facts. Examples of summarising that could be used are:

> *You have said you are interested in...*

> *It seems from what you have said that you would prefer to attend the day centre twice each week...*

Discussion point

How is summarising different from paraphrasing?

Activity 6

Helpful hints

1 Provide advice to new care workers to help them understand how to empathise with service users.

2 Explain the purpose of summarising, giving two examples of its use.

3 What does assertive communication mean?

4 Give an example of when and how a care worker might find it necessary to be assertive when communicating.

What behaviour fails to value people?

Some service users may feel **vulnerable** when they meet with care workers and view any proposed communication as a threat to their self-esteem, as they are not in control of the situation they find themselves in. This could be because of what they learned when they were growing up or could be the result of a poor past experience. Viewing the service user as being 'equal' is an important aspect of any communication. Service users need to feel safe and know from a care worker's tone of voice and body language whether they are being sincere and honest.

Service users will not feel valued if a care worker:

- tries to exert power over them
- does not give them full attention
- uses an unfriendly tone of voice
- does not address them by their preferred name
- appears too busy
- shouts or uses verbal abuse.

What is the role of body language when communicating orally?

The term 'body language' is also known as 'non-verbal communication', and refers to the bodily movements which accompany speech and which add meaning to interactions.

The role of each of these components of body language is outlined in the table opposite.

Body language is important as it can confirm what a person is saying or it can contradict the words they are using. For example a care worker might ask a service user how they are. The service user may say, 'Yes, I'm fine', but this may not be the message that the service user's body language is saying. Their facial expressions, positioning and lack of smiles may indicate that they are far from being fine! Reading body language can be a 'problem solving' exercise for care workers, which if perfected can be a skill that can help build trusting relationships between service users and care workers.

> **Discussion point**
>
> *What is meant by the phrase 'service users may feel vulnerable'?*
>
> *How can care workers provide support for service users who feel vulnerable?*

> **Discussion point**
>
> *How does body language help communication?*

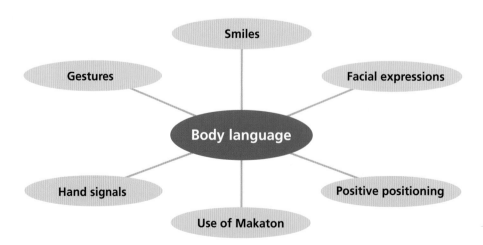

Figure 2.17 *Components of body language*

Body language	Role
Gestures	Gestures add meaning to language by conveying a range of positive or negative responses. Examples of gestures are: shrugging the shoulders to indicate that you are not sure or that you don't know about something, or nodding the head up and down to show that you are in agreement with what is being said
Smiles	Smiling indicates a warm and friendly approach. The role of smiling is to help people feel comfortable and to let them know that you are not likely to be aggressive
Facial expressions	Facial expressions add meaning to language by conveying a range of positive or negative responses. They can include raising an eyebrow, frowning, or pulling the mouth into different shapes. They can also show that you have questions you want to ask about what a person is saying
Hand signals	Hand signals also add a range of meanings to language. These can be **subtle** or sweeping movements of the hand. They can be quite significant in the message they convey, for example a wide sweep of the hand in an outward movement away from the body could mean, 'Don't ask me, I don't know'. Sign language is another form of hand signal where the hands are used to make signs that help convey meaning
Use of Makaton	As already stated earlier in this unit, Makaton is used to help people with hearing impairment understand verbal communication. It involves using an established set of hand movements to convey meaning
Positive positioning	Sitting side-by-side with the body slightly leaning forward towards the person with whom you are speaking shows that you are interested in what they are saying

Activity 7

Using body language

1 Explain what is meant by the term 'body language'.

2 For each of the following situations, give an example of body language that could be used, and explain why it would be suitable.
  a Meeting a service user for the first time.
  b Explaining to a service user what a piece of equipment looks like.
  c Listening to a service user who is telling how they nearly slipped and fell.
  d Listening to a service user who is speaking very quietly.

3 Explain how using body language can enhance communication.

Assessment activity 2.2

Skills for communicating

Mary is an older service user who is living in a residential home. She has severe arthritis and needs help with dressing.

As a care worker you are helping Mary to choose some clothes to wear.

1 Make notes of the conversation that you are likely to have with Mary, including any open or closed questions.

2 Using the notes, make a checklist in the form of a table of at least four verbal skills that you are likely to use in the conversation with Mary, giving examples. Your table could look like the sample given below:

Skill	Example
Open question	Mary, what do you think you should wear today?

3 Think about the body language you might use in the conversation with Mary. Make a list of those you think you are likely to use and state how and why you might use them.

4 Make a checklist of verbal and non-verbal skills that could be used by an observer who is assessing you while you are having the conversation with Mary. Your table could look like the sample given below:

Skill	Observers comments
Open question	

5 With another person role-play the conversation, taking the part of the care worker. Ask another person to observe the role-play and to complete the checklist of skills you used by filling in the 'Observers comments' column.

What factors aid effective listening?

> Listening, therefore, is 'hearing a great deal and often saying not much.'
>
> (*Verena Tschudin, 1991*)

Listening is an essential part of oral communication. To be effective when listening, care workers need to be sure that they are 'actively listening'. Active listening is a way of **maximising** effectiveness when communicating. Active listening not only means listening attentively but making sure that the other person knows the care worker is listening.

mean staring continuously but making eye contact at appropriate places to indicate interest. It helps the person to whom we are speaking realise that we are concentrating on what they have to say rather than on a conversation that is happening across the other side of the room.

Have you ever had an experience where you have been talking to someone but they have been looking at a magazine or concentrating on what another person is saying? If you have you may have stopped the conversation, perhaps in the middle of a sentence, and they may not have even noticed! You probably felt hurt or angry and could only think that what you had to say was boring or not of value to the other person.

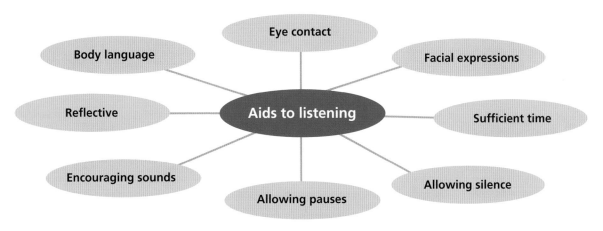

Figure 2.18 *Aids to listening*

Body language, eye contact and facial expressions

When care workers use body language, such as leaning forward to show interest, and using facial expressions such as smiling, service users know that they are listening and will be encouraged to continue speaking. You may wish to look back and re-read the information given earlier in this unit.

Eye contact is also a way of showing that the person who is listening is interested in what is being said. The term 'direct eye contact' does not

> **Discussion point**
>
> *How can the use of effective body language, eye contact and facial expressions contribute to effective listening?*

Allowing sufficient time

Allowing sufficient time means not rushing a conversation. Care workers need to let service users they are talking to know that the focus of the communication is on them. If they talk to a service user while doing another task, or while moving away – for example, continuing to walk down a corridor – it is unlikely that they are listening effectively and the service user could feel insecure. This could mean that a really important piece of information which could influence that person's care is not given to the care worker because the service user feels that he/she is not considered to be important.

Not interrupting service users and allowing them to say all they want to say is also a sign of effective listening, as is avoiding jumping to conclusions. For example, a care worker must never be in such a hurry that they make assumptions on behalf of a service user by finishing a sentence for them.

Making encouraging sounds

To make encouraging sounds is to say such things as: 'well!' or 'um!' or 'do go on'. Such responses indicate to service users that you are interested in what they are saying, and can often be used to gain more information or to encourage an exchange of views or opinions. The person talking is encouraged by signals that the listener wants to know more!

Allowing pauses and silences

An important part of listening is not being afraid of pauses or silences. For example, a care worker should give a service user the chance to consider what they have said and how they feel and what they want to say next. Care workers who are listening effectively should be quite comfortable with pauses and silences and should not try to rush a conversation on.

Being able to be comfortable with silence when listening and communicating is the sign of effective listening skills. It shows that the listener is able to contain their own anxiety or thoughts (if any), and are willing to concentrate on the other person. If the listener is anxious to 'rush to help' the other person with words or gestures, it is probably an attempt to deal with their own awkwardness or embarrassment. An acceptance of silence is recognition that the service user might need someone to 'be there' rather than for 'something to be done'.

Reflective listening

When we indicate that we have heard what someone is saying, we provide reassurance for the speaker, encouraging them to speak freely and openly. For example, nodding our head confirms that we are listening, as does repeating part of a phrase or sentence that has been spoken by the service user. This is known as reflection (see also page 74). An example of reflection is shown in Figure 2.19 below.

Figure 2.19 *Effective listening*

The example of careful use of reflection in Figure 2.19 shows that the care worker is listening and has taken on board what has been said. This can be very reassuring and can help to build trusting relationships.

> ## Discussion point
>
> *How does 'reflection' support active and effective listening?*

Listening requires **flexibility**. Listening can be at three levels:

- **Level 1** – at this level a person is only partially listening to the other person.
- **Level 2** – the listener is very well 'tuned-in' to the person who is speaking.
- **Level 3** – this level of listening has been called 'global listening', as the person is able to identify fully with the one talking.

> Nature gave man two ears but only one tongue, which is a gentle hint, that he should listen more than he talks!
>
> (*Davis, 1972*)

> ## Discussion point
>
> *What are the differences between Level 1 and Level 3 listening?*

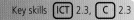

Activity 8

Key skills ICT 2.3, C 2.3

How to listen

1 Explain why listening is important when communicating with care workers.

2 Explain what is meant by the term 'reflection', and give an example of its use.

3 Prepare a handout to give 'Helpful tips' to new care workers about how to be effective when listening.

4 Work with another member of the group to prepare and carry out a two to three minute role-play as a care worker and a service user in a playgroup. Make sure you use body language, hand signals, eye contact and that you are assertive.

5 When you have completed the role-play, write down examples of how you used **each** of the following skills:
   a Body language.
   b Eye contact.
   c Hand signals.
   d Assertiveness.

Assessment activity 2.3

Effective listening

Janice has been asked by her manager to give a training session to care workers in a day care setting about how to improve their listening skills.

1 Explain how a care worker can listen effectively, giving examples of how this can be applied in any care setting.

2 Identify at least **four** factors that can aid listening, and explain how and why these contribute to effective listening.

How can care workers practice in an anti-discriminatory way to promote equality and diversity?

We are all unique and, therefore, have different needs. Promoting equality means making sure that people have equal access to care, so that all their needs are met. Care workers must ensure that assumptions are not made about service users. To make sure that equality and diversity are promoted, care workers should:

- develop self-awareness of their own attitudes, views and opinions, as this makes them confident in their interactions
- not devalue minority cultures, e.g. consider people from minority cultures not to be as good as others
- not show disregard for significant aspects of people's lives, e.g. religious practices
- not express racist attitudes and actions
- not become a barrier to good practice, e.g. encouraging trainees to develop discriminatory attitudes.

An example of becoming a barrier to good practice would be an experienced care worker telling a young trainee care worker:

> *Don't bother asking Rayish what activity he would like to participate in on the activity afternoon, as he has dementia and doesn't know what he's doing anyway.*

This is an example of a care worker influencing another not to support service users' rights, not to be sensitive to diversity, not to promote equality and not to follow good practice. It is training others to discriminate and showing a lack of value for individuals.

Care workers' practice needs to be **ethnically sensitive**. It must respect:

- cultural values
- cultural practices
- cultural needs.

Anti-racist practice recognises discrimination and **oppression**. This combines with ethnically sensitive practice to recognise further cultural needs and differences. Each care worker must be responsible for developing their own awareness of these issues. For example, by:

- being aware of stereotyping, i.e. always responding to the uniqueness of an individual
- taking steps to learn about other cultures and perspectives on life, i.e. learning about other life experiences and other values, beliefs and practices (They could do this by attending training sessions or by looking information up on the Internet, or by talking with service users from different cultures)
- making sure that they focus on fostering and maintaining the dignity of service users, e.g. addressing them by their preferred name
- empowering service users, i.e. enabling them to take control of things such as decision-making by providing choices (Some care workers enjoy the feeling of having 'power' over service users, and this can often lead to discrimination. Working in 'partnership' can prevent dependency, boost self-esteem and raise service users' confidence)
- reviewing their own practice, i.e. to promote healthy attitudes, to look critically at what they are actually doing in their day-to-day tasks, and to encourage reflection
- seeking to update their training so that they can consider issues and learn from sharing with others
- knowing how to challenge discriminatory practice, e.g. by reporting direct and indirect discriminatory behaviour.

Examples of *direct* discrimination:

A care worker serves meat and vegetarian sandwiches on the same plate.

A care worker has served food with a spoon that has been in contact with non-halal (forbidden) meat.

Example of *indirect* discrimination:

A nursery in a multicultural area only produces leaflets giving information about nursery events and management in English.

Activity 9

Promoting equality and diversity

1 Explain what is meant by the term 'promoting equality'.
2 Give an example of direct discrimination that could occur in a playgroup.
3 Give an example of indirect discrimination that could occur in a hospital.

Why do we need to recognise cultural differences when communicating with others?

Culture is about the way people live, think and relate to each other. It is often linked to society and the community of the people with whom we grow up, such as parents, extended family and our neighbourhood. An example of cultural difference is that in this country young women are accustomed to making their own health decisions, but in other cultures young women are less likely to make health decisions for themselves, but would do so after talking with senior members of the family.

Culture can have a great influence on the way in which people communicate, for example, certain hand gestures in this country which are acceptable, can be considered totally rude and unacceptable in another country.

How can we recognise service users' personal beliefs and identities?

Personal beliefs

Personal beliefs about the spiritual aspects of life can be part of a person's culture. For example,

they might have been brought up to believe in a certain religion – or they might have made their own decision to follow a certain faith. The main religion in the UK is Christianity, although only a minority of people go to church. Examples of other religions practiced in this country are: Islam, Sikhism, Hinduism, Buddhism and Judaism.

In any one health, social care or early years setting there are likely to be service users who have different beliefs. Care workers need to respect the beliefs and religious traditions of others even if they are different from their own. They can do this by, for example, making sure that a place is available for a service user to pray, or that food served is appropriate to their religious beliefs, or by finding information about different religions to enable conversation with service users on this topic.

Care workers also need to examine their own attitudes and opinions about other faiths to make sure that these do not demonstrate prejudice or discrimination. Care workers must not make any service users feel, through the communication that they have with them, that they are not valued as individuals as a result of personal beliefs, as this would lower the service users' self-esteem.

Case study

Hashim

Hashim is living in a nursing home. He speaks very little English. He is a Muslim and is unhappy about the food that is being served because it does not meet the requirements of his religion.

1 Carry out research to find out which foods Muslims can have and which they should avoid.

2 Explain three practical ways in which care workers could promote Hashim's cultural and religious beliefs.

3 What is meant by the term 'culture'?

4 What would you do if someone told a racist joke in a care setting?

Personal identities

Personal identities are shaped by a range of genetic, social and emotional factors. Identity is how we think of ourselves and how others see us. Other people identify us through the factors shown in Figure 2.20.

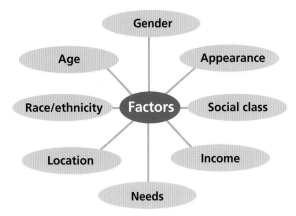

Figure 2.20 *Factors that contribute to personal identity*

For example, we may recognise a person by his red hair which is like his father's and his grandfather's. A child at a playgroup could be recognised because she is female. An older person at a day centre could be recognised because of her physical characteristics, such as wrinkled skin – or she could be recognised simply because of the location, for example a day care centre for older people. All service users are different and can be identified as a result of combinations of interlinking factors. For example:

- age/location
- sex/colour of skin
- language/ethnic group.

It is important for care workers not to make assumptions about service users when first meeting them. For example, a service user may seem brusque and demanding simply because they feel insecure and do not know what to expect on their first day. As they become familiar with their surroundings and the people around them, they may become more secure and not be at all aggressive.

> **Discussion point**
>
> *Why is it important that care workers are aware of their own attitudes and prejudices?*

How can service users' rights and choices be supported?

Service users have rights, many of which are upheld by law. These include the right to:

- their own GP
- choice
- confidentiality
- protection
- fair and equal treatment
- consultation.

These rights are examined in more detail in Unit 1.1. Care workers need to make sure that they support service users to maintain these rights. For example, the right to choice could be supported by:

- encouraging service users to choose what they would like to wear
- helping service users to choose from a menu the foods they would like to eat
- giving service users a choice of activities to participate in
- explaining different treatments service users could have and the differences and effects of each
- providing a range of information so that service users can make choices.

> **Discussion point**
>
> *How could care workers support service users rights and choices in a hospital?*

Supporting service users rights is part of the care values (these are discussed in Unit 1.6). The care values are principles that are derived from human rights. In health and social care settings the three care values that underpin the work of care workers are:

- fostering equality and diversity
- maintaining confidentiality
- fostering individual rights and beliefs.

The table below shows some of the smaller parts or components that the care values can be broken down into.

Note that in early years care and education settings the three care values are incorporated into a wider range of 'principles'. These are listed in Unit 1.6, page 43.

Applying the care values should be a natural part of all care workers day-to-day tasks. They are not part of legislation or **codes of practice** but are values that help to make sure that quality care practice is maintained.

> ## Discussion point
> *How does the application of the care values show service users that care workers want to empower them?*

Why is it important to maintain confidentiality?

> Confidentiality is to ensure that private and personal information is kept safe and out of reach of unauthorised persons in the workplace and beyond.

Service users have the right by law, under the Data Protection Act 1998, to have confidentiality maintained. Confidentiality means that personal and private information should not be disclosed without the service user's permission.

Confidentiality can only be broken if:

- a service user is likely to harm themselves or others
- if the law has been or is about to be broken.

Component of the care values	Examples of application in care settings
Communicating effectively	Speaking in a tone and manner that a service user can understand when giving information. Not telling them that what they are saying is silly or nonsense
Supporting dignity	Not calling service users 'love' or 'dear', and addressing them by their preferred name
Supporting respect	Listening to a service user when they are speaking and not turning away from them
Supporting choice	Allowing a service user to decide when they wish to go to bed or which television programme to watch
Supporting trust	Not making promises that cannot be kept
Supporting privacy	Pushing the bathroom door to almost closed when bathing a service user so that they cannot be seen by others
Supporting protection	Making sure service users are not abused either verbally, physically, sexually or emotionally

Activity 10

Key skills [C] 2.1a

Applying the care values

1 Marti is being taken to the toilet as he has mobility problems. How can the care worker promote Marti's dignity?

2 A district nurse is attending to an ulcer on Jamie's leg. How could the district nurse apply the care values when carrying out this task?

3 Richard has learning disabilities and lives in a residential home. What rights does Richard have and how could his care worker promote these rights?

Maintaining confidentiality is an important aspect of building a trusting relationship with service users. Care workers need to make sure that:

- they do not tell service users' personal business to others either at work or at home
- they do not talk about service users by name in front of others
- they do not leave notes about service users lying around where others can read them
- information that is personal is locked away securely
- information kept on computer is only kept for the permitted length of time
- only authorised care workers have access through use of a password to service users' information

- only relevant information can be kept
- only those with a relevant interest can receive a service user's information, e.g. others involved in providing care for the service user, and even then it is on a strictly 'need-to-know' basis.

Discussion point

Why should a service user's personal information be kept confidential?

Assessment activity 2.4

Applying the care values

Angus is a trainee social worker. He visits Mount Pleasant day care centre as part of his training. While he is at the day care centre he notices:

- the computer is left on with personal information displayed in the main community lounge
- one service user is assisted to go to the toilet but the door is left open and there is no answer when he shouts that he needs help
- a group of care workers are talking loudly in the dinning area about a service user who attends on a different day, freely using her name and discussing her personal information
- Madge is told that she does not need to see the lunch menu as she takes too long to decide what she wants and she always makes the same choice anyway

- several service users' files are left open on the top of the piano in the community room
- Majid asks for a quiet place to pray but is told there is nowhere he can use
- Megan, who is sitting in the community room surrounded by other people, is given some personal information about the health treatment she needs.

1 Identify **two** components of the care values (other than confidentiality) and explain how each is being broken by care workers in the case study. What actions should the care workers take?

2 Describe how confidentiality is being broken and explain how confidentiality should be applied in each situation given in the case study.

How can care workers successfully communicate with service users?

There may be a number of reasons why care workers would need to communicate with service users. This could include to:

- obtain information, e.g. about a service user's history to find out about their likes and dislikes
- give information, e.g. about treatment or diet
- exchange ideas, e.g. about possible activities the service user would like to do.

Communication can also fulfill intellectual needs, as people have to think about what they are saying and about what is being said to them. Communicating can be informative and interesting because both parties may learn something new from the conversation. By communicating with care workers, service users can develop a sense of achievement and fulfilment. Communicating can be:

- on a one-to-one basis
- with a group, e.g. more than one person.

Before communicating with service users it is often best to be prepared by:

- making a plan
- arranging the area to be used, e.g. seating arrangements
- deciding what you are going to talk about, e.g. what information do you need to obtain or what ideas need exchanging?

Discussion point

What are the reasons for communicating with service users? Give some examples.

Making a plan

A plan for an interaction is important because it helps to organise thoughts and to put them in the correct order or sequence. It also enables the person who is collecting information or exchanging ideas to think about what information they will need, the skills that they will need to use, how body language may help the communication and how to ensure that active listening is encouraged. Factors that can influence communication also need to be thought about.

Planning involves asking:

- Who will I have the conversation with?
- What will I talk about?
- What are my aims and objectives?
- Where will I have the interaction?
- What communication skills am I likely to use?
- What body language am I likely to use?
- How can I apply the care values?
- Do I need to consider any cultural issues?

Thinking about the environment for the conversation

Care workers need to decide whether a one-to-one communication they are planning is going to be formal or informal, as the seating arrangements will need to reflect this. Decide what room will be suitable. For example, would it be best to have the conversation in a separate room or in a larger room where there are other people, but in a position where the conversation will not be overheard? The latter may be the better option in some circumstances, as the person with whom the care worker is conversing may tend to speak more freely with others having conversations around them. Look back at section 2.1 where it discusses 'What factors influence oral communication?', and think about them when planning the environment for the communication you will have.

Figure 2.21 *Why is this room poorly arranged for a meeting?*

In the plan shown in Figure 2.22, the chairs have been arranged alongside one another, but with sufficient room to allow for personal space. They have not been placed either side of the table as this would make the communication too formal. The table will be helpful when the care worker is making notes and to put refreshments on. A window is open very slightly to make sure the room is well-ventilated, but not draughty.

> **Discussion point**
>
> *Why is it important to prepare a room correctly before having an important conversation?*

Communicating with a service user

All interactions or conversations, however long, have three main parts:

- the first contact or initial introduction
- the main content, maintaining contact with the service user
- the winding up or ending of the interaction.

Making first contact

First impressions are very important and can influence the whole of an interaction with a service user. In the introduction or first contact, care workers will probably use some closed questions, a few open questions and

Figure 2.22 *A good environment for a conversation*

appropriate body language. For example, here is an outline or **transcript** of a conversation (with notes) of the first contact between Jake (care worker) and Fiona (service user). It is Fiona's first visit to the day care centre:

Jake	Good morning, my name is Jake and I am your key care worker while you are at the care centre. How would you like to be addressed while you are here?
Fiona	I prefer to be called by my first name, Fiona.
Jake	Would you like a cup of tea?
Fiona	Yes, please.
Jake	I'll get you one. Do you take sugar?
Fiona	Yes, one please. Where shall I sit?
Jake	Shall we sit over there in the window seat?
Fiona	Yes.
Jake	How do you feel about coming to the day care centre?
Fiona	A bit nervous really, I don't really see why I have to come. The social worker thought I ought to get out of the house more.
Jake	I shall need to get a few details from you for my records and then I will introduce you to some of the other people who are attending today. Did you say one sugar?

This opening conversation would have been accompanied by positive body language, such as smiling, extending the hand in greeting, direct eye contact and gestures.

The care worker would have used a friendly, warm tone and would have been careful not to overwhelm the service user by being too loud or confusing them by speaking too quietly.

Jake would have spoken at an appropriate pace, not speaking too quickly, and would have given Fiona time to think. He would have given Fiona his complete attention and showed that he is interested in her and values her as an individual. He has greeted Fiona in a friendly manner, finding out her preferred name.

Figure 2.23 *First impressions count*

Case study

Communicating with children at a nursery

As a nursery nurse you are working with Katrina, Catlyn and Chris. They are going to use different types of materials to make a picture.

1 Write **two** closed questions that could be used while working with the children during the introduction to the activity.

2 Write **two** open questions that could be used when working with the children during the initial contact to the activity.

3 Give some ideas of the body language that would be appropriate to use while working with the children at the introductory stage of the activity.

4 Prepare a transcript of the conversation during the first contact with the children when doing the activity. Indicate which:
   - are closed questions
   - are open questions
   - is an example of reflection.

5 What other factors would you take into consideration when communicating with the children to make sure the communication with them is as effective as possible?

Main conversation and maintaining contact with the service user

Once the first contact has been made, the main part of a conversation can take place. Care workers should decide before starting a conversation what the main purpose is to be. For example:

- to obtain information
- to give information
- to exchange ideas.

In the main part of the conversation the care worker in our example (Jake) is likely to use more open questions so that the service user (Fiona) can expand the information she is giving. Some closed questions will be used in order to gather specific information. Skills such as clarifying, reflecting and summarising will be used, as will appropriate body language.

Sometimes a conversation needs some help to 'move it along' or to continue, as the person speaking may run out of steam or be stuck on a particular thought. Examples of phrases that can be used to help a conversation along are:

> Please continue.
>
> Do tell me more.
>
> So...
>
> Um-hum...
>
> I see...

If a service user has given quite a lot of information and has included some ideas and thoughts that are muddled or confusing, the care worker may need to **clarify** or check what the service user is actually saying or wanting. Examples of clarifying are:

> So, do you mean...?
>
> Do I understand that you...?

Within conversations, whether in a group or on a one-to-one basis, care workers may need to summarise. That is, they may need to bring together all that has been said in a short sentence or two which 'sums up' a particular part of the conversation. Examples of summarising are:

> Just to make sure that I have understood what you have agreed...
>
> You seem to prefer...

Here is an example of part of the main conversation that Jake might gone on to have with Fiona:

Jake	Here is your tea. Now I will need a few personal details from you. Can we get these down on the form while we are having our tea?
Fiona	Yes, what do you want to know?
Jake	Can you give me your full name and address?
Fiona	Fiona Martin, 26, Ashcroft Drive, Martinstown.
Jake	Telephone number?
Fiona	02567 48569 – that includes the Martinstown code number.
Jake	Thank you Fiona. Who is your GP?
Fiona	Dr Chesney who is in the Fordingbridge practice.
Jake	Good, that's the formal information finished. Now let's think about what you would like to do while you are at the centre. Are there any activities that you particularly like doing?
Fiona	Well, I used to like painting, but I haven't done any for a long while.
Jake	What type of painting did you like doing?
Fiona	Oh, watercolour. Pictures of places I had visited or of the local area. I wasn't very good though.
Jake	Watercolour you say?
Fiona	Yes, I found watercolours easier to work with than oil.
Jake	Well, we do have an art group on Wednesday afternoon. How do you feel about joining the group?
Fiona	Well, I could give it a try I suppose?
Jake	Let me tell you what else we have going on here. On Wednesday mornings there is a choice of two activities. The computer group meets from 11 to 12 and the craft group from 10.30 to 12. You couldn't do both activities, but do either of these interest you?
Fiona	I've always wanted to learn the computer, but I don't think I'd be very good at it!
Jake	What makes you think you would not be very good?
Fiona	Well, I've never learned to type.
Jake	I don't think you need typing skills. Now, let's see if I've got this right. You would definitely like to join the art group on Wednesday afternoon and in the morning you will try the computing session?
Fiona	I think so. If...

From this transcript of the main part of the conversation between Fiona and Jake it is possible to see that Jake used a wide range of skills to gather the information he needed. During the conversation he would have tried to help Fiona to feel relaxed by leaning slightly forward when speaking, and through showing a genuine interest in what she was saying. He would have actively listened, and used reflection to show that he was listening.

Case study

Communicating with Fiona

Read the transcript of the conversation again.

1 Select **three** closed questions and explain why they have been used.

2 Select an example of 'reflection', and give its purpose.

3 Select **two** open questions. What is their purpose in this particular conversation?

4 Continue the conversation between Jake and Fiona. make sure you use at least **two** closed questions, **two** open questions and include an example of clarifying or summarising.

Winding up the conversation

Bringing a conversation to a close or to an end successfully, requires the use of thought and appropriate skills. Service users should feel that a conversation has reached a natural conclusion.

How care workers end a conversation can have a positive or negative effect on service users and this has consequences for the relationship between them. For example, if a conversation is ended abruptly the service user may feel guilty, thinking they have done something wrong, and then they are not likely to willingly communicate with that care worker again.

A conversation is often ended by one of the participants sending a 'signal' that they are ready to stop talking. This could be in the form of a sigh or increasingly long pauses, or body language such as restlessness, less eye contact or even physically moving away from the other person.

It is important that these signals are noted and appropriate action taken to end the conversation. It can be very annoying when the signals are ignored and a person carries on talking, being insensitive to the body language that is being displayed.

Figure 2.24 *Finishing a conversation*

Phrases that can help with the ending of a conversation are:

I very much enjoyed talking to you

I hope we meet again

I found that conversation very interesting

Let me know how you get on with...

Any phrases that are used should be accompanied with a smile and a tone of voice that indicates you are being sincere.

Conversations are built around the use of complex behaviour. They involve anticipation of own behaviour and the behaviour of others. Care workers must:

- plan what they are going to say
- try to understand what others are saying
- know how to finish.

Case study

Winding up the conversation with Fiona

Jake has collected from Fiona all the information he needs and feels that Fiona should now meet some of the other service users who are attending the day care centre.

1 Make a transcript of the conversation that Jake might have with Fiona to end their conversation.

2 Why is it important to end communication with service users in a positive way?

At some time or another care workers all experience difficulty in managing communication, but the more aware they are of the skills involved and the more communication they have with people, the more they are likely to perfect the skills and be successful.

Assessment activity 2.5

Key skills [C] 2.3, [ICT] 2.3

Communicating with service users

A Ida is a service user who has mobility problems but she is living in her own home. You are a care assistant who will be helping Ida with daily living tasks, such as cleaning, shopping and preparing snacks. You have arranged the first visit with Ida.

B You are leading a ten-minute activity with three children in the reception class of the local primary school or at a playgroup or at a nursery. The activity can be on any topic related to health and well-being. For example, eating healthily, how to keep fit, good hygiene.

1 a Prepare a handout to help explain to trainee care workers how you would prepare for the communication with Ida.

b Make a plan to show how you would prepare for the communication with the children.

For both tasks: remember to think about:

- factors that could influence the conversation
- barriers that could inhibit the conversation

- how you will apply the care values in the conversation
- the skills you will use, e.g. verbal, body language, listening.

2 Make a diagram of the seating arrangements for **each** communication, giving reasons for the way you have set out the room.

3 Produce a table to show the verbal skills and the body language you will use for **each** communication.

4 Make a transcript for **each** of the ten-minute conversations that you will have. Indicate which part of the conversation is included in:
- the initial contact
- the main content
- the winding up.

5 Stage the two ten-minute conversations (e.g. one-to-one and group). Remember to arrange for your tutor to observe you having these conversations.

Figure 2.25 *Evaluating*

How can we evaluate the effectiveness of our communication skills?

Evaluating oral communication skills for a care worker involves:

- thinking about what they have done and how they have done it
- considering the skills they have used and the reasons why they used them
- asking themselves questions about how effective they have been when using these skills and whether they achieved the outcomes they wanted. In other words, did they achieve the aims and objectives they set and how well did they meet them
- thinking about any improvements they could have made
- planning how to improve their skills.

When evaluating, care workers should use skills such as the ones outlined in the table on the right.

Skills	Examples
Reflection	Thinking about what they have done
Analysis	Examining what they have done in detail
Drawing conclusions	Making a decision about how well they have completed the tasks or skills
Planning	Thinking about how to improve those tasks or skills

To help when evaluating, a care worker may decide to use the help of others. For example:

- their assessor/tutor
- their peers, e.g. those people who are in their group or class.

The feedback care workers receive from others can help guide them to think about any improvements that they may want to make for future communication with service users.

Reflection

When care workers reflect, they should think about a whole conversation they have had from start to finish. Here is an example of reflection by Jake who has communicated with Fiona at the day care centre. He is thinking or reflecting on the first part of the conversation he had with Fiona:

> My introduction was clear and my tone of voice was friendly and welcoming. I established a good relationship with the service user. I think this was because I smiled at her and extended my hand so she could shake it. I also offered her some refreshment which helped to break the ice. I am pleased that I arranged the seats so that they were side-by-side and not facing one another. I think this helped Fiona to feel more relaxed. I needed to put Fiona at ease so that I could collect accurate information about what she wanted to do and check her personal details.

In this example Jake is thinking about his aims and objectives, what he actually did and how well he did it. He is going over in his mind what actually took place. It often helps if care workers make notes at this stage to remind them of what they did.

Analysis

When care workers analyse, they should think through and clearly remember all the parts of a communication they have had. They should think about particular things they have done and/or the skills they have used and how well they have used them. To do this they need to make **judgements** or decisions, for example, about the skills they used and how they used them. Here is an example of an analysis of the skills Jake used:

> I think my tone of voice was appropriate because I did not have a raised voice, neither was it too quiet so that Fiona couldn't hear. I made frequent eye contact so that Fiona knew I was interested in what she had to say and that I was focusing on her and not on others. I used quite a number of open questions, for example, one I used was 'How do you feel about that?'. This gave Fiona the chance to talk about her feelings. I also used reflective comments to show Fiona that I was actively listening. For example, '...so you like watercolour painting'. I did summarise during the conversation because at one stage Fiona was jumping from topic to topic and I wanted to make sure that I had understood her correctly. I said, 'so have I understood correctly, you would like...'

Jake has considered and analysed the skills he used in his conversation with Fiona, and given examples to illustrate the points he is making. He has seen how his knowledge about skills and how they should be used helped him make decisions. He is able to think about the skills against the 'theory' he has learned. Thinking about each component part within a task or activity is part of the analysing process.

Drawing conclusions

When drawing conclusions, care workers should make 'informed judgements'. That is, measure something against the knowledge they have of the subject.

If they draw conclusions and explain them, they will be making 'reasoned judgements'. If they examine the facts and knowledge supplied by others who may be experts, they will be making 'informed judgements', using the facts, opinions and views of others. This could be the views of 'theorists' or other people who have knowledge and opinions of the subject, or they could be using the feedback they have received from their assessor or peers, they could even include their own opinions. Here is an example of Jake drawing conclusions from his conversation with Fiona:

> In my opinion I used prompts very successfully as Fiona moved the conversation forward as a result of my saying 'so, which do you think you would like to join, it's a difficult choice to make'. If I had not done this it is likely that Fiona would have continued to talk around the subject without making any decisions. In her feedback my assessor confirmed that this was appropriate.
>
> I was not afraid of silence. Fiona had one long silence during the conversation. I think she was thinking back over past activities that she had done. Jan Sutton and William Stewart in their book Learning to Counsel state that 'silence can be threatening but it can also be constructive'. In Fiona's case I think it was constructive because she was recalling memories of pleasurable activities, which helped her to arrive at a decision.

In this example, Jake is expressing his own opinions and referring to the opinions of others. He is considering the skills he used and their purpose, and discussing the reasons for points in the conversation. In a full evaluation Jake would discuss a range of skills used, drawing conclusions about their effectiveness.

How should care workers plan for improvements in their communications?

Assessing own skills

Having drawn conclusions, good practice is for a care worker to think about the ways they can improve the skills used in their communications. They could identify issues for improvement by considering:

Aspect of communication	Evaluation
Purpose	Did the skills used enable the purpose of the communication to be achieved?
Reasons for use	What were the reasons for using the skills chosen? Were there other skills that would have been more suitable?
Effectiveness	Did the skills used enable both the care worker and the service user to understand and have a meaningful exchange of information?
Achievement of outcomes	Did the skills allow the outcomes to be achieved? Could the service user have benefited if something had been done differently?

Planning for improvement

If care workers do not think about how they can improve the things they do, they could not get any better in the tasks they are carrying out. Care workers should always be thinking about their own 'professional development'. In other words, 'How to do things better'. When planning for such improvements they need to think about:

- what needs improving
- the order in which the improvements should tale place
- the timescales.

Using a checklist within assessment of own skills

In Unit 2.2 there is information about skills to use during an interaction. From this it would be useful to create a checklist for use during an evaluation, in order to compare what skills were planned to be used and which skills were actually used. Care workers might also like to think about why they used them (purpose) and how effective they were (did they help to achieve the outcome).

The contribution of others in assessing own skills

Having a person who is observing during a communication is always helpful. The person who is observing, perhaps an assessor or someone from the same peer group, will not be actively involved in the interaction and is, therefore, more likely to record which skills were used and whether they achieved their purpose. To do this effectively, those who do the observing need a document on which to record their observations. This could be a similar document to the checklist used for self-assessment, providing that there is space for comments.

Videoing the communication is also a very good idea, as long as permission has been obtained from the participants. A video can be played back and the pause button used to help the consideration of each skill used and its effectiveness. This is a great aid when trying to evaluate own performance.

Assessment activity 2.6

Evaluating communication skills

1 Reflect on both the one-to-one and the group interaction that you did as part of Assessment activity 2.5. Make notes or use spider diagrams to help you think about what happened. Use the following headings to help you:

- purpose
- skills used
- reasons for use
- effectiveness
- achievement of outcomes.

2 Write up your reflections as the first part of the evaluation.

3 Refer back to the skills checklist that you drew up for both communications. Analyse the skills used making reference to any assessor comments, peer feedback and your own self-analysis. Draw some conclusions about the effectiveness of the skills used.

4 Make a plan for improving any skills that need further practice, giving reasons for the improvements suggested. Your plan could look like the example given in the table below:

Skill	How to improve skill	Reason for improvement
Clarifying	Find out more about how to clarify and the purpose. Write out a role-play with clarifying statements included. Practice in a role-play to use the skill more	Only used once in the communication with service user as I wasn't clear about its purpose
Tone of voice		
Applying care value		

Glossary

Acronym: a word created from the initial letters of other words

Analyse: to examine in detail and make decisions about

Assertive: being confident and direct in dealing with others

Assumptions: guesses, or pre-empting something a person is going to say

Bereavement: suffering a loss of someone through death

Braille: a system of raised dots used to enable people who have visual impairment to read

Clarify: to make absolutely clear

Clinically depressed: a state of unhappiness which is severe and which is recognised as a medical condition

Codes of practice: a standard set by occupational sectors; guidelines

Component: a part, a smaller unit

Condenses: to reduce or diminish

Contact: to get in touch with or make oneself known to another

Convey: pass on or give, for example, to pass on a message to another

Co-ordination: to bring together, to combine, to oversee

Decode: to interpret or make understandable

Dependency: to rely on another; not being in control of ones own life

Disclosing: to make known or reveal.

Dismissive: refusing to take something seriously

Diversity: difference, being dissimilar

Empathy: to see from another persons perspective, to see things as they do

Emphasis: to give weight to something

Encode: to wrap up, to put within something

Ethnically sensitive: being aware of other people's culture

Expand: to make larger, to give more detail

Flexible: not rigid; willing to change ones position on a topic

Focus: to concentrate on; the main emphasis

Formal: to follow an approved or an acceptable approach or method

Gesture: body movement usually using a hand to make a signal

Impact: an impression

Implied: to hint at

Informal: casual, not following a set pattern or routine, no set pattern

Inhibited: preventing someone from participating or from joining in

Insight: awareness, understanding, discernment

Interaction: making a connection with another, for example, talking to another person or persons

Interpret: to make sense of, to unravel

Jargon: slang, not using the standard words

Judgements: to make decisions

Labelling: applying a stereotype to a particular person

Makaton: a simple form of sign language that follows a pattern

Maximising: to make the most of

Medical history: an account of all illnesses and conditions experienced by a person during their lifetime

Non-judgemental: not making judgements about people, not condemning people because of their opinions or beliefs

Oppression: hardship; to abuse; being severe

Peer/peers: people who are equals in age or social standing

Perspective: a view of; looking at something from a particular point of view

Potential: showing ability

Rapport: being in harmony, building relationships, having a good understanding or affinity

Retain: to remember, to hold on to

Reflection: to look back, to think about what has passed

Socio-gram: a diagram or drawing which shows how people are arranged when having a conversation

Stereotyping: thinking that all people in the same group are the same

Subtle: mysterious, hard to grasp

Technical terminology: language used by people who are knowledgeable about a topic or subject

Unambiguous: clear, not muddled

Unique: the only one in existence; special

Vulnerable: at risk, insecure

Withdrawn: quiet, reserved, not joining in

Empowering the service users means involving them

When carrying out practical tasks such as helping to choose clothing or serving meals, care workers should provide the highest possible standard of care. One responsibility of care workers is to make sure that any practical care they give will not make the service user become dependent on them. They should ensure that a balance is achieved between giving the care needed and allowing service users to do as much as possible for themselves. Practical care involves:

- empowering service users by maintaining dignity and providing choices
- applying the care values in the day-to-day tasks that are carried out, e.g. maintaining confidentiality.

Skills and qualities required for practical caring vary according to the task. For example, all care workers need to have effective communication skills, but not all care workers require scientific skills. Knowing the skills and qualities that they already have is extremely useful for care workers and often helps to guide their choice of career.

> ## Discussion point
>
> *Think back to a situation when you have received care from a professional care worker. What skills did they use? What qualities did they show?*

Care workers in different care settings are likely to demonstrate a range of skills. For example, a care assistant in a residential home or a hospital for older people may need to help service users with dressing. This will mean using interpersonal and communication skills as well as practical skills when helping the service user to dress. Problem solving will also be needed as dressing a person is not as easy as it may seem, particularly if they have severe **arthritis**!

In a different setting, for example a playgroup, a nursery nurse also needs to communicate and interact with service users. He or she may need to help with the putting on of coats or shoes, but other practical skills, such as using play equipment, and being creative when using paint or when preparing the interest table will be needed.

A large number of service users need support to maintain mobility. This type of support is not just confined to older people, but to young people and adults with disabilities or service users who have been involved in an accident. Knowing about aids that help with mobility and how to use them can be extremely useful for care workers. Helping service users to choose meals, and serving a meal so that it looks appetising, is a very important aspect of practical care. It is part of the role of care workers in all care settings.

What will we learn in this unit?

Learning outcomes

You will learn to:

- Describe how to empower service users when providing practical care
- Review the skills and qualities that contribute to effective practical caring
- Provide support for service users when choosing clothing, dressing and when putting on outer garments
- Investigate and provide support for service users to maintain and improve mobility
- Assist service users to choose meals and serve simple meals to service users
- Evaluate the success of the practical care provided.

How can service users be empowered?

Empowerment is allowing service users to have as much control over their own lives as possible.

Prior to the early 1980s, service users admitted to a hospital or to a residential home were not allowed any say in what was done to them, nor were they consulted about the type of care they were to receive. There was no requirement to ask their permission before practical care was given and very little, if any, discussion about what care was to be provided. As a result of this attitude, service users would very quickly become **dependent** on care workers and were, over a period of time, unable to do anything for themselves.

Those working in health, social care and early years settings soon realised that this 'dependency' was not helpful, and as a result policies were introduced that required care workers to encourage service users to take more responsibility for themselves. To do this it was recognised that care workers needed to *empower* service users. In other words, to encourage them to take some control of what was happening to them.

To be able to empower service users, certain ingredients are needed. Examples are given in Figure 3.1 below.

Figure 3.1 *Ways of empowering service users*

Providing choice

The National Minimum Standards for care homes forms the basis of standards of care for older people. One of the topics within these standards is related to choice. Older service users must be allowed to choose the home that they wish to live in. Other pieces of legislation, for example, The Care Standards Act 2000, The 1990 NHS and Community Care Act and the NHS Improvement Plan (June 2004), all contribute to making sure that not just older people, but service users of all age groups and from all backgrounds have the opportunity to make choices, as far as is possible, within the existing provision of services. For example:

- the NHS and Community Care Act 1990 makes it possible for service users to choose to remain in their own homes and to receive support
- the Care Standards Act 2000 has as part of its provision, the need for providers of services to have a complaints procedure in place. This allows service users the right to choose whether they are satisfied with the service they are receiving or whether to complain
- the NHS Improvement Plan encourages choice by:
  - empowering local communities, i.e. giving local people the choice of the services required
  - encouraging diversity of provision, i.e. providing a wider range of services from which to choose
  - getting information to the patient – so that by having information, service users can make informed choices.

By making it possible to choose, control has been given to the service user. This **philosophy** has been extended to day-to-day activities in care. settings. For example, service users can choose the things given in the table below.

Discussion point

Why is it important to empower service users?

Giving service users respect

Care workers can show respect in a number of different ways. For example, by:

- listening carefully to service users
- not ignoring service users
- accepting that service users may have different cultural and religious beliefs
- accepting that service users may have different sexually orientation than themselves
- addressing service users by their preferred names.

To respect someone is to show that they are valued. Providing practical care requires interacting with others. When we interact we have an **influence** on one another and can affect how others are feeling. Care workers need to be aware of the effects that they can have on other people, and the ways in which others can affect them. If a service user's behaviour makes a care worker angry, and the service user ends up being shouted at or disregarded, he or she is being shown a lack of respect.

Being respectful does not mean that a care worker must agree with everything the service user says and does. Neither does it mean that a care worker does not have to stand up for themselves. A weak person will not be respected. Respect has to be earned. It is earned by:

- being just and fair
- trying not to hurt the feelings of others

Services users' choice	Responsibility of service provider to:
What they eat	Provide a menu with a choice of foods that has options acceptable to all service users whatever their culture or belief
What they wear	Allow service users to select the garments they wish to put on
Which activities they participate in	Organise a programme of activities that provides mental stimulation
When they have a bath	Within reason provide choice for hygiene routines
When to carry out their religious duties	Provide time and space for service users to pray or celebrate religious events

- not creating fear
- expressing open and honest feelings, but expressing these in a sensitive way that will not cause hurt to others
- not **demeaning** people or making them look foolish
- being willing to share information.

Care workers should work towards creating an atmosphere of acceptance and openness when providing practical care. They must make sure that they have 'no hidden agendas' in order to **cultivate** respect between themselves and service users.

Encouraging service users to participate in decision-making

What sorts of decisions do service users need to make? The answer is that there are many which vary according to the type of service needed. Examples of decisions that service users might need to make and the reasons why it is important for them to be involved are given in the table at the top of the next page.

To participate in decision-making is to be involved; to be part of the decision-making process. Service users feel good about themselves if they can be involved and are more likely to

Figure 3.2 *Respect can lead to sharing and improved self-esteem*

respond positively rather than feeling that things are being decided for them. Participation in decision-making leads to a positive self-concept.

In order to make decisions, service users need to be given as much information as possible. They need to know what options they have and the advantages and disadvantages of a particular approach or way.

> ### Discussion point
>
> *How could a care worker show respect to a service user who is being verbally aggressive?*

Decisions	Why service users need to be involved
Whether to move into residential care or nursing care	It is a service user's life that is going to be affected and he or she must have a say in what and where they think is appropriate
Whether to have one form of treatment or another	If service users feel comfortable with one particular type of treatment, giving them the option to choose it could affect the outcome positively
How to organise the care plan and who will be involved	Service users may have certain preferences, for example, whether to attend a day centre each week or whether to have Meals on Wheels at home. They cannot control what happens entirely in the care plan but they can express preferences if choices are offered
Which recreational activities to take part in and when	Service users are more likely to benefit from an activity, whether it is providing intellectual stimulation or whether it is creative, if they have made the decision to do it
What routines to follow and when	Co-operation is more likely when service users have been given a framework in which things can happen, and are then allowed to make decisions within that framework, e.g. when to go for a walk or when to visit a friend

Care workers need to remember that service users may not know what information they need to ask for. They may not know that certain services exist and as a consequence may not think about asking what is available. For service users to be able to participate in decision-making means that care workers need to listen very carefully to them and make suggestions, for example, 'have you thought about...'. However, offering something that is unrealistic or impossible to a service user could have disastrous effects and lead to poor relationships.

Discussion point

How can taking part in the decision-making process empower service users?

Maintaining service users' rights

Look back to Unit 1 where service users' rights have been covered in depth before reading on. Service users' rights are enforced by legislation, policies and codes of conduct/practice. Legislation that supports these rights includes that given in Figure 3.3 below.

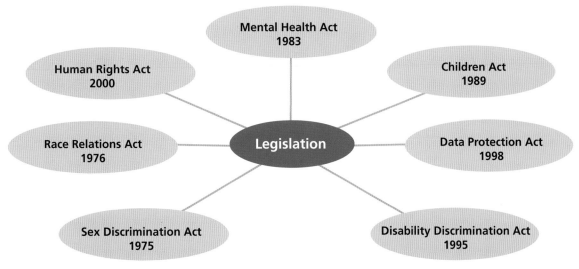

Figure 3.3 *Legislation that supports rights*

These pieces of legislation mean that all care workers, whatever health, social care or early years setting they are working in, must uphold the rights of service users. These rights can be summarised in this way:

Service users' rights

Some rights of service users in a hospital. The right to:
- be admitted by a specific date
- complain against the NHS, to have the complaint investigated and to receive a prompt written reply
- know quality standards and maximum waiting times
- be given clear information about any proposed treatment
- choose not to take part in research.

Some rights of service users in an early years setting. The right to:
- be heard
- safety and security
- have their wishes considered
- confidentiality
- be provided with stimulating activities.

Some rights of service users in residential or nursing homes. The right to:
- choose their own GP
- equal and fair treatment
- consultation
- protection
- make a complaint.

All service users have the right to:
- confidentiality
- choice
- not to be discriminated against
- practice their cultural and religious beliefs
- make a complaint
- have access to own health records
- equal and fair treatment.

Activity 1

Empowering service users

1 Which of the following three statements are correct? Empowering service users means:
   a Doing everything possible for the service user so that they feel dependent.
   b Making the service user do everything for themselves.
   c Asking relatives to do as much as possible for the service user.
   d Allowing the service user to have as much control over their care as possible.

2 Maria is confined to a wheelchair as she has had a serious accident. She has to have an operation on her leg. Describe **three** choices that Maria could be given by care workers while in hospital.

3 How could care workers show Maria respect during her stay in hospital?

4 Explain how care workers could encourage Maria to participate in decision-making while she is in hospital.

5 Explain how care workers could uphold Maria's rights while she is in hospital.

How can the care values be applied when looking after service users?

The care values have been clearly detailed in Unit 1.6. Look back and remind yourself about what they are and why they are important.

Care workers apply the care values in their day-to-day tasks through the three main components of the care values. These are:

- fostering equality and diversity
- maintaining confidentiality
- fostering rights and beliefs.

These components form a set of values or principles that underpin all work carried out by care workers. On top of page 105 there are some examples of how they work in practice.

How the care values are applied

Fostering equality and diversity
- Providing services that are equally accessible to all
- Meeting individual needs – having a person-centred approach
- Accepting service users with different sexual orientations
- Following anti-discriminatory practice

Maintaining confidentiality
- Not gossiping about service users
- Keeping information safe
- Storing written records securely
- Making sure access to electronic records is limited to specific care workers who have a password
- Not talking about service users by name at home or in public

Fostering rights and beliefs
- Accepting different cultural and religious beliefs
- Making provision for service users with different beliefs to celebrate their events
- Providing appropriate foods
- Providing a place for service users to practice their religious beliefs

The care values underpin care work to ensure that all service users are treated consistently, fairly and in a way that care workers would want to be treated themselves. They are valued for themselves.

Discussion point
Why is it important for care workers to apply the care values?

Case study

Bridget

Bridget is 35 years of age. She has learning difficulties and lives in a community home. Her care workers help her to dress and assist her with her personal hygiene, such as bathing and washing. Myra, her key care worker, always asks Bridget when she would like her bath and which soaps and shampoos she would like to use. Myra always gives Bridget some time to herself when she is having a bath and holds up the towel so that she has some dignity when getting out of the bath.

Bridget attends a resource centre from Monday to Friday where she is learning to cook and to make dried flowers. Myra helps Bridget to choose which dishes she would like to make even though this takes some time. Myra sits with Bridget and helps her to make the flowers by reading the instructions with her and showing her how to put them together.

Sometimes when she finds things difficult, Bridget flies into a temper and shouts at Myra, but Myra tries to distract her by showing her something interesting in the instructions or suggesting different flowers that could be used.

Myra keeps a written record of Bridget's actions and behaviours. She writes these up in her office and stores them in a locked filing cabinet. Case conference notes are kept on computer and only Myra and one other person has access to these.

Bridget is a member of the Salvation Army and likes to attend the service on Sunday mornings. Myra or another care worker goes to the service with Bridget, even though it is not their own faith.

Sometimes Myra's own family ask about her work at the community home, but Myra is very careful not to talk about Bridget or any other people living in the home by name.

1 How has Myra fostered the care values in her dealings with Bridget? Find examples from the case study for each of the main components of the care values.

2 What would Myra have done differently if she were not fostering the care values? Think about this in terms of:
- providing choice
- giving respect
- fostering beliefs
- anti-discriminating
- maintaining confidentiality
- communicating effectively.

Care workers must behave in a **non-judgemental** way, working to the principles of good practice by valuing service users for their individuality and diversity, enabling them to direct their own lives. All service users should be met with an open mind and accepted as they are. They should not be judged by the standards which govern any care worker's life. Personal values should be put to one side so that service users are accepted for how they are, not as care workers would like them to be.

Figure 3.4 *Valuing a person for who they are, not what we want them to be*

Assessment activity 3.1

Key skills ICT 2.1

Empowering service users

Hermione is a trainee nurse whose placement is at Gray's Nursing Home. The nursing home cares for older people and also takes service users who are recovering from amputations.

Hermione has been asked by the Nursing Home to produce a 'Guide' based both on the practice observed in the home and on secondary research, to show how care workers can empower service users, and to give guidance on how the care values should be applied.

1 Carry out secondary research to find out how care workers can empower service users. Include information about **four** ways from:
  • providing choice
  • giving respect
  • maintaining dignity
  • participating in decision-making
  • maintaining rights.

2 Prepare questions that could be used to interview a care worker to find out about methods used by their particular setting to empower service users, and about the ways in which they apply the care values in their day-to-day tasks. For the care values, include information about:
  • fostering equality and diversity
  • maintaining confidentiality
  • fostering rights and beliefs.

3 Arrange to visit a care setting or ask a care worker to visit your centre (with your tutor's permission), to find out how care workers empower service users and how they apply the care values.

4 Produce information for the Guide using both primary and secondary information to identify **four** ways that service users can be empowered, giving examples to illustrate the points made.

5 Information is needed for the Guide to show how all **three** components of the care values could be applied by care workers in their day-to-day tasks. Remember to give some scenarios or case studies to illustrate the points being made, as well as showing how care workers' own attitudes and opinions should not be allowed to influence their actions when providing practical care for service users.

What are the skills that contribute to practical caring?

Making sure that service users get the correct pills

There are many skills needed to provide practical care, but here we are going to consider four groups of skills which are likely to arise in job roles in each of the three main sectors of health and social care, that is:

- health job roles
- social care job roles
- early years job roles.

What is a skill?

A **skill** is something a person can do. A skill can be learnt and practised until it can be done well.

For example, an infant is not born with the skill of being able to walk. He or she watches the people around them and then starts learning the skill by first pulling themselves up into an upright position. Then, when he or she has learnt how to do this, they try moving, first by holding on to furniture. After much practice they have learnt to stand up and then they want to move. The parent holds on to the infant and guides the walking in the first instance. Gradually the parents reduce the amount of holding they are doing and soon the infant is walking unaided and independently.

Learning any skill follows a similar pattern. That is:

- watching others
- copying
- practising
- being able to do the skill.

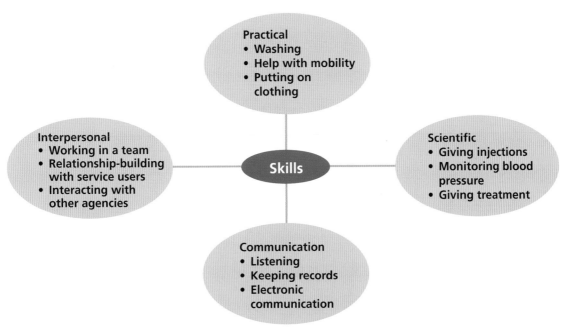

Figure 3.5 *Examples of skills required by care workers*

Once a person has learnt a skill it is more than likely that they will not forget how to do it, however long they may not have used it for. This is like having once learned the skill of riding a bicycle. Even if a person does not ride a bicycle for twenty years, they would still know how to do it. They may need to practice for a while, but the knowledge of how to do it comes back quite quickly.

Learning skills for work can be achieved through:

- actually doing the job, e.g. on-the-job training
- through training, e.g. in school, college or HE.

> ## Discussion point
> *Why is it important to practise skills?*

Skills that are needed for practical caring

Skills of a nursery nurse

A nursery nurse is concerned with the care, education and well-being of children up to the age of eight years. They take responsibility for the children in their care. What duties they have depends on the age of the children for whom they care. For example, if they are caring for toddlers and pre-school children, they have to focus on developing language skills and exploring through the world of play. If they are caring for children who are between two and four-and-a-half years old, nursery nurses have to organise and supervise outdoor play. If they are caring for babies, then quite a lot of practical and physical caring is involved, for example, feeding, cleansing and changing nappies.

Nursery nurses may also be involved in keeping general records for the children for whom they care, as well as records to do with observing and assessing them. Meeting and talking with parents, main carers and other professionals is likely to be part of their work. They also have to be involved in organising, planning and managing activities for the children. Nursery nurses can be employed in:

- day nurseries, playgroups and crèches
- schools, where they provide support for teachers
- hospitals, where they are involved in caring for infants and children who are ill
- as nannies in private homes.

The day-to-day tasks and skills needed by a nursery nurse who is providing care and education for children between two and four-and-a-half years old are outlined in the table below.

Tasks carried out by a nursery nurse	Skills required to carry out the tasks
Greeting children and parents	Oral communication skills, listening skills
Putting up play equipment	Practical skills, problem-solving skills
Planning activities with others	Interpersonal skills, communication skills, organisational skills
Storytelling	Communication skills, interpersonal skills
Preparing practical activities, e.g. playdough, paint	Scientific skills, creative skills, practical skills, mathematical skills
Talking with children and answering questions	Oral communication skills, listening skills, problem solving skills
Keeping records	Written communication skills
Comforting children	Interpersonal skills, oral communication skills
Giving basic first aid	Scientific skills, interpersonal skills, practical skills, oral communication skills

The tasks carried out by a nursery nurse require many skills

From the list of tasks it is possible to see that a large number of skills are needed. Some of these skills could be learnt while actually doing the job, while others may need to be learnt while training. Others would probably be present in the nursery nurse already, as people often choose jobs that they 'are good at' and for which they already have shown some **aptitude**.

From the table it can be seen that the main skills needed by a nursery nurse are:

- communication skills, e.g. the ability to speak clearly and listen carefully
- interpersonal skills, e.g. when relating to children and parents
- practical skills, e.g. in providing help with activities
- scientific skills, e.g. an awareness of health and safety, first aid

A nursery nurse also needs additional skills such as being able to:

- work well as part of a team
- organise, present and manage
- problem solve, e.g. knowing how to cope in difficult situations and find solutions.

Skills of a registered general nurse

In contrast to nursery nurses, registered general nurses care for service users (patients) who are over the age of 16. They do a lot of practical nursing such as checking temperatures, blood pressure and respiration rates. They often assist doctors with physical examinations as well as giving drugs, injections, cleaning and dressing wounds. Taking **clinical histories** and helping to draw up care plans in consultation with doctors and others is part of the role of a registered general nurse, and frequently they are required to counsel service users and relatives, providing emotional support to help them cope with their current situation. Sometimes nurses in a hospital are responsible for supervising health care assistants.

Some of the day-to-day tasks and skills needed by a registered general nurse are shown in the table below.

Tasks carried out by a registered general nurse	Skills required to carry out the tasks
Greeting service users and talking with them	Communication skills, interpersonal skills
Taking temperature, pulse and monitoring blood pressure	Scientific skills
Recording the health measurements taken	Communication skills
Hygiene routines	Practical skills, communication skills
Cleaning a wound, changing a dressing	Practical skills, scientific skills
Admitting new service users to the ward	Communication skills, interpersonal skills
Helping with the physical examination of a service user	Practical skills, scientific skills
Working with others, e.g. nurses, doctors, physiotherapists	Interpersonal skills, communication skills
Planning care for service users	Organisational skills, communication skills

Some of the skills used by a general nurse are very similar to those used by a nursery nurse. Both use communication, interpersonal, practical and scientific skills. It is likely that a general nurse would use more scientific skills than a nursery nurse because of the tasks that he or she carries out.

Some skills are known as **transferable skills** because they are used in a large number of job roles and are not specific to a particular job. They are necessary for most job roles. Skills that are transferable are:

- communication
- Information and Communication Technology (ICT)
- working in a team
- interpersonal skills (customer/service user care)
- planning and organising
- time management
- problem solving.

What qualities are required in practical caring?

Qualities are what someone is like as a person. They are partly the result of a person's **genetic** make up that is inherited from their parents. Qualities are also the result of factors that have influenced a person's development, for example, family, education, income, social class and where they live.

No one thing contributes to our **uniqueness.** People are the way they are because of inherited factors and the experiences that they have had.

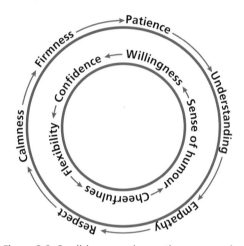

Figure 3.6 *Qualities can enhance the care we give*

For example, a person brought up in a large family is more likely to share things with others than a person who is an only child. A person whose mother is always calm in a crisis may inherit the same **trait** from her. A person who is honest may be so because they have been influenced while growing up by family members who placed a great deal of value on an open and honest approach.

Qualities contribute to people's **characters**, and often reflect the things that are important to them; the things that they value. They are things people do naturally because they are part of their make-up or **characteristics**.

When providing practical care for service users, qualities that come naturally enhance the care that is provided.

The qualities that most help when providing care are:

Qualities	How they could help when providing care
Patience	Care workers who are patient are less likely to get angry if a person asks the same question over and over again. They will understand that some people need time to make up their minds before they are able to make a decision, e.g. about when to have treatment, what to wear, and what they would like to eat
Understanding	Understanding enables care workers to see things from another person's point of view or perspective, e.g. a service user who is upset because their pet has died should not be told 'well you knew it was going to happen soon'. Instead the care worker should listen and respond in a way that shows that they can identify with the pain that the service user is feeling. They might say, for example, 'Well Joan, think about some of the happy times you and Sam had together. Do you remember when he stole the meat from Betty's plate? He was so pleased with himself, he looked as though he was grinning at the time!' This approach is likely to help establish good relationships between the care worker and service user
Empathy	To be able to empathise with service users means to see and feel things in the same way as them. Care workers are able to put themselves in the same position as service users. Service users will recognise this by the way a care worker speaks to them and the words that they use
Respect	Care workers who show respect value service users for who they are, not what they think they should be. They find out what service users prefer to be called instead of calling them 'love' or 'dear'. They listen to what they have to say and do not walk away in the middle of a sentence
Willingness	Care workers who are willing to be helpful are always appreciated by both staff and service users. Such care workers do not mumble and complain about the tasks they are given and often offer to do something without waiting to be asked. Service users appreciate such an attitude and are likely to trust and value a person with this quality
Sense of humour	Care workers who have a sense of humour are always appreciated. They can often see the funny side of a difficult or embarrassing situation, e.g. a service user told a care worker that he had taken cat worming tablets by mistake when he should have taken a headache tablet. The care worker replied 'well at least you'll be ready for a night on the tiles!' The situation was lightened by the care worker's reply
Cheerfulness	Cheerful care workers are easily recognised. They usually have a friendly approach which is conveyed by tone of voice. They greet service users in a manner that shows that they are pleased to see them and are genuinely interested in them. Care workers who are cheerful are much more likely to have a more positive experience with service users

Activity 2

Key skills [C] 2.2

Skills and qualities

1 For each of the following tasks, which skills would be needed by a dental nurse when completing the following task?
   a Greeting a service user.
   b Helping to put a protective apron/gown on a service user and getting them seated.
   c Mixing materials for a filling.
   d Handing equipment in support of the dentist while treating a service user.
   e Cleaning a service user's teeth.

2 Explain, using examples, which transferable skills could be used by a care assistant when carrying out tasks in a service user's own home.

3 Explain, by using examples, which qualities would help a nurse who had to give distressing news to a service user?

4 How would a care worker show empathy?

How can skills and qualities be used when caring for service users?

When skills and qualities are used together to provide practical care, the results are more likely to be effective as the skills will **enhance** the qualities and vice versa.

For example, Amnita, a nursery nurse, has to settle a dispute between two children in the playgroup who are quarrelling over a toy. Amnita uses her skills of communication to talk to both children to find out exactly what the problem is and to suggest a solution. Amnita is very calm (quality) and is also very good at listening (skill). She is also firm (quality) and quickly makes it clear to the children that she is expecting them to listen to what each has to say. Because she is patient (quality), she does not try to rush their explanations. Amnita uses communication (skills) to encourage them to explain exactly what has happened.

The result is that both children feel that they have been heard. No favouritism has been shown as both have been provided with time to say what they want. Amnita also uses her problem solving skills by asking each child to suggest what they think should happen, in other words to find a solution. In this situation, skills and qualities have been used together to find a solution to a difficulty.

Using skills and qualities when providing practical caring

The text that follows is an example of practical care duties.

Tejpal is a nurse caring for Rupert who is recovering from surgery to his hip. Rupert's temperature and pulse need to be monitored. Tejpal greets Rupert cheerfully, making conversation about a TV programme Rupert watches. Tejpal explains to Rupert that he needs to monitor his temperature and pulse. He asks Rupert's permission before carrying out the monitoring. The thermometer is correctly prepared and Tejpal places it in Rupert's ear, asking Rupert how he is feeling while he is doing this task. He takes the measurement and reads the result. Tejpal then finds Rupert's pulse and counts for 15 seconds. He calculates the reading and records the results. Tejpal tells Rupert that both are normal and reassures him that he is recovering as expected.

When carrying out this practical task Tejpal has used both skills and qualities to make sure that the practical care he is giving is carried out quickly and efficiently. He has used:

- communication skills to explain what he is going to do and has demonstrated respect (quality) by asking permission to carry out the tasks
- scientific skills in using the thermometer correctly
- practical skills to take temperature and pulse without causing distress to Rupert

- interpersonal skills to relate to Rupert and to provide support to prevent him from worrying by telling him what the measurements are. He has also shown the quality of cheerfulness in his approach.

Using skills and qualities when in intellectual care situations

Here is an example of an intellectual care situation:

> Robert is a social worker who has made an arrangement to make an assessment of need for Sheila as she has mobility problems. Robert carefully explains to Sheila that he needs to ask her some questions and observe her doing some tasks to find out exactly what she can do and what she cannot do. He shows Sheila the form he has to complete and asks her if there is anything she does not understand.
>
> Robert starts to ask Sheila some of the questions from the form. As he progresses through the form Sheila finds it quite hard to understand the questions. Robert realises this and **reframes** the questions. He waits and gives Sheila time to answer and to think before she answers.
>
> Robert explains to Sheila that he would like to observe her making a cup of tea. He jokes with Sheila and says that he has found that 'this is the best method to use to get a cup of tea while on the job'.
>
> Sheila has difficulty reaching for the cups and saucers and drops one. Robert remains very calm when Sheila gets flustered by what has happened. He reassures her, telling her 'I can see how difficult it is to reach up for the cups', and goes to fetch the dustpan and brush to clear up the broken china.

In this situation, Robert has used a number of skills and shown several qualities. He has:

- used communication skills to explain what the purpose of his visit is and to reassure Sheila about what is going to happen
- demonstrated the quality of 'respect', by showing Sheila the form and allowing her to see the questions
- demonstrated the quality of 'understanding' by rewording questions, so that Sheila can understand them
- demonstrated the quality of 'patience' by giving Sheila time to answer the questions and by not rushing her
- used interpersonal skills and demonstrated the qualities of 'cheerfulness' and 'sense of humour' by joking in order to **defuse** tension
- demonstrated the quality of 'willingness' in brushing up the broken china.

In this situation the main focus was on providing intellectual caring skills as an assessment of need was being carried out. This meant that Robert had to make informed judgements about Sheila's needs and how best to meet those needs. He achieved this by thinking about the best way to help Sheila, and the skills and qualities he demonstrated worked together both to obtain the information he needed and to act in Sheila's best interests during the assessment of her needs.

Using skills and qualities to support the emotional needs of service users

All care workers at some time in their career need to provide emotional support for service users. For example, a service user in a care home could receive some upsetting news, or a child at an early years setting could be upset because they miss their parent or are not feeling well, or a service user in a hospice could require emotional support because their loved one is dying. Whatever the situation, both skills and qualities have to be combined by care workers to meet service users' needs.

When someone is upset, a person's first instinct is to go up to them and to put their arms around them to provide comfort. For care workers this may not be the best method to use, as to take such action is to invade a service user's personal space. Sometimes just sitting alongside a service user in silence is a good way to provide emotional support. The service user will be aware of the care worker's presence and can talk if they feel they want to. When providing emotional support, care workers must not:

- say 'Oh, I know how you must feel'
- start telling the service user of a similar situation that has occurred in their own life
- finish sentences for the service user if they are overwhelmed with grief.

Emotional upsets do not just involve a person crying. Situations can arise where service users show emotional disturbance through:

- displaying anger
- being aggressive
- acting in a threatening way
- being withdrawn
- seeking isolation
- laughing too much
- being hysterical.

In all of these situations care workers need to demonstrate qualities of calmness, respect, understanding, patience and a sense of humour when it is appropriate. A sense of humour, if correctly used, can often be used to defuse a situation.

Using skills and qualities to support the social needs of service users

Whatever their age, from children through to older adults, service users need some form of social integration and stimulation. Some service users find interacting and socialising with others very difficult. They may be very private people in their personal lives and may worry that they have nothing to say that others will want to hear. Care workers have a responsibility to help service users to become **socially integrated**, whether they

Figure 3.7 *Just sitting side-by-side in silence can be emotionally comforting*

are users of day care facilities or in residential care.

The skills and qualities which care workers need to support service users' social needs include:

- communication skills, in order to help people start talking to one another and to join in any activities that are being provided
- the quality of 'willingness', in order to encourage others to interrelate, e.g. taking part in an activity with a service user until they feel confident to continue by themselves. This may be time consuming but it is very rewarding when the desired outcome is achieved. Another example is showing a willingness to listen, even if the care worker has heard an account several times previously. This helps build trusting relationships and as a result the social needs of the service user will have been partially met.
- the quality of 'patience', because it may take time to persuade a service user to join a group or an activity.

Meeting Joan's social needs

Joan, aged 78, was admitted to a residential home after being in hospital for three months. She had previously lived alone in her own home, but she had a fall and broke her hip. While in hospital Joan caught the **MRSA bug** and was kept in isolation for two months of her three-month stay. When she was discharged from hospital Joan really wanted to return to her own home, but she realised that she could not look after herself and reluctantly accepted that she needed 24-hour care and support. She was given a very nicely decorated, but small, room at the residential home, shown the lounge and introduced to the other residents.

Joan, however, retreated to her bedroom and would not come out. She would not go to the dining room for meals, she would not go to the lounge. For three weeks staff served her meals on a tray in her room. Other staff took it in turns to sit with her for half an hour at a time to try and get her talking and to encourage her to come out. They talked about her home life before the accident, enquired about her childhood, shared experiences of local places, and talked about programmes that were on the television. Still Joan would not budge!

After a fortnight the staff left the door to Joan's bedroom open while they talked and conveniently forgot to close it when they left. One or two residents put their heads around the door as they passed and said 'hello'. One, resident, Pat, found that she and Joan had some common experiences, and stayed to chat about these. A care worker brought both Joan and Pat a cup of tea while they were talking. After three weeks Joan eventually emerged from her room and joined the residents for a midday meal. A few days later she sat in the lounge with some of the other residents and soon took over as their 'spokesperson'.

1 What skills did the care workers use to achieve a successful outcome for Joan?

2 In what way did the care workers use the qualities of patience, understanding, empathy, respect and willingness to build up Joan's confidence?

Assessment activity 3.2

Key skills [C] 2.2, [ICT] 2.3

Skills and qualities in practical care

Ann-Marie is a health care assistant who works in a Trust hospital on a surgical ward. As part of her day-to-day tasks she monitors patients' health, makes beds and attends to patients' hygiene needs.

Roger is a teacher in a reception class. He organises play activities, and encourages the children to learn basic literacy and numeracy skills. He supervises outdoor play and makes sure the children eat their lunch. Roger also greets parents and talks to them about the children's achievements.

Kara is a care assistant at a day care centre for older people. As part of her duties she is required to greet the service users, help them to choose their lunch from the menu and organise activities for them such as bingo and community singing.

Kara spends time talking with the service users. She also has to help take them to the toilet if they have mobility problems.

1 Use primary and secondary sources of information to describe the skills and qualities that each care worker would use for each of the case studies. Give examples to illustrate the points you are making, trying to show as many connections as possible between the skills and the qualities.

2 Explain the likely effects on service users when skills and qualities are used to provide practical care.

3 Prepare an aid that could be used when training care workers to show how skills and qualities can help to build good relationships with service users.

How should service users be encouraged to participate in choosing clothing to maintain appearance?

Choosing what to wear and putting on clothes are all part of a person's daily living **routines**. It is something that they do without thinking very much about it. For people who lack mobility or who have broken or amputated limbs or a sensory impairment, the process is much more difficult. They may not be able to:

- see what clothes they have to choose from
- reach the place where the clothes are stored
- put the clothes on even if they could reach them
- do the clothes up even if they were able to put them on.

The process of choosing clothes is quite a complicated process.

Just thinking about choosing clothing takes time and effort and requires decisions to be made. Some service users, particularly those who are confused, need help with this task. It is possible that some service users need to be reminded of which clothes they have to choose from. Care workers can select items and hold them up for the service user to see, or if the service user has sight impairment the care worker could describe some items.

Care workers could make a list or lay clothes out in the order in which they are to be put on, if service users have difficulty in remembering which garment to put on first.

If a service user insists on wearing the same set of clothing each day, several sets of the same clothing will need to be bought.

Figure 3.8 *Service users have a lot to decide*

Figure 3.9 *Now George, will it be stripes or check today?*

Care workers need to make sure that any clothes chosen:

- fit comfortably
- are suitable for the activity
- are clean.

Having chosen the clothing, the next stage is to help the service user to put on the items. The amount of help required depends on the service user's ability to participate. Service users could be unsure about which item to put on first, or which way round a garment needs to be. Involving service users is very important. The table below gives some suggestions as to how this could be achieved.

Stages in the dressing process	How care workers can involve the service user
Deciding the order for putting on garments	Either encourage the service user to lay the garments out on the bed in the order in which they will be put on, or help them to do so
Put on undergarments	Talk to the service user while they are putting on the items of clothing and gently encourage them, making suggestions about how to manage the situation, e.g. a care worker could say, 'would it be easier if you sit on the edge of the bed to put on your knickers Mel, otherwise you could fall over'.
Putting on top items of clothing, e.g. trousers, skirts, blouse, shirt, jumpers	Provide practical help, for example by holding up a jumper and arranging it so that an arm can be put in first. Or advise the service user to step into a skirt or pull it over the head. Give assistance to put the clothing on as easily as is possible
Doing garments up	Provide practical support by helping to do up zips and buttons if this is needed
Getting shoes on	Provide an aid and show a service user how to correctly use the aid if this is needed. If aids are not available, ask the service user if they would like assistance with putting on and/or doing up their shoes

During the dressing process care workers need to make sure that they are communicating effectively with the service user. This means making sure that the pace, tone and vocabulary are appropriate and not patronising the service user. Qualities of calmness and patience should be shown as the service user may not be very quick when dressing. Before giving practical help the service user should be asked if they require support and how best the care worker can be of assistance. By taking this approach service users are less likely to become totally dependent and will have been empowered to take some control over their lives.

What aids exist to support service users when dressing, and how are they used?

Everybody experiences difficulty at some time or another with either doing up buttons or trying to do up a zip. This may be because we have a cut on one of our fingers or we have sprained a wrist. For service users who have difficulty every day with routine tasks, aids can improve the quality of their lives considerably.

An aid is a piece of equipment or materials that can be used to make daily living tasks easier. Daily living tasks are all those activities that are

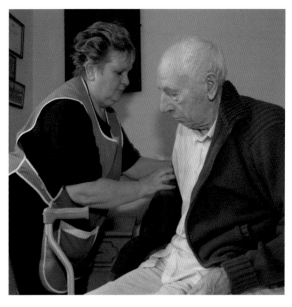

Helping a service user to get dressed

> ### Activity 3　　　　Key skills [C] 2.3
> #### Choosing clothing
> Barbarella is ten years of age. She has an arm and hand in plaster and her knee is heavily bandaged as she was recently involved in a car crash with her parents. Barbarella is recovering in the children's ward of the hospital.
>
> **1** Why is it important to involve Barbarella in choosing the clothes she will wear?
>
> **2** Explain how a nursery nurse could help Barbarella choose items of clothing to wear.
>
> **3** Explain how the nursery nurse could help Barbarella to dress, making sure that she empowers Barbarella.
>
> **4** Describe how a care assistant could help an older service user, who is confused, to dress.

routine and which are carried out every day of our lives. Examples of daily living tasks are dressing, feeding and washing. Aids make daily living tasks easier for service users who have specific needs and who are not able to easily carry out day-to-day routines independently. For example, trying to dress without using both hands can be very difficult indeed, as can putting on a sock or a pair of tights without being able to bend because of a broken hip. Aids help service users to be more independent, that is, less reliant on others.

However, it should be remembered that using an aid correctly can often take considerable practice. A range of aids are available to help those who experience difficulty. Some are shown at the top of the next page.

Shoehorn

Finding suitable footwear may be difficult for service users who cannot bend because of **rheumatism** or some such condition, or others who have difficulty gripping the shoe because of **arthritis** or other condition. Many service users choose slip-on shoes for these reasons while others may prefer shoes that can be fastened

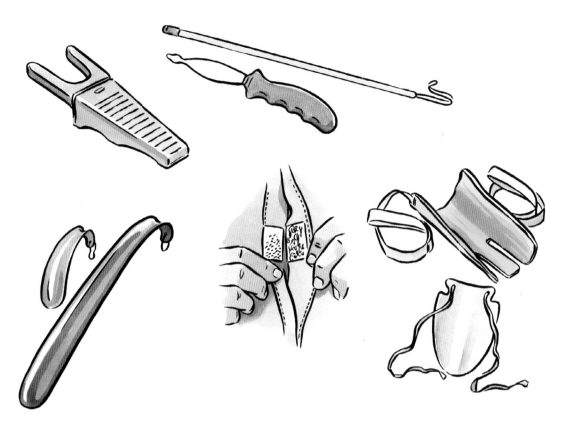

Figure 3.10 *Aids that can improve the quality of life for service users*

because they give a better grip. Whatever type of shoe is preferred, service users are greatly helped by having access to a shoehorn.

A shoehorn is an aid that can help service users to put on shoes. There are a variety available, ranging from short to long-handled shoehorns. The purpose of a shoehorn is to help someone who cannot bend easily to put their shoes on without the back of the shoes being walked down. A simple shoehorn can be a 'best friend' when it comes to putting on shoes or boots, as it can save time and money because the footwear is not damaged by being constantly pressed down at the heel when being put on.

The long-handled model of shoehorn helps to prevent having to bend. When buying a long-handled shoehorn it is important to check that the point where the handle joins the horn is strong and unlikely to break. When using a shoehorn service users should be encouraged to push their shoe up against the wall or a solid piece of furniture. This helps with stability when putting the shoe on and using the shoehorn.

To remove shoes, a 'bootjack' can be very useful. This aid requires the service user to put the heel of their foot between prongs and then to pull their foot out of the shoe. Look at the illustrations of aids and find the different types of shoehorns and the bootjack.

Try it!

Obtain a short and a long-handled shoehorn. Try using each. Which was easier to use?

Stocking and sock aids

Stocking and sock aids work on the same principles. These aids are intended to help service users who have difficulty bending forwards or who do not have the use of two hands, to put on socks, stockings and tights. If a person has a broken arm or is recovering from a hip or knee operation, putting on socks, stockings or tights can be an impossible task.

Try it!

Get a sock or a pair of tights. Secure one arm at your side so that you are not tempted to move it. Now try putting on the sock or tights. Can you do it?

Try it!

Obtain a sock/stocking aid from an aid centre or other source and try using it. How easy is it?

Most manufacturers produce two types of sock or stocking aid:

- the flexible version
- the rigid version.

The flexible version is perhaps the more difficult to use, but both need practice by service users. The flexible version is cone shaped and made of plastic or material. It has two holes and tapes or ribbons at the top. Look at the illustration of aids to see how this version is actually used.

The rigid version is made up of a plastic semi-circle with handles. The semi-circle part is known as the 'gutter'. See Figure 3.11 for how to use the flexible equipment.

Use of Velcro

Velcro is self-adhesive material that enables two surfaces to be brought together to stay in the position in which they are required. It is often used when service users have limited movement and are unable to fasten buttons, skirts, trousers or shirts, or to do up shoelaces.

Velcro can be used to help young children fasten their clothing or service users who have had an accident, for example, amputees. It is also useful for service users with conditions such as rheumatism or arthritis.

Discussion point

How can the use of Velcro improve the quality of life for a service user?

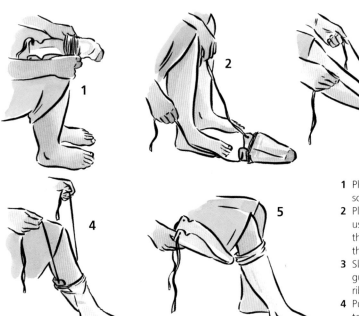

1 Place the gutter between the knees, putting the sock or tights onto the gutter.
2 Place the gutter on the floor in front of the person using it. If the service user is doing this themselves, they should use the ribbons or tapes attached to the gutter in order to avoid bending.
3 Slide the foot into the sock or tights and ease the gutter over the heel and up the leg using the ribbons. The sock or stocking is gradually pulled up.
4 Pull the gutter up by the ribbons until it is possible to reach it by hand. The sock or stocking is now in reach and can be easily pulled further up by the service user.
5 Remove the gutter. The sock or stocking can be pulled to the required height.

Figure 3.11 *How to use the flexible sock or stocking aid*

How can service users be supported in choosing and putting on an item of outer clothing?

When providing support for service users who want to put on an outer garment, some useful points to remember are:

- do not tell them what to do
- involve them as far as is possible
- allow them to make the decisions unless the decisions are likely to be harmful to them
- give them time to choose and to put on the clothing.

Supporting service users to put on socks or shoes

Support from care workers should take the form of:

- giving verbal support, e.g. encouragement, advice and guidance
- giving practical help, e.g. placing the shoe or sock in a position which enables a service user to put it on
- interacting with the service user, e.g. seeking opinions about how best to help.

Service users should be verbally encouraged to decide which shoes or socks they would like to wear. Care workers can help them by reminding them:

- what socks and shoes they have to choose from
- the purpose for which they are required, e.g. going to the shop or for medical treatment or for a walk
- the best position to adopt to make the task as easy as possible.

Supporting a service user to put on a cardigan, coat or jacket

When providing support for service users who want to put on a cardigan or jacket or coat, a care worker's role is as follows:

Choosing clothing and putting on outer garments	Care workers' role when providing support
Assess the situation	Find out what the service user's needs are and what specific help they are most likely going to need
Find out what item the service user wants to put on	Remind the service user of the choice they have
Work out which way to put the garment on	Explore with the service user whether it is best to put the left or right arm into the garment first
Decide if the garment needs to be fastened	Discuss with the service user whether they are likely to feel cold if the garment is not fastened or whether this will make them too hot. Ask what is more comfortable – fastened or not fastened?

To take an example of a care worker demonstrating this role, let us consider a conversation involving Ingrid, who has been to see a consultant at the local hospital. She is recovering from having a broken left arm. The consultant has asked Ingrid to remove her cardigan so that he can see how easily Ingrid can move the arm after having had

Case study

Supporting Bagicha to put on his shoes

Bagicha is at the day care centre. On arrival he removed his shoes and put on his slippers as he finds these more comfortable. It is now time to return home and Bagicha needs support to put his shoes back on.

How can the care assistant provide support for Bagicha when putting on the shoes?

1 Describe the practical steps that would be required to support Bagicha to put his shoes back on.
2 While supporting Bagicha through practical help, a care assistant would be giving verbal support. When would verbal support be most appropriate and why? Give three examples which cover different aspects of support.

several weeks of physiotherapy. The health care assistant helps Ingrid to put her cardigan back on.

> **Care assistant** How would you like to do this Ingrid?
>
> **Ingrid** I think I should put my left arm in first.
>
> **Care assistant** OK, Shall I hold the cardigan in position for you so that you can slip the arm into the sleeve?
>
> **Ingrid** Yes, that would be helpful, I won't be struggling with it then.
>
> **Care assistant** Good, that's one arm. Now I'll drape the cardigan round the back of you. I think you will need to bend your right arm slightly backwards to get your arm in the other sleeve. Do you think you can manage that?
>
> **Ingrid** Lets try, we'll soon find out!
>
> **Care assistant** The arm is in Ingrid, but can you push it just a little and I will gently pull the sleeve on all of the way?
>
> **Ingrid** Thank you so much.
>
> **Care assistant** Would you like any help with the buttons?
>
> **Ingrid** Yes please! It's a bit chilly out.

From this conversation it is possible to see how the health care assistant works closely with Ingrid to put on the cardigan. She does not tell Ingrid how to put the cardigan on, but instead asks Ingrid how she would like to approach the task, and then supports her decision, while gently providing suggestions.

In this situation the health care assistant has:
- empowered the service user by encouraging her to make her own decisions
- provided choice by letting the service user decide which approach she would like to use
- used effective communication skills by using open and closed questions
- provided practical care by holding the cardigan in position and helping to do up the buttons
- formed good relationships with the service user by using effective interpersonal skills.

The service user has had a positive experience and has been part of the decision making process.

> **Discussion point**
>
> *Why did the health care assistant want to empower Ingrid?*

Assessment activity 3.3

Key skills **C** 2.3, **ICT** 2.3

Supporting service users to dress themselves

Tanni is 76 years of age and lives in a residential home. She is unable to dress herself without support as she has severe mobility problems and uses a wheelchair for mobility. She is not totally dependent and likes to do as much as possible for herself. A care assistant helps Tanni to dress each morning.

Becci is five years old and is in the reception class at primary school. She has a broken wrist and cannot get dressed after PE lessons. She finds putting on her shoes and coat very difficult. Becci is helped with this task by the nursery nurse who assists with the reception class.

1 Prepare a short guide that could be used by **either** the care assistant for Tanni or the nursery nurse for Becci, to help them understand how to encourage service users to participate when choosing clothes and dressing. Try to link theory to what actually happens in practice, and discuss how the support provided will encourage service users to participate in the process.

2 Tanni and Becci need to use aids to help them with dressing. Choose **three** aids from those listed below and clearly describe how each should be used. Choose from:

- shoehorn
- stocking aid
- sock aid
- Velcro.

Explain how each aid chosen will provide support.

3 Correctly demonstrate how **three** of these aids would be used. Remember to arrange for your tutor to assess the demonstration.

4 Choose **one** service user from the given case studies and give a practical demonstration (simulated) to show how a care worker would provide support when helping a service user to put on items of clothing (including sock or shoes, and cardigan or coat or jacket).

Remember to arrange for your tutor to assess you when carrying out this practical task.

What are the benefits of remaining mobile?

For all service users, remaining mobile is very important as it allows them to have some control over their own lives and is a basic human right. Some older service users develop **deformities** through conditions such as arthritis, which means they can no longer straighten their arms or legs. Other service users may not be able to move from a bed to a chair either because of illness or conditions that prevent movement, or because of accidents that have caused damage. Lack of mobility often means that service users can no longer look after themselves and sometimes this necessitates moving them into a nursing or residential home. Other service users may need the support of community care services in their own homes or may be cared for by family, relatives or friends.

When people do not remain mobile they can become totally dependent on others. Lack of mobility can have a very bad effect on service users' physical and mental health as they can:

- put on weight
- develop a low sense of self-esteem
- have joints that seize up
- lose interest in what is going on around them
- become withdrawn and depressed.

> ### Discussion point
> *Why are service users who are not mobile likely to become dependent on others?*

Figure 3.12 *Remaining mobile enables service users to do more*

If a person is not mobile they often consider themselves to be a **burden** to those who are caring for them and this can cause them a great deal of distress. The possible effects of not remaining mobile are:

Parts of the body	Effects of lack of mobility
Feet and ankles	Can become swollen
Legs	Can develop blood clots (thrombosis)
Lungs	Have a high risk of developing chest infection through not being able to breath deeply
Bowel	Can become constipated as movement helps the bowel to contract
Muscles	Can become weaker and strength is rapidly lost

Care workers need to be very **sensitive** when helping service users with mobility. Care must be taken to ensure that time is given to enable service users to move at a speed with which they are confident, and to assist them rather than doing everything for them. For example, if a service user can walk a little, a care worker should not **automatically** provide a wheelchair because it is quicker!

What is the range of mobility aids available to service users and their purpose?

Walking sticks

Walking sticks are used for service users who are slightly **unsteady** on their feet or when they lack confidence and feel that they will lose their balance and fall over.

Walking sticks must be the correct height for a service user, otherwise the service user could begin to stoop which can lead to loss of balance and a fall.

The purpose of a walking stick is to:

- provide support
- help maintain balance
- give confidence
- prevent loss of balance

- prevent falling
- encourage independence.

When using a walking stick a service user should:

- hold the stick, by placing the right hand firmly but comfortably over the top of it (if the person is right-handed)
- place the stick slightly in front of themselves so that they can take a step forward
- using the stick as support, move the opposite foot from the stick forward to the same position as the stick
- move the foot that is on the opposite side of the stick past the stick
- repeat the moves again.

Try it!

Obtain a walking stick. Try using it. How easy is it to use the walking stick?

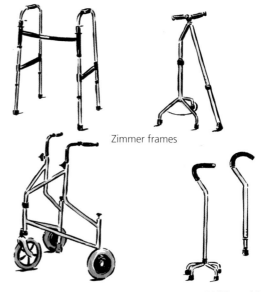

Zimmer frames

Walking sticks

Wheelchairs

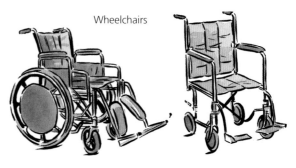

Figure 3.13 *Aids for mobility*

Zimmer frame

The Zimmer frame is the commonest form of walking aid for service users who require the help of two care workers when walking. The purpose of a Zimmer frame is to:

- help service users who are quite unsteady on their feet
- help service users feel confident
- make mobility more stable
- encourage independence.

Zimmer frames are made in a variety of heights and widths and on some frames it is possible to adjust the height. Service users are measured before being provided with a Zimmer frame, so that a frame is selected that is correct for their height. If a person has to reach up they could lose their balance and fall. A frame that is too low could cause a service user to fall over because they have to bend over the frame. Service users living in nursing or residential homes that have Zimmer frames must have their names marked clearly on the frame so that they are not used by the wrong person, as this can lead to accidents.

Each Zimmer frame has four legs with rubber ends on. These ends are known as **ferrules**, and have patterns of raised rubber on the base. These prevent the frame from slipping. Care workers should check these patterns every few months to make sure they have not worn off.

Using a Zimmer frame involves slightly lifting the frame off the ground in order to move forward. Service users:

- place the Zimmer frame a short distance in front of themselves so that they can lean on it with their arms stretched almost to the full
- move one leg forward and then the other with the second leg moving past the first. The service user will lean on the frame for support.

Some service users do not have the strength to lift the Zimmer frame, and therefore they need the type of Zimmer frame that has wheels attached.

Tripod

A tripod is often used by service users who have had a stroke and who may have weakness or **paralysis** on one side. Service users must be measured to make sure that a tripod is the correct height for them. If a person has paralysis or weakness on their left side then they need a right-handed tripod, similarly a person affected on the right side needs a left-handed tripod.

The tripod is used in a similar way to the Zimmer frame and has the same purpose, the main one being to encourage independence. The three legs of the tripod provide support for the service user when moving. Some service users can move without assistance from a care worker as a result of using a tripod.

> ### Try it!
>
> Obtain a Tripod and try using it. How does it compare with the Zimmer frame for ease of use?

> ### Activity 4
>
> Key skills 2.3
>
> #### Anika
>
> Anika, who is 55 years of ag,e has recently had her left hip replaced. She is recovering well from the operation but needs an aid to help her walk. Her husband Kia also needs some slight support when walking as he is afraid of losing his balance.
>
> 1 Explain how using a walking stick could help Kia and instruct him on how to use it correctly.
>
> 2 The hospital has suggested that Anika uses a tripod. Why do you think this aid has been chosen?
>
> 3 Work with another person and role-play being Anika who is using a tripod. Your partner should be the care worker who provides support.
>
>   Using no more than half a side of A4, write instructions for Anika on how to use the tripod correctly.
>
> 4 Practice using a Zimmer frame correctly. Ask a friend to observe your demonstration and to advise on improvements.

How can correct use of mobility aids be demonstrated?

Care workers need to show service users how to use mobility aids correctly, so it is important that they know how each type of aid is used. They will, at some time in their career as a carer, be required to give a demonstration showing how to use one or more mobility aids.

In order to be a success, a demonstration needs to include:

- an explanation of the correct way to use each aid
- a demonstration of how to actually use each aid correctly.

Part of the preparation for a demonstration is thinking carefully about what should be included. When planning for a demonstration, care workers should:

- choose the aid(s) they are going to demonstrate
- practise using the aid(s) and write down each step as they use it
- prepare a handout (based on the notes) for those observing
- prepare a document to help them analyse their own performance in terms of:
  - aims and objectives
  - skills they will use
  - qualities they will use
  - time they will take
  - outcomes they will achieve.
- practise the demonstration to see if any changes are needed and how long it will take
- Make sure they have got the date, time and place correct for the demonstration!

Once the demonstration has taken place, good practice would be for care workers to analyse their performance in order to better it for any future occasion. Information about how to do this appears in Unit 3.6.

How is a wheelchair correctly used?

For some service users, mobility aids such as walking sticks, Zimmer frames and tripods are not an option because their condition or impairment means that they have to use a wheelchair.

The main types of wheelchair are:

- **self-propelling** wheelchairs
- **non-self-propelling** wheelchairs
- electric wheelchairs.

Self-propelling wheelchairs have large wheels which have circular handgrips on them. The person in the wheelchair uses the handgrips to push themselves along. This often takes quite a bit of practice, but the outcome is worth it because it means service users are less dependent on others.

Some service users cannot move themselves around in self-propelling wheelchairs, and need to be pushed around by a care worker or family or friends. These wheelchairs have smaller wheels and are often lighter and can be folded for storage.

Electric wheelchairs are very much more expensive but increase the amount of independence achieved as service users can control where they wish to go and when.

It is important that all wheelchairs are fitted with the correct type of cushions as some service users may spend a long time in them. Wheelchairs must be regularly maintained.

For wheelchairs that are self-propelling or non-self-propelling it is important to make sure that:

- the tyres are regularly checked and are at the correct pressure
- the brakes are working correctly
- the wheels move easily and are not impeded in any way, e.g. because the tread on the tyres is worn.
- Electric or battery-operated wheelchairs must be regularly maintained by recognised representatives of the manufacturer or a local responsible dealer.

When using wheelchairs it is very important to make sure that the brakes are on before **transferring** service users to them. This is to prevent the wheelchairs from moving during transfer.

Points to remember when using a wheelchair

Remember to:

- unfold the wheelchair by pushing down on the outer edges
- place the wheelchair in the position required, as near to the service user as possible

- make sure the brake is locked
- lift or swing away the footrests
- if possible remove the side from the wheelchair to make it easier for the service user to gain access
- encourage the service user to place one hand on the wheelchair and one hand on the chair from which they are moving, in order to steady themselves
- encourage the service user to slide into the wheelchair, providing support if required.
- encourage the service user to sit back in the chair
- make sure the service user is comfortable and warm
- ask if the service user is ready to move, release the brake and push the chair at a reasonable speed
- make sure the service user's elbows are not outside the wheelchair so that they are not hit by people who are passing or caught on narrow door frames. When moving a wheelchair up a curb, tip the wheelchair by stepping onto the bar at the rear of the wheelchair (next to the wheels). Move the small wheels onto the curb and then lift the back wheels up.

How should a service user be assisted to use a wheelchair?

'Walking people' often talk down to people sitting in a wheelchair. When assisting a service user who is in a wheelchair, care workers should try to be more aware of their body language by kneeling or bending down to meet the service user's eye level when talking to them. Care workers should try to be more aware of the needs of wheelchair users, especially if such users cannot propel themselves or have **sensory impairment** or memory problems.

When assisting, care workers must check the position of a person in a wheelchair to prevent pressure sores and injuries. The person should sit in the most comfortable position possible, making sure they are sitting as far back as possible. Both feet must be placed properly on the footrests. The hands must be placed into the lap to ensure that the fingers cannot be caught in the wheels.

The person assisting needs to ask a service user in a wheelchair whether they are comfortable and need to inform them how and when the wheelchair will be moved. The aim should be for a smooth and steady movement of the wheelchair. Rough handling, rushing and quick turns should be avoided, since this can frighten a service user in a wheelchair.

Before **tilting** a wheelchair, the service user sitting in it must be informed. The wheelchair must not be tilted too fast backward and forward, or too fast forward and backward. If a wheelchair gets stuck, the chair should not be forced, but the obstacle should be removed first.

Care workers assisting a service user in a wheelchair should beware of people who stop to talk to them as though the wheelchair user were not present. They should draw service users into any conversation whenever possible.

Figure 3.14 *Ignoring a wheelchair user*

Activity 5

Sophie

Sophie is 50 years of age. She is confined to a wheelchair because she has rheumatoid arthritis which means she cannot move very far without assistance because her limbs are no longer straight.

1 List three different types of wheelchair.

2 Identify **three** checks that should be made when maintaining a wheelchair and explain why each is important.

3 Obtain a wheelchair. Working with another member of the group demonstrate how to get the wheelchair up a curb. Now reverse the roles. How easy was it? What improvements could be made?

4 Produce a handout that could be given to a care worker to remind them of points to remember when assisting a service user to use a wheelchair.

What are the sources of aids that support mobility?

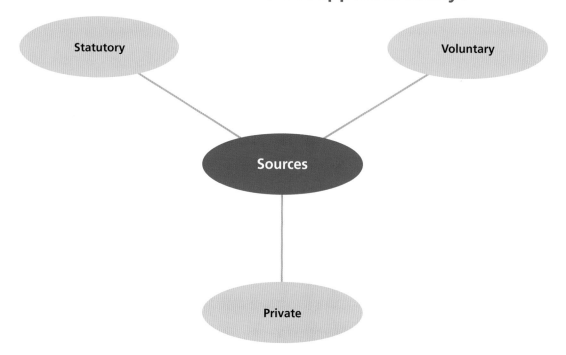

Figure 3.15 *Sources of aids*

Statutory sources

Statutory provision of aids can be through:

- the NHS
- local authority (social services)
- community care (NHS or local authority).

A GP could recommend that a service user should be **assessed** to see which mobility aid would best suit them. The GP could, for example, refer the service user to a physiotherapy department or to an occupational therapist.

Alternatively, a service user could be visiting a day clinic at their local hospital, particularly if they are recovering from a stroke or if they have rheumatoid arthritis or have had a knee or hip replacement. At the day clinic they would be assessed to see how much support they require and which would be the most suitable aid. The whole topic of which aid would be best would be discussed with the service user before decisions were made. The service user may be encouraged to 'try' several different types of aid to see which they felt more comfortable with.

Service users need to be measured to make sure that they receive an aid that is suitable for their height. If a service user has decided to have a Zimmer frame, the care worker measuring should ask the service user to stand against the frame, leaning slightly forward holding the frame. If the frame is the right size, when the service user's feet are level with the back legs of the frame, their arms should be very slightly bent.

When measuring for a walking stick, care workers should make sure that the person's hand is at the same height as the top of their thigh. If the stick is adjustable, the inner part of the stick can be moved up and down until the correct height is reached. If the service user prefers a wooden stick, a measurement will have to be taken. The stick should then be cut off at the correct height and a rubber ferrule placed on the bottom to prevent the stick from slipping. Figure 3.16 outlines how to measure service users for a walking stick.

Local authorities provide aids for people who wish to remain in their own homes but who need support, or who live in residential and nursing homes.

It is possible that a local authority social services department could carry out an assessment of need by **liaising** with the NHS through the community physiotherapist. Or the social service department could ask a GP to write a letter of referral to the community physiotherapist, who would then assess the service user and complete an order form for the aid. The community physiotherapist would then visit the service user in their own home or in the residential or nursing home to check that the aid is the correct height and to instruct the service user about the correct way to use it.

Voluntary sources

Some voluntary groups supply aids for service users, usually for a very small charge. The Red Cross and St Johns Ambulance have 'loan centres' for mobility aids in some areas of the country. If a person needs an aid for a very short time, perhaps because they are recovering from a car or motorbike accident, they can hire a mobility aid for a week, month or several months. When they no longer need the aid they can return it to the centre. If borrowing or buying aids from a voluntary group, it is very important to make sure the aid is at the correct height for the person.

Private sources

A private source of mobility aid could, for example, be a shop, the Internet or a private hospital. Buying an aid privately means that

Figure 3.16 *Measuring a service user for an aid*

service users are required to pay for it, and it will always remain their own to do with as they choose. The number of shops that sell mobility aids are increasing, and while they may not keep in stock every type of mobility aid, they have brochures to illustrate the aids which provide information about their use and cost. It is best to study these brochures and to investigate all sources of aids before making a decision to buy. Bear in mind that a service user's needs may change and the mobility aid that they currently have may no longer be suitable in a few months time. This could mean additional expense for the service user.

Assessment activity 3.4

Key skills ICT 2.3, C 2.3

Mobility aids

Note: During this task you are required to keep a log relating to the demonstrations that you need to carry out. The log should show how theory links with practice and should give reasons for the actions taken.

1 Prepare a presentation for a group of new service users to explain the benefits of remaining mobile. Make sure you link theory to actual practice.

2 Choose two walking aids from:
   • walking sticks
   • Zimmer frame
   • tripod.

   Arrange a demonstration of each of your chosen mobility aids aimed at a group of new mobility aid users. Arrange for your tutor to assess the demonstrations. Remember to follow the recommended steps. These include:

   • prepare a handout for those observing
   • analyse your performance at this demonstration in terms of
     – aims and objectives
     – the skills you have used
     – the qualities you have used
     – the time taken
     – the outcomes achieved.

   This last point will help you for Assessment activity 3.6.

3 After you have demonstrated how to use the two aids correctly, demonstrate to the service users how to use a non-propelling wheelchair.

4 Produce materials to explain to the service users how to assist a service user who is using a non-propelling wheelchair.

5 Present information to the care workers about sources of mobility aids.

How can service users be assisted to choose meals?

Eating and drinking are essential if service users are to stay alive. If service users need help with any part of the eating and drinking process, care workers should be careful to offer help in a way that maintains their dignity.

Reading

Some service users may have difficulty in reading a menu. This could be because they:

- have poor eyesight and may not be able to read the packaging on foods or menus, e.g. the size of the print may be too small
- may not understand the vocabulary used in the menu, i.e. they may not have the **literacy** skills necessary
- may have a disability that prevents them from holding or reading the menu.

Care workers need to be aware of such difficulties. Often service users do not want anyone else to know that they are unable to cope, and do everything possible to cover up their difficulties. If they cannot read the menu, service users may end up eating the wrong thing. Signs that show a service user could be having difficulty in reading a menu would be if they:

- choose foods they do not like and leave them
- say they are not hungry and do not order anything
- experience eating difficulties.

Some reasons that service users may have difficulties are shown in the table below.

If a care worker suspects that a service user may have difficulty in reading the menu, they need to make time to sit and read the menu with them. This can be done sensitively as shown in the conversation at the bottom of this page between a care worker and Maise at a day care centre.

Reasons	How care workers can help
Dysphagia (which causes difficulty and discomfort when swallowing. It can effect people who are older, are stroke sufferers or who have Parkinson's disease)	Give liquid foods or semi solid foods
Sore mouth and throat	Avoid foods that are hard and need chewing because of difficulty swallowing, and give soft foods such as soup, jelly or ice cream
Poor appetite (nothing appeals to the service user)	Use 'concentrated foods' which have a lot of nutrients, e.g. milk shakes or powdered foods such as Complan
Vomiting	Give rice, noodles and other bland foods in small amounts. Do not offer solid foods and liquids at the same time

Care worker Well, here's today's menu, Maise. Let's have a look and see what they're offering us today. I'm hungry already so I'm hoping my favourite will be on there.

Maise What's your favourite then?

Care worker Fish 'n chips!

Maise I used to like them, but I've gone off them because of the bones! Stick in your throat they do.

Care worker We've got the choice of tomato soup or pâté for starters, Maise. I'm going to have the soup. What about you?

Maise I think I'll have the soup. It will slip down easily.

Care worker Let's see if my fish 'n chips are on today. Yes, I'm in luck. What have they got that you would like, Maise? I can offer ham, egg and chips, macaroni cheese or sausage with mash and peas.

Maise I like macaroni cheese. It's a long time since I've had one of those. I think I'll order that.

From this conversation you can see that the care worker:

- involves herself by suggesting that she is also choosing her own lunch, so the service user does not feel patronised that the menu is just being read for her benefit
- clearly reads what is on the menu and does so at a pace that is appropriate for Maise by not hurrying her
- gives Maise time to think by saying what she is going to have first
- has a very friendly approach and has obviously built up a good relationship with Maise, bringing a touch of humour to the situation.

The menu is read in a way that does not offend Maise, making her feel valued. From the care worker's perspective, Maise has been provided with the opportunity to order food she likes and which she will not have difficulty swallowing.

Other service users may just ask to have the menu read to them. If this happens, care workers should:

- read the menu slowly and carefully
- repeat the name of each dish
- explain any dishes that service users are unsure about
- check that the order when taken is what the service user thinks he or she has ordered.

Advising

Sometimes a service user needs advice about what foods to choose, for example at a day care centre or in their own home.

Before providing advice it is important for care workers to know whether the service user:

- has any **special needs**
- has any eating difficulties
- has any religious or cultural preferences
- has any likes or dislikes.

Care workers who are providing advice need to be aware of the nutritional needs of the service user. Any advice given must take into consideration:

- **the nutritional value of foods**, e.g. protein, carbohydrate, fats, vitamins, fibre, water

- **Dietary Reference Values (DRVs)**, e.g. the recommended requirements according to age, sex, body size and activity levels
- **present levels of intake**, e.g. the foods and nutrients the service user is having currently.

Care workers may need to take advice from a supervisor or seek the aid of a dietician if asked to give detailed advice about choosing meals and diets.

Allowing choice

It is a service user's right to be able to choose the foods they eat. If service users have a condition that affects the foods they are able to have because of an illness or a condition, there may have to be some **restrictions.** For example, if a service user has an allergy to nuts, then to allow them to eat foods which contained nuts would not be a responsible action.

Service users are more likely to eat foods if they have chosen them than if they are given no choice. If food is put in front of them which they dislike or which does not appeal to them they are not likely to eat it.

Menus need to provide service users with a choice of dishes, which include at least one:

- meat dish, e.g. roast lamb
- fish dish, e.g. fish pie
- vegetarian dish, e.g. macaroni cheese
- dish from a different culture, e.g. humus
- hot dish, e.g. goulash and rice
- cold dish, e.g. salad.

Service users may request items that are not on the menu. If these are simple things which can be produced without too much trouble, care workers should enquire whether the chef could produce the dish for the service user. For example, if a service user asks for an omelette, it may be possible for the chef to make one as only eggs and a little milk would be needed. However, if something more complicated is requested, such as a curry, such a request would probably be refused.

Some service users may have difficulty in reading or remembering menu choices, as has already been discussed in this unit. Ways of helping service users to choose could include for example:

- producing the menu in large print
- using pictures to illustrate the menu
- allowing service users to choose their meals as near as possible to the time when the meal will be served
- reading the menu to the service user
- noting services users' likes and dislikes in their care plan.

To allow service users choice means:

- helping them to feel that they have some control over their lives
- empowering them
- valuing them
- helping them to participate in the decision-making process.

Making notes

Try it!

In 15 seconds write down different reasons for making notes.

Notes are used:
- to help remember facts
- as a reminder of something that has to be done

- to find out about something
- to pass on information to others
- to record important information.

Care workers should make notes for all the reasons given above, particularly when helping service users to choose meals. For example, a service user may tell a care worker that they are not able to eat a particular food because of their medical condition. The care worker should make a note of this to pass onto others on a 'need-to-know basis'.

Care workers should also take notes to record what different service users have chosen to have from the menu, in order to remember who wants what!

Notes can be very useful when a service user has enquired about which ingredients are in a certain dish. The chef may give the care worker a list of answers that need to be recorded so that the care worker will have a **memory jogger** when passing the information to the service user.

Some notes can be written up at a later time by care workers onto **permanent** records, so that others who are involved in caring for the same service users will have a formal record. Notes help care workers to include all the important facts when this task is being completed.

Activity 6

Key skills (N) 2.2

Vessha

Vessha is in the reception class at Highgate Primary School. He has not yet learnt to read so he cannot read the lunch menu that is on display in the canteen. Also, he has only recently arrived in this country, and is not familiar with Western dishes.

1 Write out a possible conversation between Vessha and the reception class teacher showing how the teacher could help Vessha choose from the lunch menu.

2 List **three** points to be remembered before giving advice to a service user about choosing a menu.

3 Work in pairs to plan a lunch menu for a five-year-old child who is reasonably active.

4 Use Dietary Reference Values to explain why the menu in Question 3 is suitable.

5 Complete this sentence. Allowing service users a choice of menu means:
   a having control over service users' lives for their best interests
   b not treating one service user more favourably than another
   c encouraging service users to participate in the decision-making process
   d providing a menu with restricted choices.

6 Explain how making notes can contribute to the effective choosing of dishes from a menu.

What preparation is required to help service users eat and drink?

Meal times should be a pleasant occasion and should provide service users with the opportunity to enjoy a meal and to chat with others in a relaxed situation. Care workers need to make an effort to make sure that eating is an enjoyable experience. Many residential and nursing homes encourage service users to eat lunch in the dining room so that they can talk with others. Hospitals too, encourage those who can walk to sit at a communal table to share their meal. In an early years setting children meet in the canteen or cafeteria or sit round in a group to eat their packed lunches.

Service users enjoying their lunch

Care workers need to make sure that service users have been correctly prepared to make sure that they are comfortable when eating. To prepare service users:

- make sure that they have been to the toilet before they eat
- **minimise** noise and distraction while they are eating, although playing music quietly in the background can help to create a relaxing atmosphere
- if they are in bed and need help with feeding, make sure they are sufficiently supported and are sitting comfortably. Care workers should make sure they are sitting at arm's length from the service user and should ask them what they would like to eat first

- if they are not able to leave their room but can sit out at meal times, make sure that they are given plenty of time to move from the bed to the chair and that they are supported when sitting. This should be done before the meal is served, so that the food does not go cold while the moving is taking place.
- if they are able to eat with others but have a special need, for example, have to have their food cut up, this should be done before the food is brought to the table, so that they are not embarrassed.
- If they are able to sit at the table but need to be fed by a care worker, the care worker should sit down next to them to feed them, rather than towering over them. This is more encouraging for the service user and draws less attention to their special need. It also helps the service user to feel more relaxed and less hurried.

How should a main course be served to a service user?

When preparing and serving food and drink it should be remembered that 'we eat with our eyes'. Presentation is very important. If the food served looks attractive and appealing to service users, they are more likely to eat it. When serving a main course to service users, care workers need to think about:

- colour, e.g. including foods in a variety of colours that compliment one another
- appearance, e.g. serving food that is not overcooked
- texture, e.g. making sure there are a variety of textures
- flavour, e.g. making sure the food tastes good.

Care workers also need to consider the appearance and setting of the table where the meal is to be served.

Colour is important when serving a meal. If a plate of food looks attractive it is likely to **stimulate** the taste buds of service users and they will want to eat it. An attractive meal has different colours, as shown in the photo on page 135.

An attractive, colourful meal which has a variety of textures

In this menu the care worker has given thought to the colour. When served this looks attractive. A variety of **textures** have been included which will enhance appearance.

Care workers need to be sure that portion sizes are not too large as an overfull plate is likely to put service users off from eating. Serving large portions is not a good idea as service users who are not likely to do too much exercise could quickly become overweight and this could add to any health problems they may have. Food should be prepared hygienically and hot food should be served at 63°C. A meal that should be served hot and is cold when it arrives is less likely to be eaten.

When setting the table care workers should ensure that the place setting matches the requirements of the meal to be served. Solid, single coloured plates are less distracting than those with decoration. Any specialist aids, such as special cutlery should be included when laying the table. The table should be laid as follows:

- a placemat which is non-slip should be used, one for each service user
- the fork should be placed on the left of the placemat
- the knife should be placed on the right of the placemat
- the spoon and fork for the dessert should be placed above the placemat with the spoon on the outside of the fork. The handle of the spoon should be at right angles to the knife
- a glass for water should be placed above and a short distance from the knife
- a table napkin should be placed to the left of the fork
- **condiments** should be placed near the middle of the table
- A jug of water should also be placed near the condiments
- Flowers, real or artificial can be added to give an aesthetic finishing touch.

Figure 3.17 *A well-set table for two service users*

When serving a meal at a table to service users, the plated food should be put down for the service user from their left side and the empty plates should be taken from their right side.

If a care worker is actually feeding a service user they should sit next to the service user. The care worker should ask the service user which food they would like to eat first. They should then put small amounts of food on the fork and place it gently in the mouth. Time should be allowed for the service user to chew and to swallow the food before putting in the next mouthful.

What actions should be taken if feeding goes wrong?

Certain conditions can occur to cause service users serious difficulty when eating and drinking. These include those outlined in Figure 3.18.

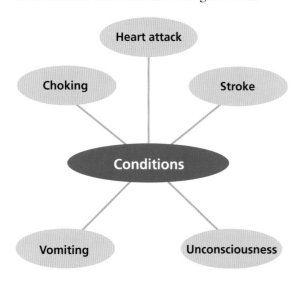

Figure 3.18 *Conditions that cause difficulties when eating and drinking*

Choking

If a service user is choking try to encourage them to cough up the lodged piece of food. If this is unsuccessful a care worker who is giving first aid should:

- bend the person forward
- give five sharp slaps between the shoulder blades

- check the mouth
- stand behind the service user and put one fist between the bottom of the navel and the bottom of the breastbone
- grasp their own fist with the other hand and pull sharply inward and upwards for up to five times
- check the mouth
- repeat the stages until the obstruction clears
- if it does not clear call an ambulance.

Heart attack or unconsciousness

For situations where service users may have had a heart attack or have become unconscious, a qualified first aider should be called to the scene immediately. In any emergency situation the first seven steps are:

- assess the situation, e.g. are there any risks to self or to the casualty?
- check the casualty, e.g. are they conscious or unconscious?
- check the casualty's response, e.g. do they respond to hearing a voice or to gentle stimulation?
- open the casualty's airway and check their breathing
- if the casualty is not breathing, breathe for them
- assess the casualty's circulation
- start **CPR**. Do not attempt this unless you are a qualified first aider.

Vomiting

If a service user starts to vomit, care workers should stop feeding them immediately and if possible turn them away from the table or food. Provide a receptacle for the person to be sick into, or if one is not immediately to hand, offer a paper napkin.

In all situations where service users experience difficulty with feeding, a qualified care worker should be asked to check them, however minor the incident.

Assessment activity 3.5

Assisting service users for meals

Ben is 77 and is living in a nursing home. He is unable to feed himself as he has had a stroke and has no movement in one arm and only restricted movement in the other. He stays in bed in the morning but likes to sit out to have his lunch in the afternoon. Ben can communicate with care workers and is a very cheerful person.

Margarite attends a daycare centre twice each week. One day while having her lunch Margarite starts to choke. A care worker rushes to help her.

1 Prepare information to explain to new care workers how to assist the service users above to choose meals. Make sure you include information about:
   - reading menus
   - advising service users
   - allowing choice
   - making notes.

2 Demonstrate how to help a service user choose a meal. (Remember to arrange for your tutor to assess you for this task.) The task can be simulated.

3 Prepare materials that could be used to train new care workers in how to prepare both service users in the examples above for eating and drinking. Give as much detail as possible, giving reasons for the actions taken.

4 Prepare information for the new care workers to explain what actions should be taken in the case of Margarite.

   The information for Questions 1 to 3 could be presented in the form of a display, written report, presentation or materials for inclusion in a resource pack.

How should care workers evaluate their own performance?

Care workers need to evaluate the practical care they undertake. In this unit, the practical skills to be evaluated are:

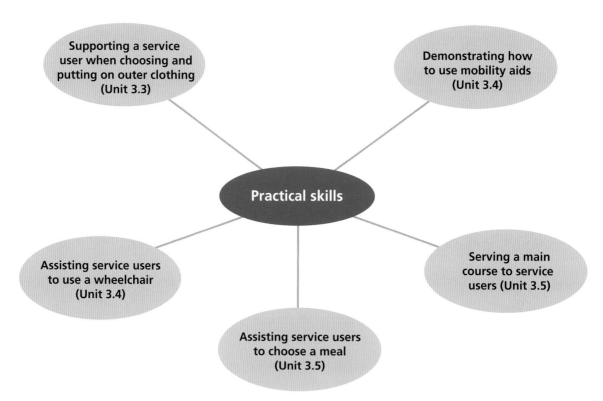

Supporting a service user when choosing and putting on outer clothing (Unit 3.3)

Demonstrating how to use mobility aids (Unit 3.4)

Practical skills

Assisting service users to use a wheelchair (Unit 3.4)

Serving a main course to service users (Unit 3.5)

Assisting service users to choose a meal (Unit 3.5)

Figure 3.19 *Practical skills to be evaluated*

Practical skills

When evaluating care workers need to:

- *reflect*, e.g. think about what they have done and how well they did it
- *analyse*, e.g. consider what they did against the 'theory' (the correct way of carrying out the task)
- *draw conclusions*, e.g. how well they completed

the task when judging it against theory or the opinions of others such as a tutor, or the service user or peers
- *think about improvements*, e.g. could they have done anything better or to a higher standard?

At each of these stages specific facts need to be included and judgements made about them. An example of how this could be done is given in the table on page 139.

Facts to be considered	Judgements
Aims	What was the aim? How was it met or why was it not met? Was the aim appropriate?
Objectives	What were the objectives? Were they achieved? Were the objectives appropriate?
Skills used	What skills were used? (e.g. practical, communication, scientific, interpersonal?) How well were they used? Should other skills have been used? Were they effective? Were they used in the same way as suggested by theory?
Qualities shown	Which qualities were used? How did they enhance the skills used? Were there other qualities that would have been helpful?
Time	How much time was allowed for each task? How long did each task take? Are there any recommended timings that judgements can be made against?
Achieving outcomes	What outcomes were intended? Were these outcomes achieved? What were the benefits to the service user?
Improvements	Where could improvements have been made? Why? What could have been done differently? What do others suggest about improvements that could have been made?

An example of an evaluation

Joanne, a care worker, is evaluating the skills she used when demonstrating the use of walking sticks. She writes:

Joanne has reflected on what she has done, analysed by making judgements and drawn conclusions. She has also thought about improvements that could be made.

My aim was to make sure that the service user knew exactly how to use the walking stick, so that they would not lose their balance when walking and had confidence when using the stick. To achieve this aim my objectives were: to make sure the service user knew the different parts of the walking stick and their use; to make sure the service user knew the correct position for their hand when using the walking stick; and to show the service user the correct movement when using the walking stick.

I achieved my aim, as the service user could use the stick at the end of the demonstration, but stated that they were not confident about the correct movement. As this was one of my objectives, I think I could have been clearer on how to use the stick during movement. I think I was not clear in the vocabulary used when explaining this part. I could improve this by working out the instructions more clearly and using words that would help the service user to understand. My communication skills for this could have been improved so that all the objectives were met.

I thought this whole process would take ten minutes as I had watched a care worker at the day care centre do this and she took six minutes. I concluded I would be slightly slower as I was not so experienced. I took nine minutes, so I was very near the estimated time.

The skills I used were...

Assessment activity 3.6

Evaluate all the practical tasks so far
In this unit, you have been asked to:

- support a service user to put on outer clothing
- demonstrate the use of three mobility aids
- support a service user in using a wheelchair
- assist a service user to choose a meal from a menu
- serve a simple meal.

Evaluate all the practical tasks you have demonstrated, making sure for each you include in the evaluation:

- aims
- objectives
- time
- skills
- qualities
- achieving outcomes
- improvements.

Glossary

Arthritis: condition of swelling up of joints

Assessed: to find out about needs; to establish what can or cannot be achieved

Aptitude: having an ability for

Automatically: without thinking or reference to another

Burden: a weight, a nuisance

Characters/characteristics: people's natures/the trait or quality that makes something the way it is

Clinical histories: what has happened medically in the past

Condiments: seasonings for food, e.g. salt, pepper, ketchup etc.

Cultivate: to encourage to grow; to foster

CPR: Cardio-Pulmonary Resuscitation

Enhance: to improve; to make better

Deformities: an abnormality; not as normal

Defuse: to calm down, to remove tension or anger

Demeaning: making to look small, silly; not giving value to

Dependent: to rely on; not to be able to do things for oneself

Ferrules: rubber tips placed at the end of walking sticks, Zimmer frames etc. to prevent slipping

Genetic: inherited from the genes, which we are born with and which determine certain things about how we develop

Influence: to effect others, to have some control over

Liaising: working in partnership with

Literacy: ability to read, write and orally communicate

Memory jogger: something that acts as a reminder; to help a person remember

Minimise: to make something as small/unimportant as possible

MRSA bug: Methycillium Resistant Staphylococcus Aureous – so-called 'super-bug', this is resistant to all known antibiotics and is caught in care settings

Non-judgemental: not to make a judgement on; not to condemn

Non-self-propelling: unable to move without help; needing another to operate

Paralysis: unable to move

Permanent: to last forever

Perspective: a mental view or way of looking at something

Philosophy: way of thinking; principles or values

Reframes: puts something another way

Restrictions: limits

Rheumatism: a disease causing swollen and painful joints and muscles

Routines: procedures or acts that are carried out regularly and always the same

Self propelling: can be moved by the person without help or assistance; no one else needed to operate

Sensitive: careful; not to offend a person

Sensory impairment: a disability affecting the eyes, hearing, smell, taste or touch, or more than one of these

Skill: something learnt and practised until done well

Socially integrated: to be able to mix and get on with other people

Special needs: having additional needs to the norm

Simulate: to pretend or act

Stimulate: to make of interest

Textures: different materials, structures, different composition

Tilting: to lift at an angle e.g. to lift up or down

Trait: feature, quality, attribute

Transferable skills: skills that can be used in more than one job e.g. ICT, Communication

Transferring: moving from one place to another or one position to another

Uniqueness: different from anyone or anything else

Unsteady: not firm; likely to loose balance

Washing hands regularly helps to stop the spread of infection

Hygiene and safety are probably two of the most important aspects of a successful care setting. They affect every person in the care setting and if they are not followed they can cause ill-health and a great deal of pain and suffering. Knowing what causes infection and how infection is spread helps care workers to reduce the risks to themselves and to others. When caring for another person it is very important that care workers do not act in a manner that is harmful to their health by spreading infection. Being aware of safe practices relating to hygiene routines and the preparation of food helps to reduce the risks.

The importance of health and safety has been highlighted in the media by the stories about the MRSA bug in care settings, particularly hospitals.

It seems that the only way to reduce the deaths and illness from this virus is for care workers to apply good hygiene practices in their day-to-day tasks.

It is important that all care workers are aware of the risks` and hazards that can exist in care settings. Risks can arise, for example, from the use of unsafe equipment, hazardous substances, ignoring correct procedures and environmental hazards. Such risks can be reduced through carrying out safety surveys, staff training and the implementation of safety features, all of which can contribute to a sense of health and well-being in service users. Making sure that service users are safe and feel secure is a priority for care workers.

What will we learn in this unit?

Learning outcomes

You will learn to:

- Describe the risk of the spread of infection in a care setting
- Describe the measures needed to prevent the spread of infection
- Recognise basic food hygiene practices required in a care setting
- Identify basic hazards and describe ways of reducing risks in care settings
- Investigate safety and security measures required in care settings

What are the risks of a spread of infection?

All human beings are at risk in the course of daily life because they are in contact with many different forms of living **organisms**, which can create hazards. Most of the time they cause us little or no risk, especially when the correct hygiene and safety procedures are followed, for example, hand washing after visiting the toilet. There are, however, risks to ourselves and others when care is not taken. A large number of diseases are easily spread to others by poor hygiene in care settings. Accidents often happen both at work and in the home from failure to act in a sensible manner. This can cause major problems for older, very young, pregnant or ill service users. People who fit into one of these groups are known as '**vulnerable**'.

Care workers have a duty to those in their care to help them remain healthy, recover if they have had a medical condition, and to remain safe. Understanding the types of infections that might occur in care settings and how their spread can be prevented, is an important part of care workers' responsibility. This allows the promotion of safety in care services and the people that use them.

What are the major disease-causing agents?

Infection can be spread in many ways. The most common disease-causing agents are:

- bacteria
- viruses
- fungi.

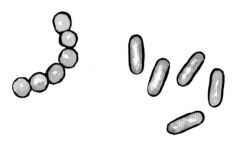
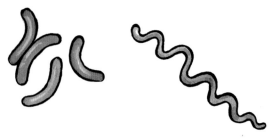

Cocci
(e.g. sore throats)

Bacilli
(e.g. tetanus)

Vibrios
(e.g. cholera)

Spirochaetes
(e.g. syphilis)

Figure 4.1 *The four basic bacterial shapes*

The **micro-organisms** shown in Figure 4.1 cannot be seen by the human eye, they can only be seen by viewing them under a microscope. In the environment around us there are billions of micro-organisms, many of which are harmless. Those that are harmless are called **non-pathogenic**, but others that are harmful are called **pathogenic**. Pathogenic micro-organisms can cause problems like the common cold or can give people life threatening diseases such as hepatitis or tuberculosis.

Bacteria

Bacteria are tiny living creatures that are sometimes referred to as germs. They are about one-thousandth of a millimetre long and are so small that it is not possible to see them with the naked eye. Through the microscope bacteria are usually seen as being small and round, rod or comma shaped.

Most bacteria are harmless; in fact some bacteria are even beneficial to humans, for example, large numbers of bacteria in the gut assist with the digestion of food. There are other families of bacteria that can cause a variety of effects. They are known as **putrefying** bacteria and affect food that may be eaten. They do this by slowly **decomposing** the food making it unpleasant, inedible and sometimes **toxic**.

Bacteria have an important role to play in nature by decomposing dead animal and vegetable matter, helping the recycling process. They multiply best between 5 and 63°C but are killed at temperatures above 70°C. At temperatures below 5°C, most bacteria multiply very slowly or remain **dormant,** that is they are not active, as if 'sleeping'. With the right conditions however, they can become active again. At very low temperatures some bacteria die, but many survive and multiply again if the conditions and food are right.

To multiply, bacteria need:

* *time* – bacteria can multiply rapidly in small amounts of time
* *temperature* – bacteria grow best in a temperature range of 5 °C to 60°C
* *food* – bacteria prefer dairy products, eggs, fish products, meat and poultry as nutrients on which to grow
* *water* – with no water, growth slows down. Drying, therefore, is a good way of preserving food.

Some harmful bacteria can be found in food and water and can cause serious diseases, even in very small numbers. Typhoid fever can be spread in this way, but is fortunately a rare occurrence in the United Kingdom today. Other diseases caused by bacteria are boils, food poisoning, whooping cough and diphtheria.

> ### Discussion point
> *Why are dormant bacteria a threat to human beings?*

Viruses

Viruses are very small particles which infect humans, animals and plants. A virus particle can make copies of itself. Viruses must infect a living **host** in order to make more copies of themselves. A virus is the smallest living organism.

As viruses are small and very **variable** it often makes them difficult to treat. Many of them are best dealt with by the body's immune system, but others have to be treated chemically.

Viruses can invade all types of body tissue, but certain viruses prefer certain types of tissue. A good example of this is the herpes virus which infects the skin.

In nurseries, some viruses cause problems that last only a short time. The common cold is one of these and for most of us the effects only last for about one week. Other viruses have a much longer-lasting effect and can last from a week to a lifetime.

Viral infections can be divided into two types:

* **local** – occurring at the site of infection, e.g. the common cold which affects the nose area, and gastro enteritis which is often found in

care settings, affecting the intestine to cause pain and diarrhoea

- **systemic** – viruses that have the ability to affect the whole of the body and not just one area, e.g. HIV which causes many problems with the immune system in its later stages. Some viruses (e.g. HIV) also have the ability to remain in the system for years without causing any problems.

Many common and childhood diseases are caused by viruses, for example, mumps, measles, chickenpox (vaicella), hepatitis, herpes and influenza. All of these diseases are now controllable and can be successfully **vaccinated** against.

> ### Discussion point
> *How are viruses different to bacteria?*

Fungi

Fungi are small organisms that feed on both living and dead organic matter. Although they are very small they are not microscopic and can often be seen with only a magnifying glass. They usually reproduce by budding or spore production which allows the fungus to spread from place to place. Included in this family of organisms are also molds and yeasts. Not all of these organisms are dangerous; some are very beneficial to us. Yeast is a very useful fungus, as it allows us to make bread and beer. Another very useful fungus is penicillin. This can be used to combat different types of infection. As this fungus grows, the chemicals that it produces can kill off dangerous bacteria and stop further infections.

Fungi can cause diseases such as ringworm, athletes' foot and candida. All of these infections tend to be superficial skin surface infections. In severe cases they can get into the body system and become a systemic infection.

What diseases can be spread in a care setting?

Diseases are caused by:

- food poisoning (bacteria-spread)
- infection (virus-spread).

Bacterial diseases

Bacteria are the main contributors to different types of food poisoning. The most common disease-causing bacteria are shown in Figure 4.3.

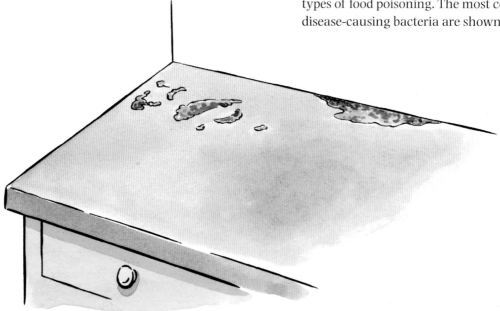

Figure 4.2 *Fungi can grow almost anywhere*

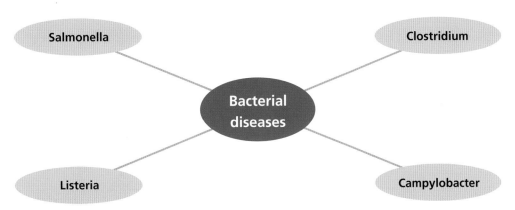

Figure 4.3 *Disease-causing bacteria which result in food poisoning*

The characteristics of these bacteria are shown in the table below.

Type of bacteria	How they affect human beings
Salmonella	• This family of bacteria was discovered by an American vet in 1885. It is responsible for a large proportion of the food poisoning outbreaks in Britain • These bacteria live in the intestines of animals. The animals are not affected by the bacteria but are just carriers
Clostridium	• Bacteria that live in the intestines of animals • Clostridium can cause service users problems especially if they have a deep wound, for example after a surgical operation • Clostridium welchii bacteria can infect a wound and start to produce gas that is foul smelling. They also produce a toxin that destroys muscle. If left unchecked this could cause a patient with an infected limb to have it amputated to stop further spread. With modern medicines and antibiotics this problem is often reduced
Listeria	• Symptoms include fever, muscle aches, and sometimes nausea or diarrhoea.
Campylobacter	• Causes gastroenteritis. This means that the small intestine gets infected by the bacteria

Did you know?

Each year it is estimated that as many as 5.5 million people in the UK may suffer from food borne illnesses – that's 1 in 10 people.

Sometimes groups of people can be infected at the same time with food poisoning, particularly if they have eaten contaminated food at a residential home or nursery school, or if they have eaten from a batch of contaminated food being sold in different places. The worst cases of food poisoning can kill but fortunately such occurrences are rare.

Food poisoning is more likely to affect service users with lowered resistance to disease, whereas healthy service users may show mild symptoms or none at all. Older service users who are sick, babies, young children and pregnant women are particularly vulnerable to food poisoning. Extra care should also be taken in care settings when preparing food for these vulnerable groups. Following good food hygiene procedures helps to reduce the risk of their coming into contact with food poisoning bacteria, especially in nurseries.

Infectious diseases

Influenza

We all know influenza as 'flu' and the symptoms can be the same as the common cold. This is why people often misdiagnose themselves as having flu (influenza) when they merely have a bad cold. Influenza is usually transmitted by airborne droplet infection and is more common in winter when people's resistance is lower.

The virus is very difficult for the body to control because it has the ability to change its appearance (**mutate**). This prevents the immune system recognizing it as something it may have dealt with before. Influenza is so infectious (**contagious**) that it can cause epidemics where thousands of people can be infected.

> ### Did you know?
> In the 1920s an influenza epidemic killed more people in Britain than the First World War did.

Measles

This is a very infectious viral disease and is spread by droplet infection. It is normally a childhood disease but can be caught by adults. The **incubation** period (the time it takes to develop in a person's system) is 10–14 days. It begins with flu-like symptoms such as a headache, fever, runny nose and a cough. A rash then appears on the face and spreads to the rest of the body. The rash tends to be patchy and even appears on the palms and the soles of the feet. The lymph glands enlarge and the eyes become inflamed and sensitive to light. Within a week the symptoms subside and the rash fades. Sometimes complications set in and bronchitis can develop. More seriously pneumonia or meningitis can also develop. In the western world measles kills approximately 1 in 1000 infants. Children are usually vaccinated with a triple vaccine known as the MMR vaccine (Mumps, Measles and Rubella).

Chickenpox

This is a highly contagious airborn viral disease. It is most common among school-age children but can also be caught by adults. Once a person has chickenpox the body usually develops enough immunity to stop them getting it again. The main symptoms usually appear after 13–17 days. A rash starts on the body and then spreads to the arms and the face. The rash takes the form of little red bumps that turn into clear blisters on the bumps. Scratching and breaking these can lead to lifelong scarring.

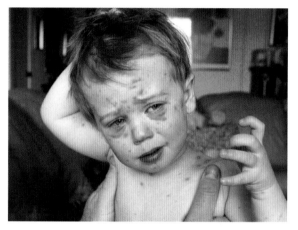

Chickenpox can be painful

Hepatitis

Hepatitis is an inflammation of the liver which reduces its ability to function. When caused by viruses it can be infectious and there are seven different hepatitis viruses which are labeled A through to G.

Hepatitis A is the most common form and is spread orally and through faecal contact. This means that a person who has come into contact with contaminated **faeces** may be handling food to be fed to others. People can also be infected by drinking water that has been contaminated with sewage. The time between exposure and symptoms developing is 28 days. A vaccine is available to those who are considered at risk, and provides ten years of protection.

Hepatitis B is more serious as the virus can remain in the body for many years. It is spread through unprotected sex, sharing needles during drug use and on rare occasions through blood transfusions. If left untreated it can become chronic and lead to permanent liver damage such as **cirrhosis** or liver cancer. Symptoms take between 40 days and six months to appear after exposure. A vaccine is available that provides protection for up to five years. Hepatitis A and B are currently the most common forms. Hepatitis C was only discovered in the 1980s and is spread most commonly by those sharing needles. Hepatitis D is very different as it is spread by being carried by the Hepatitis B virus and can only occur at the same time.

Hepatitis E and F are spread in a similar way to hepatitis A and have a similar effect. There are few chronic cases and treatment is usually rest for two weeks. Hepatitis G was first reported in 1994 and is spread in the same way as B and C. People who work in high risk professions especially health care should consider being vaccinated against hepatitis.

Herpes

The herpes family of viruses includes the viruses responsible for cold sores, genital herpes, chickenpox and glandular fever. The herpes simplex virus has two types. The first (HSV-1) causes cold sores and is spread by close personal contact. It can hide in sensory nerve cells, resurfacing when we are run down or exposed to sunlight.

The second (HSV-2) is mainly spread by sexual transmission and therefore produces genital herpes. This usually takes the form of small itchy blisters which burst and turn into sores. These infections cannot be totally cured but there are many remedies that can be used to control the condition.

Ringworm (Tinea)

Ringworm is a skin infection caused by various fungi and develops into a red ring-shaped rash. In fact it is not caused by a worm but by fungi called dermatophytes.

The fungi invade the top layer of skin and affect the tissue underneath. Ringworm is particularly common among children and is usually treated with non-prescription anti-fungal creams and powders. Stronger prescription medicines can be used in more severe cases.

Attention to personal hygiene and keeping skin clean and dry can help prevent this infection. Because ringworm is highly contagious, clothing, hairbrushes and other personal items should be cleaned and dried after use.

Ringworm can cause complications by producing secondary infections that can spread to other parts of the body. These can occur in the scalp, groin and nails. Another common and well-known form of tinea is athlete's foot.

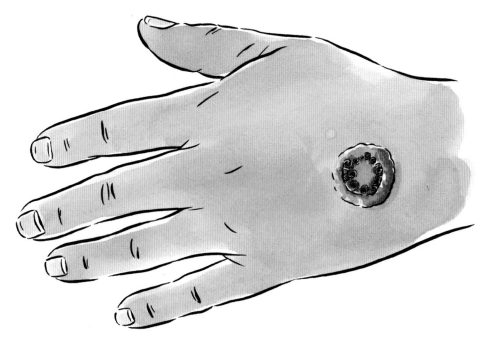

Figure 4.4 *Ringworm can be embarrassing for service users who contract it*

What are the main routes of infection?

There are three main routes of infection:

- respiratory route, i.e. inhaled through our lungs
- digestive route, i.e. taken into the body when food is eaten or drunk
- blood, i.e. contact with blood and infected body fluids.

Respiratory route

The respiratory route means that bacteria is breathed in through the nose and mouth. Bacteria can live in a variety of places but especially in dust and in liquids. This means that they can become airborne and there is the chance that they can be breathed in without the person knowing. This is normally not a problem as the body's **defence mechanisms** will deal with them fairly quickly, but bacteria can move about even faster. Occasionally an infection can be caused from very active bacteria. **Tuberculosis** is a very contagious and damaging disease and is spread by the respiratory route.

When they have favourable conditions, for example, food, warmth and liquid (e.g. water),

bacteria **reproduce** themselves by dividing into two. This process is called **fission**. The bacteria keep dividing into two and so millions of bacteria are produced. One germ can multiply to more than four million in just eight hours.

Digestive route

It is probably safe to say that there are bacteria on everything that is eaten and drunk. Not all bacteria are bad and some actually help with the digestion of our food. For the ones that are a possible danger the digestive system has developed methods of dealing with them.

The digestive process uses very strong acid in the stomach and an alkali in the small intestine. The production of acids and alkali is one mechanism that helps to destroy certain bacteria. For the bacteria that the body cannot cope with there are a number of ways to make food and drink safe to consume.

Examples of these are:

- *cooking* – thorough cooking is important to destroy harmful bacteria, although some bacteria can withstand boiling for at least 30 minutes
- *sterilising* – where liquids are subjected to very high temperatures which kills any bacteria
- *pasteurising* – a process that kills bacteria, by one of two main methods: high temperature for a short time, where milk is heated to 72°C for 15 seconds and cooled to 10°C, or it is heated to between 63 and 66°C for 30 minutes and then cooled rapidly to 10°C
- *dehydrating* – a process of removing water from foods which prevents moulds, yeasts and bacteria from growing
- *irradiating* – a method of killing pathogenic bacteria by using X or gamma-rays, which is infra-red light or ultra-violet light that is passed through food.
- *pickling* – a method of preserving foods in vinegar, which is acetic acid that destroys the bacteria.
- *freezing/chilling* – a method not of killing the micro-organisms in food but of preventing them from multiplying, by keeping the temperature of the food low. For freezing, the temperature is

17°C. For chilling it is just above freezing point. Frozen food can be kept for up to one month.

Preserving food by these methods helps to prevent the spread of dangerous bacteria and disease-causing agents.

Blood

Blood and body fluids are a route of infection. Coming into contact with other people's blood and body fluids puts a care worker at risk of becoming infected. Body fluids such as blood, saliva and droplets from sneezing provide a warm, moist environment for bacteria to develop in. This means that humans are all effectively carriers of many different sources of infection.

The following are potentially dangerous body fluids:

- diarrhoea and faeces
- saliva
- droplets from sneezing
- vaginal discharges
- seminal fluid.

All body fluids and waste such as urine, vomit, blood and saliva must be cleared and flushed down a **sluice drain.** The area must be cleaned with **disinfectant** immediately to prevent the spread of bacteria. When carrying out such tasks care workers must wear protective clothing such as a disposable apron, gloves, overshoes and in some circumstances, a mask.

It is essential to remember to wash your hands between dealing with different service users and different incidents.

Discussion point

Why do care workers need to wash their hands when working in a care setting?

What are the symptoms of infection?

When suffering from infections, food poisoning and other diseases caused by bacteria, viruses or fungi, the general symptoms experienced by service users are:

- sickness and vomiting
- diarrhoea
- high temperature
- stomach cramps and abdominal pain.

The specific symptoms for different diseases and conditions have been covered in the 'Infectious diseases' part of this unit (see pages 146–147).

What are the basic procedures to prevent spread of infection?

According to the British Medical Journal 'Nursing homes are responsible for 78 per cent of outbreaks of infective diarrhoea in the UK and may be 'reservoirs of MRSA', with up to 27 per cent of residents being affected by the infection'.

Infections are a major cause of human suffering and premature death. The costs to the health care system of providing care for those with infection are enormous. For these reasons prevention and control of infection are issues of very great practical importance for every health care professional.

To prevent and to help reduce the risks of infection, it is important to follow certain basic procedures of cleanliness.

Disease-causing organisms live in and on the body and can affect others if high standards of personal hygiene are not maintained. Attention to personal hygiene is therefore important. Regular washing and wearing clean clothes helps to protect people against infection. Looking after self is a priority when caring for others. Wounds such as cuts, grazes scratches and boils can easily become infected. The best way to stop this

happening is to keep wounds properly covered with a suitable waterproof dressing. In this way both carer workers and service users are protected from infection.

Cleanliness for care workers must be applied to:

- self, e.g. personal hygiene
- equipment, e.g. the items used to provide care and to treat service users
- the environment, e.g. floors, furniture
- food preparation,e.g. preparing, cooking and serving meals.

When considering personal cleanliness care workers should pay attention to all parts of their body. This includes the factors listed in Figure 4.5 below.

Dress

When working with service users it is appropriate to wear clothing that has been provided by the care setting or approved by them. Clothing provided often takes the form of a uniform. Besides providing protection from the spread of infection, a uniform makes care workers easily recognised. In the ideal situation, work clothing should not be worn outside of the work environment as this helps stop the spread of any infection from one environment to another.

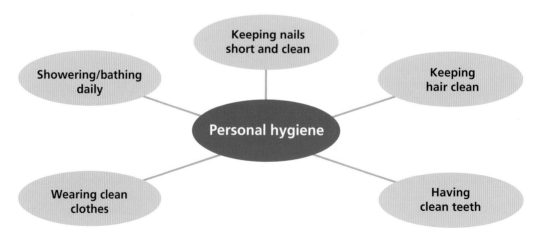

Figure 4.5 *Personal hygiene*

> **Discussion point**
>
> *Why is it important to have different clothes to work in than those worn for leisure?*

It is not a good idea to wear rings, bracelets or watches while working in care environments. The skin area under the watch or jewellery can warm up and encourage the growth of infectious organisms, increasing the risk of infections that can be passed on.

It is important that a care worker wears clothing that is suitable for the tasks that they have to carry out. For example:

- trousers may be more suitable than a short skirt for a female care worker if working in a nursery school where equipment has to be put out and put away and where there is a likely to be a lot of bending
- a loose-fitting skirt for a female care worker may be more appropriate in a day care centre

or hospital as free and unrestricted movement will be necessary.

Whatever clothing is worn, it must be clean.

Protective clothing

In addition to wearing a uniform, care workers may also be supplied with other forms of protective clothing. These are there to help protect care workers as well as service users. Protective clothing can include:

- masks – paper masks help to prevent the spread of infection through the respiratory route
- aprons – barriers to infection made of latex so they can be disposed of after each use
- gloves – excellent barriers to infection made of latex, so they can be disposed of after each use
- overshoes – used for one area only, in order to prevent the spread of infection from one room or one area to another
- theatre hoods or caps – to contain hair when in the operating theatre
- theatre greens – these are now not always green and are used to perform or assist surgical procedures.

Figure 4.6 *Protective clothing helps to prevent the spread of infection*

It should be remembered that all protective clothing should be changed when moving from one service user to another. This greatly reduces the risk of **cross-infection**. Care workers may often find that they have to change their apron or gloves part way through a task. It is important that they do this especially if that garment has become heavily soiled. It should be done as a matter of safety and good practice.

Hand washing

Did you know?

Germs can stay alive on hands for up to three hours. Damp hands spread more germs than dry ones.

A very large quantity and variety of germs are carried on people's hands everyday. Unfortunately, a few of these can cause illnesses like diarrhoea, colds and other, more serious, sometimes even life-threatening, diseases. When people forget to wash their hands, or don't wash their hands correctly, they can spread these germs to others.

Hand washing, when done correctly, can help everyone stay healthy and avoid spreading and receiving germs. Hands should be washed when:

- preparing or eating food
- treating a cut or wound or tending to someone who is sick
- inserting or removing contact lenses
- cleaning after using the toilet
- handling uncooked foods, particularly raw meat, poultry or fish
- changing a nappy
- blowing the nose or coughing or sneezing
- playing with or touching a pet
- handling rubbish.

How hands are washed is just as important as when they are washed, especially when it comes to getting rid of germs. Just rinsing them quickly is not enough. When care workers wash their hands, they should:

- massage palm to palm
- rub right palm over back of left hand and vice versa
- rub palm to palm
- massage backs of fingers in opposing palm
- rotate right thumb clasped in left palm and vice versa
- rotate fingers of left hand in right palm and vice versa
- rinse hands with water.

The hand washing process should take no longer than 30 seconds.

Figure 4.7 *Step-by-step hand washing*

Hair care

Disease-causing organisms can live in hair and on the scalp. Unwashed hair can carry many bacteria that can easily fall onto service users or their food or into a wound if hair is not correctly managed.

Long hair should always be kept under control and not left loose. If care workers keep touching their hair then there is a risk of transferring bacteria to service users.

To practise correct hair care:

- shampoo hair frequently
- keep hair tied back or covered if necessary
- avoid touching hair
- never comb hair in the presence of others especially service users
- do not comb hair in food preparation and cooking areas.

Hair that is left hanging and not tied back could become caught up in equipment and cause injury.

Footwear

Care workers should aim to have footwear that is only used for work. This is for the same reasons that care workers have specific clothing for work as it decreases the risk of the spread of infection. Shoes that provide support are probably safer to wear when in care settings. Also if care workers are on their feet for long periods of time, flat shoes are usually more comfortable. Footwear should be kept as clean as possible.

Oral and facial hygiene

Bacteria live in the nose, mouth, throat and ears. By repeatedly touching these areas bacteria can be transferred to work surfaces, equipment and service users. It should be remembered that if a person sneezes or coughs they should always cover their nose and mouth, preferably with a tissue. Droplet infection from a sneeze can travel up to four metres in certain environments.

Always:

- avoid coughing and sneezing directly onto people and equipment
- avoid touching your face and head – particularly the mouth, nose and ears.

Figure 4.8 *What you wear on your feet is important*

Sneezing and coughing without covering the mouth is a way of spreading infection

What conditions require reporting when working in care settings?

Disease

Hospitals and other residential health care settings have specific problems relating to infection control for a number of reasons:

- they have a high density of people who are susceptible to infection because of illness or **debilitation**
- they have many sources of infection because people with severe infection are often hospitalized
- there is a high level of close interpersonal contact between care professionals and service users.

For these reasons most care providers now pay particular attention to control of infection.

In care environments there is always a need to be constantly aware of the effects of disease. A number of diseases are what is known as 'currently notifiable' under the Public Health (Infectious Diseases) Regulations 1988. These diseases include:

- malaria
- measles
- plague
- rabies
- rubella
- salmonellosis (other than typhoid or paratyphoid)
- smallpox
- sexually transmitted diseases
- tetanus
- tuberculosis
- typhoid and paratyphoid
- typhus.

These are just some examples of the many notifiable diseases that are considered to place the public at risk.

Under the regulations, medical practitioners are **obliged**, as soon as they become aware or suspect that a patient is suffering from, or is a carrier of an infectious disease, to notify in writing the local medical officer as soon as possible. However, *immediate* notification is obligatory in the case of certain infectious diseases such as cholera or where a serious outbreak of infectious disease is suspected. At the end of each week, returns of all diseases notified are sent to the Department of Health and Children.

It is therefore important that care workers play their part in making sure that their managers and appropriate **clinicians** are made aware of any new disease outbreaks.

Illness

Whether the illness is that of a service user or a care worker the correct people need to know. If the service user develops a new illness then their medical practitioner needs to know. This is always done in the best interests of the service user and in confidence. If a care worker develops an illness then it is their personal responsibility to notify the appropriate people. This may be their GP and their manager. This is because they have a duty to their service users and others.

Conditions

Various environmental conditions need to be reported in the interest of public safety. Overflowing drains and sewers should always be reported as soon as possible in order to limit the spread of infection. Unsanitary conditions in general should always be reported, if necessary to the Environmental Health Department of the local council. Environmental health officers have far-reaching powers that allow them to shut down offending environments, especially where they think there is a serious danger to public health. Airborne pollutants can also be a problem, and include escaping chemicals and gases. These chemicals and gases can be toxic and can cause diseases such as asthma and bronchitis. They may also carry disease-causing agents such as bacteria or viruses.

> **Discussion point**
>
> *What is a notifiable disease?*

What universal precautions are needed to prevent the spread of infection?

Universal precautions are those taken by **clinical** staff to limit the risk of the spread of infectious diseases. Such precautions mainly apply to blood and other bodily fluids. In the UK, the Department of Health regularly sets guidelines for health authorities to follow. Precautions have long been established for limiting the risks associated with Hepatitis B and more recently Hepatitis C, and similar precautions are now taken for the control of human immunodeficiency virus (HIV).

The guidelines are safeguards aimed at reducing the risk of transferring infections from patient to practitioner, patient to patient, or practitioner to patient. Universal precautions for care workers are:

- Wash hands before and after contact with each service user and before putting on and after removing gloves.
- Change gloves between dealing with different service users.
- Cover any wounds or breaks in skin with waterproof dressings. If you have extensive broken skin then wear gloves all the time.
- Wear gloves when coming in contact with blood or other bodily fluids.
- Exercise care in handling disposable sharp instruments, including scalpels, needles, scissors etc.
- Do not wear open footwear in situations where blood or other bodily fluids may be spilt or where sharp instruments or needles may be dropped. Wear footwear which encloses the feet.
- Clear up any spills of blood or bodily fluids promptly and disinfect the area.
- Wear gloves when cleaning equipment, before sterilization or disinfection and when clearing up spillages.
- Follow any safety procedures for the disposal of contaminated waste.
- Where there is potential for blood to splatter, wear protective eyewear. Eye wash should be available and should be used immediately if there are any accidents.

(Adapted from: Care: S/NVQ by Yvonne Nolan Level 3)

> **Discussion point**
>
> *Why do you think these measures are called universal precautions?*

How can an environment be cleaned and sterilised?

Cleaning

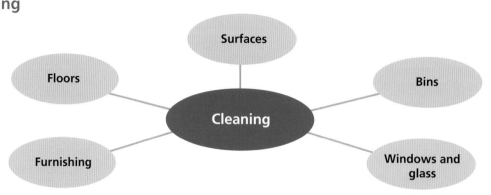

Figure 4.9 *Cleaning a care environment*

The purpose of cleaning is to remove micro-organisms and dirt or other objects from surfaces or equipment. Cleaning is usually carried out by using water, with or without **detergents**. Cleaning is the first stage of making sure that the environment or surroundings are free from dirt and micro-organisms.

Areas used by service users and for the treatment of service users should be cleaned daily or more frequently if there are spillages. Sometimes different equipment is used for different areas in a care setting. For example:

- red buckets are used for cleaning away blood or bodily fluids
- yellow buckets are used to mop corridors and floors
- blue buckets are used in operating theatres.

For most cleaning, a detergent solution is adequate for surfaces and furniture.

Basins and taps should be cleaned after use with a detergent solution. Bins should not be allowed to become overfull and should be cleaned daily with a detergent solution. Carpets should be vacuumed daily. There should be a schedule for cleaning carpets at least every six months. Cloths and dusters should be disposable and thrown away at the end of each day. A colour-coding system makes this process easier to operate. By using a different colour for each day of the week it is possible to make sure that cloths and dusters are changed regularly.

Furniture and other hard surfaces should be damp dusted daily with colour-coded disposable cloths.

Mops should have detachable heads. They should be washed after use in hot, soapy water, then wrung out and stored, mop upside down.

Figure 4.10 *Cleaning is the first stage of any process to help reduce the risk of infection*

Table tops and feeding trays must be cleaned immediately prior to serving food.

The air filters of vacuum cleaners should be changed regularly according to the manufacturer's instructions. Detachable tools should be wiped with a detergent solution.

Disinfecting

A disinfectant is a chemical used on objects and surfaces to reduce the number of pathogenic micro-organisms. It was thought that liberal splashing of disinfectant around hospital wards and clinics would kill 'germs'. However, it is now known that overuse of antibacterial agents is an important cause of some kinds of hospital-acquired infection. This is because the causes of some infections slowly become more resistant to its effects. Disinfection does not mean that all micro-organisms are killed and in particular, bacterial spores are frequently not killed.

It is now generally accepted that good maintenance and thorough cleaning of floors, walls and ceilings is sufficient except in specific instances. The approach now should be to only apply disinfectant where it is specifically indicated by the policy of the setting to do so. Disinfection is never an alternative to cleaning.

Chemicals used to 'disinfect' are available under a variety of commercial names, but floors and surfaces are normally cleaned with sodium hydrochloride (bleach) or sodium dichlorisocyanurate. The latter comes in granules.

In some care settings alcohol wipes are used to disinfect equipment that comes into contact with service users.

An example of where disinfection would be important, is the disinfection of toilet seats and handles when there is an outbreak of diarrhoea. Care workers must make sure, however, that disinfection solutions are rinsed and dried off the seats and handles of toilets, in case service users rub the excess fluid into their eyes or in case the disinfectant irritates their skin.

Sterilizing

Sterilization means making an object free from all micro-organisms including spores. There are many methods available for sterilization. Sterilization may use exposure to:

- heat
- radiation
- chemicals.

The most common form of heat sterilization is 'autoclaving' or moist heat. Autoclaving involves exposure of objects to superheated steam. Water boils at 100°C when at atmospheric pressure. At higher pressure the boiling point is higher. Most modern autoclaves use pressure at more than three times **atmospheric pressure** giving steam at 134°C, which achieves sterilization in about three minutes. Items for autoclaving are cleaned and wrapped in porous paper. The paper is sealed with a sticky tape called 'Bowie Dick' tape. The tape has pale white diagonal stripes. The stripes change to a dark brown colour at high temperature. This allows the operator to see easily that the wrapped instrument has been in the autoclave. Only materials which can withstand exposure to steam at high temperatures are suitable for autoclaving.

High temperatures without steam can achieve sterilization, but much higher temperatures and longer periods of exposure are required.

Equipment that is used to penetrate the skin or to enter the body must be sterilized. Such instruments can be reused many times as long as they have been through the sterilization process each time.

Plastic pieces of equipment cannot be sterilized because the temperature would cause them to melt. Such items can be sterilized by the use of gas or chemicals. The chemicals may be used in combination with temperatures of 50 to 70°C.

Dealing with spillages

All spillages of bodily fluids (blood, urine, vomit or faeces) should be dealt with immediately. Gloves (disposable) should be worn and as much of the spillage as possible should be mopped up with absorbent toilet tissues or paper towels.

These can be disposed of into a plastic waste sack or flushed down the toilet if there are only small amounts. For spillages indoors, clean the area with a detergent, e.g. washing-up liquid and hot water, then rinse and dry. For spillages outside (e.g. in the playground), sluice the area with water. Gloves should be disposed of and hands washed after taking off the gloves. Spillages on carpets and upholstery should be cleaned with warm soapy water or an appropriate carpet shampoo.

> ## Discussion point
> *How is disinfecting different from sterilization?*

Case study

Key skills ICT 2.3

Rob

Rob is working in a nursing home. He has been asked to:

- clean a service user's bedroom
- disinfect equipment in the treatment room
- sterilize some equipment.

1 Prepare a handout that would give Rob the information he needs to successfully clean the service user's bedroom.

2 Explain why the equipment will need to be sterilized.

3 Describe how Rob should sterilize the equipment.

4 What are the following used for?
   a Blue buckets.
   b Disinfectant.
   c Red buckets.
   d Alcohol wipes.

Disposal of waste

An important element of infection control is appropriate disposal of waste. Care establishments generally use a colour-coded bag system for waste disposal:

- *Yellow bags* are used for clinical waste. Transport of clinical waste must be strictly

controlled and it must be disposed of by **incineration**. The costs of this process are very high.

- *Black bags* are used by hospitals and other care settings for domestic waste.

- *Hard-walled containers* are used to dispose of sharp objects to avoid puncture injuries to those subsequently involved in the disposal process.

- *Bed pans* should be carefully emptied down a toilet or sluice. They should be washed in hot detergent solution, rinsed, dried and wiped thoroughly with Pre-Sept (**hypochlorite**) solution. A **designated** sink not used for food preparation should be identified for this 'dirty' task.

Medication disposal

Medication that is no longer required or has become out of date should, where possible, be returned to a **pharmacist**. This is so it can be disposed of in a safe and appropriate manner. Medication should never just be thrown in the waste bin in case it falls into the wrong hands. Liquid medication can be washed down the sink with the aid of running water if necessary. Tablets can normally be disposed of down the toilet. Both of these actions should only take place if you are certain that there will be no damaging effects on the environment. If there is ever any doubt professional advice should be sought.

> ## Discussion point
> *Why should care be taken when disposing of medication?*

Cleaning medical equipment

Equipment should be cleaned on a regular basis according to manufacturer's instructions. Using a detergent solution and drying is adequate for most surfaces.

Where water-based cleaners are not suitable then certain alcohol-based solutions can be used providing a risk assessment has been carried out.

Examples of how certain items of equipment should be cleaned are shown in the table below.

Equipment	How it should be cleaned
Hoist	Warm water and detergent
Scalpel	Sterilized
A drip pole	Detergent and warm water
Plastic tray	Alcohol wipe

What are the procedures for sending specimens to the laboratory?

Within any care environment there should be procedures in place for sending specimens to the laboratory. The main reasons for the procedures are to ensure that the specimen:

- reaches the laboratory in a testable condition.
- is labelled with the correct service user details.
- is packaged in a manner that makes it safe to transport and handle.

For these reasons specimens should always be placed in the correct container. The specimen should be labelled so that it accurately identifies the service user and where they are located. The contained specimen should then be placed in the appropriate transportation packaging. This should carry a **biohazard** warning to allow it to be recognised. It should be sent by the correct courier service to the laboratory in as short a time as possible. Where this is not possible in the same day the specimen should be stored in a fridge until departure. On no account should it be stored with food or other medication, in case it is confused with them, which could have dangerous consequences. It must also be remembered that it is illegal to send infected and toxic substances through the postal system.

Remember, always follow the correct local procedures, and if in doubt ask for advice.

Figure 4.11 *Sending specimens to the laboratory*

Preventing the spread of infection

Julia has an illness that must be reported. The doctor has advised that the room should be kept as clean as possible and that both universal and special infection control precautions should be put in place where appropriate. All waste products from the room must be treated as infectious until the doctor is satisfied that Julia is free from infection. All members of staff and visitors must wash their hands before and after entering Julia's room.

1 Explain how good personal hygiene can prevent the spread of infection, and how poor personal hygiene can influence the spread of infection. Give examples to illustrate the points made. Try to use a variety of sources to help you with this task and record those used.

2 Explain which conditions need reporting in health and social care settings.

3 Describe 'universal precautions', explaining how the use of these can prevent the spread of infection.

4 Explain how Julia's room would be cleaned and sterilized, giving reasons for the actions taken.

5 It has been decided that specimens from the hospital must be sent to the laboratory. Explain how this would be done giving reasons.

6 Explain how infectious waste from Julia's room should be disposed.

4.3 Recognise basic food hygiene practices in care settings

What are the basic hygiene practices for food preparation and cooking?

Surfaces

Food poisoning affects thousands of people every year and many of these cases go unreported. The exact number of cases of food-related illness that occur each year are unknown. This is because many people do not seek the help of their doctor when they develop symptoms. Food poisoning can be extremely dangerous especially for the very young, older service users and those who are ill or infirm. It is therefore important that care workers' actions do not increase this problem. To prevent contamination of food it is necessary to follow recognised hygiene procedures to make sure that risks are kept to a minimum.

Cleaning and disinfection chemicals are available to maintain the correct standards of cleanliness. Usually these chemicals are added to water to make a cleaning solution. Some come ready to use in spray or **aerosol** bottles for convenience.

Substances used for cleaning food preparation areas fall into three categories:

- *detergents* – dissolve grease and assist in the removal of stains and dirt. It must be remembered that detergents do not kill bacteria
- *disinfectants* – chemicals that are designed to destroy bacteria. They reduce the bacteria to a safe level. Disinfectants are not effective for removing grease. They can have a strong smell and can affect the taste of food if used in excess. The use of them should be limited
- *sanitizers* – chemicals that combine the roles of detergent and disinfectant. They are designed to remove dirt and grease and disinfect all in one action.

The combination of the above chemicals and very hot water provide an effective way of keeping surfaces clean.

Any work surface that is used for food preparation must be:

- strong
- durable
- easily cleaned
- resistant to stain or to absorbing liquids
- not easily damaged.

In professional food areas stainless steel tables are used for food preparation activities. They are usually on wheels which have brakes so that they can be moved easily which also allows for ease of cleaning.

It is vital that work surfaces are kept clean and bacteria free. To do this the 'clean as you go' approach should be used. This means that all equipment and surfaces should be cleaned as soon as they have been used. Any spills should also be mopped up immediately they occur. Work surfaces should be left clean and clear when work has finished.

The stages of cleaning work surfaces are:

1 Remove food particles and spillages with a damp cloth.
2 Use a solution of detergent and very hot water to remove grease and general stains and soiling.
3 Rinse surface thoroughly with very hot water.
4 Apply a suitable sanitizer in very hot water and allow sufficient time for the solution to do its work.
5 Rinse again using very hot water and allow the surface to dry naturally or with disposable paper towels.

If the soiling is very light, stages '2' and '3' could be bypassed, but do not do this if the surface has been in contact with raw meat, poultry, shellfish or eggs.

Equipment

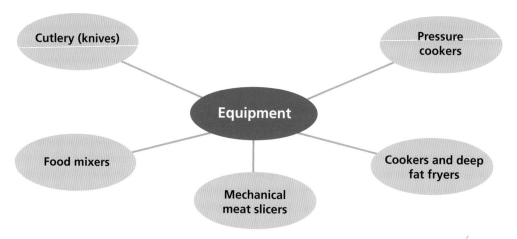

Figure 4.12 *Examples of equipment*

Never attempt to clean equipment unless you have been trained to do so. This is especially important where the equipment has sharp cutting surfaces and/or moving parts that are run by electricity. Care should also be taken with equipment that is hot or generates a lot of heat, for example cookers and deep fat fryers.

When training has been completed some basic steps should be followed when cleaning equipment.

The basic steps are:

- disconnect the equipment from the power source
- take extra care when removing any blades
- remove all waste food
- thoroughly wash and sanitize all parts
- reassemble the equipment taking care to fit all components correctly in case they fly off during use
- sanitize again those parts that will come into contact with food
- ensure that all safety guards are refitted correctly.

All other small items of equipment like pots, pans, cutlery, plates and glassware can be cleaned in the usual way. This may either be in a dishwasher or by hand using detergent and hot water.

Activity 3

Key skills C 2.3

Trish

Trish works in a Trust hospital and is responsible for supervising the hygiene practices and procedures for the preparation and handling of food. She is giving a presentation to a group of staff who are responsible for cleaning surfaces and equipment in the hospital kitchens and dining areas.

1 a What is a cleaning solution?
   b In what form can they be obtained?
   c What is a santizer?
2 Produce a simple handout that Trish could use to show the stages of cleaning surfaces.
3 List **three** pieces of equipment that would be used in the hospital kitchen that would require cleaning.
4 Explain the method(s) that would be used to clean the equipment listed.

Sell by dates

Foods that are likely to go off quickly are known as **perishable**. They normally have a 'sell by' date on them and a 'use by date'. It is an offence to sell food after the sell by date has past. The food can be used up to and including the date shown. Most other foods carry a 'best before' date. This indicates the month up to which it will be in its best condition for eating.

Some foods are not required by law to carry a date mark. These include fresh fruit and vegetables and meat from the butcher.

Food

It is important that certain precautions are taken when providing food for service users. The table below is a guide as to what you should and should not do and why!

Packaging of products gives sell by dates

What should I do?	Why should it be done?
Wash hands: • before entering a food area • after using the lavatory • between handling different types of food, e.g. cooked and raw meat • before and after touching food • after coughing into the hands or using a handkerchief • after touching face and hair • after carrying out cleaning or handling rubbish	Many bacteria live on the surface of the skin. Many of these are harmless but some that are transferred can cause illness. Bacteria can be acquired from other sources and can contaminate food. Handling raw meat and poultry and then handling cooked meat is very dangerous unless hands are thoroughly washed between tasks.
Avoid touching your nose or coughing and sneezing over food or preparation areas	Personal cleanliness is essential or bacteria will be transferred to the food.
Avoid touching the food with your hands. Where possible wear gloves or use tongs	The less hands are in direct contact with food, the less chance there is of contamination
Avoid touching dishes or cutlery that are to come into contact with food	This cuts down the transfer of bacteria
Keep the hair covered with a net or hat and do not comb hair in the food area	Hair and scalp carry bacteria that can fall into the food
Do not smoke in the food area	This is against the law and can contaminate food
Keep cuts and grazes covered with a brightly coloured dressing	Wounds are infected with bacteria and if the dressing comes off it can be easily found
If you are ill do not handle food	A person who is ill could infect food
Wear clean protective clothing	There are fewer bacteria on clean clothes

Cooking

Heat kills bacteria and this is why food must be cooked thoroughly. Most bacteria will not survive in food that has been cooked at a temperature of at least 70°C.

Meat and poultry should be cooked thoroughly all the way through. Large pieces of meat take longer to heat up to the centre. The need for sufficiently high temperatures reaching the centre is very important.

It is bad practice to mix previously cooked food with newly cooked food. Topping up soup lowers the temperature and increases the risk of bacteria growing. It is much safer to make up food in smaller quantities as and when it is needed.

Eggs can carry salmonella. To safeguard service users, eggs should be cooked for around seven minutes at 70°C.

High-risk foods like eggs and chicken that are eaten immediately after cooking are safe providing the temperature is high enough. If there is going to be a gap in time between the food being cooked and being eaten, it must be kept hot. Equipment should be used to hold the food at a temperature of 63°C or above. This could be a heated tray, trolley or service counter.

When using this type of equipment:

- heat the equipment to at least 63°C before loading the food
- ensure the food is already fully cooked and at a minimum temperature of 63°C
- never use the equipment to heat up cold or partially heated food.

Reheating food can increase the risk of food poisoning. Some food handlers often make the mistake of thinking that because food has already been cooked it is free of bacteria. They believe that it only needs warming up. If this happens, bacteria has ideal conditions for growth, (i.e. food, warmth and liquid).

Guidelines for food that needs reheating:

- don't get the food out of the refrigerator too soon and leave it lying around
- handle as little as possible and keep it covered
- divide larger items into smaller portions where possible
- heat the food to at least 70°C at its core
- serve quickly following reheating
- never reheat cooked food more than once
- if reheating ready-made meals from a shop, follow the manufacturer's instructions in addition to the above advice.

Storing

Bacteria flourish at body temperature (37°C), which means that even one piece of food left out for a couple of hours can contain millions of bacteria. The reason foods are stored in a refrigerator is because bacteria and viruses don't multiply below 6°C. The correct temperature for a refrigerator is between zero and 5°C.

Chilled foods should be put away quickly but don't overcrowd the refrigerator as it raises the temperature. With cooked food, let steam evaporate first before covering and placing in the refrigerator. Always keep the refrigerator clean by washing the inside surfaces with warm soapy water.

Never thaw then refreeze food. To slowly defrost, take the dish out of the freezer and leave it in the refrigerator overnight rather than on the counter top. Place meats on a plate on the bottom shelf. When defrosting with the microwave, cook the dish immediately. Never freeze food that has gone beyond its 'use by' date, and discard old food regularly.

Keeping the refrigerator at the right temperature helps prevent bacteria from multiplying. The correct temperature for a refrigerator is below 5°C and a freezer should be kept at minus 18°C. Check both the refrigerator and freezer temperatures regularly with a reliable thermometer. To maintain a constant temperature, keep the door shut whenever possible.

When storing food in a refrigerator:

- don't allow the juices from raw meat, fish and poultry to spill or drip onto other foods. If you plan to use only part of the meat or poultry, store it in a secure container and tightly wrap any remaining parts destined for the freezer
- put fruit and vegetable items into the salad drawer
- keep milk and fruit juices on the bottom rack in the door
- place dairy products, dressing, spreads, sauces, cream and convenience foods on the centre and top shelves
- store raw meat, fish and poultry on the bottom shelf of the refrigerator. This prevents **cross-contamination** as the blood and other liquids from the meat and fish cannot drip down onto other foods.
- cooked foods should be kept on the top shelves of the refrigerator.
- mayonnaise and ketchup should be kept in the refrigerator after opening
- never place food in an open tin in the refrigerator. Use secure containers instead and throw the food out after two or three days
- keep seafood either in the refrigerator or in the freezer until you are ready to prepare it .

Figure 4.13 *Correct storage of food in a refrigerator*

Most frozen foods should be thrown out after three to six months. When storing food in the freezer, remove it from the wrapping and place it in a labelled and dated freezer bag. Remember to **expel** all the air from the bag before sealing it.

After a power cut, foods that have started to defrost should be thrown out. If the power comes back on and if there is any doubt about which foods have defrosted and refrozen, the food should be thrown away.

Recommended refrigeration storage temperatures for some foods		
Food	**Storage temperature °C**	**Shelf life in the home**
Seafoods	3	3 days
Crustaceans and molluscs	3	2 days
Meat	3	35 days
Minced meat and **Offal**	3	23 days
Cured meat	3	23 weeks
Poultry	3	3 days
Fruit juices	7	714 days
Milk	7	57 days
Cream	7	5 days
Cheese	7	Variable (13 months)
Butter	7	8 weeks
Oil and fat	7	Variable (6 months)
Margarine	7	Variable (6 months)

Cross-contamination occurs when food is put in contact with other contaminated foods. An example of this could be the blood from a piece of chicken dripping onto a plate of cooked food. Cross-contamination means that bacteria or other pathogens have been transferred from an infected food item to an uninfected food item. They both become infected or contaminated.

If food looks or smells in any way, throw it out. A sure sign of spoilage is mould. Most mouldy foods should be binned along with leaking cartons and food that has passed its 'use by' date.

Food that does not need keeping cold should be kept in sealed containers in a cool dry cupboard or larder. It should never be stored on the floor. Vegetables can normally be kept in a cool, dry place in loose paper bags or racks, but not in plastic bags. This makes them sweat and rot more quickly.

Assessment activity 4.3

Hygiene practices

Sunny View Nursery School has been recently built and is about to open. Children attending will be between the ages of six months and four-and-a-half years old. Some of the service users will stay all day and will need to be given meals and snacks. The kitchen manager is having a training day with all those responsible for the preparation and cooking of food in the nursery school to give them training about basic food hygiene that will be required in the care setting.

1 Try to arrange to visit a care setting or invite a care worker from a care setting to the centre to find out about the measures used to promote good hygiene practice when preparing and handling food.

Alternatively you could approach an Environmental Health Officer to help find the information you need and/or take the Basic Food Hygiene Course which would provide you with the knowledge for this section of the portfolio work.

2 Work with others in the group to prepare questions to help you find out about the hygiene practices used by the care setting when preparing and handling food.

3 Prepare materials that could be used for the Sunny View Nursery School training day to give a comprehensive and detailed account of the procedures for handling and preparing food to prevent the growth and spread of micro-organisms. When preparing the materials try to link theory to practice to illustrate the points you are making.

Remember to include information about:
- surfaces
- equipment
- sell by dates
- food
- cooking
- storing.

What are the basic hazards in a care setting?

A hazard is anything that can cause a person harm. Hazards can be found in any environment and especially at work. It is important that care workers recognise hazards in the workplace as this helps reduce risks and prevent accidents.

Unsafe equipment

Unsafe equipment can be the cause of many accidents at work from minor injuries such as cuts and bruises to major injury and death. For this reason the Health and Safety Executive (HSE) have rules that employers have to follow when they provide equipment. These rules state the equipment must be:

- suitable for the intended use
- safe for use, maintained in a safe condition and, in certain circumstances, inspected to ensure that it remains safe
- used only by people who have received adequate information, instruction and training
- accompanied by suitable safety measures, e.g. protective devices, markings and warnings.

Equipment that is unsafe or broken should always be reported. It is potentially dangerous and should not be used.

Examples of equipment that must be checked in care settings are shown in the table below.

Equipment	What should be checked
Hoists	<ul><li>belt fastenings for loose fittings</li><li>pistons for oil leaks</li><li>cables for wear</li><li>slings to make sure they are not broken</li></ul>
Slides in a playgroup	<ul><li>stability (is it well-anchored)</li><li>edges for sharp or jagged areas</li><li>joints for rust and wear</li><li>slide surfaces for water, dirt or excessive wear</li><li>that the slide has been put up according to the manufacturer's instructions</li><li>the area beneath the slide for inappropriate materials (it should be that recommended and not hard concrete)</li></ul>
Wheelchairs	<ul><li>tyres for leaks – they should be inflated to the recommended pressure</li><li>brakes for faults – are they binding?</li><li>bearings for wear</li><li>fabrics for wear and tear or dirt</li></ul>
Drip stands	<ul><li>castors for freedom of movement</li><li>telescopic extensions should run freely and lock off tightly</li><li>that all attachments are present and functional</li></ul>
Beds	<ul><li>wheels so they run freely</li><li>breaks for faults</li><li>the steering bar for faults</li><li>mattresses for dirt or damage</li><li>back rest and elevation mechanism for correct function</li></ul>
Fire extinguishers	<ul><li>expiry date</li><li>weight (if appropriate)</li><li>hoses and cylinders for wear and leaks</li></ul>

Hazardous substances

Hazardous substances can cause a variety of effects that include:

- skin irritation or dermatitis as a result of skin contact
- asthma as a result of developing an allergy to substances used at work
- losing consciousness as a result of being overcome by toxic fumes
- cancer, which may appear long after the exposure to the chemical that caused it
- infection from bacteria and other micro-organisms.

Hazardous substances include:
- substances used directly in work activities, e.g. pharmaceuticals, cleaning agents
- substances generated during work activities, e.g. fumes from sterilizing or disinfecting
- naturally occurring substances, e.g. dust
- **biological agents** such as bacteria and other micro-organisms.

The HSE have designed a set of regulations called the Control of Substances Hazardous to Health (COSHH) Regulations 2002. So that hazards can be identified and the risks reduced, the guidelines give eight steps to follow:

1 Assess the risks to health from the hazardous substances used or created by your workplace activities.

2 Decide what precautions are needed.

3 Prevent or adequately control exposure.

4 Ensure that **control measures** are used and maintained properly and that safety procedures are followed.

5 Employers are to monitor the exposure of employees to hazardous substances, if necessary.

6 Carry out appropriate health surveillance where an assessment has shown this is necessary or where the COSHH regulations say it is necessary.

7 Prepare plans and procedures to deal with accidents, incidents and emergencies involving hazardous substances, where necessary.

8 Employers are to ensure employees are properly informed, trained and supervised.

If the content of a package or container is hazardous, it will have a label explaining what should or should not be done when using the substance. Any substance about which care workers are unsure should be treated as a hazard until they know that it is not.

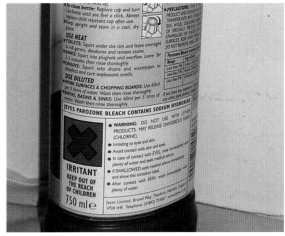

Example of a biohazard label

Hazardous locations

Notes that many of the following examples of hazards in specific locations can apply to more than one location.

Kitchens

Kitchens are well-known for being dangerous places if they are not correctly maintained. Items that can cause danger in a kitchen include:

- cookers – can cause burns and scalds (cooker guards can help to prevent children from burning themselves and pulling saucepans off)
- knives – put away so that children cannot cut themselves
- cables – can be tripped over or can lead to electric shock if damaged
- cleaning materials – should be stored where small children cannot get access to them and where they cannot be mistaken for consumable items
- wet floors – can lead to slips and falls and can increase the risk of electric shock if there are damaged cables present
- electric kettles – should be stable with coiled flex to avoid them falling and scalding people
- cupboards – should be childproof if children are present.

Bathrooms

Dangers in a bathroom include:

- slippery surfaces – avoid uneven floor surfaces and mats, and floors should be non-slip
- cleaning materials (especially liquid cleaners) – should be stored away from items such as shampoo, to reduce the risk of service users mistaking one for the other
- running the hot water before the cold – can lead to scalds if service users are unaware
- lack of an emergency alarm – can make service users feel vulnerable and alone. There should be either a panic button or a personal alarm that they can use.

> ## Discussion point
> *Where else might an emergency alarm be useful to service users?*

Stairs

Stairs can be dangerous and falls can seriously injure service users and could be fatal. Care workers should ensure:

- stair coverings are non-slip and fixed – so that they do not slide about or cause service users to slip
- no obstacles are left on stairs – these could cause a person to trip

- lighting is sufficient – to allow service users to see clearly where they are going both during the day and at night
- a rail or banister exists – to provide support for service users.

Bedrooms

Dangers in a bedroom include:

- lack of smoke alarms
- smoking – should be discouraged because of the danger of fire. If it is not possible to do this then it should only be allowed in designated areas where the furnishings are fire resistant
- lack of fire instructions – should be placed where they can easily be seen
- lack of safety catches – should be fixed to windows.

Community rooms

Dangers in community rooms include:

- floor coverings – should be non-slip and rugs and mats should be fixed so that they do not slide about or cause service users to slip
- furniture – should be stable and fixed in place where possible
- electrical equipment such as televisions – should be turned off when not in use to reduce the risk of fire
- electric sockets – should not be overloaded. Plastic covers should be placed on electric sockets when they are not in use.

Figure 4.14 *Spot the hazards in the residents' community room*

Entrance halls

Dangers in entrance halls include:

- packages – should not be left unattended as they may cause an obstruction. Also, as the country is in a state of heightened alert due to terrorism all suspicious packages have the potential of being explosive devices
- unauthorised access – security pads should be in use on the front door.

To conduct a health and safety risk assessment, follow these steps:

STEP 1: Look for the hazards and the associated risks.

STEP 2: Decide who might be harmed and how.

STEP 3: Evaluate the risks and decide whether the existing precautions are adequate or whether more should be done.

STEP 4: Record the findings.

STEP 5: Review the assessment and revise it if necessary.

Activity 4
Key skills 2.2

Hazards in care settings

Russell is going to carry out a safety check of the entrance hall and stairs at Blake Residential Home.

1 List three checks that Russell could make for the entrance hall. For each explain why it could be a risk.

2 Describe how stairs can be a risk to service users, giving examples of the hazards that could cause injuries.

3 Explain how unsafe equipment could be a hazard to both service users and care workers, using examples to illustrate the points made.

4 Produce a handout to give advice to care workers about how to store hazardous substances.

How can risks be reduced in care settings?

Safety surveys and audits

Safety surveys and audits are used to assess the risks that can arise from hazards in the workplace. To do this employers and staff have to involve themselves in what is known as risk assessment.

Risk assessments are nothing more than careful examinations of what, in the care setting, could cause harm to people, so that the health and safety officer can weigh up whether enough precautions are in place. The aim of a risk assessment is to make sure that no one gets hurt or becomes ill.

Employers are legally required to assess the risks in their workplace. The important things that have to be decided are whether a hazard is significant, and whether the control methods that are in place are sufficient.

Staff training

Staff involvement and training is a key element of the Health and Safety Commission's 'Strategy for Workplace Health and Safety in Great Britain to 2010 and beyond'. An organisation's greatest asset is its workforce. **Employees** are often best able to spot issues and bring about real improvements. They can also influence health and safety through their own actions and by accepting personal responsibility. Trained workplace health and safety representatives operating in partnership with management are an important part of maintaining health and safety benefits. Staff training in health and safety is essential to ensure that everyone including the service users are not at risk from injury.

Safety features

Many pieces of equipment have safety features. When equipment is designed correctly often these features are not noticeable. An example of this is the swivel chair used with a computer. Originally these were made with a base that had four struts with wheels on. It was found that they were prone to tipping over. Now, by European Union law they have to have a base with five struts. This makes them more stable.

Examples of other safety features are:

- smoke alarm – alerts people
- fire alarm – gives people time to evacuate the building
- window catch – prevents unwanted intruders
- firefighting equipment – can prevent fire from spreading.

Regular checking of equipment

All equipment should be either serviced or checked on a regular basis. If the equipment has to be serviced then the manufacturer will have made recommendations as to the time intervals between each service. Failure to observe these recommendations is often be dangerous. For example, if the hoist in a care establishment is not serviced on a regular basis it can become worn or hard to use. This then poses a danger to both service users and care workers.

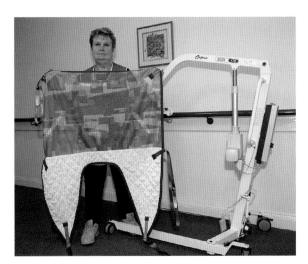

Careful examination can prevent accidents

Following rules and regulations

Rules and regulations must be followed because safety depends on them. They usually come from one of two sources:

- they may be local and designed by the employer
- they may have been designed by the government.

Wherever they come from, it is important that they are followed as they are put in place for the good of everyone.

One of the main sets of rules and regulations is The Health and Safety at Work Act 1974. This act provides the basis of health and safety law. It places general duties on all people at work, including employers and employees.

All rules and regulations are monitored by specialist health and safety enforcement officers who are appointed to specifically enforce health and safety legislation. They are either from the Health and Safety Executive, or the local authority. All health and safety officers have far-reaching powers and have the ability to close an establishment down, impose fines or take employers and occasionally employees, to court.

Putting policies in place

Because all places of employment are subject to health and safety law, employers must have relevant policies in place. These will be locally designed versions of the official regulations. They must be designed for a particular place of work so that all of the staff can follow them and comply with the safety laws. Most care establishments have the following policies:

- fire policy
- lifting policy
- hazardous waste policy
- drugs and medication policy.

Providing safety and warning notices

Safety and warning notices are used to make people aware of risks and hazards. Their purpose is to prevent accidents by making people aware of what is around them.

All signs are designed to guidelines laid down by the British Standards Institute. They are based on a standard combination of shapes and colours. They have to be manufactured in accordance with British Standard BS 5378. By doing this all signs throughout the country are easily recognised because they have been standardized.

There are three main types of sign:

- a black triangle with a black picture on a yellow background. This indicates a warning
- a red circle with a red crossbar containing a black picture on a white background. This indicates a prohibition which means you must not do something
- a solid blue circle with a white picture built into it. This is an instruction sign.

Signs should be provided at eye level where they are needed, so that they are easily visible.

Figure 4.15 *Examples of safety and warning signs*

Try it!

See if you can recognise the signs!

Correct storage of hazardous substances

It is important that all hazardous substances are stored in the correct way. Information on the type and method of storage is usually provided by the manufacturer. Whatever is being stored, it needs to have certain information to identify it for health and safety reasons. This information includes:

- the identity of the substance including trade names and code numbers
- possible hazards of using, transporting or storing the substance
- safety precautions
- emergency actions
- first aid
- supplier's name and contact details.

All portable containers must be labelled if there is any possibility someone else may use the container. Hazardous substances should be kept locked away.

What are the benefits of reducing hazard risks?

To the service user

Every service user has the right to live and be treated in an environment that is safe. The last thing they want is to come out of a care setting in a worse condition than when they went in!

If the environment is unsafe and has risks and hazards, this can cause service users to worry. Service users' clinical conditions can be affected by worry. It can often make their condition worse or slow their physical and mental progress. Service users who are worried about their care become anxious and may experience increases in blood pressure. This, as we know, can be physically damaging to service users.

To staff

Thousands of working days are lost each year due to injury, all of which could be prevented. One of the main benefits of a safe environment is that staff enjoy their work and care about what they do. Staff are supported by the fact that they are safe in the environment that they are working in. The fact that there is someone who is making sure that the environment is safe can often boost morale. It is a well-known fact that happy staff work better and tend to stay longer at their place of employment. This has a benefit to both service users and employers. It provides **continuity** of care for service users. This means that they do not see continuous changes in the staff. It allows them to bond with members of staff and provides them with a level of security. For employers, staff staying longer builds the reputation of the organisation as a universally caring environment.

Assessment activity 4.4

Key skills **C** 2.1a, **ICT** 2.3

Hazards and ways of reducing the risks

Figure 4.16 *Hazards in the playroom of a play area of a nursery school*

Six months after the opening of Sunny View Nursery, the Health and Safety Officer is conducting one of her regular safety survey/audits of the playroom.

On this occasion she finds the hazards shown in the picture above.

1 List five hazards shown in the picture above. For each, give a safety measure or action that could reduce the hazard.

2 Arrange to visit a different type of care setting to find out about hazards that could exist and ways used to reduce the hazards.

3 Work with others in your group to prepare questions to ask while at the setting to help you find out about possible hazards and the ways that could be used to reduce the hazards.

4 Think about a different care setting. Are the hazards likely to be different or are there likely to be any additional hazards? Discuss these and explain the safety features that could be used to reduce the risks.

5 Explain how warning or safety signs could be used in settings, giving examples to illustrate the points made.

6 Give a presentation to explain to new trainees:
   • what are hazardous substances
   • how hazardous substances should be stored.

7 Explain how health and safety policies and following rules and regulations can help to reduce the risks in settings.

8 Prepare materials to explain to new trainees in care settings the benefits of reducing the risks in care settings. You should consider the benefits to:
   • service users
   • staff.

How can we identify and reduce the safety and security risks?

Identifying hazards

Good security is the best way to reduce the chances of people in a care setting becoming victims of crime and stopping intruders. A lot of crimes are done on the spur of the moment, as a burglar may see an open window or other easy point of entry and take their chance. It is therefore very important that all care workers are aware of the problems that can arise when security is lax because staff are not vigilant and consider that it is not their problem. If care workers make the effort they can reduce the instances of property theft and violent attacks.

Reducing the risks

A care setting should always be secure especially when there are only a few staff on duty. The following actions are important:

- shut ground floor windows during the night
- don't leave a key under the mat
- leave a light on in the evenings
- use sensor-controlled outside lighting that is activated by movement
- window and external door alarms should be turned on at night
- take the obvious precautions and challenge all strangers and unauthorised visitors
- ask the local police for advice about security.

The first thing to do to reduce risks to safety and security is to carry out a risk assessment. As we have seen, risk assessment is the process of identifying hazards in the workplace and assessing the risk of them causing harm. Through looking closely and accurately at areas of risk and developing measures to reduce hazards, risks in the workplace can be reduced.

In Unit 4.4 some basic steps were shown for carrying out a health and safety risk assessment. The following five steps can be used to assess any sort of risk. Here they are used to assess risks to safety and security:

STEP 1: Look for the security risks

These are often easy to spot. Something that looks like a breach in security is a potential risk.

STEP 2: Decide who might be a risk, or at risk, and how

For example, they could be:

- young workers, trainees, new and expectant mothers, or anyone who may be vulnerable to being attacked or robbed
- cleaners, visitors, contractors, maintenance workers, or anyone who may need to be monitored to make sure that they do not pose a security risk
- members of the public, or people you share your workplace with, or anyone who could be compromising security and/or involved in criminal activity.

STEP 3: Evaluate the risks and decide whether the existing precautions are adequate or whether more should be done

Once a security risk has been discovered the existing security measures that are being used have to be looked at to see if they are working. If it proves that they are not adequate then they must be improved.

STEP 4: Record your findings

Nothing can be changed unless the assessment that has been made is recorded in writing. A description of the security problem and the risks that it poses are always required as a starting point. This description can include sketches and diagrams to help explain the problem.

STEP 5: Review the assessment and revise it if necessary

Reviewing the problem and the risks that it poses should be carried out on a regular basis. This depends on how great the risk is. Don't be overcomplicated. In most care environments the risks are few and simple. Checking them is common sense, but necessary. For example, most care workers would know if their setting had any weak points in building security or if there was an awkward entrance where someone could slip in unnoticed. If there was, they should check to see what reasonable precautions had been made resolve this problem. It is straightforward to understand what is involved, and so most people can carry out an assessment (they don't have to be an expert on crime). Care workers who work for larger care environments, for example hospitals, always train a responsible employee as a security officer to help reduce risks. These officers do regular checks in as many areas as possible. But they cannot be everywhere at once. They have to rely on the staff helping them by being observant of what is happening in the work environment.

Always remember that everyone is responsible for maintaining security and for identifying risks and bringing them to the attention of the appropriate staff.

What fire safety measures are required in care settings?

Fire risk assessment is something virtually all employers are required to carry out under The Fire Precautions (workplace) Regulations 1997 as amended 1999, which runs alongside the Fire Precautions Act 1971. The assessment is used to discover whether there is a risk of a fire occurring in the **premises**, and the effects it would have on all staff and visitors or contractors.

For those businesses that employ five or more people, the assessment must be recorded in written form. It is also a requirement that the assessment of areas that have been highlighted as a significant risk within a business is ongoing. Having a policy showing preventative and protective measures for adequate fire safety and reassessing risks for continuous improvement is just part of what is involved in a fire risk assessment. Other areas that such an assessment should cover are shown in Figure 4.18.

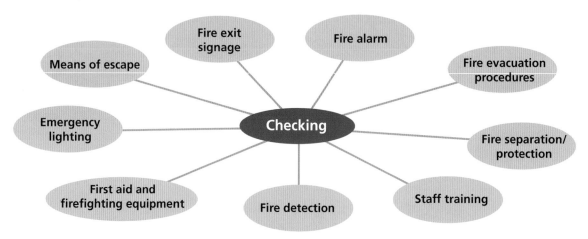

Figure 4.18 *What a fire risk assessment involves checking*

Failure to do a fire risk assessment could render a person liable to pay certain penalties. For employers and/or certain staff under some fire safety legislation, penalties include a £2000 maximum fine and/or three months imprisonment for each offence, rising to a maximum of two years imprisonment.

A fire risk assessment involves identifying potential sources of **ignition** in the workplace, the **combustible** materials that are present as part of the business operations, the furnishings and the building in which the business is carried out. The aim is to reduce these to a minimum. Opportunities may be taken to **eliminate**, **substitute**, avoid or transfer the various hazards that have been identified. Once this has been done the residual sources of ignition and combustible materials that form the core of the day-to-day patterns of work must be separated as far as is practicable.

People who use the premises must also be considered. These include staff, customers, visitors or members of the public. The means of escape, equipment for detecting and giving warning in case of fire and firefighting apparatus must be appropriate for the premises and the numbers of people present. Consideration also has to be given to the age, agility and health of the people who may be on the premises. For example, different factors have to be considered for crèches than for residential care homes.

Alarms

Every care environment should have its own dedicated fire alarm system. This should be in the form of a bell, a claxon or some other audible device. The way in which it rings can be used to indicate what event is happening. An intermittent alarm could indicate that the fire is not in the immediate building but elsewhere on site. One short alarm could indicate a test.

Fire alarms are normally activated by a red 'break glass' box that should be visible in an accessible position. Once activated, they can only be turned off from a central control box within the building. Often these alarms are directly linked to the local fire station.

If necessary, another method of alerting people to fire is by shouting 'Fire!'. This sounds a bit obvious, but often people get so panicked when they discover a fire that they forget to do it.

If necessary another method of raising the alarm is to use the internal telephone system. In larger care establishments there should be a special short telephone number that will be answered immediately if rang.

Equipment

Fires do not just happen, a fire needs three things to make it occur.

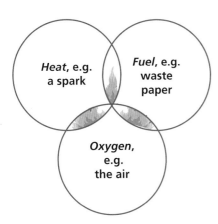

Figure 4.19 *The elements of a fire*

Remove one of the elements of a fire and the fire risk disappears. Good fire safety practice can remove some of these factors, but once a fire has started it is the role of fire extinguishers to tackle a fire by attacking one of its elements.

All care environments should provide fire extinguishers of various types (and, where appropriate, fire blankets) throughout their buildings. There are several types of extinguisher available and they work in different ways. Basically, they all interrupt the fire process by either removing heat from the fire (as in the case of a water extinguisher) or by removing oxygen from the fire (as in the case of CO_2), or both (as in the case of foam). They each have different advantages and problems.

A person should never attempt to tackle a fire unless they are confident that they can do so safely, for example, when:

- they have already raised the alarm.
- they have a clear unobstructed route away from the fire in case it grows larger
- they are confident of their ability to operate the extinguisher
- they have the correct type of extinguisher.

Types of extinguisher

There are the following types of fire extinguisher (there are also additional specialist extinguishers available but these require specific training and are not available for general use):

- water (red)
- foam (cream)
- CO_2 (black)
- dry powder (blue).

Extinguishers conform to one of two colour-coding systems. If they are new they are red with coloured handles or a coloured 'shoulder' or band on the cylinder. If they are older, the whole cylinder is coloured with the indicator colour.

Fire extinguishers are marked as to which fires they may or may not be used on. The fire extinguisher selected should always be marked for the type of fire that it will be used on.

Extinguishers come in a variety of types

Types of fire

There are three common types, or classes, of fire:

- *Class A* – involves ordinary combustibles such as wood, paper, cloth, rubber and many plastics
- *Class B* – involves flammable liquids, such as gasoline, oil, grease, tar, oil-based paints, lacquer and flammable gases
- *Class C* – involves energized electrical equipment, such as wiring, fuse boxes, circuit breakers, machinery and appliances.

What type of fire extinguisher should be chosen to deal with a particular kind of fire can be summarized in the table shown on page 178.

Type	Best for	Dangers
Red (water)	• Solids – wood, cloth, paper, plastics, etc.	• Do not use on burning fat or oil • Do not use on electrical appliances
Blue (dry powder, multi-purpose)	• Solids – wood, cloth, paper, plastics, etc. • Liquids – grease, fats, oil, paint, petrol, etc. • Electrical equipment	• Do not use on chip or fat pan fires • Does not easily penetrate equipment – fire may re-ignite • Does not cool fire well – fire may re-ignite • Smouldering material – fire may re-ignite
Blue (dry powder, standard)	• Liquids – grease, fats, oil, paint, petrol, etc. • Electrical equipment	• Do not use on chip or fat pan fires • Does not easily penetrate equipment – fire may re-ignite
Cream (foam, multi-purpose)	• Solids – wood, cloth, paper, plastics, etc. • Liquids – grease, fats, oil, paint, petrol, etc.	• Do not use on chip or fat pan fires
Cream (foam, standard)	• Limited number of liquid fires	• Do not use on chip or fat pan fires
Black (carbon, dioxide CO_2)	• Liquids – grease, fats, oil, paint, petrol, etc.	• Do not use on chip or fat pan fires • Does not cool well – fire may re-ignite • Fumes from CO_2 extinguishers can be harmful if used in confined spaces
Red (fire blanket)	• Especially for clothing and chip and fat pan fires • Solids – wood, cloth, paper, plastics, etc. • Liquids – grease, fats, oil, paint, petrol, etc.	• If blanket does not completely cover the fire, it will not extinguish the fire

Using fire extinguishers

The ways to use the different types of fire extinguishers are summarised in the table on page 179. In all cases:

1 Take the extinguisher to where it is to be used.
2 Pull out the pin. (This will also snap the coloured plastic tag.)
3 Aim the hose or nosel.
4 Pull the trigger.

In the case of some old water extinguishers the procedure is different. For these, remove the top cover, aim the hose, and then strike the knob on the top of the cylinder.

Safety procedures

In all care environments there should be set procedures that have been designed to maintain safety. To safeguard everyone, they should always be followed and updated when necessary. The following are areas where care workers may find safety procedures applied.

Flammable materials

Flammable materials that are used in care settings should always be kept to a minimum. These can be items as innocent as surgical spirit or alcohol-based hard surface cleaner. All flammable items should be stored under lock and key when not in use. There should be a specific cabinet or cupboard which, preferably, is fireproofed.

Rubbish

Stairs and corridors should always be kept clear of rubbish. Bags of rubbish should not be left lying around for people to trip over. They can also be a cause of spread of infection, especially in warm weather.

Type	How to use	Works by
Red (water)	• Point the jet at the base of the flames • Keep it moving across the area of the fire • Ensure that all areas of the fire are out	• Cooling burning material
Blue (dry powder)	• Point the jet or discharge horn at the base of the flames • With a rapid sweeping motion, drive the fire towards the far edge until all the fames are out • After using the shut-off control (if the extinguisher has one) wait until the air clears. If the flames are still visible, attack the fire again	• Knocks down flames by smothering the fire • Provides some cooling effect
Cream (foam)	• For fires involving liquids, do not aim jet straight into the liquid • Where the liquid on fire is in a container, point the jet at the inside edge of the container or on a nearby surface above the burning liquid • Allow the foam to build up and flow across the liquid • For fires involving solids, point the jet at the base of the flames • Keep it moving across the area of the fire. Ensure that all areas of the fire are out	• Smothers fire with foam film on surface of burning liquid • Has a cooling action with a wider extinguishing application than water on solids
Black (carbon dioxide CO_2)	• The discharge horn should be directed at the base of the flames • Keep the jet moving across the area of the fire • Do not hold the horn as it gets very cold	• Vapourising liquid gas which smothers the flames by displacing oxygen in the air
Red (fire blanket)	• Place carefully over the fire • Keep your hand shielded from the fire • Do not waft the fire towards you • If blanket does not completely cover the fire, it will not extinguish the fire	• Smothers the fire

Piles of rubbish in hidden places should be avoided; all rubbish should be deposited in the correct place. If it does not go directly out to the bins there should be a central collecting point for it. Equipment should not be left in corridors as it may pose a fire risk for those trying to exit the building.

Gas and electrical equipment

All gas and electrical equipment should be checked regularly. This is compulsory under health and safety law. Heavy fines and even prison sentences can be given to those who do not maintain their equipment properly.

In the event of fire

Everyone should know how to raise the fire alarm. The alarm system should be checked and tested weekly. Fire alarms and extinguishers should be serviced every 13 months and fire doors and exits should be kept free from obstructions and clearly marked. Procedures should be in place so that regular fire drills take place and all fire instructions must be clearly displayed. All staff should be trained how to use the different fire extinguishers.

Below is an example of the procedure used in the event of a fire.

If fire breaks out at work:
- operate the nearest fire alarm
- ensure the fire brigade is called
- attack the fire with a suitable extinguisher if it is safe to do so
- evacuate the building
- report to the assembly point
- do not re-enter the building until informed it is safe to do so.

Instructions should be given to maintenance staff, setting out the action they should take in the event of fire. The instructions should include bringing all lifts to ground level and stopping them. Someone should shut down all services not essential to the escape of occupants or likely to be required by the fire brigade. Lighting should be left on unless it the cause of the fire.

End-of-day checks

Procedures should be in place so that care settings can have end-of-day checks where necessary. These may include the following:

- the building is secured by a named individual at the end of each working day
- doors and windows are secure
- no combustible material is left lying around
- no unauthorised people are on the premises
- alarms are switched on
- external lighting is switched on
- flammable liquids are locked in the proper store.

Fire drills

Fire drills are designed to ensure that all employees know how to leave the premises in the event of fire. Repeated practice is desirable and fire drills should be held at regular intervals and preferably twice a year.

Employees should be trained:

- to recognise the fire alarm when it sounds
- to act in accordance with the evacuation plan
- to leave the premises quickly by the nearest possible route
- to go to the designated assembly point
- to assemble for roll call.

Departmental managers (or their equivalent) should make sure that their departments are completely evacuated. Management should evaluate performances during fire drills and in particular should investigate the causes of any

delays in evacuation. With this information they should take steps to make sure delays are **eliminated**.

How can the security of buildings be maintained?

How to prevent access to unwanted callers

There are recognised ways to prevent access to unwanted callers. The most common is to keep all outside doors locked and have a door bell. This can be done if the door locks comply with the fire regulations. However, many care settings use a range of methods to prevent access to unwanted visitors. If a care setting is big enough, it may have a reception so that everyone entering and leaving signs in and out. This has two benefits: it allows the monitoring of visitors and supports the fire procedure by listing everyone in the building.

Safety requires good security – not people falling asleep on the job

Security of the building

To help maintain the security of the building, doors that are not in regular use should be alarmed. This identifies if anyone is coming in or out, unannounced. Closed circuit television may also be employed to monitor the coming and going of all staff and visitors. It is important that everyone who works in a building is aware about security and follows the security procedures, as this benefits the safety of all.

Keys

To help maintain security the number of keys issued should be limited. There should be a list of the people who hold keys and the access that they have. Such people are called 'key holders'. By doing this the safety of the building is increased. Keys should always be looked after and not left laying about for anyone to pick up.

Some care environments do not have keys. Access can be obtained by having door code entry systems which require a secret combination to be typed in. The other option is an electronic card entry system. In this system a magnetic card is used that is similar to a credit card. This is swiped through the lock and the door releases. These can often be combined with a personal identity card.

Suspicious packages

Unaccompanied packages pose a risk, due to the heightened state of alert that has been caused by terrorism. It is therefore important everyone is aware of any suspicious items that are left. This could be in the form of luggage, packages, boxes or other unexpected containers.

A suspicious package that cannot be identified should not be moved or opened until it has been identified. The vast majority of these objects prove to be perfectly harmless. In the event that a suspicious package is discovered, care workers and service users may be asked to evacuate the building. The quickest and easiest way is to use the fire drill procedures that were discussed earlier in this unit. In this instance both the fire brigade and the police would need to be contacted. They would alert the appropriate authorities and services (e.g. bomb disposal) if necessary.

Such actions should not be taken by care workers acting alone – where possible they should alert their manager to the incident and let them manage the situation. If they have to act alone, the priority is to act in the best interests of all who are present and act in a way that maintains the safety of all. It is far better to be safe than sorry.

How can the security of people be maintained?

To maintain security, identity cards can be issued to help identify who visitors and staff are. These are usually produced with a picture of the individual on them and they also contain their name and details about where they work or who they are.

Temporary cards can be issued to people who are visiting or who have come to make repairs or service equipment. These cards often do not have a picture of the individual on them. People who come from some outside companies may have an identity card of their own to support their identity.

This allows the registration of all people moving about the building and helps to identify who they are.

Many employers identify their staff by giving them a uniform and a name badge. This, together with an identity card, makes identification immediate.

Assessment activity 4.5

Key skills [C] 2.3

Maintaining safety and security

Ferdinand is responsible for safety and security at Sunny View Nursery School. He needs to make sure that the all those using the nursery school are protected from harm.

1 Identify the possible safety risks to the service users, care workers and visitors that could exist in the nursery school, explaining how these could be reduced.

2 Arrange to visit a different type of care setting to find out how safety and security is promoted.

3 Work with others to prepare questions to use when visiting the setting to find out about

safety and security measures used in the setting. Remember to ask questions about:

- safety risks
- security measures
- fire safety
- security of buildings
- security of people.

4 Visit the setting and ask questions to find out about the safety and security measures used.

5 Carry out a safety and security survey/audit of **one** care setting. Arrange for your tutor to make an assessment of the survey.

Draw conclusions from your findings. Try to link theory to practice in the evidence you present.

Glossary

Aerosol: A spray liquid often found in bottles or cans, can be under pressure

Atmospheric pressure: the weight of air on the earth's surface

Biohazard: Something that is biologically infectious or dangerous

Biological agents: compounds or chemicals that are biologically active or alive

Cirrhosis: a disease of the liver that causes it to fail

Clinical: of or for the treatment of patients

Clinicians: people who treat patients

Combustible: capable of or used for burning

Contagious: a disease that is infectious and easily contracted and spread to others

Contamination: to be coated with or to have a disease or infective process

Continuity: being continuous, unchanged, unbroken

Control measures: ways of controlling how something happens

Cross-infection: simultaneous infection by something that originates from a source other than themselves

Debilitation: to make an existing condition or ailment worse

Decomposing: breaking down

Defence mechanisms: systems for protecting something, e.g. antibodies to attack viruses

Designated: given a purpose or use

Detergents: strong cleaning chemicals, e.g. washing up liquid

Disinfectant: liquids to kill infections

Dormant: sleeping, waiting to act

Eliminate/eliminated: to remove completely

Employees: those who are given paid work by a company or business

Expel: to eject or throw out, often done with force

Faeces: waste products expelled from the large bowel via the anus

Fission: process or division by which bacteria multiply

Host: a thing that has guests; they can be unwanted, i.e. parasites

Hypochlorite: A type of strong bleach used to kill germs

Incubation: the period of time before a germ causes symptoms

Incineration: destruction by fire

Ignition: spark that starts something off

Local: contained in one small or specific area

Medication: a general term for pills or drugs used to cure illness and disease

Micro-organisms: Microscopically small living material e.g. viruses and bacteria

Mutate: to change into something else

Non-pathogenic: harmless micro-organisms

Obliged: something that you must do

Offal: the less valuable edible bits of an animal, such as guts

Organisms: small living creatures

Pathogenic: harmful micro-organisms

Perishable: a product that will go off or go rotten quickly

Pharmacist: a person who dispenses prescribed drugs and other medicines

Premises: a building or place of work

Putrefying: making something go rotten

Reproduce: to produce members of a species by natural causes

Sluice drain: a place for rinsing things into

Sterilization: making an object free from all micro-organisms

Substitute: something that can be used instead of

Systemic: something that can affect the whole system, e.g. a disease

Toxic: something that is very poisonous

Tuberculosis: a disease of the lungs that can spread to other parts of the body and can kill if not treated. Was once known as consumption

Vaccinated: made immune from a disease

Variable: something that does not remain constant or the same

Vulnerable: to be easily affected by a disease process because you have a weakness

Becoming a parent can bring people together

Becoming a parent is probably one of the most exciting and fulfilling life events that can happen to anyone. Being a parent carries a lot of responsibility and yet the role is one that many feel least prepared for. Successful parenting is not something that comes naturally to everyone but with the right preparation being a parent can be a very enjoyable and rewarding experience.

If the correct preparation is carried out and if the mother in particular understands what is happening in her body, pregnancy can be easy. It is important for the mother to consider her diet and the amount of exercise she takes. This is to make sure her body is as healthy as possible so that she can provide nutrients for the baby and cope with the strain of pregnancy on her body. **Antenatal care** is also an essential part of the preparation process as it informs the mother and father of what to expect both during pregnancy and after the birth.

Parents need to understand how children develop and about the care children require in order to help them meet their needs. Providing the correct physical care, love and attention during the first three years of a child's life has an effect on the way the child develops in later years. It is therefore very important to 'get it right'.

Recognising the **milestones** of growth and development and patterns of development can help parents to give the support and encouragement required for their children to progress to the next stage.

Development is divided into four main areas:

- physical
- intellectual
- emotional
- social.

This is often referred to as P.I.E.S.

An understanding of the care needs of a new baby including feeding, keeping a baby clean, having the correct **layette** (clothing) and equipment, helps parents to cope when their baby is born.

A well-designed nursery for a new baby is also important. The nursery should be designed to be safe and easy to use. It is important for equipment to be placed where it is easy to reach so that a baby can be cared for efficiently. The nursery should be a room where babies can be cared for and sleep in a relaxed atmosphere and where they can feel safe and secure.

What will we learn in this unit?

Learning outcomes

You will learn to:

- Recognise the responsibilities of parenthood
- Describe the milestones in physical development from birth to three years
- Describe milestones in intellectual development from birth to three years
- Describe the milestones of emotional and social development from birth to three years
- Review the care needs of a new baby
- Design a nursery for a new baby, evaluating its suitability

How should a mother prepare for parenthood?

Before and during pregnancy a mother must make sure her body is well-prepared to cope with the pressures of pregnancy and birth.

Diet before and during pregnancy

A healthy diet containing **adequate** amounts of energy and essential **nutrients** is important both before a woman becomes pregnant (**conception**) and during pregnancy. The mother needs to prepare her body so that she will be able to provide nutrients to the **foetus.** A balanced, healthy diet is not only necessary for the unborn child but also has an effect on the child after it has been born. A baby with a low birth weight is likely to remain small.

Figure 7.1 *A healthy diet*

During pregnancy, a woman has an increased need for **folic acid** as it is removed through her kidneys at four times the normal rate. Taking a daily dose of 400mcg of folic acid is recommended for three months before trying to conceive. This can come from folic acid capsules, folic acid milk drinks available from chemists or by eating folic acid rich foods, such as green vegetables, oranges, and foods that have had folic acid added, such as some bread and breakfast cereals.

Folic acid reduces the risk of having a baby with conditions known as 'neural tube defects', such as spina bifida (a condition where parts of the backbone do not form properly, leaving the baby with a gap or split which causes damage to the baby's nervous system).

> ## Discussion point
> *What foods would you recommend a woman to eat before she conceives? Why?*

During pregnancy, a woman's nutritional needs are greater because the diet must provide enough energy and nutrients:

- to meet the mother's needs and provide extra for the growth of the breasts, **uterus** and **placenta**
- to meet the needs of the growing foetus
- for the mother to have a store of nutrients to help the growth of the foetus, and for producing milk.

Nutrients and oxygen pass to the foetus from the mother through the placenta, via the **umbilical cord**.

To achieve a balanced diet pregnant women are advised to eat:

- plenty of fruit and vegetables (ideally five servings a day), e.g. apples, oranges, bananas, peas, carrots and salad
- plenty of starchy foods, e.g. bread, pasta, rice, breakfast cereals and potatoes
- calcium, e.g. milk and milk products

- protein and iron, e.g. lean meat or alternatives to meat, such as fish (especially oily fish such as mackerel), chicken, eggs or pulses (beans and lentils). This group of foods provides iron, red meat being a very good source.

If iron intakes are low because iron-rich foods are avoided, **anaemia** can result, which is not good for pregnant women.

If dairy products are left out of the diet, it is much harder for pregnant women to get sufficient calcium that is needed for the development of bones. Almost two-thirds of the calcium needed each day comes from diary products. A pregnant woman should have 700mg per day.

The government recommended daily nutrient requirements of pregnant women are:

Nutrients	Recommended daily intake
Protein	51g
Vitamin A	700mcg
Folate (folic acid) B9	400mcg
Vitamin C	50mg
Calcium	700mg
Iron	14.8mg

Drinking alcohol during pregnancy can damage the unborn child, so pregnant women may prefer to avoid alcohol. The Department of Health advises that to minimise the risk to their unborn child, women who are trying to become pregnant or who are at any stage of pregnancy should not drink more than one or two units of alcohol once or twice a week, and should avoid heavy drinking sessions. Recently a government report suggested that having any alcohol at all can affect the development of an unborn child both while growing and after the birth.

> ## Discussion point
> *What foods and drink would you recommend a woman not to have during pregnancy? Why?*

Exercise during pregnancy

A mother copes with pregnancy better if she is fit and healthy. Being pregnant puts a strain on a woman's body and **stamina** is needed for the birth. One way to prepare is to exercise so that the mother's body systems are in a good condition. That does not mean a woman who wants to become pregnant should become an exercise fanatic!

Exercise also helps with:

- constipation
- backache
- fatigue
- varicose veins
- circulation problems
- meeting other mums-to-be.

This is because exercise stimulates body systems, strengthens muscles and is a sociable activity where the expectant mum can meet others in a similar situation.

To be effective the exercise should be:

- carried out regularly both before and during pregnancy, e.g. exercising for 20 minutes three times a week
- not too strenuous so it does not make the mother over-tired (this could have a negative effect), e.g. the mother may not be able to get enough sleep
- within reason, i.e. a mother can keep up her chosen activities for as long as she feels comfortable. At the first signs of discomfort the activity should be stopped, e.g. if she gets too breathless or is in pain.

Suggested activities include those shown in Figure 7.2 below.

Exercising in water is safe and enjoyable during all stages of pregnancy unless the mother has been advised not to do so by her GP. It is particularly good for late pregnancy backache. This is because the water supports the whole body, and the pregnant woman can be as energetic or relaxed as she wants. Many public and private pools offer aqua-natal classes, often run by trained midwives or physiotherapists. Most classes begin with a sequence of gentle warm-up exercises, followed by stretches and a swim. Swimming several lengths gives a good, safe workout.

Antenatal class

Pelvic floor exercises are very important during pregnancy and should be carried out regularly. The pelvic floor is formed of layers of muscle that

Figure 7.2 *Different types of exercise*

support the uterus, bowel and bladder. Pregnancy and childbirth put pressure on these muscles, and pregnant women may find that they leak urine when they sneeze or cough. This is called 'stress incontinence'. The pelvic muscles can be toned so they maintain their strength and it is known that by doing these regular 'invisible exercises' the pelvic muscles return to normal quicker after birth.

To carry out pelvic muscle exercises a pregnant woman should:

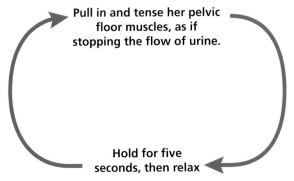

Pull in and tense her pelvic floor muscles, as if stopping the flow of urine.

Hold for five seconds, then relax

Figure 7.3 *Pelvic muscle exercises*

Ten sets of exercises (five each time) should be done each day.

These exercises can be done almost anywhere – no-one can tell they are being done!

Care needs to be taken with activities like horse riding, aerobics, scuba diving, water skiing and contact sports as these could damage the foetus or even cause a miscarriage. A pregnant mother should consult with her GP or midwife before doing on any of these sports.

Activity 1
Key skills [C] 2.3

Exercise for Sophie

Sophie wants to have a baby and has done very little exercise since she started work. She likes to curl up in a chair and watch the television when she gets home from work.

1 Suggest ways Sophie can make sure her body is fit before she conceives.

2 How should Sophie change her exercise routine when she is pregnant?

2 How could exercise benefit Sophie before, during and after pregnancy?

Clothes during pregnancy

A pregnant woman's normal clothing quickly becomes tight and uncomfortable when she is pregnant. When the stomach expands as the baby develops it is important not to wear clothes that are very tight and restrict movement.

Some women prefer not to show off their 'bump' when pregnant, others are very proud and like to 'show their bump off'. Loose clothing can discretely cover the bump so that other people are unaware of the pregnancy. Tighter, fitted clothing is more fashionable and preferred by some expectant mothers.

Whatever clothing the expectant mother wears it should be comfortable. Clothing, including underwear, must not restrict the growth, development and movement of the developing baby.

Activity 2
Key skills  2.1, [C] 2.1b

Clothes for pregnant mothers

Sophie likes to wear fashionable clothing. She wears short skirts and high heels during the day. When Sophie goes out she wears tight trousers and skimpy tops.

1 Use pictures from catalogues and magazines to create two posters: what to wear and what not to wear during pregnancy.

2 Prepare and give a short talk to a group of expectant women, including Sophie, about what to wear during pregnancy. Use your posters to help you explain to the group the advantages and disadvantages of dressing each way.

Emotions while pregnant

Being pregnant can sometimes feel like being on an emotional rollercoaster. This is due to the huge increase in hormones in the body during pregnancy, which makes most pregnant women feel like they have less control of their emotions. One minute they may feel over the moon about becoming a parent and the next they may dread the day they are due to give birth. Many worry about whether they are going to cope from day-to-day and whether they will make a good parent.

Some pregnant women burst out crying for no reason at any moment, even in front of complete strangers. Often, minor incidents may seem like the end of the world, and it is quite normal for a pregnant woman to feel low, anxious, and tearful sometimes during pregnancy.

Most pregnant women feel anxious at some point, whether it is when they go for their first **ultrasound scan** or when thinking about coping with labour pains. As the birth of their baby draws closer they may become anxious about whether the baby will be born healthy and whole.

Tests can be done during pregnancy to put a mother's mind at rest. Blood tests, blood pressure, height, weight and urine tests are straightforward and check for conditions that mothers can develop during pregnancy, for example, diabetes and pre-eclampsia. For older mothers or women who develop complications further tests can be carried out, for example **amniocentesis** to check for Down's Syndrome.

To cope with emotional changes a pregnant woman should take time to talk to her partner, midwife, friends and other mums-to-be about their fears. Often, just talking about things will make them feel much better.

Being stressed during pregnancy can cause a pregnant woman's blood pressure to rise, which is harmful for their baby. It is important for them to avoid stressful situations, slow down and relax more by reading, listening to music, taking gentle walks and exercising.

Activity 3

Emotional changes

Sophie has found it difficult to cope with the first few weeks of her pregnancy. One minute she is very happy and looking forward to the birth, the next she is bursting into tears for no reason at all.

1 Prepare and perform a role-play in pairs. One is to be the midwife, the other Sophie. During the role-play the midwife should give advice to Sophie about how to cope with her emotions at this time.

2 Explain how emotions can change during pregnancy.

Physical changes in pregnancy

During pregnancy there are many physical changes. The table below shows some of these and when they occur.

Changes during pregnancy	When the changes occur
Breasts enlarge and become uncomfortable	From 2 weeks after conception
Nipple darkens in colour	Week 4 onwards
Tiredness and irritability	Week 6 onwards
Morning sickness	Weeks 2 to 12
Need to pass urine more often	Week 8 onwards
Constipation	Week 12 onwards
Stomach bulge	Week 14 onwards
Sleepless nights	Week 22 onwards
Backache	Week 22 onwards
Swollen hands and ankles	Week 24 onwards
Heartburn and shortness of breath	Week 24 onwards
Stretchmarks may develop	Week 26 onwards

Discussion point

What can a pregnant woman do to help her cope with the physical changes in pregnancy?

Antenatal care

The care provided to a mother and her unborn baby before a birth takes place is called **antenatal care**.

0–8 weeks

Pregnant women should make an appointment with their GP as soon as they think they are pregnant. The GP refers them to a midwife or midwifery team. The midwife gives health advice relevant to early pregnancy, such as the importance of taking folic acid as well as information on early screening tests.

8–12 weeks

If a pregnant woman is unsure of her dates or has had a small bleed, the midwife is able to refer her for an ultrasound scan. If there is a need for a special scan, for example to detect Down's Syndrome, they must be referred by the midwife before the 13th week of pregnancy.

12–16 weeks

During this time a pregnant woman will be 'booked-in' with her local maternity unit so they know that she is expecting a baby. The midwife either visits the woman at home or she may need to attend a booking clinic at the local hospital or health centre. The process may take about an hour (or longer) and includes the woman giving information about her health, having blood taken and giving a urine sample. The midwife explains what is going to happen during pregnancy, discusses any worries the woman may have and gives her her own personal set of antenatal notes.

16–24 weeks

The second antenatal session with the midwife is usually at about 24 weeks, and sets the pattern for future appointments. The midwife checks blood pressure, tests urine and measures the 'bump'. They also check the baby's movement and are able to check the baby's heart rate.

24–30 weeks

A pregnant woman should have an antenatal appointment with her midwife or doctor (depending on the arrangement) once a month from 24–32 weeks, and then every two weeks after that, although this does depend on the area they live in. Usually, the total number of antenatal appointments is around six, unless there is a problem with the pregnancy. By 28 weeks the woman should have received her 'MatB1' form from her midwife, enabling her to claim maternity benefits.

30–36 weeks

Most mums-to-be start antenatal classes around this time, run by local midwives. However, they could choose to attend those run by the National Childbirth Trust or by an Active Birth Centre.

36 weeks onwards

A pregnant woman is likely to have an appointment every week from 36 weeks. At these appointments a close check is made on the size and position of the baby. If the midwife has any concerns she refers the woman for a scan or to see the obstetrician.

What is the father's role in preparing for childbirth?

Becoming a father for the first time is a fantastic experience, something that is never forgotten. Men are often worried about how their life will change and how they will fit in with their new family. There may be a fear of the unknown and a fear of failure. It is very important for them to get involved, to learn as they go along and to trust their instincts that they will do the right thing at the right time. The sooner the father gets involved, the quicker and easier they will build up their confidence and form a bond with their baby. Fathers can be very helpful during pregnancy. Just because they are not actually carrying the baby does not mean they cannot help.

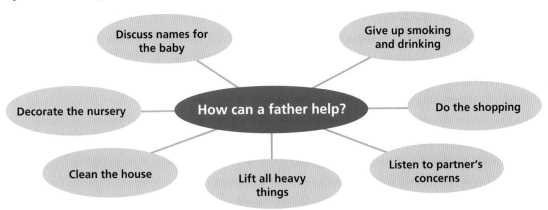

Figure 7.4 *How a father can help during a pregnancy*

Assessment activity 7.1

Key skills ICT 2.1, 2.3, C 2.3

Antenatal preparations

You have been asked to produce a guide for new parents that could be used by a local health centre, entitled: 'The Responsibilities of Parenthood'.

The information could be presented in a variety of different ways, for example, posters, displays, leaflets, flyers. Complete the following tasks and include them in your guide.

1 a Carry out research to find out what a woman should include in her diet before and during pregnancy. You could do this by talking to a midwife, health visitor or by visiting an antenatal clinic.

  b Prepare materials that could be displayed in the health centre to offer guidance to women about their diet before and during pregnancy. You should include as much detail as possible.

2 a Research different types of exercise which can help women during pregnancy.

  b Prepare posters that could be displayed in the health centre to encourage women to carry out the right types of exercise during pregnancy. You must describe why exercise is important.

3 a Visit the maternity clothing department of a local store. Find out what clothing pregnant women like to wear.

  b Produce materials that could give guidance to pregnant women about the clothing they should wear during pregnancy. Explain why it is important for clothing not to be too tight.

4 a Prepare information for pregnant women to explain how their emotions could be affected by pregnancy.

  b Give examples of how a woman could cope with her emotional changes.

5 a Produce **three** case studies to show how women can experience different changes during pregnancy.

  b Produce materials that could be displayed to help women cope with changes experienced during pregnancy.

6 a Visit an antenatal clinic or interview a midwife (with your tutor's permission) to find out the antenatal care available to pregnant women in your area.

  b Design and make a leaflet that could be given to pregnant mothers in your area to explain what antenatal care is available and why it is important.

7 a Produce **three** case studies to show different ways fathers could provide support to their pregnant partner.

  b Use the case studies to provide guidance materials to explain the father's role during pregnancy.

Every child is individual and develops at its own pace. Some children reach milestones more quickly than others do. This can be for a variety of different reasons including:

- the **genes** the child has inherited from its parents

- the amount of time, encouragement and interest given by the parents

- whether the child has any illnesses.

When a child is 'slow' in one area of development it is often quicker or 'forward' in another. There is usually no need for parents to get concerned because their child has not reached a milestone by the suggested 'normal age'.

What are the key features of physical development?

There are two strands to physical development:

- *growth*, which covers the increase in size, height and weight

- *development*, which covers how a child gains skills and is able to control the actions their body makes.

Birth to one year
Reflexes

When babies are first born they are able to carry out several movements called **reflexes**. These reflexes are made automatically and babies do not have any control over them. Reflexes help babies to live until they gain control of their body and can make movements for themselves. The table below describes basic reflexes.

Reflex	Description
Swallowing and sucking	Babies automatically suck when a finger is placed in their mouth. This helps them to feed as they suck on the breast or teat when it is put in their mouth. This reflex disappears when they are six months old
Rooting	When babies' faces are stroked gently with a finger, they turn their head towards the finger. This looks like the baby is trying to find a nipple or teat and is expecting a feed. This reflex also disappears after six weeks
Grasping	Babies curl their fingers around an object placed in their hand. This may seem like they are trying to hold onto the object. This reflex disappears after three months
Walking	When babies are held in a standing position with the bottom of the feet resting on a hard surface they make stepping movements as if trying to stand up straight. If the shins are placed against the edge of a table the baby seems to 'step up' as if trying to climb on the table. This reflex disappears after six months
Startle	If babies are exposed to loud noises or bright lights they close their hands to make fists and bend the elbows to bring the hands close to the shoulders. Sometimes they may cry as well
Falling	When moved suddenly babies feel like they are being dropped. This makes them open their hands and throw their arms backwards. They then bring their arms inwards as if they are trying to catch a ball
Blinking	When babies are first born they blink when a light is shone directly into their eyes

A baby's reflexes are checked when they are born. If a baby does not have the normal reflexes this can be a sign that there is a problem.

Head control

As the muscles in the neck develop, babies gain control of their head movements.

Newborn babies have no control of the head because the muscles are very weak. If they are lifted into a sitting position the head falls backwards. It is very important to always support a baby's head so that it is protected from injury.

At *three months* old babies begin to have control of the head. The head wobbles slightly if babies are held in an upright position. If babies are pulled upwards into a sitting position the head will still drop back, but this is much less.

By the time babies are *six months* old they have complete control of the head. The head does not fall back when babies are pulled into a sitting position. Once in the sitting position babies can hold the head up and have a good look around.

Sitting up

Sitting up requires a baby to have control of the muscles in the neck and back. The ability to sit unaided is developed during the first year.

Age	Development of sitting
Newborn	When newborn babies are held in the sitting position they roll forwards. The back bends and the head falls forward
3 months	Babies need to be supported in the sitting position. The back is held much straighter and although the head is wobbly babies keep the position for a short time
6 months	Babies can sit up straight with the support of a chair or pram. It is possible for babies to sit unaided for a short time with their hands on the floor between their legs to give support. The muscles are still weak and this position cannot be held for long
9 months	Babies are now able to sit without support and can pull up into a sitting position unaided
1 year	Babies can now sit unsupported for a long time. They can turn to the side and stretch out to pick objects up without falling over

Lying on the stomach (prone position)

When lying on their stomach babies develop strength in their arms and legs. It is from this position that babies learn to crawl.

When *newborn* babies are laid on the stomach the head turns to one side and the legs curl under the stomach, similar to the position babies adopt in when in the womb. At around *one month* babies start to hold the head up and the legs start to straighten. At *three months* babies lie with the legs straight and push up on the arms to lift the head and shoulders up. The arms gain strength and are straight at *five months* so that babies can lift both head and chest off the floor. Babies can also roll over from front to back. By *six months* old babies can roll back onto the front again. At *nine months* babies start to move about the floor, often by shuffling on the bottom in a sitting position, by pulling with the arms on the front or by rolling. A *one year* old is usually crawling quickly on hands and knees or even hands and feet. Sometimes children miss out the crawling stage and walk straight away.

Freedom!

Walking

The legs of newborn babies are not strong enough to carry the weight of the body, and the muscles in the legs, hips and thighs are too weak to be supportive. Babies also have to be able to co-ordinate the muscles and the movement of the legs to be able to balance.

Newborn babies appear to walk during the first few weeks but this is simply a reflex action that they have no control over. At *three months* old babies have developed some strength and can support a little of their weight with support. The knees and hips quickly give way and babies tend to crumple. Babies enjoy being bounced up and down at *six months* old and can support their body weight. From *nine months* onwards babies start to walk. Often this is sideways at first, holding onto furniture or with both hands held. Babies can pull themselves up into a standing position using furniture or trousers for support! By the time babies reach *one year* old they can

walk holding one hand for support. They usually keep their feet wide apart to give a wider area of support and they fall over a lot.

One to three years

Between the ages of one and three years children begin to develop control over their movements. They learn to move when they want to and become more independent. The perfection of hand and eye co-ordination helps children to play with a wider range of toys.

Activity 4

Key skills ICT 2.3

Norms of growth

Parents are often confused about when a baby should reach the stages of development.

1 Design a poster which parents could use for easy reference to show the stages of development for a baby up to the age of one year.

Figure 7.5 *The different stages of walking*

Walking

Usually by the time babies are *fifteen months* old walking becomes more steady and falling over quickly becomes a thing of the past. Some children walk much earlier than this and others walk later. They often hold their hands in the air to help them to balance and find stopping and turning corners difficult. Looking down can result in a fall. Crawling up stairs is fun but standing up and leaning backwards has painful results. At *eighteen months* children can walk up stairs holding on the rail tightly to balance. They can climb the stairs putting two feet on each stair.

At *two years* old children walk up and down stairs keeping two feet on each stair. They can kick a ball without falling over and have developed the balance required to stand on tiptoe and jump. Children often land with one foot at a time. By the time children reach *three years* old they are able to walk up stairs in an adult manner with one foot on each stair. Coming down is still a problem and both feet are needed to balance on each stair. Jumping off the bottom stair is great fun! Children may be able to balance on one leg and start to hop around.

Learning to walk is fun

What are the milestones of physical development?

Gross motor skills

Gross motor skills involve the use of muscles to control the body and larger muscles. Children learn to control the muscles used for balance and large movements, for example rolling over, sitting, crawling and walking, during their first year. Control is gained first at the head and moves down the body to the shoulders, arms and then the legs.

Age	Gross motor skills developed
Newborn	• has stepping reflex but loses this after six weeks • head has to be supported when lifted • rolls in a ball when sat up • lies on tummy with head on one side and knees drawn up underneath
3 months	• can lift head when lying on front • can turn head from side to side when lying on front • pushes up on arms and lifts shoulders off the floor • kicks legs strongly • can hold larger objects, e.g. rattle
6 months	• lifts head and chest above the floor • supports upper body on straight arms • can sit for long periods supported by a chair, pram or cushions • can sit unsupported for short periods of time but falls over easily • able to roll from front to back • can sometimes roll from back to front • starts trying to crawl
9 months	• crawls backwards first and then forwards • pulls into standing position using furniture to hold on to • walks sideways around furniture • can sit unsupported for longer periods of time • some start to crawl upstairs
1 year	• crawls very quickly • walks holding one hand or pushes along toys • some may be walking unsupported • can sit unsupported for long periods of time • crawls upstairs forwards • crawls downstairs backwards • can sit down from standing without falling over
15 months	• able to walk without support but swings arms to keep balance • can crawl downstairs on bottom, feet first • throws a ball • able to kneel without support • can stand without holding onto anything
18 months	• can walk with confidence • can pick things up from the floor without falling over • can sit on 'haunches' (squat) without falling over • can walk up and down stairs with support • runs but is unsteady • can use push along toys confidently • pulls toys along
2 years	• can walk up and down stairs without support two feet to a step • climbing on furniture is fun • able to kick a ball • runs without falling over
3 years	• can run and walk without problems • can balance on tiptoes • can throw a ball • can catch a large ball with arms straight • can walk upstairs properly one foot to each stair • comes down stairs with two feet on each stair • can hop • can pedal a tricycle • able to jump with two feet together

Age	Fine motor skills developed
Newborn	• has a grasp reflex which disappears after a few weeks • hands are kept closed in a fist most of the time
3 months	• hands are held open • looks at hands • plays with fingers • holds objects for a short time that are placed in the hand then drops them
6 months	• able to grasp an object without it being placed in the hand • grasps toys with whole hand (**palmar grasp**) • passes objects from hand to hand • turns objects over • puts objects into the mouth • splashes water in the bath • plays with toes when lying on back
9 months	• uses fingers and thumb to grasp an object (inferior/primitive pincer) • deliberately drops things on the floor • looks for fallen objects • picks objects up with index finger and thumb (**pincer grasp**) with difficulty
1 year	• uses pincer grasp easily to pick up small objects • points to objects wanted using index finger • starts to show a preference for using one hand • able to place small objects into a container • throws things on purpose • able to bang bricks together
15 months	• claps hands • can place one block on top of another • drinks from a cup using two hands to hold it • grasps crayons with whole hand and makes marks on paper • holds a spoon but often misses mouth • turns spoon upside down before it reaches mouth
18 months	• can turn the pages of a book several at a time • able to build a tower of three blocks • can put large beads on a string • uses pincer grasp with confidence • begins to hold pencils and crayons properly • can take shoes off but not put them on
2 years	• can turn pages of a book one at a time • can put shoes on • able to draw simple pictures • can turn door handles/knobs • able to build a tower of six bricks • can undo a zip • holds a pencil properly and can draw circles, lines and dots
3 years	• holds small crayons properly • can draw a face • eats with a spoon without dropping food • able to build a tower of ten bricks • able to use toy scissors • able to dress but needs help with buttons • tries to undress but finds it difficult

Fine motor skills

Fine motor skills involve co-ordination of the hand and eye to control movement of the hands and fingers. Children learn to use the smaller muscles to pick objects up and drop them. As control is gained precise movements allow children to point, draw, do up shoelaces and write. These skills are often clumsy at first and gradually develop to become more accurate.

> **Discussion point**
>
> *Is it really necessary for a child to crawl before they can walk? Why?*

What is the pattern of physical development?

Children usually develop gross and fine motor skills in a particular order or **sequence**. This follows the way their bodies gain control of their muscles. It is like climbing a ladder – they usually climb one rung at a time!

Sometimes children grow at the same rate as other children but their control and development does not follow the expected development pattern. This is usually because they have a disability that affects their progress.

> **Discussion point**
>
> *Do you think children without brothers or sisters develop more quickly or slowly than children with brothers or sisters? Why?*

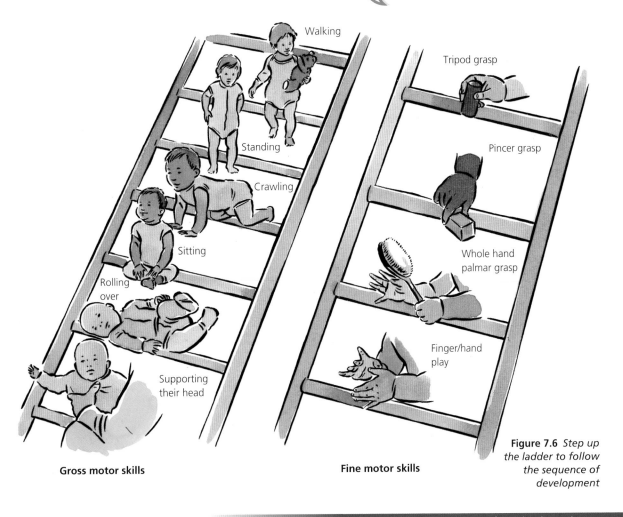

Gross motor skills

Walking
Standing
Crawling
Sitting
Rolling over
Supporting their head

Fine motor skills

Tripod grasp
Pincer grasp
Whole hand palmar grasp
Finger/hand play

Figure 7.6 *Step up the ladder to follow the sequence of development*

Activity 4

Children developing

Arrange to visit a nursery or playgroup (with your tutor's permission) or organise a children's tea party.

1 Observe children playing. Record their different stages of development. Remember to include physical, intellectual, emotional and social observations of play (P.I.E.S.), but place most emphasis on physical.

2 Discuss your observations with other members of your group.

3 Give reasons for the differences in development.

Assessment activity 7.2

Physical milestones of development

You have been asked by the local antenatal clinic to produce materials that could be put on display or be part of a Resource Pack to inform parents of the physical milestones of development.

Complete the following tasks and include them in your display.

1 Make a poster or use another method (e.g. Resource Pack) that includes detailed information of the milestones of physical development (gross motor skills and fine motor skills) at:

- three months
- six months
- nine months
- one year
- two years
- three years.

Your material must be factually correct, informative and eye-catching. You could get your information from books, childcare workers etc.

2 a Choose a child who **must** be at least three years old.

Make a questionnaire to find out when the child reached milestones of physical development. You must find out about:

- gross motor skills
- fine motor skills.

Use the questionnaire to help you find out the information you need when talking to the parent.

b Design and use a chart to record the information.

3 a Compare the development of your chosen child with the 'milestone norms' of physical development. Describe how the child followed the pattern of development. Ask yourself:

- Was the child quicker or slower to reach the milestones?
- Did the child follow the normal sequence of development?

b Explain why there may have been differences.

Intellectual development refers to the development of the mind. A child's mind is very active right from birth. As children learn to think, reason and explain, their intellectual development is progressing.

Discussion point

What activities could help children to learn?

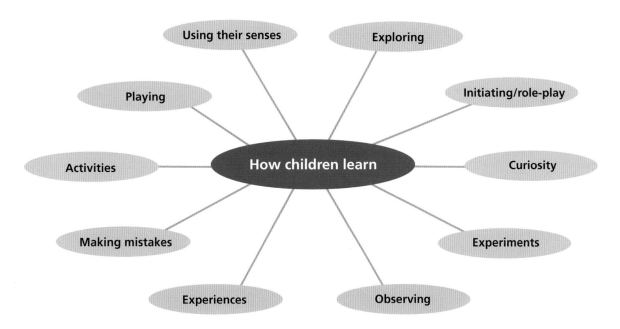

Figure 7.7 *Children learn in different ways*

What are the key features of intellectual development?

Intellectual development can be divided into two main strands:

- cognitive skills (understanding)
- language skills (communication).

The development of these is very closely linked to the other aspects of development – physical, social and emotional.

Birth to one year

During their first year babies develop an understanding of their surroundings, their carers and communicate their needs through crying. They are totally dependent on their carers and can do nothing for themselves. The table on page 200 describes this development.

Age	Key features of intellectual development
Newborn	• aware of feeling of hunger and responds by crying • recognises mother's or main carer's voice • explores using senses and movement • copies adults who open their mouth or stick their tongue out • responds to high-pitched tones by moving limbs • responds to brightly coloured or shiny objects
3 months	• uses mouth and touch to explore • looks around to explore surroundings • smiles in response to speech • shows an interest in playthings, e.g. mobiles, rattles, chime balls • likes to explore different textures, e.g. on an activity mat or play gym • laughs and vocalises with meaning
6 months	• makes noises to voice displeasure or satisfaction • understands objects and knows what objects can do, e.g. toys that make a noise • learns by using senses like smell, taste, touch, sight, and hearing • repeats actions and copies sounds, e.g. animal noises. • puts things in the mouth to explore
9 months	• recognises and looks for familiar voices and sounds • understands the meaning of 'no' • focuses eyes on small objects and reaches for them • recognises familiar pictures • looks for fallen toys • explores objects by touching, shaking, banging • babbles expressively as if talking
1 year	• finds objects which have been seen and then hidden away • plays 'peek-a-boo' • enjoys looking at picture books • uses trial and error to learn about objects • watches and copies actions of others, e.g. 'clap hands' • scribbles to and fro

One to three years

Children progress quickly in their intellectual development between the ages of one and three years. They gain an understanding of their surroundings and the foundations for future learning are made. The table on page 201 describes this development.

What is the pattern of intellectual development?

The pattern of intellectual development usually follows the same sequence. It is necessary for children to pass through one stage before progressing on to the next. Intellectual development relies on the development of physical skills. Before babies are mobile only the immediate surroundings can be explored. As soon as the baby can crawl this opens up a whole new world, and when they can walk their experiences expand and so does their understanding.

Intellectual development can be affected by inherited patterns of development. If there is a family history of 'late-development', this may be repeated. There may also be inherited learning difficulties, which could affect the sequence of intellectual development.

How does communication develop from birth to three years?

How children learn to talk

The way children learn to speak depends on the opportunities they have to practise and use

Age	Key features of intellectual development
18 months	• can identify pictures of named objects, e.g. cup, ball, dog • looks for objects that are out of sight • can point to parts of the body • starts to show a preference for using one hand • can take things out of a container one by one • able to scribble on paper • refers to themselves by name
2 years	• learns by trial and error • able to put together a 3-piece puzzle • able to match different textures • starts to use everyday objects for pretend play, e.g. a cardboard box • able to stack beakers in order • scribbles in circles, may make vertical lines and V-shapes • knows their full name • interested in the names of people and objects
3 years	• listens attentively to short stories and books • enjoys repeating simple rhymes/stories • understands concepts of time; 'now, soon, and later' • asks who, what, where and why questions • able to put together a 6-piece puzzle • can sort objects into simple categories • understands the concepts of 'one' and 'lots' • can count up to ten • can identify primary colours; red, blue and yellow • able to distinguish, match and name colours • knows his/her age • knows and can name correctly three different shapes, e.g. circle, square, triangle • can copy a circle • drawings of people may have a head and one or two features

language. Children learn to speak by watching and copying those around them. Babies quickly learn that smiles are nicer to experience than frowns, and imitate them.

Babies love to communicate with other people, and from a very early age use various ways of getting their message across:

• using their *eyes* to make contact with their carers
• using varying *tones*, e.g. crying, screaming and gurgling
• using *facial expressions* to show they are happy, unhappy, content
• using *gestures*, e.g. pointing, throwing, pushing, pulling to inform others of their wishes.

Frustration is common in babies before they begin to talk as they find it hard to get their message across to their carers. Communication makes life much easier for a child.

To be able to talk takes a lot of practice in order to get the sounds right and to express them in a way which has meaning. Certain activities can help with the development of speech:

• people talking to them
• listening to voices
• practicing sounds
• copying sounds
• learning what different sounds mean.

> ### Discussion point
> *How can parents and carers help babies develop their speech?*

Pattern of the development of speech

Individual children learn to talk at different speeds. The differences are much more noticeable than in any other area of development. Some children are well ahead of the average ages for developing speech, others may be a long way behind. Girls usually talk at an earlier age than boys do.

The development of speech can be divided into two distinct stages: **pre-linguistic** and **linguistic**. The pre-linguistic stage occurs between birth and 12 months. At this time babies cry, smile, use facial expressions and cry to gain attention. The linguistic phase is when speech develops and words are used to label objects, for example, dog, cup or ball. These progress on to simple and then onto more complex sentences. The following table shows the pattern of development of speech.

How can communication be encouraged?

Children need a lot of encouragement to help them learn to communicate effectively. This encouragement can be given in a variety of different ways – all involve spending time with the child.

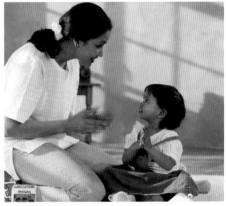

Talking helps communication to develop

Age	Speech development
Newborn	Babies cry to communicate. At one month small sounds are made in the throat called **guttural** sounds. By 5 or 6 weeks of age babies start to coo and gurgle when someone is speaking to them. At around 8 weeks babies move eyes and head towards a sound
3 months	Babies raise the head in response to sounds. They learn to control the muscles in the lips, tongue and voice box (larynx) and can make a wider range of sounds. Gurgling and babbling occur more often and there seems to be a two-way 'conversation' with other people
6 months	Cooing may stop. The variety of sounds babies can make increases. The noises made can seem to represent words, 'goo', 'adah' (often thought to be the first use of 'dada'), 'der', and 'ka'. Babies laugh, chuckle and squeal when playing, and scream when annoyed
9 months	Babies begin to copy the sounds made to them by adults. They can repeat the same word several times, 'dad-dad', 'mum-mum' and 'bab-bab' being favourites. These are not usually spoken with meaning, more often because babies are getting used to making sounds. They imitate sounds, e.g. blowing raspberries
1 year	Words are spoken with understanding and sometimes in response to instructions, for example babies might respond to 'give it to daddy' with 'dad-dad'. Babbling sounds more like speech. Babies imitate simple words. They begin to point, which shows understanding of words, e.g. when asked 'where is the ball?', they point to the ball
2 years	New words are learnt very quickly. Toddlers can use 50 or more words and can put together two or three words to make simple sentences, e.g. 'me want ball'. They start to use pronouns, e.g. 'me', 'I', 'you'. At this time, questions are asked constantly
3 years	Vocabulary is large. A simple conversation can be held with longer sentences being used. Children often talk non-stop. They use language to describe experiences and express their feelings. Sometimes they get the ending of words wrong, e.g. 'drawed', 'sleeps'. They ask inquisitive questions, e.g. 'Why?', 'Where?', 'What?', 'How?'

Effects of talking with others

A child's speech develops by imitating other people, so it is essential for other people to talk to them. As soon as babies are born others instinctively talk to them. At this early stage it does not matter that they do not understand what is said, what is important is that someone is talking to them. Often people use a high-pitched tone and talk nonsense. Babies recognize this as communication and respond by cooing and babbling. Even though words are not actually spoken there seems to be a two-way 'conversation' held.

Babies listen carefully when being spoken to. As they get older sounds are learnt and eventually the ability to copy words develops. As responses are made to the sounds, children develop their skills further. Children copy what they hear. If they hear English, they speak English, if they hear a different language, they speak that language, if they hear swear words, they learn those as well. If children are not spoken to, they do not learn to speak very well.

Children learn the art of conversation through talking to adults and other children. They ask questions and from the responses given their language skills and range of words develops.

Role of books

Reading books to children helps to develop their vocabulary. It is important to start by looking at pictures and telling a child what the picture is, then progressing on to telling stories and asking questions. Children can have great fun using books to help with their communication.

Visits

Children who have a range of experiences develop language and communication skills at the same time. Going on visits helps children to learn the vocabulary that matches where they go. Children enjoy visits to the seaside, farms, the country, shops, the zoo etc. Wherever they visit it is important to talk to them about their experiences, tell them about the things they can see and get them to ask questions.

Figure 7.8 *Visits help children to learn about the world around them*

Emotional barriers

Children may have difficulty speaking because they are very shy. Sometimes parents or careers place pressure on children by correcting them constantly and never allowing them to make mistakes. If children are afraid of making mistakes, they may not want to speak because they do not want to get it wrong.

Children who are not encouraged to speak or given praise by their parents do not experience the pleasure of success and could give up trying to talk.

Interacting with others

Children need to interact with others to practice their communication skills. They can interact with others in various ways:

- visiting family
- playing with friends
- parent and toddler groups
- going to a playgroup or nursery.

Interacting with other people helps children to gain confidence in their ability to communicate. This confidence encourages further development of their skills. They could be answering questions, asking for help or doing a variety of activities. Children also learn how to speak in appropriate ways to different people in different situations by interacting with them.

Cultural barriers

Children who are brought up in a family where their preferred language is different to that of the country in which they live can experience communication difficulties. They may go to a nursery or playgroup and not be able to communicate with their carers because they do not understand what is being said. Children who have to learn two different languages may get confused.

Children may develop strong accents depending on where they live, or mix with others who have a different accent to their own. Communication problems can be caused because people do not understand them or they could use local phrases which have no meaning to others.

The cultural background of children can affect their ability to communicate. Children who have different beliefs and experiences use language which reflects this.

What are the barriers to communication?

Physical barriers

Children who are deaf may find speaking difficult because they cannot hear other people speak, and so they are not able to mimic the sounds.

Children who have a cleft palate cannot press their tongue against the roof of the mouth to make sounds needed to speak clearly. Damaged vocal cords may mean that a child cannot make the various sounds necessary to communicate clearly.

Children who stammer or stutter a lot can become self-conscious if people make a fuss and this can make the problem worse.

Children with damage to the part of the brain that controls language can find communication difficult.

Activity 5
Key skills (C) 2.1a

Encouraging communication

1 Work in pairs. Each pair should take a different barrier to communication. Produce a role-play of a child being given support to overcome communication barriers.

2 Explain why it is important for children to be given positive encouragement to communicate.

Assessment activity 7.3

Intellectual milestones of development

You have been asked by the local antenatal clinic to produce materials that could be added to your display or put into a Resource Pack to inform parents of the milestones of development by including intellectual development.

Complete the following tasks and include them in your display or Resource Pack.

1 Make a poster or handout that would explain to parents the milestones of intellectual development at:

- three months
- six months
- nine months
- one year
- two years
- three years.

Your poster or handout must be factually correct, informative and eye-catching. You could get your information from books, childcare workers etc.

2 a You need to find out more information about the development of your chosen child who must be at least three years old.

Make a questionnaire to find out when the child reached milestones of intellectual development. You must find out about:

- the pattern of the development of speech
- how the child was encouraged to communicate
- any barriers to communication the child had including, physical, emotional and cultural. Use the questionnaire to help you find out the information you need when talking to the parent.

b Design and use a chart to record the information you found out.

3 a Compare the development of your chosen child with the 'milestone norms' of intellectual development.

b Explain why the development of your child may be different to the 'milestone norms'.

Include information about:

- ways the child was encouraged to talk
- barriers to communication experienced.

7.4 Describe the milestones of emotional and social development from birth to three years

Emotional development is all about the way people feel about themselves, other people and the things they do. Children have feelings of fear, excitement, affection, pride, jealousy, sadness and contentment. They show these and many more depending on their experiences. It is important that children develop the ability to recognise and control their feelings through their emotional development.

Everyone likes to feel they belong and get on well with the people around them. The ability to mix with others is referred to as 'socialising'. If children lack the skills and attitudes necessary to socialise with others in their community they are likely to become very lonely. Children are happier and healthier if they get on with the people around them.

What are the key features of emotional and social development?

Birth to one year

During their first year babies quickly develop an emotional bond with their parents and carers. Their personality begins to emerge and they start to socialise with those close to them. The table on the right describes this development.

Age	Key features of emotional and social development
Newborn	• enjoys feeding and having cuddles • likes to feel close to mother • imitates facial expressions • gazes into parent's or primary carer's eyes • moves their whole body to express enjoyment • shows signs of inborn temperament (excitable or placid) • smiles at parents • enjoys being talked to
3 months	• smiles and coos to express enjoyment • likes to be cuddled • recognises familiar people • smiles at strangers • shows enjoyment at different activities, e.g. bath time
6 months	• enjoys playtime • laughs when enjoying activities • wary of strangers • gets upset when mother leaves • recognises other people's emotions, cries and laughs when others do • will pass toys to others • able to feed self with fingers
9 months	• prefers to be near a familiar adult • can distinguish between family and strangers • expresses fear of strangers by crying • content with own company • enjoys songs and action rhymes • comfort objects, like a blanket or teddy, become important • enjoys being noisy • expresses likes and dislikes at mealtimes • dislikes going to bed • can drink from a cup with help
1 year	• shows affection for family • likes to be with people they know • plays alone • able to wave goodbye • shy towards strangers • plays games with others, e.g. pat-a-cake • often depends on comfort objects • may have mood swings – happy one minute, upset the next • enjoys social side of meal times • learning to feed self • may help with dressing

One to three years

When children reach three years old they have become very sociable individuals with strong self-identities. They are able to express their feelings and become more confident. The following table describes this development.

Age	Key features of emotional and social development
18 months	• happy to play on their own, but like to be near a familiar adult • shy of strangers • wants to be independent • can take clothes off and try to dress self • can use a cup and spoon reasonably well • shows emotions clearly, e.g. fear, anger, joy, happiness • temper tantrums start • may start to be toilet trained • senses others concerns for them, e.g. when walking or climbing • may get frustrated easily • enjoys repetitive stories and rhymes • begins to use words to express self
2 years	• able to express their feelings • keen to try out new activities • can be very clingy and dependent on carers • can be confident and independent • gets frustrated easily if cannot express self • temper tantrums are common • able to dress themselves • able to feed themselves without spilling much • can go to the toilet on their own, may need help to pull pants up • likes to help with chores • likes to have their own way • strong sense of self-identity
3 years	• begins to show interest in making friends with other children • plays with others children • understands gender and age • can show concern for others • gaining confidence • likes to be independent and do things for self • shows feelings for younger bothers/sisters • able to use the toilet alone • happy to share toys and take turns • fears develop, e.g. of the dark • able to pretend and imagine • enjoys pleasing adults and helping out • can use a fork and spoon to feed self

What are the milestones of emotional and social development?

Inborn temperament

The genes inherited by children from their parents often control their inborn temperaments. The way children control and demonstrate their emotions is influenced by their temperaments. It is temperament that controls whether a child is placid and quiet or excitable, shy or has a lot of self-confidence, worries a lot or has no worries at all.

Environmental influences

The surroundings children grow up in can have a big impact on their emotional development. The way children live at home and the behaviour they see affects their emotional development. If children have a calm atmosphere at home they are likely to be calm and have control of their emotions because they learn from their experiences. If children live with constant arguments and disruption they are likely to have difficulty controlling their own emotions because they have not been taught how to do so.

Bonds of affection

When children develop strong feelings for the people who care for them they form bonds of attachment. This is often referred to as **bonding**.

Shyness

Children have different levels of shyness. Newborn babies do not understand who different people are. Up to the age of six months children are usually friendly towards strangers. By the time they are a year old, they often show definite signs of shyness, hiding behind their mother or covering their eyes with an arm. They think that if they cannot see the person then the person cannot see them. Older children may not talk to people they do not know and can become shy and withdrawn. Shyness usually disappears as children get older and mix with more people.

Emotional reaction to stress

Stress is hard for anyone to deal with but even more so for children. A range of events can trigger stress. These include:

- starting playgroup, nursery or school
- the arrival of a new baby
- being apart from parents
- parents getting divorced
- death of a relative or even a pet
- moving to a new house
- physical or emotional abuse.

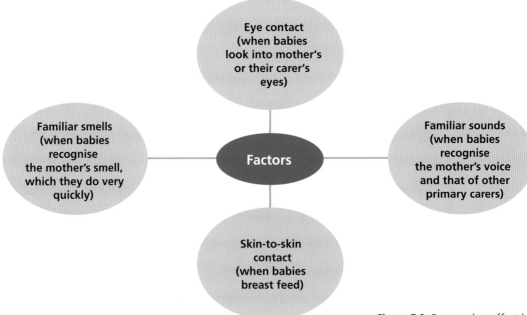

Figure 7.9 *Factors that affect bonding*

A child's emotional development may not be advanced enough to cope with the feelings these events may give them. Their level of understanding is not high enough to be able to control their feelings.

Discussion point

Why is it important for children to express their feelings?

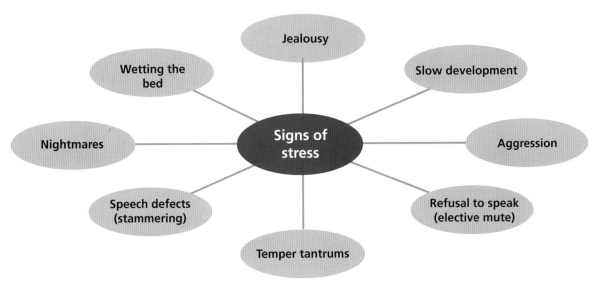

Figure 7.10 *Signs of stress in children*

Parents can help children to cope with stressful situations by talking to them and allowing them to express their feelings. It is important for stress to be dealt with quickly to prevent the effects lasting longer than necessary and becoming an even greater problem.

Activities which help children to cope with stress include:

- playing with playdough
- sand play
- hammer and pegs
- drums and percussion instruments
- books and stories
- singing
- drawing and painting
- role-play/pretend play.

Activities like these help children to express their feelings, especially when they are not able to talk about them.

Security and insecurity

Children feel secure if they are loved and have someone who cares for them. This is because they feel safe, happy and wanted. Feeling this way helps children to progress in their development.

If children feel unloved and unwanted and are left alone for long periods of time they feel insecure. This is because they do not have the comfort of knowing that they are cared for and they do not feel safe. Children who are insecure may become withdrawn or behave badly to get the attention they want. Their behaviour problems and lack of attention have an impact on their development.

Fears and nightmares

All children experience fears at some time in their lives. Young babies cry if there is a loud noise. At nine months old babies develop a fear of strangers. From the age of two years other fears may develop, e.g. a fear of dogs, the dark, heights and almost anything they do not understand. Fears are linked to the fact that children's imaginations are developing and they get carried away. Adults can make children afraid of things by making threats to them or talking about scary things like ghosts and fires.

Figure 7.11 *Children have nightmares linked to their fears*

Some children have regular nightmares, others rarely have them. Nightmares can develop from a child's fears, for example a child who is afraid of dogs could have nightmares about being chased by a dog. To young children a nightmare is real, they may cry out in fear and can even be woken up. When children have nightmares, an adult should comfort and reassure them.

> ### Discussion point
>
> *Discuss nightmares and fears you may have had as a child. Why do you think you had them? How did you get over them?*

What is the pattern of social development?

Babies are born with the need to have company and are very sociable. Babies who are lonely cry for attention and can usually be consoled by being cuddled by their carer. A baby's social development follows a particular pattern.

1 Interaction with their main carer – making eye contact, smiling and babbling.
2 Knowing that they are part of a family – recognising the difference between people they are familiar with and strangers.
3 Mixing with other people in a group and co-operating – following instructions, copying actions, playing with other children and sharing.

At first, children's social skills are developed with their parents or main carers. These skills then progress to enable the children to develop the social skills required to interact with other people.

How can self-esteem be encouraged?

Self-esteem is the way a person thinks of and values themselves. Self-esteem helps children to have confidence in their ability to cope with any situation, and gain independence. Key ways for parents and carers to encourage children's self-esteem are summarised in the table on page 211.

Ways of encouraging self-esteem	Effect on children's self esteem
Praise	Children who are praised when they do something well and when they try, feel good about themselves. This encourages them to do well because being praised raises their self-esteem
Learning new skills	Learning how to do things for themselves and having the skills to be independent raises children's self-esteem. Children feel pleased when they learn new skills. This gives them a high 'feel-good factor'
Choices	When children are given choices they are able to make decisions for themselves. This makes them feel important and raises self-esteem. The choices could be about the clothes they wear or the toys they play with
Expression of feelings	Children who are allowed to talk about the way they feel are given a sense of importance. The value of giving their opinions is seen in their high level of self esteem. Children feel special and loved
Independence	As soon as children can do things for themselves they feel that they have more control over their own lives. This independence raises their self-esteem because they no longer have to depend on others. Children who are allowed to try things for themselves even if they fail have high self-esteem

What factors inhibit the development of self-esteem?

Poor relationships

Children who feel unwanted or not liked by their parents or carers do not feel good about themselves. If children find it hard to make friends and feel left out they develop low self-esteem. Children may believe there is something wrong with them and this reduces their self-confidence.

Discipline

Being over-strict with children and correcting everything they do has a negative impact on their self-esteem. They quickly feel that they cannot get anything right and may even give up trying. Children could begin to 'put themselves down' and develop a dislike of themselves.

Physical appearance

Children whose physical appearance is different can have low self-esteem. This could be because:

- they have a physical disability, e.g. partially sighted or a wheelchair user
- of their race
- of the clothes they wear.

Lack of pride

Children who are constantly criticised feel that they cannot do anything right. This lowers their sense of pride and has a negative effect on their self-esteem. Children should be encouraged to feel proud of their achievements no matter how small they are.

Activity 6

Development of self-esteem

A child's self-esteem can be affected by a variety of different actions.

1 In pairs discuss the differences between actions which inhibit and those which encourage self-esteem.

2 Write a guideline for parents entitled 'How to support your child's development of self-esteem'.

What is the role of play on development?

Play gives pleasure and makes a very important contribution to the social and emotional development of children. Children who enjoy

Solitary play allows children to explore and try things out

exploring and trying things out. They are happy to do this on their own as social skills have not yet been developed.

Parallel play

Children like to play alongside others from the age of two years old. They are often parallel to others and there is little, if any, interaction between them. Children know that others are playing close to them but are not able to co-operate as they can only think of themselves.

Looking on play

Looking on play usually happens when children are around three years old. They watch carefully what other children do and then try to copy them. Observing other children can give them the confidence to try and do the same activity for themselves.

Joining in play

Children join in games organised by adults but do not take the responsibility for themselves. Through joining in play children learn how play can be more interesting when others are involved as well. They begin to develop social skills of interaction and like to join in with their 'friends' and play the same games. They are not yet able to co-operate fully.

playing are likely to be happy and contented because they feel a sense of achievement and pride. Play also helps children to learn about the way others behave and how to mix and share responsibilities.

Solitary play

Children play on their own between zero and two years. They are not interested in interacting with others because they are only able to think of themselves. Children at this stage of play enjoy

Figure 7.12 *Play is a child's work*

Co-operative play

Children play together happily, taking turns and sharing, from three years onwards. They co-operate with each other and take on different roles. Sharing may only last for short periods of time and there are often arguments as children of this age like to take control. Co-operative play helps children to learn the importance of being honest, and they quickly learn that cheating and anti-social behaviour like kicking is not tolerated and leads to them being excluded.

Playing co-operatively helps develop a range of skills

Assessment activity 7.4

Key skills ICT 2.1, 2.3, C 2.3

Emotional and social milestones of development

The local antenatal clinic is very pleased with the work you have completed so far and want you to produce materials that could be added to your display or Resource Pack to inform parents of the milestones of development by including emotional and social development.

Complete the following tasks and include them in your display.

1 Make posters or handouts that could be added to your display or Resource Pack to explain to parents the milestones of emotional and social development at:

- three months
- six months
- nine months
- one year
- two years
- three years.

Your material must be factually correct, informative and eye-catching. You could get your information from books, childcare workers etc.

2 a You need to find out more information about the development of your chosen child who must be at least three years old.
Use a questionnaire to find out when the child reached milestones of emotional and social development. You must find out about:

- the inborn temperament of the child
- environmental influences
- bonds of affection

- how the child was affected by shyness
- how the child reacted to stress
- security and insecurity
- any fears or nightmares experienced by the child.

b Design and use a chart or other materials to record the information you found out.

3 a Did your chosen child develop ahead of or behind the 'milestone norms' of emotional and social development?

b Explain the development of your child's social skills.
Include information about:

- social skills with the main carer
- social skills with a significant other, e.g. child minder, teacher, friend, relative.

4 Use the information you have gathered to explain how your chosen child developed their self-esteem. Think about:

- How was the child's self-esteem encouraged?
- What factors inhibited the child's self-esteem?

5 Explain how play has helped the emotional and social development of your chosen child.
Include information about:

- solitary play
- parallel play
- looking on play
- joining in play
- co-operative play.

What does post-natal care involve?

Post-natal care is the care given to mother and baby after the birth. The aim of this care is to make sure that mother and baby have the best possible start to this stage of their lives.

The role of professionals

The responsibility for post-natal care is shared between different professionals.

Midwife

For the first ten days after a birth, a midwife provides care and support. While in hospital the care is provided by the hospital midwives. When mothers and babies return home the care is provided by a community midwife attached to the mother's GP's practice, who calls daily until babies are ten days old.

Paediatrician

A paediatrician checks a newborn baby's progress in the hospital and provides information about any problems for mothers.

Health visitor

A health visitor checks on mothers and babies at home when they are discharged by the midwife at around ten days after a birth. She then makes visits to check progress, offer advice and provide support. The health visitor gives mothers their contact number so that they can be called if mothers have any concerns.

GP

Mothers see a GP for their post-natal examination six weeks after a birth. At this time GPs also examine babies to make sure they are healthy.

After six weeks, mothers and babies are usually left to settle into their own routine. Health visitors or GPs can still be called if mothers have any concerns.

Formalities after birth

Every birth has to be **notified** to the local health authority within 36 hours. The doctor or midwife who assisted at the birth usually do this.

Babies also have to be **registered** within six weeks of birth in England or three weeks if a baby is born in Scotland. Parents must choose a name for their baby and this is then given to the Registrar of Births. When the baby is registered, a birth certificate is issued.

> ### Did you know?
> If the parents are married, either of them can register a birth, but if they are not married the mother must register the birth on her own and the details of the father can be left off the birth certificate.

When babies have been registered, the parents receive a medical card which allows them to register their baby with their GP. Babies are then issued with their own NHS medical card.

Figure 7.13 *The role of a health visitor*

Tests for the baby

One to five minutes after birth babies have their APGAR score checked. There are five different checks carried out in the test, and each is given points between zero and two. If babies score over seven they are in excellent condition. A score of less than four indicates there are problems and the baby may need to be resuscitated.

Check	Result	Score
Appearance	Blue	0
	Pink and blue	1
	Pink	2
Pulse	No pulse	0
	Below 100 beats a minute	1
	Over 100 beats a minute	2
Grimace	No response to noise	0
	Small movement/whimper	1
	Crying loudly	2
Activity	Limp and floppy	0
	Some small movements	1
	Active/moving well	2
Respiration	No breathing	0
	Slow or irregular	1
	Breathing well	2

Twenty-four hours after birth babies are examined by a paediatrician (children's doctor). The doctor listens to the heart and lungs and checks the baby's eyes, ears and nose. The mouth is checked for a **cleft palate** and the doctor makes sure there are no swellings around the neck. The abdomen is pressed to check that the liver and spleen are a normal size. The movement of the hips is checked for 'clicks' which could indicate dislocation and needs treatment straight away to prevent permanent abnormality. The paediatrician also checks a baby's reflexes.

Seven to nine days after birth babies have a 'Guthrie test' to check for PKU (phenyl-ketonuria). A few droplets of blood are taken by pricking the baby's heel and this is then put onto a card to check the level of phenylanine. If PKU is diagnosed babies are treated for the condition immediately by giving them a special milk substitute. They also need to eat a special protein diet when weaning. If PKU is not treated, babies can suffer brain damage.

The 'thyroid function' test is carried out at the same time. Again, small droplets of blood are placed on a different test card to check the level of the hormone thyroxine. Children who do not produce enough thyroxine will not grow normally and can suffer with learning difficulties. If an abnormality is detected a child is given doses of the hormone to get the balance right.

A hearing test may be carried out in the hospital for any babies at risk of being deaf. This could be because their parents are deaf or they have been born prematurely (before their expected date).

Tests for the mother

When in hospital a gynaecologist checks a mother's health and well-being after birth. Hospital and community midwives maintain this checking for the first ten days after birth. This role is then taken over by health visitors.

Six weeks after the birth of a baby mothers are given their post-natal examination by their GPs. During this examination mothers:

- are weighed
- have their blood pressure taken
- have their urine tested
- have an abdominal examination to check that their reproductive organs have returned to their original size
- are asked questions about their emotional state of health to check for post-natal depression
- have their **perineum** checked to make sure it has healed properly and any stitches have dissolved
- are offered a smear test to check for infections or abnormalities
- are given advice regarding contraception.

> **Discussion point**
>
> *Why is it important for a mother to go for her post-natal examination?*

Child health clinics

A child health clinic (baby clinic) is run by a local health authority and is sometimes attached to a GP surgery. The clinics are usually held at regular times each week and parents can choose to go to them. Going to the clinic gives new mothers the chance to meet others in the same situation as themselves as well as being for checking progress.

Activity 7

Key skills [C] 2.1a

Child health clinics

Arrange a visit to a child health clinic. Observe the activities that take place there.

1 Discuss your observations in your group.

2 Why are child health clinics necessary?

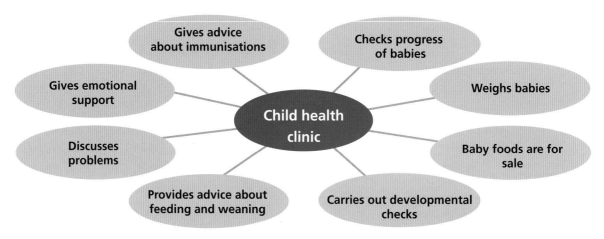

Figure 7.14 *What happens at a child health clinic?*

Parent-held records

A Personal Child Health Record folder is given to every new parent. The record is a useful way of keeping track of the health, growth and development of their child. There is also a section which gives advice and information for parents. The parents fill in the baby's personal details, address, date of birth, GP and when the child reaches developmental milestones. Doctors and other health professionals fill in the sections to record the baby's height and weight, hearing tests, immunisations etc.

The records help parents and professionals caring for chilren to see how well they are developing. It is also easier to notice if there are any developmental problems.

What does a newborn baby look like?

Size and shape

Every baby is unique and there are many variations in size and shape. Small parents often

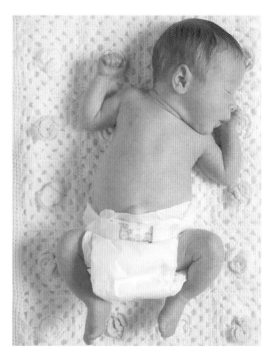

A newborn baby

have small babies, boys are usually slightly larger than girls are, and first babies often weigh less than the brothers or sisters that follow.

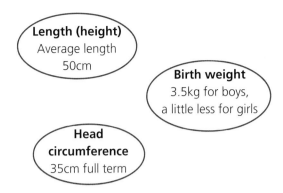

Length (height)
Average length 50cm

Birth weight
3.5kg for boys, a little less for girls

Head circumference
35cm full term

A new baby has a head that is large in comparison to the rest of the body. The legs are short in relation to the body and the tummy seems to be swollen. There is a layer of fat under the skin which makes the arms and legs seem 'chubby'.

Physical appearance

There are characteristics which are easy to observe in the appearance of newborn babies. Starting from the head and working down the body these are:

- some babies have a lot of hair, others have no hair at all
- the pulse can be seen beating clearly underneath the scalp where the soft spot called the **fontanelle** is. This is where the bones of the scalp are not yet joined
- the eyes appear to be swollen due to the pressure of passing through the birth canal and are kept closed most of the time
- Some babies have 'stork bites' on their eye lids or back of the neck. These are small reddish marks which usually fade as the baby gets older and eventually disappear altogether
- 'strawberry marks' start as small red spots and can grow into raised red lumps. These are harmless and usually shrivel and disappear completely by the age of two years
- the face may have small white spots called **milia**, or 'milk spots', caused by small sebaceous glands being blocked. They usually disappear without treatment
- the arms and legs curl up tightly as if the baby is still in the womb
- the umbilical cord is cut and clamped after the birth. It shrivels up after the birth and drops off after a few days

- dark-skinned babies often have bluish coloured marks, called 'Mongolian spots', around the cheeks of their bottom or back. These gradually fade and eventually disappear on their own
- parts of the body may be covered with fine hair called **lanugo**. This usually falls out shortly after birth
- a whitish, greasy substance known as **vernix** can be found on the skin. This protects the skin while a baby is in the womb and is thought to give natural protection from infection so is not washed off immediately
- birthmarks can be found anywhere on the skin. These are usually caused by small blood vessels under the skin and do not hurt or cause babies any harm.
- 'port wine stains' are caused by dilated capillaries and can appear anywhere on the body. They are usually bright red or purple and do not disappear.

How should a new baby be fed?

When babies are born and for the first few months of their life milk is the only food they have. The milk a baby drinks contains all the nutrients it needs.

Breast

Breast-feeding is the most natural way for babies to get the food they need to survive. A mother's breasts prepare for feeding during pregnancy and in last few weeks of pregnancy they may leak a yellowish liquid called **colostrum**. As soon as babies are born their mother's breasts start to produce milk and by three days after birth the flow of milk is usually good.

At about four or five days after birth babies seem to be very hungry and want to be fed around ten to twelve times in 24 hours. The sucking action of a baby helps the flow of milk to become established although it can make mothers very tired. Feeding on demand can continue for several weeks before babies settle into a routine of being fed about six times a day, every three to five hours. At about three months old the time between feeds gradually increases and babies may give up the night feed.

Mothers should try to continue breast-feeding for the first two weeks and if possible for at least four to six months. As babies are weaned onto solid food and nutrients are supplied from another source the need for breast milk decreases.

Some mothers find that they cannot breast-feed because they do not have enough milk. Others may have medical reasons, but some simply do not like the idea of breast-feeding. If mothers can possibly breast-feed for a few days, their babies will benefit from the antibodies contained in the colostrum to fight infections.

Bottle

Manufactured 'formula milk' is available as dried milk or in liquid form which is made to be a close replacement for breast milk. Most have vitamins and iron added to make sure babies get the nutrients they need. Mothers should ask their midwives, health visitors or GPs about which type of milk to use for their babies.

The manufacturer's instructions about how to prepare the feed must be followed strictly. There is no reason why babies who are bottle-fed should not develop into healthy active children. The chart below compares breast and bottle feeding.

Discussion point

'Breast is best'. Discuss this statement. Present your arguments for and against breast feeding.

What equipment is needed for feeding babies?

Bottles

Bottles for feeding babies are available in a variety of shapes and sizes. A mother should choose a bottle which she feels comfortable using. Bottles should be a good design, including:

- a wide neck to make cleaning easy
- clear plastic/glass so that the cleanliness of the inside can be easily checked
- graduated measurements in millilitres or fluid ounces to help with accurate making of feeds
- a tight fitting cap to protect the teat
- a sealing disc which fits into the top to prevent spillages
- a shape that babies can easily grasp when old enough to feed themselves.

Breast feeding	Bottle feeding
It is safe and natural	Baby can be fed anywhere without embarrassment
No special equipment is needed – can feed on demand	Bottles have to be prepared accurately
Contains natural antibodies to fight infections	Baby could be prone to infections
It is cheaper	Feeds can be expensive
Gives time for bonding to develop	Less skin-to-skin contact
Baby is less likely to become overweight	Mother knows exactly how much milk the baby is having
Baby is less likely to become constipated	Baby could get an upset stomach if bottles not sterilized thoroughly
Baby is less likely to develop eczema or nappy rash	Baby could suffer from stomach pains caused by wind
Helps the mother to lose weight	Baby could become thirsty because feeds are too strong
Mother's womb shrinks back to normal size more quickly	Strict sterilizing routine is needed
Periods take longer to restart	Other people can feed the baby
Mother is more contented	Father can feed baby and become close
Nipples can become sore or even cracked	Hole in teat must be right size or baby could choke

Sterilizing equipment

Hygienic equipment is essential for the health of babies who are bottle-fed. All equipment used must be sterilized. Bottles must be cleaned before they are sterilized. Different methods can be used to sterilize equipment, it is down to the preference of parents. There are also cost implications. Here are the different methods:

1 Cold water sterilizing involves all equipment being placed in a chemical sterilizing solution. Special tablets or liquid are dissolved in water. The equipment must be completely covered and left for at least 30 minutes. Fresh solution has to be made up every day to maintain the sterilizing effect. All equipment must be rinsed in cooled boiled water to remove all traces of the sterilizing solution. This method is safe for bottles, teats, plastic spoons etc. No metal equipment can be sterilized in this way. The sterilizer costs from £15 and tablets/liquid also have to be bought.

2 A special electric steamer designed to sterilize bottle-feeding equipment can be bought. The equipment is placed in the sterilizer, cold water added and the steamer turned on. The process takes about 10–15 minutes. This is a more expensive way of sterilizing with sterilizers costing £25–£50.

3 Microwavable sterilizers work on the same principle as steam sterilizers. The equipment is placed in the steamer with sterilized water. The microwave is turned on for 8 minutes and steam is produced. The high temperature kills any germs. Microwave sterilizers cost around £20.

4 Placing the equipment in boiling water for at least ten minutes also kills off any germs using the high temperature of the water. This method simply uses a saucepan and water which most people already have.

Try it!   Key skills [N] 2.2

Compare how much it would cost to sterilize bottle feeding equipment for one year using each method.

How should a baby be kept clean?

Cleanliness of babies is especially important for the first six months as a baby's immune system has not developed and fighting infection is difficult. Germs grow on milk and food, and are also present in urine and stools.

All babies rely on their parents and carers to keep them clean and to maintain their hygiene. This

Figure 7.15 *Bottle feeding equipment*

involves washing and bathing, cleaning feeding equipment, clothing, bedding and nappy changing. Babies cannot help getting dirty; after having their feed they often bring up a little of the milk, they wet and soil their nappies, and when they start to feed themselves they get very messy!

Changing the nappy

Babies need their nappies changing several times a day. Whether they are wearing a disposable or washable nappy a hygienic routine must be followed to prevent germs spreading:

1 Check that all equipment needed is close at hand
2 Wash hands thoroughly
3 Place baby on their back on a changing mat or plastic sheet to prevent surfaces underneath getting dirty
4 Hold baby by the ankles with one hand and remove the nappy with the other
5 Clean baby's bottom using tissues, wipes or cotton wool
6 Dry baby's bottom thoroughly
7 Smear baby's bottom with a barrier cream (zinc and castor oil cream or similar cream made especially for this purpose)
8 Place clean nappy under baby's bottom while lifting baby up by holding the ankles
9 Put the legs down and fasten the nappy securely
10 Plastic pants can then be put on over washable nappies
11 Wash hands after disposing of the nappy

Nappy care

Disposable nappies

Put any cotton wool, wipes or tissues that have been used to clean inside the nappy. Wrap this up and seal with the tapes and throw away in a lined bin. Nappy sacks can be bought which have a pleasant smell and can be tied to seal the nappy inside. These are very useful when out and about. Nappies should be disposed of carefully so that others do not have to smell the contents and germs are not spread.

Washable nappies

Washable nappies can be used over and over again as long as they are cleaned thoroughly.

Any solids on the nappy should be removed straight away. This can be done by holding the nappy under the flush of a toilet. The nappy should be soaked for several hours in a sterilizing solution following the instructions given by the manufacturer. A bucket with a lid is good for this as it keeps the smells inside. The nappies should then be washed in hot water (at least 60°C) using a mild non-biological soap powder. Nappies can be boiled to restore whiteness but this is not necessary every time they are washed. Nappies must be rinsed thoroughly to remove all soap and sterilizing solution so that babies do not suffer from an allergic reaction. Softener can be added to the final rinse to soften the nappies. They should be dried thoroughly, preferably outside or in a tumble drier.

Coping with nappy rash

Nappy rash, also known as ammonia dermatitis, occurs when a baby's skin is left in direct contact with stools or urine for long periods of time. The redness of nappy rash is caused by the bacteria in the stools reacting with the urine and ammonia being produced which burns and irritates a baby's skin. The longer a baby is left in a nappy the more time there is for ammonia to be produced.

Nappy rash can be prevented by:

- changing the nappy regularly
- applying a layer of barrier cream after changing the nappy to reduce contact between the skin and urine
- leaving the nappy off for a while to let the skin breathe
- washing nappies thoroughly to remove all traces of urine and stools
- using one-way liners which allow urine to pass through and be absorbed by the nappy but do not allow it to go back and get in contact with the skin.

When babies develop nappy rash a strict routine is needed to help the rash to heal. Following the above points is particularly important. If the rash does not clear up within a week or starts oozing, medical advice should be sought.

Babies are more prone to nappy rash when:

- they have been immunised
- their diet has changed
- they have an upset stomach and diarrhoea
- they are teething
- they are feeling unwell.

Protecting the baby through parent cleanliness

Parents and carers should be very particular about their own personal hygiene routines to protect babies from harmful germs and bacteria. Parents and carers must make sure that they wash their hands:

- after using the toilet
- before preparing feeds
- before feeding baby
- before and after changing nappies
- after blowing their nose and before handling the baby.

They must also take care to wash their clothes regularly, and to keep the house clean, particularly concentrating on floor coverings when the baby is starting to crawl.

How should bath time be conducted for babies?

Bath time should be fun and enjoyable for babies. It is important for parents and carers to relax as tension can be passed onto the baby. New parents are often scared of bathing their baby as they are unsure and lack confidence. This is unnecessary if everything is prepared in advance.

Babies can be bathed at any time of the day. Some have their bath in the morning, others may have it in the evening before bedtime. Whenever the time is, it is important that there is no rush as that is when accidents can happen.

Preparation

To make sure bath time is enjoyable careful preparation is important:

- The room should be warm and free from draughts as babies lose body heat quickly. Close the windows and doors.
- Put the baby bath (if you are using one) on a firm surface or bathstand – the floor is a good choice (so is inside the big bath).
  - Always put cold water in the bath first and top up with hot water to give a comfortable temperature, around body temperature 37°C. The temperature can be tested using an elbow. If the water is too hot on the elbow it is too hot for the baby! If hot water is put in first, the bottom of the bath could be too hot and burn the baby's back and bottom.
  - Collect together all the equipment that is needed for bathing, drying and dressing the baby before the baby is put into the bath.

Figure 7.16 *Bath time should be fun*

Figure 7.17 *Bath time equipment*

Bath time routine

Babies feel secure if they follow a routine at bath time.

> 1 Wash your hands thoroughly.
>
> 2 Undress baby and wrap in a towel to keep warm.
>
> 3 Clean the baby's face with damp cotton wool. Do not use soap on the baby's face. Wipe each eye with a clean piece of cotton wool from the bridge of the nose to the outer corner. This will prevent any infection passing from one eye to the other.
>
> 4 Tuck the baby under one arm supporting the back and head. Hold the baby's head over the bath and wash the scalp with water. Soap or shampoo does not need to be used every day as this dries out the skin.
>
> 5 Take off the nappy and clean the nappy area.
>
> 6 Place the baby in the bath water with one hand supporting the head and neck, the other supporting the bottom.
>
> 7 Allow the baby to relax in the water, holding the baby's shoulder with one hand and the head resting on your arm. Babies often like to kick and splash so be prepared to get wet. Talk to the baby all the time, some people even sing to babies while they are in the bath.
>
> 7 Use the free hand to wash the baby, make sure all creases and folds are carefully cleaned.
>
> 8 Lift the baby out of the bath and dry carefully by patting and not rubbing. Make sure all crease and folds are dry especially the neck, groin, armpits, behind the knees and behind the ears. If creases are left damp sores will develop.
>
> 10 Smear nappy cream on the baby's bottom and put on a nappy before dressing him.

When babies are six months old they have grown out of a baby bath and need to use a normal bath. When using a normal bath, a bathmat should be placed in the bottom to prevent babies from slipping under the water. Cold water should be put in first and topped up with hot. Check the temperature before putting babies in the water. DO NOT allow babies to stand up in the bath and NEVER leave a baby alone in the bath!

Topping and tailing

If it is not possible to bath a baby every day they should be 'topped and tailed' to keep the face, hands and bottom clean. When doing this:

> 1 Make sure the room is warm and draught free.
>
> 2 Undress the baby down to their vest and nappy.
>
> 3 Wash the baby's face using cotton wool balls and warm water in the same way as bathtime.
>
> 4 Wash the baby's hands and feet and dry them carefully.
>
> 5 Take off the nappy and clean the baby's bottom using warm water and cotton balls or baby wipes. Dry thoroughly.
>
> 6 Put a clean nappy on and get the baby dressed.

What should babies wear?

The clothing babies wear when they are first born is called the 'layette'. Babies need to have enough clothes to keep warm and allow for washing them often. Babies grow quickly in the first few months and the layette is quickly grown out of.

Do's and don'ts of a baby's first clothes are shown in the table below.

The layette should	The layette should not
be loose fitting and comfortable	be tight, and should allow for movement
be easy to put on and take off	have drawstrings or ribbons near a baby's neck
be easy to wash and dry	be loosely-knitted or holey garments as these can cut off the blood supply to fingers and toes
be lightweight	include hairy or itchy fabrics
be soft and warm	include thick layers of clothes
be flame resistant	have heavy buttons or zips

Basic items

The basic items of the layette should be bought before a baby is born so that they can be taken into hospital and worn straight after the birth. Mothers can have great fun buying clothing for their baby but they should not get carried away as the size of the baby is not known and small clothing does not fit a baby for long.

Additional items

When babies are first born there is no need for separate day and night clothes as they spend so much time asleep.

Outer clothing and coats are not essential as babies are usually well wrapped up in a blanket when out in a pram.

If babies have long fingernails some parents choose to buy thin cotton scratch mittens for them to wear to prevent them scratching and marking their face.

Bootees are not essential when babies wear a sleep suit with integral feet; however some parents put these on over the top of the sleep suit to keep the baby's feet warm.

Swim nappies can be bought for babies to wear in the swimming pool.

Care of baby clothes

Most clothing bought in the shops can be machine washed. The instruction labels on the clothing should be followed carefully.

Woollen clothing is warm to wear but should be washed by hand.

Figure 7.18 *Examples of items contained within a baby's layette*

Cotton clothing can be washed in hot water. Coloured cotton may fade. White cotton can be boiled and bleached to restore whiteness if necessary.

Man-made fibres and mixed fabrics need washing with care so follow the directions on the labels.

What nursery equipment is required for a new baby?

All nursery equipment must be safe to use. Look for **Kitemarks** to check that minimum standards have been met.

For sleeping

Cots

Safety aspects of a cot are especially important when babies reach the age of six months and can move around. Cots should have bars between 45 and 65 mm apart to stop babies getting their head trapped. The mattress must fit the inside of the cot frame so that babies cannot get their arms, legs or head trapped and should be firm to prevent suffocation. If the cot has a side that drops down the release catches must be childproof.

Carry-cot

Useful when a baby first comes home and up to six months later. The sides and hood protect babies from draughts. A carry-cot can be used as a pram as well as a bed.

Moses basket

Useful for very young babies but they soon grow out of them.

Travel cot

A good idea if the parents work and when on holiday. These can also be used as a play pen if the mattress is taken out.

Blankets and sheets

Recommended for babies under 12 months. They need to be washed regularly as babies often dribble in their sleep.

Duvet or cot quilt

Should not be used until the baby is 12 months old because they are very warm and baby could overheat.

For going out

Pram or pushchair

Choosing a pram or pushchair can be a difficult decision as there are so many different styles available in the shops.

Large prams are not seen very often as they are heavy and difficult to manoeuvre.

Pushchairs which do not allow a baby to lie flat are not recommended until the baby is able to sit without help.

A carry-cot which fits onto a wheelbase is useful as it allows baby to lie flat and can often be converted into a pushchair when the baby is older.

Baby nests are very cosy and like a small sleeping bag. They keep baby warm and can be used in a pram or carry cot.

Figure 7.19 *Equipment for babies comes in all shapes and sizes*

Car seats

Fit onto a wheelbase and later convert into a pushchair. Where possible, car seats should be fitted by a professional into a car so that there is no risk to the baby if the car is in an accident.

Baby carriers or slings

Allow babies to be carried close to their parent leaving their hands free to do other things. Babies feel secure when carried in this way.

For bathing
Baby bath

Should have no sharp edges. Some are made from moulded plastic. This is not an essential item as babies can be bathed in a sink or even the normal bath as long as the parents make sure the baby is safe. A rubber bath mat should be used to prevent the baby from slipping and the taps should be covered so that the baby does not get burnt.

Moulded sponges

Can be bought to put in the bottom of a normal bath in order to bath a baby. These allow the parent to have both hands free.

Gadgets are available which have sucker on the feet and help baby to sit up in the bath unaided. These should not be used until the baby is able to sit up out of the bath and are only a precaution.

> REMEMBER, babies must NEVER be left alone in the bath as they can easily drown.

Bath toys

A wide range of bath toys can be bought, for example boats, cups etc. These should be safe and give babies the opportunity to play and have fun.

For playing
Baby bouncers

Can be hanged from a doorway and allow babies to bounce up and down. This gives good exercise for their arms and legs. Babies weighing over 12 kg should not use a bouncer.

Baby walkers

Are like a seat on wheels with a tray in the front. They allow babies to have freedom to move around before they can walk. The tray can be used to put toys on and babies can have fun. Babies over 23 kg should not use a walker. Babies should not be left alone when in a walker or bouncer, or use them for long periods of time as their legs can be affected.

Playpens

Are useful when babies start to get mobile and move around a lot. They keep babies safe while parents are busy or go out of the room. Again, babies should not be left alone in a playpen for long periods of time. The sides of a playpen should be sturdy enough to hold a baby's weight when in a standing position. If babies start climbing they should no longer be left in a playpen as accidents can happen. If a playpen has bars on the sides these should be no more than 45–65mm apart to prevent a baby's head from being trapped.

Assessment activity 7.5

Key skills ICT 2.1, 2.3, C 2.3

Post-natal care

The local antenatal clinic are very pleased with the work you have completed for them so far on child development. You have now been asked to produce a guide or material for a Resource Pack which can be given to new parents called 'Caring for a New Baby'. Complete the following tasks and include them in your guide.

1 You need to provide the expectant parents with information which will help them to prepare for when their baby has been born. You must explain:

- the roles of a midwife, health visitor, paediatrician and GP
- what formalities have to be completed after the birth
- the tests a baby has and why they are important
- the tests a mother has
- parent-held records.

2 a Arrange to visit a child health clinic or arrange for a speaker to come and talk to the group (with your tutor's permission) about a child health clinic.

b Write a report to include in your guide which explains what happens at a child health clinic.

3 Use pictures or diagrams to explain to the new parents what to expect when their baby is born. You must include details about:

- size
- shape
- physical appearance.

4 a Parents have to make the decision about whether to breast-feed or bottle-feed their baby.

Design a chart or other materials to include in your guide which would help them make their decision.

b Describe the equipment that would be needed for bottle-feeding.

5 Write instructions the parents should follow when:

- changing a nappy
- cleaning up after a nappy change
- preventing and treating nappy rash
- protecting their babies through parent cleanliness.

6 New parents who have never bathed a baby before can get very nervous. Help to calm them by giving detailed instructions for:

- preparing for bath time
- the bath time routine which should be followed.

7 a Use a catalogue or other materials to find pictures of the basic items which should be bought before a baby is born to include in your guide. State how much each item would cost and give a total cost so the parents know how much they may need to spend. Include a section of additional items which they could buy if they can afford to.

b Explain how baby clothes should be cared for.

8 Nursery equipment can be very expensive. Provide guidance for the parents about different equipment available for:

- sleeping
- going out
- bathing
- playing.

Provide advice about what to look for when buying items of equipment for each purpose.

What design features should be considered when designing a nursery?

The design of a nursery for a new baby is an exciting opportunity for prospective parents. The preparation of a nursery is one of the most interesting things they can do for their unborn child. It is important that the design features are carefully considered to make sure the nursery will be a safe, comfortable and relaxing environment.

It is a good idea to prepare a nursery before the baby arrives because after the birth time will be taken up with providing for the baby.

Ergonomics

The **ergonomics** of the design of a nursery is all about how easy and safe the room is to use. The furniture should be placed so that the person using it feels comfortable and safe, good posture is promoted and movement around the room is easy. Equipment and accessories should be easy to reach without creating hazards.

Remember:
- shelves should be put up at a level where everything can easily be seen and the parents do not have to over-stretch to reach things
- powders and creams should be close to the changing area but out of a baby's reach
- there should be no obstructions between the changing area, bath, chair and cot
- the chair should be a comfortable height which is easy to get out of and has good back support for night feeds
- the changing area, whether a tabletop, chest of drawers or specially designed changing unit should be the correct height. If too low this could cause backache and if too high it would be difficult to change the nappy.

Safety issues

The design of a nursery must make sure that both baby and carer are safe at all times. All equipment and furniture bought should carry a safety mark to show that it meets minimum standards.

Figure 7.20 *Consider ergonomics when designing a nursery*

Consideration needs to be given to the following safety aspects:

Safety features	Purpose
Flameproof fabric for all upholstery, bedding and curtains	To prevent fires spreading
Non-toxic, lead free paint for walls and furniture especially baby's cot	To prevent babies getting lead poisoning and becoming ill
Safety locks on windows	To prevent babies falling out the window when able to climb
Childproof covers on sockets	To prevent foreign objects being poked into them
Childproof safety catches on drawers and cupboards	To prevent fingers being trapped
Non-slip floor covering	To prevent slipping over, especially if babies are bathed in the nursery
Easy to clean surfaces	To maintain hygiene
No splintered wooden surfaces	To prevent babies getting splinters
No rugs or small mats	To prevent tripping
No trailing wires	To prevent tripping and electrocution
The cot should have bars between 45 and 65 mm apart	To stop babies getting their heads trapped
Cots with sides that lower should have childproof catches	To prevent babies getting their fingers trapped
Use non-slip mats in bath	To prevent babies slipping
Adequate lighting	To enable parents to see what they are doing

Equipment

The equipment placed in a nursery should be suitable for meeting the needs of a newborn baby:

- babies need to have somewhere to sleep in the nursery. Refer to Unit 7.5 for detailed information on suitable sleeping equipment
- a chest of drawers with a sturdy frame is useful for both storage and nappy changing. It should be about hip height so that a baby can be changed without discomfort. A chest with at least three drawers is a good idea so that baby-changing equipment and clothing is close at hand
- a plastic bin with a lid is useful for disposing of dirty nappies
- Wall shelves allow baby equipment and supplies to be stored neatly. These can be used later for storing books and toys
- a chair with a straight back allows babies to be fed in comfort in the peace of their own nursery environment
- a small table or bedside cabinet is useful to place items on when sitting in the chair
- lighting should be adequate to check a baby while they are asleep during the night. A dimmer switch could be fitted to the main overhead light so that the level of brightness can be adjusted. A night light could be used or even a lamp, but care should be taken with trailing wires
- flooring should be hard wearing and non-slip. Vinyl or laminate flooring is easy to clean. Cork or carpet tiles are easy to clean and can be replaced individually
- walls could be painted with non-toxic, washable emulsion paint. This would allow colour schemes to be changed quickly and easily. Wallpaper if used should be able to be wiped clean
- curtains or blinds should non-flammable and block out daylight so that a baby can sleep well during the day.

Purposes

During the first few weeks after delivery babies may sleep in the same room as their parents. However, there should also be a room which is designated as the nursery for the baby to move into and which can be used to provide for the baby's care needs. The nursery should have enough room and equipment for sleeping, feeding, bathing, nappy changing and dressing.

Babies are stimulated by a brightly-coloured environment. The colour scheme should be chosen to allow a baby to sleep peacefully yet be entertained when they wake up.

The room should be kept warm so that a baby cannot catch a chill when bathed or changed. The temperature should be a constant 16–20°C (60–70°F). Ideally a thermostatically controlled heater or radiator should be installed. The room should be well ventilated to prevent an accumulation of stale air, but must be free from draughts.

Designed for comfort – fit for purpose

Assessment activity 7.6

Key skills [ICT] 2.3, [C] 2.3

Design a nursery

1 Draw a design for a nursery using A4 card or paper. Your design must include:

- a plan of the nursery
- a list of all equipment and furnishings
- cutouts to show colour schemes and fabrics to be used.

You must consider the following design features:

- ergonomics – the position and height of equipment
- safety issues – safety of equipment, paint, fabrics, flooring

- equipment – what is needed and why
- purposes – what the nursery is to be used for.

2 Write a detailed evaluation of your design.
   a Explain why your design is fit for the purpose.
   b Explain the ergonomics of your design and why equipment has been placed in certain positions.
   c Explain how safety issues have been addressed in your design.
   d Explain how and why your nursery would be easy to use.

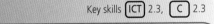

Glossary

Adequate: enough for the purpose

Amniocentesis: when a long needle is inserted into the womb to extract amniotic fluid for testing

Anaemia: a blood deficiency which leads to paleness and tiredness

Antenatal care: the care provided to a mother from conception to birth

Bonding: the feelings of love between parents and their baby

Cleft palate: a hole or spit in the roof of the mouth

Colostrom: first 'milk' produced in mother's breasts, contains antibodies

Conception: the moment the egg becomes fertilized by a sperm and a woman becomes pregnant

Co-operative play: play that involves children joining in with other children

Embryo: a developing baby up to six weeks after conception

Ergonomics: design features of a room which make it easy and comfortable to use

Fine motor skills: skills involving fine movement of the hands and fingers including writing, drawing, using a knife and fork

Foetus: a developing baby from six weeks after conception

Folic acid: high levels are needed in a woman's blood to prevent spina bifida, folic acid is found in fruit and vegetables

Fontanelle: a temporary gap between the bones of the head which is covered by a tough membrane. The fontanelle closes over between 12 and 18 months of age.

Genes: inherited from both parents, the genes give the baby it's features e.g. hair colour, height, eye colour etc.

Gross motor skills: skills involving the use of large muscles in the body including walking, running, climbing

Guttural: throaty, harsh-sounding

Kitemark: official mark to show that an object has been approved by the British Standards Institution

Lanugo: fine hair covering baby's body straight after birth

Layette: baby's first set of clothes

Linguistic: when children begin to use recognisable words to communicate

Looking-on play: play involving one child alongside another when they demonstrate awareness of each other but do not actually interact

Milestones: achievement of particular skills or ability

Milia: small white fatty spots that can appear on baby's face soon after birth

Nappy rash: soreness which can develop when baby's skin is left in contact with urine or stools for a long period of time

Notified: informed or given notice of

Nutrients: substances that give food for the maintenance of life

Paediatrician: a doctor who specialises in the care and treatment of children

Palmar grasp: using whole hand to pick objects up

Perineum: area between the anus and the birth canal

Pincer grasp: using index finger and thumb to pick objects up

Placenta: a large disc shaped organ which enables oxygen and food to pass to the foetus and remove carbon dioxide

Post-natal care: care provided after the birth of the baby

Pre-linguistic: the phase before babies start to talk when they communicate by crying, smiling, using facial expressions, cooing and grunting

Reflex: an automatic response to a stimulus

Registered: put on an official list

Self-esteem: the way a child feels about himself or herself

Sequence: coming one after the other

Solitary play: when a child plays alone without taking any notice of others who may be near

Stamina: strength; endurance

Tripod grasp: using thumb and two fingers to pick objects up

Ultrasound scan: sound waves bounce off the mother's abdomen sending a black and white picture on to a screen showing baby's development

Umbilical cord: a pale white twisted cord with red blood vessels which links to the placenta. The cord transports oxygen and food to the baby and removes carbon dioxide.

Uterus: also known as the womb, the place where baby develops before birth

Vernix: a whiteish, greasy substance found on baby's skin following the birth

Working with young children can be very rewarding

In this unit we will consider the different types of provision available for families with young children exploring how the physical, social, emotional and intellectual needs of young children are met. Caring for children should be in a way that promotes health and well-being and, therefore, early years workers must have a wide range of skills and qualities.

When considering a career in childcare early years workers must be able to apply the care values as these provide the foundation for quality care, and they need to be aware of health and safety issues, knowing how to promote a safe learning environment where children can play effectively.

The play environment needs careful planning so that the different stages of play can be catered for and a variety of activities can be offered. Early years workers need to know how to plan activities for children's learning and development and be able to evaluate them and make decisions about any changes should they repeat the activities. Early years workers also need to know how children have benefited from taking part in play activities.

What will we learn in this unit?

Learning outcomes

You will learn to:

- Identify the different types of care and education provision for young children and how it meets their needs
- Describe job roles and the skills and qualities required when working with children
- Recognise how to promote and maintain a safe environment for young children
- Investigate how the role of play contributes to the development of the child
- Design a suitable layout for a care and education setting for young children
- Plan and carry out an activity to intellectually stimulate young children and evaluate the success of the activity

What provision exists for young children?

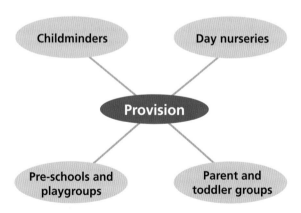

Figure 8.1 *Care and education provision for young children*

Families need a range of services to provide support for themselves and their children. Parents have different reasons for choosing childcare. These could include:

- wanting some personal space, e.g. time for themselves and to catch up with household chores or to participate in recreational activities

- having to work for **economic** reasons, e.g. so that there will be enough money to buy wants as well as needs
- choosing to work for personal reasons, e.g. having a sense of fulfilment
- considering that it will help their child **socialise** if they mix with other children, e.g. learning how to share with others
- lack of choice as childcare may be linked to child protection issues, e.g. the safety of the child
- feeling it would be beneficial for their child to experience a wide range of equipment and activities that might not be available at home, e.g. outdoor play items
- promoting independence by being away from the main carer for a time, e.g. being supervised by others who are not members of the family
- wishing to become involved in early years experiences with their child, e.g. learning with others.

It is important to remember that parents will chose the type of provision that best fits their lifestyle and childcare requirements.

Day nurseries

There are a range of different types of nursery provision from which parents can choose. For example:

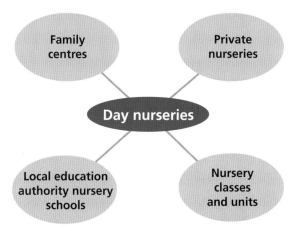

Figure 8.2 *Different types of day nursery*

Private day nurseries

The increase in working parents has led to more private day nurseries and workplace crèches, which cater for babies and pre-school children during the normal working week. Day nurseries in the private sector charge a fee and may offer part or full-time care. OFSTED has been responsible for the inspection of day nurseries since 2001, whereas previously this was a responsibility of the local authority. Under the Care Standards Act 2000 all childcare providers must be registered by OFSTED and must meet the National Standards.

Family centres

Social Services are responsible for some family centres and day nurseries. These care and education settings cater for families with particular needs and in some areas they offer **subsidised** places in the day nursery, to enable the parent to work or to return to study. They may offer full-time or part-time provision and might work closely with health services and other agencies. Parents or main carers of children who attend family centres and day nurseries are actively encouraged to be involved in all aspects of childcare for their children.

Most social service nurseries operate a 'key worker' system where one of the early years practitioners works closely with an individual child. In this way the child always has a familiar person at hand and develops a close relationship with that person. In addition, the key worker gets to know the child and the family and can become a valuable link in all aspects of the child's care. The **funding** is primarily from social services and the staffing ratios are usually very high.

Nursery schools

Nursery schools are run by the Local Education Authority (LEA) and have their own head teacher, class teachers and nursery nurses. The **staff/child ratio** is usually 1 : 15 and children normally attend five half-day sessions per week. Staff from nursery schools, classes and units often meet to discuss common issues and organise specific training and development.

Nursery classes and units

Nursery classes and nursery units are usually attached to a primary school, the head teacher of the primary school also having authority for the class or unit. Parental involvement is actively encouraged. Children are involved with the Foundation Stage of the National Curriculum with long, medium and short-term plans developed for them.

Learning to socialise at an early age

Parent and toddler groups

Parent and toddler groups are often held in:

- community centres
- church halls.

They are run on a non-profit making basis with donations and or fees used from refreshments and **consumables**. Parents stay with their child all the time, and as the child is not being left in someone else's care there is no requirement for the organisers to be qualified. Such sessions are usually held twice per week and children have the advantage of free play, mixing with other children and developing social skills. The parents/carers can develop informal support groups and gain encouragement from being with other parents/carers of toddlers.

Pre-schools and playgroups

These are usually non-profit making groups that hold sessions in community centres, church halls or other accessible **venues**. Many are attached to primary schools and offer three-to-five-year-old children the opportunity to learn through play. Sessions are usually two-and-a-half hours duration each morning or afternoon and staff carefully plan a varied **curriculum** to provide opportunities for learning and the development of skills. Parents are usually required to pay a small fee per session and this may be the only type of provision available in isolated areas. Parental involvement is actively encouraged and many move on to being leaders of playgroups themselves.

Childminders

Childminders use their own home to provide care for young children during the day, or before and after school for older children. They care for children under eight years of age and the financial arrangements are private between the childminder and the parent. Many childminders carry out this work as they have children of their own. Childminders are required to register with the local authority and must comply with strict regulations and screening through the **Criminal Records Bureau (CRB)**.

Nannies are another option open to parents. Nannies are employed by families to care for a child in the child's own home. They may also use the services provided by a playgroup, nursery or parent and toddler group, but spend the remainder of the time with the child devising and carrying out activities and encouraging the child to develop skills through play and exploration. An individual may be employed as a 'live-in nanny', having their own room and private time away from the family. Other employment may be on a daily basis with the nanny arriving and leaving at pre-arranged times. Duties are usually discussed and arranged **prior** to commencing employment.

Did you know!

Rachel and Margaret McMillan in Deptford opened the first nursery in 1913 in order to provide an open-air school for the deprived children in that area.

Activity 1

Key skills [C] 2.1a, [ICT] 2.3

Which service?

Max is a one-year-old. His mother is going back to work for two mornings each week and needs care for Max while she is at work.

1 Choose two services that would be suitable, stating reasons why.

2 Explain the purpose of a 'Parent and toddler group'.

3 Explain the difference between a childminding service and the service provided by a nanny.

Mrs Singh wants her three-year old daughter, Nasreem, to mix with other children occasionally and experience activities she may not have at home. Mrs Singh is also quite keen to be involved as she enjoys spending time with her daughter.

4 What are Mrs Singh's options? Discuss which service you would choose.

5 Devise a leaflet or handout explaining to parents of young children what services are available.

What are the physical needs of young children?

All the basic physical needs of children must be met before they can fully develop and enjoy their surroundings. Maslow's hierarchy of need places very basic needs first, such as safety, warmth, food and security (see Unit 2). A hungry, cold child is not able to focus on any other activities until those needs have been met.

Fruit supplies vitamins

Food

Food is one of the most basic and essential needs and young children's diets need to be considered carefully.

A balanced diet is the best way to keep children healthy, and if they have the right diet they have an increased chance of being able to resist infections. A balanced diet consists of the food types shown in the table below.

Often, parents worry that children are not eating enough, but as a general rule if they have plenty of energy then they are having enough of the right foods.

Food type	Purpose	Where found (e.g.)
Carbohydrates	Energy providing	Bread, potatoes
Proteins	Body/muscle building Repairs injury	Meat, fish
Fats	Energy providing and helps to absorb Vitamins A and D	Butter, oil and hidden in many foods
Minerals • Calcium • Iron	 Strong teeth and bones Enables the blood to carry oxygen	 Milk, cheese Red meat, spinach, egg yolks
Vitamins • A • B • C • K • D	 Good for eyesight Good for nervous system Good for skin Helps with blood clotting Good for teeth/bones	 Carrots, milk Bread, meat, pasta Kiwis, oranges, potatoes Most vegetables Most dairy products

It may be worth considering offering children smaller portions and then offering more, rather than filling a plate and expecting everything to be eaten.

Some children and adults have food **allergies** and it is essential that those who are caring for children check with parents to find out if the child has any allergies. Some of the most common allergies are:

- nuts
- milk and dairy products
- seafood.

These allergies can be so severe in certain individuals that they may be life threatening. It is vital that early years workers are aware of these issues at all times. There are also certain medical conditions where diet must be considered, such as diabetes and coeliac disease. If early years workers are caring for children with any medical condition or allergies, they should gain more detailed information from the parents about the needs of children with this condition. For example, children with coeliac disease are not able to eat foods which contain gluten. Gluten is typically found in cereals such as wheat, barley, oats and rye, and as these are often used for breads and biscuits, it is important to check ingredients when shopping if children are affected by this condition.

Activity 2

Key skills   2.3

Shona

Shona is four years old.

1 Plan a well-balanced lunch and tea for Shona.

2 Explain why you chose the different foods included on the menu.

3 Why should children be served small portions of food?

4 How does coeliac disease affect people?

Warmth

Children need to be comfortable in order to enjoy play and activities. If they are too cold they are unhappy. They can enjoy being outside on a cold day if they are dressed appropriately, for example with warm protective clothing.

Natural fibres such as cotton or wool are better for providing warmth and they provide better absorbency. It is often a good idea to dress children in two thin layers rather than one thick, bulky layer.

Discussion point

What clothing should be worn by a child who wants to play outside in cold weather? Give reasons for your answer.

Protection

Children need to be safe and secure. A range of factors need to be considered, but these are dealt with later in this unit in more detail (Section 8.3). When considering protection of the child, the main issues that need to be addressed are that:

- the care and education setting is safe, e.g. there are no hazards, and safety features are in place
- staff are appropriately recruited, e.g. they have the qualifications, qualities and skills needed for the job role
- staff have been appropriately checked (references and CRB checked)
- equipment is safe (check Kitemarks and safety standards)
- outdoor equipment is safe and placed securely on correct surface
- children are protected from abuse
- firefighting equipment is in place and is regularly maintained
- **evacuation** procedures are in place and all staff are trained to use them
- first aid kits are available and are regularly maintained
- first aid and safety personnel have been identified.

Safety

Safety applies to every activity and action in the care and education setting. When early years workers are caring for children, it is their responsibility to keep the children from harm by every means possible. Within the setting it is important to carry out regular checks on resources to ensure that they are safe to use and that measures are in place to make sure children cannot access dangerous substances and equipment. Some safety aspects are covered in more detail later in this unit (Section 8.3). However, early years workers must always be on guard when taking children outside a setting as many children are not fully aware of the rules of the road and must be continuously reminded how to behave when traffic is around as shown in Figure 8.3.

Health

When caring for young children in a care and education setting, early years workers need to be aware of the signs and symptoms that a child is not in good health.

- *signs* are what can be seen, e.g. rash, flushed appearance, **pallor**
- *symptoms* are what the child feels and we can only find out about these if the child tells us or indicates that there is a problem, e.g. pain, **nausea**, headache.

Signs and symptoms that a child is not well:

Heavy eyes	Sleepy	Flushed cheeks
Irritable	Headache	Lack of appetite
Vomiting	Unusually quiet	Pale
Weepy	Clingy	High temperature

All early years settings should have details of the contact telephone numbers and addresses of parents or main carers. This information is collected when a child is registered to attend a setting, because if children become ill or injure themselves, the parents need to be contacted immediately. Early years workers must support an ill child in whatever way needed. Many ill children want to sleep, and providing there is not an underlying injury that will probably be the best for them.

Activity 3   Key skills [C] 2.1a, 2.3

Meena

Meena is attending a nursery school. The early years workers are taking the children out to a local animal centre. On the way back Meena cries and tells the nursery nurse that she feels unwell.

1 Discuss the safety measures the early years workers should take when taking Meena and others to the animal centre.

2 Give details of some of the signs and symptoms which would have alerted the early years workers to think Meena was unwell.

3 What action should the early years worker take if Meena is unwell?

4 Explain why it is important to have contact numbers for children who attend the nursery school.

Figure 8.3 *Road safety rules*

Hygiene

Figure 8.4 *How to reduce the spread of infection*

Hygienic practices must be developed and maintained in order to promote good health and well-being and to help prevent the spread of infection (see Unit 4). Also, people who are dirty and smelly are unpleasant to be around. It is important that a positive image is presented by early years workers as children consider them to be good role models and may copy their example.

Figure 8.6 *Personal hygiene should be encouraged*

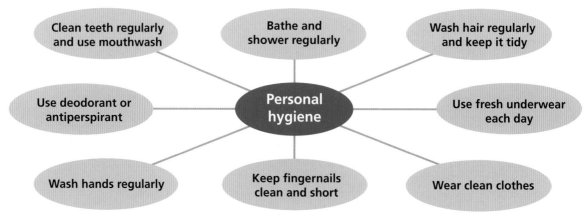

Figure 8.5 *Let's get clean!*

What are the emotional needs of young children?

Young children need an emotionally stable environment in order to develop fully and form secure relationships of their own. They are easily affected by the emotional relationships of other people close to them especially family, and any upsets or variations in consistency of care can have a **detrimental** affect on a child. It may be that at times the care and education environment is the main secure and stable one in a child's life and the early years workers provide the security needed for **holistic** development.

Bonding

Children develop a strong relationship with their parents or main carers, which begins at birth. This **bonding** process is so important that many people believe that it can affect a child's ability to form relationships with others later in life. John Bowlby (1907–90) was one of the main people to develop a theory about the needs of children in relation to their main carers. This became known as 'attachment theory'. Aspects are:

- **psychological** problems are more likely to be evident in people who have been separated from their parents early in life

- babies should form these attachments in the first twelve months, as it is an instinct which must be allowed to develop.

Young children can form very close relationships with a number of people, providing the basic, foundation relationships in their life remain secure.

Bowlby's theory eventually led to the introduction of the key worker system whereby a child has one early years worker nominated to be the main carer in a care and education setting.

Stability

Stability in the early years is important as it lays the foundation of future development. Lack of stability confuses young children and can cause them to develop a sense of insecurity. They are not be able to play effectively and form deep meaningful relationships, which affects them later in life. Many children find change difficult to cope with, and this includes when furniture and equipment are moved to alter the physical layout of a care and education setting. If this is done without the involvement of the children both in decision-making and layout, it can lead to questioning confusion. If children are involved in change and can take an active part, then they gain confidence in the knowledge that they are empowered to influence the environment.

Emotional development	
Age in years	**Development stage**
2–3	This is often a difficult time for young children and their parents and carers, as the children try to develop and come to terms with a strong sense of independence. It is a time when tantrums are evident as feelings become stronger. As children develop greater language and physical skills these displays of frustration lessen and the ability to express themselves clearly increases. Children require a great deal of support at this time
3	Children begin to build on the skills they have already developed and grow in confidence. They develop friendships with other children and take part in co-operative play, sharing and taking turns. Their concentration span increases as they become more independent, but occasional tantrums may occur when strong feelings are involved. Children become less **egocentric** and show concern for others who are upset. It is a time when children typically wish to please parents and carers and they show great affection and imitate the actions of adults they come into contact with
4–5	Play with other children becomes an important part of the daily routine and children like others to take notice of their achievements. Asking people to watch what they can do and showing pride in activities is a common attribute at this age. As children's vocabulary increases they become more confident in the use of language and are keen to learn and develop new skills such as reading and writing. There is a greater desire to experiment and explore and find out about the properties of materials in their world

Security and stability enables children to grow in confidence and to take calculated risks in exploration and experimentation. Children are able to concentrate on developing skills and knowledge with the underlying awareness that the safety, security and stability of the environment is there. It is only if these are missing that they create great problems.

> ## Discussion point
>
> *How can a care and education worker provide a stable environment for young children?*

Secure relationships

Children also need to be secure in their relationships. It is only with people they feel safe and happy with that they can move and venture into new areas. A trip to an unfamiliar place is fine if going with someone you have a good relationship with and trust, but can be traumatic with a relative stranger. Most care and education settings have a policy of staged entry so that children and families can gradually become familiar with the early years workers and the surroundings. The initial introduction to a setting may be a short visit for child and parent. The policy of many care and education establishments is to offer home visits prior to children visiting the setting, so that children meet the early years worker in the safety and security of their own home. After a few visits to the setting with their parents it may be suggested that the parent leaves for a very short time. This may even just be to another part of the building if the environment allows that. In this way children gradually develop independence whilst being with others who are by this point familiar and friendly. The length of time away from parents gradually becomes longer and the children fully settle in. This long staged entry is not always possible, but it should not be rushed, and should be carried out as sensitively as possible.

What are the intellectual needs of young children?

Jean Piaget (1896–1980) was one of the most famous psychologists to develop 'cognitive learning theory'. He spent much time studying children and developed a theory about how intellectual development takes place. He was very much committed to the promotion of 'discovery play', whereby a child discovers things for themselves and learns by first-hand experiences. He also developed his theory to include specific stages of development that all children experience. These he called the '**norms**' or '**patterns**' of development. His work affected the education process greatly and although others have developed his work, his basic ideas are still considered important today when caring for children. Piaget's norms of development for children are:

Age in years	Stage of development
2	Solitary play Imitating others Trial and error Repetitive activities Watching others
2–3	Parallel play Imitation Symbolic play (using one thing to represent another) Pretend play Starting to reason
3–4	Questioning Co-operative play Increased concentration span Starting to solve problems
4–5	Greater understanding Uses and understands symbols, e.g. writing/ reading Sharing interests and activities Understands rules Greater reasoning skills

Communication

Communication may take many forms and serve many purposes. There is more information later in this unit and in Unit 2 relating to communication.

A young child's vocabulary is very limited in the early stages of oral communication and children experience many frustrations as they are often able to understand more information than they can give back to others.

Written communication begins later when children begin to develop manipulative skills and begin to paint and draw. Gradually the skills are refined and, with help, children develop writing skills and can convey messages by picture or by symbol. These symbols represent the pictorial and are known as words.

Signing is another way of communicating and may be the main method for some children who are unable to communicate effectively in other ways, such as children who have a hearing impairment. British Sign Language and Makaton are the two most common methods of signing used in this country and many early years workers have attended classes to develop skills in these languages.

When adults communicate with children they convey important messages through body language. A child may be very confused if the words and the body language do not match, for example, if the body language is showing displeasure and the words used are trying to reassure the child. When a child is proud of a creation and brings it to an early years worker for comment, it is good practice to pay particular attention to the child, face them, get down to their level and speak enthusiastically about the product. The message should be that the child is important and what they have created is worthy of the care worker's undivided attention. The wrong message is conveyed if the carer's body is only half turned and the eyes are really looking elsewhere, and a throw-away comment is used such as 'That's lovely'. What the child is then being told is that they are not important enough for full attention!

Discussion point

Two children can hold a 'conversation' with each one talking about a totally different topic. Some adults still manage this!

Figure 8.7 *Let's talk*

Activity 4

Key skills ICT 2.1, 2.3

Melanie

Melanie is four years old.

1 Why is it important for Melanie to have secure relationships?

2 How can early years workers make sure children experience stability?

3 What is Jean Piaget's theory about intellectual development? Use a flow chart to illustrate your answer.

4 Explain what is meant by parallel play. Give an example.

5 Give an example of solitary play.

6 Explain how co-operative play can affect the development of children.

7 Devise a simple game that encourages children to take turns and talk to each other.

Stimulation

In Romania when children were discovered in forgotten orphanages it was noted that those children without any play experiences, spent much time hitting their heads against the sides of their cots in an attempt to provide some variety and stimulation. It is through stimulation that the interest of children is maintained and developed. It is useful to consider what makes an activity boring in order to **determine** what should be avoided. It may be that an activity is boring because it is repetitive or lacks excitement or variation. The activity may have been interesting to start with but it has gone on too long and the children have lost interest. When planning activities, motivational factors must be considered. Early years workers need to use **advantageous conditions**. For example, if the weather is good then why not take advantage of it? It may be that what has been planned can wait for another day. All early years workers should know that a flexible approach with all things is essential when working with children.

> ### Discussion point
> *What activities do you think would bore a child of three years of age? How could the activities be made more interesting*

Interests

Very young children develop individual interests, which can be used advantageously to develop skills in other areas. In some care and education settings, interest tables or displays are used to stimulate children's imaginations. These interest tables are usually linked to a theme or colour and can be added to each day. They provide children with an opportunity to handle materials and objects that they may not normally come into contact with, for example, artefacts from varying cultures. A small table can provide an 'interest area' in a private house. Covering the table gives added texture and if boxes are placed under this it raises some areas to make a more interesting display. Labelling the displayed items provides more interest and helps develop an awareness of language and the written word.

Challenge

Children need challenges in their lives and these can be provided by the sensitive **intervention** of early years workers. The **innate** curiosity of children means that they are always striving to achieve new goals. This is a healthy attitude and enables new skills to be developed and knowledge to be increased. It is important that challenges are within reach for a child, for if they are **unattainable**, then the child may lose the will to strive to meet these goals. They may then develop an attitude of submission and acceptance that they cannot do certain things. Challenge should not necessarily be a competitive activity as this can sometimes be destructive, especially for a child who has special needs. Challenges should be set against personal targets and built upon what a child can already do.

What are the social needs of a young child?

Human beings are, in general, social creatures who enjoy the company of other people. Young children do not like to be alone and become very distressed if they are by themselves for any length of time. However, by a gradual process, children develop individual skills of forming relationships with others. Play encourages the social side of activities, but there are times when children wish to play alone and other times when they wish to play **co-operatively**.

Co-operation

It is through co-operative play that children learn to share and take turns. At this stage meaningful conversations develop and the foundations for imaginative play are formed. Gradually, children understand the rules of games and often suggest rules of their own. They are also quite strict in enforcing the rules of a game whereas adults can be more lenient. It is through co-operative play that children learn to solve problems and to talk through and **refine** ideas. Resources within a care and education setting should be designed to encourage co-operation in its widest sense. Toys and activities for small groups of children should be preferred to those which only allow solitary play, for example, cars for two instead of one, seesaws, table-top games for small groups, cookery activities. Such activities allow for co-operative play, inter-action, the development of ideas, and the development of language and conversation skills.

Language

Initially language is immature but reaches a complex and sophisticated level by the time children are five. In order for language development to be effective, errors in grammar and structure must be corrected in a sensitive and meaningful way and without making children feel **inferior**. Simply repeating a phrase with the correct wording is often all that is required. Here is an example:

> **Child** I've bringed you this painting.
> **Adult** Have you brought that for me? That's very kind.

In this example there is no criticism and the correct term has been reinforced.

The basis of oral language can be formed at a very early stage. If a parent or carer speaks to a baby (using a particular type of language called 'motherese'), the baby responds by babbling back and keeping good eye contact. If when the baby stops, the adult responds, the child remains quiet until the adult stops and then begins babbling again. It is plain to see that the baby is learning and developing the basic skills of conversation and taking turns to speak. Children should be encouraged to talk and express themselves. It has been noted that if an adult or older sibling always speaks on a child's behalf, they might lose the will to speak for themselves and become **verbally inarticulate**.

Inter-relationships

When children play they develop the ability to relate to other people in different ways. As people grow older they have a number of varying and interconnected relationships, some of which are more formal than others. For example, relationships with close family and friends are very *informal* and are based on mutual trust and respect, whereas relationships with colleagues at work take on a different status and are usually a little bit more *formal*. Children begin to develop these skills at a very early age. Hearing a child having a pretend telephone conversation can help us to realise that they speak to different people in different ways. Play is the most important way these skills are allowed to develop. Initially, children play alone, and then alongside other children. Gradually they enter into a co-operative relationship with others and it is then that the wish to share resources and activities comes to the forefront. The caring nature of a child comes through and it is noticeable that they can see things from each other's point of view and empathise with each other. It is common to see a young child comforting someone who is hurt by giving them a cuddle or patting their back.

Assessment activity 8.1

Key skills [C] 2.2, 2.3

Meet the Brooker Family

The Brooker family are moving into your local area. The family have three children:

- Marti, who is a one-year-old
- Michelle, who is three years old.
- Bart, who is four-and-a-half years old

1 Produce a 'Directory of Services' for the family that includes at least three services that provide care and education for the children.

2 The 'Directory Of Services' should give a comprehensive account of the purpose of each service and how each meets the needs of young children.

8.2 Describe job roles and the skills and qualities required when working with children

What job roles are available when working with children?

There are a variety of job roles in the care and education sector and although each involves working with young children they each have differing requirements. Hours of employment vary, as do location and resources available. A description of the main job roles is listed in the table below.

What skills are required when working with children?

The skills required for working in the care and education sector are common to most job roles. Early years workers need to be flexible in approach and **adept** in a number of areas. The skills noted below are not **exclusive** to working with children but are also important when relating to parents and other professionals.

Job role	Description
Nursery nurse	Nursery nurses are trained to Level 3 and may work in day nurseries, private nurseries, nursery schools and primary schools. They are often employed in a supervisory capacity with nursery assistants. Many progress to roles of assistant/deputy manager or manager of nurseries. When working in a nursery class nursery nurses typically work alongside a qualified teacher and are involved in the planning, preparation and implementation of the curriculum. Additionally, many nursery nurses work as nannies and in out-of-school provision
Playgroup leader	Playgroup leaders typically hold qualifications at Level 3 in Playgroup Practice and are members of the Playgroup Association. They are in charge of a playgroup, which may be linked to a primary school or may be run in a village/church hall or community centre. They work closely with other dedicated playgroup workers and parents and often they need to physically arrange equipment at the beginning of each session
Childminder	Childminders use their own homes to provide care and education for children. The financial arrangements are private between the childminder and the parent. Many childminders move into this work because they have children of their own. Specific training for childminders can be accessed through the National Childminding Association, which joined with the Council for Awards in Childcare and Education (CACHE) to develop specific courses in this area. Childminders are required to register with the local authority and must comply with stringent regulations and screening through the Criminal Records Bureau (CRB)
Nursery teacher	Nursery teachers are **qualified** teachers who are specifically trained for working in the early years sector. Training usually takes three or four years and is at degree level. Nursery teachers are responsible for planning and preparation of all activities within their class and typically work alongside trained early years workers (nursery nurses) with children aged three to four years. Children usually work at Foundation Stage of the National Curriculum. Nursery teachers work in a nursery class, which may be attached to a primary school or nursery school or a joint education/social services establishment

Figure 8.8 *Skills required for working with children*

Early years workers must be approachable, as they need to relate to children, parents, carers and other professionals. It is important that the skills identified above are used effectively. It is necessary to communicate clearly, as there may be involvement in such activities as writing reports, notes to parents, information leaflets and posters. Active listening skills are extremely important. Occasionally, people hear only what they want to hear rather than what is actually being said. Early years workers should listen carefully and it may be useful for them to repeat parts of a conversation in their own words so that there is no misunderstanding. Early years workers must be able to plan ahead and prepare for activities in the care and education setting. These activities involve practical skills such as labelling pictures and organising materials for creative activities. Helping children develop social skills is an area which must be approached in a sensitive way as intervening

too early or too late can have a detrimental effect. There is always a great variety in care and education settings and no two days are the same. Just as adults arrive at work in various emotional states, so it is for children, and early years workers need to be sensitive toward children and parents, and be able to adapt as needed. It is challenging and very rewarding working in this sector.

What qualities are required when working with children?

Early years workers require certain qualities that will enable them to carry out their job effectively. Qualities are important and are instrumental in helping develop the good **reputation** of a practitioner. Parents and carers feel more content when leaving their children in the care of people who demonstrate some of the qualities shown in Figure 8.9 below.

Figure 8.9 *Qualities required when working with children*

Caring for children can be very rewarding

Activity 5

Skills and qualities needed by early years workers

Donna is a nursery nurse in a nursery school.
Jonathan is a teacher in a reception class.
Ros is a childminder.

1 What skills and qualities would these early years workers need when carrying out the following tasks?

  a Donna is talking to the children about items on the interest table.

  b Ros is making cakes with the children she is looking after.

  c Jonathan is showing the children how to count.

  d Ros is preparing the children to have their lunch by washing their hands and taking them to the toilet.

  e Jonathan is organising outside play for the children.

  f Donna is in the book corner with a small group of children.

2 Carry out research to find the answers to:

  a What is a skill?

  b What is a quality?

  Write a definition of each.

3 Think about your own skills and qualities. Write down **three** skills and **three** qualities that you think you have that would help you with a job in an early years care and education setting.

What are the early years care values?

Welfare of the child

The welfare of the child is of paramount importance. In order to put the needs of children first, it is necessary to have a certain level of information before taking responsibility or caring for children. The majority of people working in the early years sector have a **proforma**, into which should be put all the relevant information concerning a child. It is good practice to only hold information that is necessary and not information for interest. Early years settings must have policies and procedures relating to first aid, waste disposal and cleaning up bodily fluids so there is no risk to anyone. It is necessary for care workers to know about sickle cell anaemia, as a child may be affected by it whilst in the care of an early years practitioner.

Maintaining a healthy and safe environment

It is the responsibility of early years workers to provide and maintain a healthy and safe environment. In Figures 8.10 and 8.11 below, the health aspects and the safety aspects have been separated.

Safety is the responsibility of all who work in an early years setting, legislation being in place to ensure that laws are implemented.

Working with others

Early years workers often work as part of a team within a care and education setting. But even childminders who spend time working with children alone in their own home have some contact with other professionals and individuals linked with the welfare of the child. There are a number of aspects to **effective** teamwork, as detailed at the top of the next page.

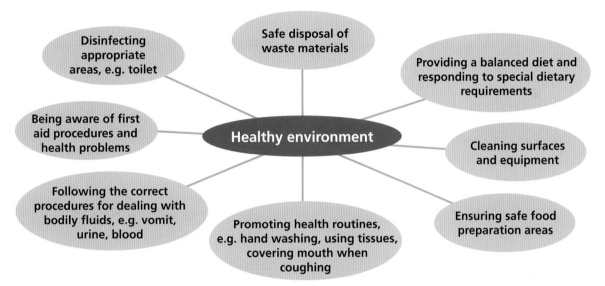

Figure 8.10 *Maintaining a healthy environment*

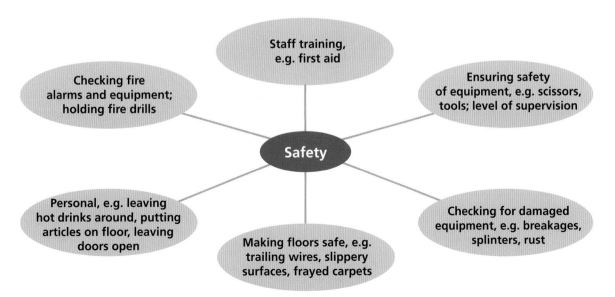

Figure 8.11 *Maintaining a safe environment*

Active listening skills	Support	Respect for each other	Avoiding conflict
Following instructions	Teamwork	Time management	Courtesy and consideration
Sharing	Confidentiality	Good communication skills	Receiving and giving feedback
Responsibility	Understanding other people's roles	Active participation	Politeness

Helping the child to meet its full potential

Play is the vehicle by which children can develop and learn. The UN Convention on the Rights of the Child states that 'children have a right to play'. Play is an enjoyable experience for children and can take place without adult input. However, for children to reach their full potential, sensitive adult assistance can be beneficial. Care and education settings provide the ideal environment for children to feel safe and secure enough to move to the next stage of development.

Children like to feel that they have succeeded at a task rather than failing and yet so often they are encouraged to attempt tasks that they cannot complete! For example, a child may have six buttons on their coat but may not have the skills or patience to fasten them all. If they fasten one and then need an adult to complete the process then they will not have succeeded in fastening the coat. However, if the adult starts the process and the child finishes the last one or two buttons then the task has been completed by the child. Success may encourage the child to repeat the process and eventually fastening a coat will be no problem at all. This same method of working can be used with all manner of activities, such as completing jigsaws, feeding activities and self-dressing.

Sensitive intervention is the key rather than taking over and preventing a child from developing self-help skills.

Valuing diversity

Figure 8.12 *Cultural diversity*

We live in a multi-culturally rich society. Care and education settings are an opportunity for children to learn from, experience and value this diversity. There are a wide range of activities available to encourage children to find out about other cultures and it is vital to be aware of variations in cultural, religious and dietary requirements. Appropriate resources enable the task of early years workers to be more thorough. Examples of how early years care and education settings can value diversity are shown in Figure 8.13.

The table on the right lists some major world religious festivals that children can celebrate.

World religion	Festival
Christian	Easter, usually March or April
Christian	Christmas, December 25th
Jewish	New Year, Rosh Hoshanah, usually September
Hindu	Holi, Spring Festival, February or March
Hindu	Divali, October or November
Muslim	Id Al Fitr, end of Ramadam
Rastafarian	New Year, usually January
Chinese	New Year, usually late January or early February

Equality of opportunity

All children should be equally valued as individuals and given opportunities to meet their full potential. This does not mean that all children should be treated the same, as some may require extra help or resources to achieve their potential.

Children must not be labelled or stereotyped. If a child is displaying undesirable behaviour then it is the behaviour that must be challenged rather than labelling the child as 'naughty'. People often have specific gender labels in mind, even with young children, for example they believe that boys play with construction toys, and girls play with dolls and buggies. Early years workers must be on guard as it can be very easy to fall into similar traps. It is also important that there are positive images relating to all aspects of equal opportunities in the care and education setting.

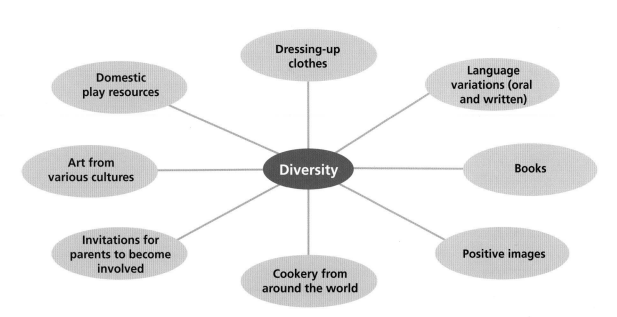

Figure 8.13 *Ways of valuing diversity*

There are a number of laws which have specific relevance to equality of opportunity.

Act	Significance for equal opportunities
Education Reform Act 1988	Introduction of the National Curriculum for all. Requirement to identify the needs of a child
The Children Act 1989	Consideration must be given to race, culture, religion and language when making decisions concerning the child
Disability Discrimination Act 1995	Rights for disabled people
Race Relations Act 1976	It is unlawful to discriminate on the grounds of race, colour, nationality, ethnicity or culture
Special Educational Needs and Disability Act 2001	Rights for disabled children

Activity 6

Key skills **C** 2.1a

Applying the care values

Sunil is a nursery nurse in a nursery school for children from six months to four-and-a-half years.

1 Explain what is meant by the term 'the welfare of the child is paramount'.

2 Sunil is responsible for the health and safety of the painting and small equipment area of the playroom. List **three** safety checks Sunil would make, giving reasons for each.

3 What would Sunil do to make sure the children have a healthy environment in which to play?

4 List **three** activities Sunil could provide to promote diversity in the nursery. Explain how each would help.

5 Discuss how you would change these phrases for the better:

> I need two strong boys to help me
>
> Be brave, boys don't cry.
>
> Girls, can you help me tidy up?
>
> Come on girls, show the boys how graceful you can be.
>
> Let the boys have the cars.
>
> Come on, dig the garden, boys. Girls, fetch the watering cans.

6 Give three examples of visual positive images that might be used in a care and education setting to promote equal opportunities.

Anti-discrimination

It is important to value a child as an individual as this encourages a sense of belonging and also helps increase self-esteem. Examples of how aspects of a child's identity can be valued and promoted are shown in Figure 8.14.

Confidentiality

Many care and education settings have a 'Confidentiality Policy' which all staff are required to follow. Parents and carers need to be able to trust early years workers and know that information about them will be kept in confidence. Early years workers learn the personal details of families and this information must not be shared freely. It is understood that professionally there are people that information can be shared with, but it is not for **indiscriminate** use. A careless word could ruin a trusting relationship. Early years workers should:

- always think before speaking
- never promise to keep something in confidence from their professional colleagues, especially if that information concerns the welfare of a child. This always comes first, especially with issues relating to child protection.

Figure 8.14 *How to value a child as an individual*

The reflective practitioner

When working with children it is always good practice for care workers to reflect or look back on what they have been involved with and consider ways of making improvements. It is useful for them to consider if the children benefited from an activity in the way hoped for and if they did not, then why not. How could things be improved upon? It is always possible to improve on own practice by attending training events, shadowing other professionals, or visiting other establishments. It is important to keep abreast with current issues and there are a number of magazines, periodicals and websites which enable early years workers to keep their practice up-to-date. The main purpose of this 'continuing professional development' is to provide the best care and education environment for children who will then have a greater chance of meeting their full potential.

Case study   Key skills [C] 2.1a

John and Nadia

John and Nadia both work in an early years setting and are on their way home after a busy day. They walk to the bus stop and while they are waiting for the bus they are joined by one of the parents of a child they work with. They begin to chat about general things and gradually the conversation gets around to working with children. The parent begins to tell them about a family living near them. As Nadia also knows the family and is working with one of the children she also begins sharing information.

1 Explain why the situation in this scenario is unacceptable.

2 What should Nadia have done?

3 What could John have done?

4 What might the consequences be?

Assessment activity 8.2   Key Skills [C] 2.3

Job roles in the early years sector

Mrs Brooker is considering having a job in the early years sector. She would like information about job roles and the skills and qualities required.

1 Within the 'Directory of Services' began in Assessment Activity 8.1, give a comprehensive account about the skills and qualities required for two job roles in the early years sector.

2 Arrange a visit to an early years care setting with your tutor's permission to find out how the care values are applied there. Write up some questions beforehand (do this together with Assessment Activity 8.3).

3 Explain in depth, how the care values are applied in the care setting chosen. Give examples to illustrate the points made.

What responsibilities do early years workers have to protect children from harm?

It is very important that when children are in care and education settings they are in a safe and secure environment and are protected from harm at all times. It is the responsibility of early years workers to ensure the setting is as hazard-free as possible as they have a legal duty of care towards the children under their protection. Ignoring a hazard is classed as negligence from a legal perspective. Protection of children from harm is not restricted to providing a safe physical environment but also includes providing well-trained and responsible care workers. All early years workers are required to submit to a check by the Criminal Records Bureau (usually referred to as a CRB check). This ensures that there are no convictions or records which would prevent someone from working with children. It is usual for references to be taken up prior to employment in the care and education sector and ideally these should be relevant to early years work. Often individuals are required to complete a health questionnaire and be prepared to undertake a medical examination if required. All of this is normally in addition to attending an interview to determine suitability for the position. These may appear to be a large number of procedures but all possible precautions should be taken to ensure that appropriate people are the ones working with children.

Once someone is employed in the care and education sector they have an additional responsibility to be alert to any indications that children are at risk of harm. It is an unfortunate fact that some children suffer abuse in various forms and the early years worker must be alert to the signs and symptoms which might be present.

They should, additionally, be aware of the reporting procedures for this, which would typically be through a line manager.

Type of abuse	Signs of abuse
Physical	Bruising; belt/buckle marks; bites; burns; aggressiveness towards other children
Emotional	Tearful; clingy; low self esteem; attention-seeking; stammering/stuttering; lying
Sexual	pain when passing urine; bruising; bedwetting; loss of appetite; genital itching; inappropriate play behaviour, e.g. sexually explicit; withdrawal
Neglect	poor personal hygiene; dirty and unkempt; failure to thrive; injury due to lack of supervision; tired; hungry

Always keep in mind the fact that very happy well-balanced children who are not being abused display some of the characteristics mentioned above from time to time. Children often have some bruises which are just linked to ordinary rough and tumble play. The early years worker needs to be aware of patterns and changes in the whole child and to report any concerns to an appropriate person.

Identification and reporting of hazards

What is the difference between a hazard and a risk?

- *hazard* – anything which might cause harm to any individual within the immediate environment
- *risk* – the likelihood of harm from the hazard.

Any environment has hazards, but extra care is needed when working with young children. Everyone working in a setting has a responsibility to ensure that the setting is as safe as is reasonably possible. When carrying out a safety survey or audit of an area all possible hazards should be considered and safety features implemented to reduce the risks. Some things are easier to remedy than others, for example, if knives are being left out on a bench, then staff training or instruction should ensure that this does not happen in the future. Staff would be considered negligent if a child injured themselves in this way. However, some things cannot be easily altered and procedures may need to be adopted to reduce the risk. For example, steps into and inside buildings may be seen as a hazard but this can be reduced by clear marking of the edges of steps, verbally informing people of their presence and placing appropriate safety/warnings and signs in obvious places.

A certain amount of risk is involved within activities. For example, a young child using hammers, nails, drills and saws at a workbench may worry adults, but this activity can be a wonderful experience for the child. If the risk cannot be substantially reduced then the activity should not take place. If the activity has a high level of supervision, with a restricted number of children, and safety rules are reinforced and strictly adhered to, then the risk factor should be reduced enough for children to be able to carry out the activity.

A hazard, once identified, should be reported and/or removed. Reporting a hazard to someone else does not remove the responsibility. A short list of potential hazards, risks and reporting procedures is listed in the table below.

Hazard	Risk	Possible reporting procedure	Possible action
Trailing wires	Tripping	Line manager Caretaker Health and safety personnel	Remove if possible. Make safe by altering layout
Water/sand on floor	Slipping	Line manager	Clear up as quickly as possible. Warn children and staff
Sharp corners on furniture	Bumping into furniture	Line manager Health & safety personnel	Recommend protective corner covers
Broken toys	Injury through sharp/broken edges etc.	Line manager	Remove toys until repaired and safe
Garden waste	Contact with contaminated products, plastic bags etc.	Line manager	Ensure waste is kept safe in secure and appropriate containers with secure lids
Animal faeces in garden	Contamination and disease	Line manager Caretaker	Keep children away from area until it has been cleaned and waste disposed of correctly

Activity 7

Spot the hazards in a childminder's home

Figure 8.15 *Kitchen hazards*

Figure 8.16 *Bathroom hazards*

1 Look at the two pictures and make a list of as many hazards as you can.

2 How might an early years worker make the areas safer for a child?

3 Identify the risks that could exist in a playgroup or a nursery class or childminder's living room. What should be done to reduce the risk?

Everyday items used regularly in the care and education setting can be dangerous if misused. For example, using scissors is an extremely dangerous activity if indiscriminate use is allowed. Pencils can become harmful especially if a child is running or has one in their mouth. Early years workers need to quickly develop skills of being watchful at all times.

Safety features

All equipment should be suitable for the age group and should meet safety standards. Check equipment for Kitemarks, which indicate that materials and design are fit for the purpose and the age range. On page 255 is a list of safety equipment and its role in creating a safe environment for children.

Equipment	Purpose
Smoke alarms	Designed for the early detection of fire and so allow swift and timely evacuation of building. They are able to detect small amounts of smoke, which trigger a piercing sound to alert individuals to potential danger
Corner covers	Designed to cover sharp corners of furniture and so reduce risk of serious injury. The plastic cover 'rounds off' the pointed, sharp corners and lessens the chance of wounds, which could puncture the skin
Electric socket covers	Designed to fit into electric sockets as a 'blank' and so prevent the insertion of other items into the dangerous live socket. Children sometimes enjoy trying to fit one object inside another and this can be extremely dangerous if it is metal and inserted into an electric socket
Plastic film on glass	Designed to prevent glass from shattering and scattering if broken. The broken glass will adhere to the film which greatly reduces the risk of harm to children. This is often used where safety glass has not been fitted
Cooker guard	Designed to prevent pans from being pulled from the cooker and spilling contents onto a young child. They are usually very easy to fit and provide a raised front to the hob and are effective in reducing risk of injury
Childproof catches	Designed to prevent young children from opening doors to cupboards or cabinets, which might contain harmful substances. They are also used on gates and other barriers used to keep children safe. Children learn new skills quickly and it is good practice not to allow a child to observe you opening a door with one of these catches attached
Gates	Designed usually as temporary measures to prevent children getting access to another room, e.g. a kitchen area when the cooker is in use, or to prevent access to stairs which could prove to be dangerous for the children. As children develop skills of balance and the ability to use stairs and steps effectively, the use of such gates may be reduced
Fire blankets	Designed for use in areas where a fire is more likely, e.g. the kitchen area. They are usually in an easy-release container and often wall-mounted in the kitchen. When placed over a burning item, they smother the flames by excluding oxygen.
Fire extinguishers	Designed to extinguish fires quickly and effectively. There are different types of fire extinguisher each with a distinct purpose (see Unit 4.5, pages 177–179). Extinguishers are usually wall-mounted and must be checked regularly by the supplier to ensure that they are still fit for purpose
First aid equipment	First aid equipment should be readily available at all times and should not be locked away. The first aid box should be clearly identified by its green colour and the white cross on it. The contents of the first aid box recommended for first aid at work is laid down by the Health and Safety Executive. It should not contain any items that, if misused through lack of knowledge, would cause harm. The kit should include various sized dressings, self-adhesive dressings, triangular bandages, and safety pins. It should not include cotton wool as this can have a detrimental affect if placed on a burn. The person administering first aid needs to wear protective equipment such as latex gloves and plastic aprons. There should also be appropriate waste disposal bags (yellow for medical waste so that it can be clearly identified as holding contaminated or dangerous waste, e.g. blood soaked tissues. There should always be someone on duty who holds a current first aid qualification. This must be renewed every three years for it to be valid. An accident book must also be provided to keep comprehensive records of accidents, treatments and the 'disposal' of the casualty. Disposal refers to what happened to the casualty next, e.g. did the child resume play, did they need to go home or were they taken to hospital? These records should always be kept safe and signed by the appropriate person
Childproof lids and caps	Designed to prevent children from opening bottles and containers containing harmful substances. Bottles containing bleach often have a cap that needs to be squeezed in a certain place before it can be opened. Medicine bottles and containers for tablets usually have caps which must be pressed down before they will turn. Others may require marks or arrows to be lined up before the container can be opened. These preventative measures can be so effective that they often pose problems for adults, but dangerous substances should not be put in any other container as it can have fatal results. Safe storage and handling of medicines is of prime importance when children are about

Regular audit checks should be carried out by a named person within a care setting to ensure that safety policies and practices are maintained and implemented. This includes, for example, spot checks on record keeping, checking first aid equipment is replenished when used, correct disposal of waste, regular fire drills, staff responsibilities and clearing of hazards. If audits are not carried out regularly then there is a danger of standards slipping and the possibility of injury is dramatically increased.

Wet floors can be dangerous

Case study

Key skills **C** 2.1a

Safety

A child had not been well and has a runny nose. Mum decides it is time to give some medication to the child to relieve the symptoms. She sits the child on the kitchen bench and carefully unlocks the childproof medicine cabinet. She removes from their package two little orange tablets, which the manufacturers promised will relieve the signs and symptoms of colds and reduce headaches, fever and runny noses. She places these beside the child and says, "These will sort out that runny nose of yours and make you feel better". She then proceeds to return the rest of the tablets to the cabinet and dutifully locks it. She turns back to the child and goes to pick up the tablets but they are not there. She looks at the child's face, still with its obvious runny nose but this time there is an orange tinge to the mucus. The child has taken the mother at her word. These tablets were to help with the nasal problem and so the logical thing to do is to place them in the nose.

1 What should the mother have done?

Risk assessment

When carrying out a risk assessment it is necessary to consider the whole care setting or area and identify the risks. It is useful if this is done from the viewpoint of a child, trying to identify what could be attractive to young children and therefore increase their risk of accident or injury. Do not assume that a child would behave in the same way if left alone as when an adult is present. When conducting a risk assessment a note should be made of risks that need attention. Suggested alterations or **control measures** need to be made. If the risk is reduced to an acceptable level then the actions taken should be documented and form part of the safety policy and procedures document. Some safety measures are simple to put in place. For example, entrances and exits should be clear and unrestricted, storage of cleaning equipment should be safe with access by children **prohibited** (this may mean that cleaning fluids etc are stored under lock and key). Play equipment, especially outdoor equipment such as climbing frames and swings should be checked before each use, the use of absorbent surface material beneath such equipment can greatly reduce injuries, particularly head injuries.

Outdoor play, especially in a garden can be an exciting environment for young children but there can be many dangers. Examples of this are shown in Figure 8.17.

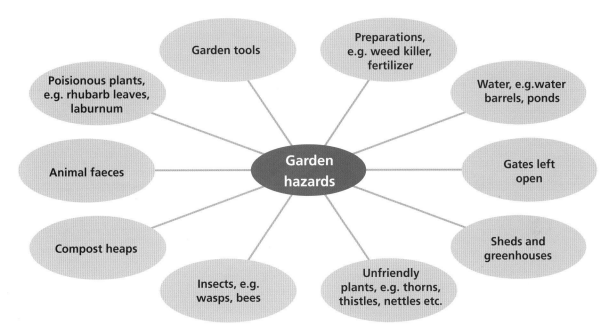

Figure 8.17 *Hazards in a garden*

Figure 8.18 *Dangerous garden*

Activity 8

The childminder's garden

Marjorie is a childminder for four children who are between the ages of one and four years of age.

1 Identify four risks that could exist in the childminder's garden.

2 Explain how each could be reduced.

3 List three actions that early years workers could take when supervising children for outdoor activities.

Attitudes

Working in the care and education sector means that all care workers must be aware of what is going on around them. Taking simple actions such as tidying away a seesaw and other items of equipment that could cause children or another worker to fall and injure themselves is important and reflects a care worker's attitude toward making sure that an environment in safe for children.

Even when working with a small group of children it is good practice to keep a watchful eye on what is happening in the setting. A skilled early years worker develops an ability to take in a vast amount of visual information from the surrounding area whilst talking with or working alongside others.

A calm and reassuring attitude is required at all times, especially if children are distressed for any reason such as injury or emotional upset. Ignoring the reason for an upset or trying to distract a child from thinking about it is not always the best thing to do. Care workers should acknowledge when children have hurt themselves, ask if they are alright and then sympathise with them and ask if there is anything they can do. They may suggest that they do not carry out activities until they are feeling more settled.

Discussion point

If an adult fell and injured their knee, would we tell them to be brave and get on with their work? Should children be treated any differently?

Early years workers must be calm, reassuring and sensitive to the individual needs of children and not frighten them.

If evacuating a building in the event of a fire or an emergency, it is also necessary to demonstrate a calm attitude. If there have been fire drills in the past, then evacuating the building is not such a daunting activity for a young child, and if the care workers are calm and organised, the children will be reassured and confident.

Legal requirements

Legislation is in place to ensure that people work in as safe an environment as possible. Some laws and regulations are given in the table below.

Legislation	Provisions
The Children Act 1989	Determines the staff/child ratio i.e. the younger the children then the more staff need to be employed to care for them
The Health and Safety at Work Act 1974	Determines what is required for an environment to be safe for work purposes
Health and Safety (First Aid) Regulations 1981	Determines how many first aiders are required, what first aid training is recommended and what should be available as first aid equipment
Control of Substances Hazardous to Health Regulations 2002	Lays down guidance regarding safe use and storage of materials. Risk assessments should be carried out on all substances which fall into this category and records of harmful ingredients and treatments must be available
General Food Hygiene Regulations 1995	Lays down guidance on the safe handling and storage of foodstuffs. If children are receiving meals in care and education settings then it is good practice that small samples are kept in case of food poisoning or infection
Reporting of Injuries, Diseases and Dangerous Occurrences Regulations 1995	Lays down specific guidance on the reporting of certain diseases and injuries. It relates mainly to communicable diseases and injuries of a serious nature which require hospitalisation and/or permanent disfigurement

It is a legal requirement that records are kept of all incidents and injuries. When safety audits are carried out it is useful to look over past records to see if there is any pattern to incidents. This may highlight:

- if a particular piece of equipment is flawed
- if a particular play area is prone to incidents
- if there are any improvements/changes to be made
- accident prone individuals.

In this way records might be seen as a useful tool to aid development rather than a record of negative events.

Assessment activity 8.3

Key skills C 2.2

Maintaining a safe environment

Arrange to visit **one** care and education setting (with your tutor's permission). Give an in-depth account of how a safe environment is provided and maintained in that setting. Provide examples to illustrate the points being made.

Remember to include information about:

- how hazards are identified and reported
- safety features that are in place
- how a risk assessment is carried out, its purpose and the checks that would be made
- the attitudes of early years workers relating to safety issues
- the legal requirements for the setting and how these are applied.

What role does play have in the development of a child?

Play is linked to the holistic development of children and it is one of the main ways through which children learn. Play has certain characteristics, as shown in Figure 8.19.

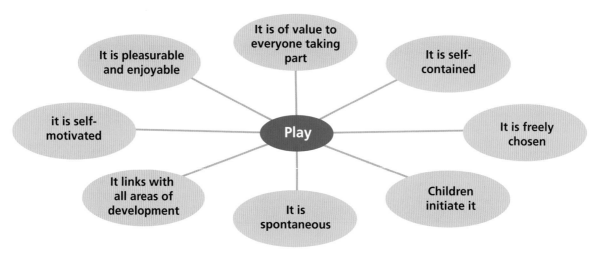

Figure 8.19 *The characteristics of play*

Socialising

Children enjoy the company of other children and as they become older they are able to share and co-operate with other children. Social play encourages children to mix, and it also teaches children that certain behaviour is unacceptable. If a child is aggressive on a regular basis then they are less likely to develop friendship bonds with other children. However, children often disagree with each other and this is a natural process during which they learn about other people's feelings and reactions. Social play also encourages language development and an increase in vocabulary.

Communicating

Children have to develop a variety of communication skills and they are often very mature by the age of three. They have learnt to communicate with each other and with adults, both at home and in a care and education setting. For example, a young child having an imaginary conversation on the telephone has already developed a 'telephone voice' and uses 'telephone language'. In a similar way, when children are reading stories to one another they use language that they would not normally hear in everyday conversations, for example 'once upon a time'. They very quickly develop a wide vocabulary and can adapt the rule for plurals and past tense to words even when it is grammatically incorrect. For example, a child may use a phrase like 'I've bringed you this'. They have taken the normal rule for past tense and applied it to the word bring. Unfortunately the English language is complex, but they have cleverly worked out the rule. They have not copied it from adults. It is important that they are not ridiculed for this but sensitively corrected. Children have a very natural and open body language and in general maintain good clear eye contact. They often become frustrated, as they understand much more than their vocabulary allows. Extremely young children understand the word NO but cannot fully communicate their thoughts. They are not be able to do this until they have developed the appropriate language skills. It is important that parents and carers talk with children as an ongoing process. They should not try to answer for children, but give them opportunity to respond.

As children develop they make friends and small group play emerges. By this time children are more skilled at using language and are more inventive and able to use dramatic play to live out fantasies.

Learning new skills

Children often appear to have limitless amounts of energy and from the moment they are born they are developing physical skills. As children increase in age they become more agile and more confident. Young children are extremely curious and love to explore. There should be an outlet for this in care and education settings. This may vary and could include wheeled toys such as cars and tricycles, to swings and climbing frames. Safety is of prime importance and impact-absorbent surfaces should be used wherever possible. It is good practice to consider health and safety issues prior to allowing physical play and to consider the level of supervision required (see Unit 8.3).

Creative play allows children to express themselves in making something original. This may involve drawing or painting a picture, making a model, telling a story or by construction of an item using different materials. It is important that parents and carers value all work and creations. Children may produce the same type of painting or model over and over again, for example a child may paint vertical lines every time they paint and then one day will move into a different type of painting. This is linked to the development of specific skills and when a child moves onto another area of development. As children develop skills in creative play they become more adventurous and create more complex items. There are problems to solve and there are occasions when children ask for adult intervention. This must be sensitive in approach and it is important to involve the child at all times and avoid the temptation to take charge.

Manipulative play involves the use of the hands in an expressive manner. Fine muscle movements are developed and refined and eventually enable children to feed themselves, dress themselves, draw and write. It is important to encourage these life skills, as children become more independent. Adults involved in care and education settings must provide safe and tested materials to enable this type of play to take place. Items such as sand, water and modelling materials help develop fine motor control.

Intellectual development

Discovery play involves first hand experiences when there is often a sense of wonder. The impact of discovery increases the likelihood of remembering and retaining knowledge. It is exciting to be present when a child experiences something for the first time. How better to learn about snow by going out into it, handling it, moulding it, collecting it and allowing it to melt. When a child is older, discovery play progresses into early science activities such as magnetism, mirrors and electricity.

Imaginative play is sometimes called make-believe play, where children happily **substitute** one item for another, for example pieces of jigsaw on a plate become a sumptuous meal. Children readily mimic the characteristics of another person and portray adults in a very clear and detailed way. Behaving as someone else helps children to understand other people's roles and reproduce role-specific language. It is through imaginative and fantasy play that children often come to terms with fears. They are able to live out things that worry them or deal with difficult situations. It is often difficult for children to express their feelings and make-believe play allows them to do this in a safe way. Occasionally, very shy and quiet children become quite outspoken when dressing up in other clothes.

Activity 9

Merrill

Merrill is four years old and attends playgroup three times a week.

1 Explain how play could affect Merrill's communication and ability to socialise.

2 At what age would Merrill have been involved in parallel play?

3 List four new skills that Merrill is likely to learn while at playgroup. Explain how each is likely to affect her development.

4 Work with another person in the group. Plan and implement an activity that would encourage intellectual development. One person should take the role of the child. Is the activity intellectually stimulating? What would the child learn?

Now reverse the roles and have a second activity. Answer the questions given above.

Was one activity more intellectually stimulating than the other? If so, why?

Recipe for 'playdough'

1 cup flour

$\frac{1}{2}$ cup salt

1 teaspoon cream of tartar

1 tablespoon oil

A few drops of food colouring in 1 cup boiling water

Add water last of all and mix well until it forms a ball of dough. If this does not happen you may need to heat it in a pan. Allow to cool. Wrap in cling-film when not in use.

DO NOT ALLOW CHILDREN NEAR BOILING WATER OR TO PLAY WITH CLINGFILM.

What are the different stages of play?

As children grow up, they pass through several stages of development (see Unit 8.1). These stages are associated with different stages in the way children play.

Solitary play

Solitary play is the first stage of play. This stage usually lasts until children are 18 months to two years old, but it must be remembered that children of all ages indulge in solitary play. Children play alone and are quite content to do so. If in the same room as other children, a child participating in solitary play pays no attention to anyone else. Young children explore by observing, stretching and reaching. Many skills are developed at this time. Later, children may stand at the edge of an activity, watching and learning but not joining in. Occasionally, children prefer to watch and gain confidence prior to joining in with an activity. This **spectator** activity can continue into adulthood, hence the appeal of watching a demonstration before attempting a new skill. Children of all ages engage in solitary play at times, but for very young children it may be the only type of play available. When an older child plays alone it does not mean that they are anti-social. It is a natural play state and children should be given the opportunity to do it.

Figure 8.20 *Solitary play*

Parallel play

Figure 8.21 *Parallel play*

During this stage of play it may at first appear that children are playing with other children whereas in fact they are playing alongside them, totally absorbed in their own activity. Parallel play can be seen from 18 months to three years, but it is beneficial to keep in mind that these stages are approximate and much depends on the nature of individual children. Children are more confident at this stage and start to rely less on their parents. Parallel play is a sign that a child is becoming less egocentric and is beginning to enjoy the company of other children. Children are very interested in their toys and often **attribute** life to them. Conversations are often with their toys and children may be totally unaware that there is someone close by engaged in a similar activity. Occasionally, children engage in parallel play but using the same equipment, for example sand or water play. There may be some interaction but it is often that they are encroaching on each other's territory rather than sharing.

Co-operative play

Co-operative play is important in the development of independent skills and attributes. During this stage of play a child usually develops a relationship with another child, and as confidence is gained more children join the activity. Children learn to share and see things from another person's point of view, and as a result are no longer egocentric. Children begin to care about how other people feel and respect their views. They will discuss options with other children and move towards solutions.

Figure 8.22 *Co-operative play*

What is the effect of play on the development of children?

It is through play that children learn about life and develop certain skills that help them deal with day-to-day issues.

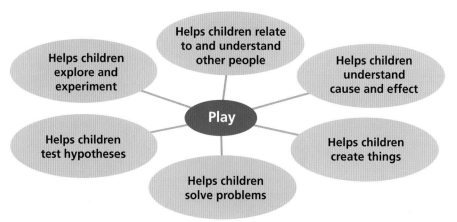

Figure 8.23 *The effect of play on children*

Play is linked to all the areas of development for a child:

- physical
- emotional
- intellectual
- social
- language.

Safety must be at the forefront of all activities and is one of the main roles of carers in a care and education setting. Children do not necessarily have the knowledge and understanding to know what is dangerous or not. Making sure that a play area is safe should not, however, inhibit play.

Discussion point

How is play linked to the development of a child?

Assessment activity 8.4

Key skills ICT 2.1, 2.2, C 2.3

Learning about play

As part of her training for a job in an early years setting, Mrs Booker needs information about the different types of play and the effect of play on the development of children.

1 Carry out primary and secondary research to find out about the role of play in an early years setting. Make notes, you may be able to visit a setting or invite an early years play leader or specialist to the centre (with your tutor's permission).

2 Produce a 'Guide to Play in Early years settings' that could be used to inform Mrs Booker about the different types of play. Remember to include information about:

- solitary play
- parallel play
- co-operative play.

Try to give examples to illustrate the points made.

3 Mrs Booker wants to know how play can affect the development of children. She needs to know how play can affect:

- socialising
- communicating
- learning new skills
- intellectual development.

You may wish to interview parents of young children to provide primary information and examples. If you do use this method make sure that the questions produced have been tried out before use and are appropriate as the information will be confidential and sensitive.

You should try to link theory to the evidence collected.

Not all establishments are purpose-built as care and education settings. It is important that when adapting an existing building for use with children that it complies with the local authority regulations and guidelines. However, it can be quite exciting to be involved with the design and layout of a purpose-built structure, for the care and education of children.

What design features must be taken into account?

There are a number of basic rules which must be followed when considering the design and layout of any setting where young children will be. These rules are all important and fit together to provide a safe, secure and user-friendly environment that is suitable for both young children and adults.

Ergonomics

This means that everything used in a setting must be designed to promote good posture, normal movement and ease of use, creating an atmosphere of independence and safety for all users of the setting. Ergonomics means checking there is enough space for ease of movement, being careful and thoughtful about the positioning of indoor furniture and considering which items should be placed next to one another. For example, having the paint and water at opposite ends of the room is not practical.

Furniture should be functional and the correct size for those who are going to use it, i.e. adults should not have to use child-sized furniture all the time and neither should children have to work at adult height. Seats for use with computers should support the back and the monitor screen should be at the correct angle so that the head of the user is not held at an uncomfortable angle. Toilets, sinks and washbasins should all be at the correct height for the intended user.

If children are expected to develop independence and access resources then these need to be easily accessible for them. Accidents occur when an individual stretches beyond their reach for something or is tempted to climb up, if the item cannot easily be reached. Looking at the environment through the eyes of a child can, in many instances prevent accidents from occurring.

> **Remember!** Prevention is better than cure!

Safety

Care and education settings must meet the local authority regulations for safety and need to be registered as being used for young children. The physical environment should be considered first. All resources should have a safety mark to ensure that they are at the right standard for use.

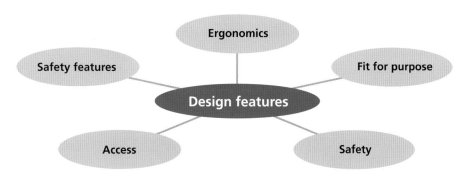

Figure 8.24 *Design features for care and education settings*

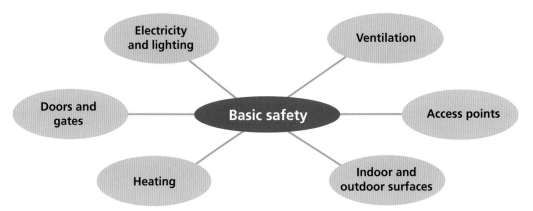

Figure 8.25 *Basic safety requirements for care and education settings*

Electricity and lighting

The whole care and education setting should be well-lit so that the entire setting is visible to all. No one should be struggling to see anything clearly, particularly if close work is being carried out. The only exception to this rule is if a sensory room is one of the features of a setting, which would cater for children with specific or special needs. Often, such rooms are darkened with soothing lighted areas to calm and relax children. There ought to be current breakers for electrical equipment so that any misuse or malfunction will result in a break in the current and so not cause electrocution for the user. All unused electrical sockets should be covered so that inappropriate objects cannot be introduced.

Ventilation

Windows should open to ensure good circulation of air and it should be possible to lock them in a safe open position. They should not be open so far that children can climb or fall out. Toughened glass is the best material for windows in buildings used for the care and education of young children.

Access points

These should be kept clear and be pointed out to adults, children and visitors in case of emergency evacuation. Labelling can also help with access so that service users know where to go.

Indoor and outdoor surfaces

All surfaces should be slip-resistant and easy to clean. Impact absorbent surfaces must be used under outdoor equipment, especially climbing frames and swings.

Heating

The temperature of buildings should be 15–18°C (18–21°C for very young children). Protection should be provided whenever there is any source of heat, such as fireguards and radiator covers. Smoke alarms should be fitted in appropriate places.

Doors and gates

All external gates and doors should be locked and coded if at all possible and such locks and coding devices should be out of reach of children. Doors should have toughened glass in appropriate panels and safety equipment should be to BSI standard.

Access

When considering access it is necessary to think about *all* users of the premises and provide for them.

Figure 8.26 *Aspects of access for safety*

Ramps/all one level

In the care and education environment, the ideal setting would be on one level. However, many buildings do not have this luxury. Ramps are one solution, as they provide easy access for all who have mobility problems, and can be beneficial for those with babies in prams or buggies.

Doors and gates

Should be wide enough for equipment to be taken outside. Many purpose-built establishments have double doors which are helpful when wanting to put equipment outside, but there needs to be a mechanism which enables doors to be kept open and not slam shut on breezy days. Doors should only be left open if they provide access to an outdoor play area and the level of supervision is such that activities and equipment can be used safely. Early years workers must ensure the safety of children and visitors, by for example, installing security pads to gain entrance.

Curbs

Should be easily seen and paths clearly marked and even. Any uneven surfaces should be reported immediately in case someone trips and injures themselves.

Railings

Should be tall enough so that children cannot injure themselves, and the spacing of the uprights should be such that children cannot put their head through and become trapped. This used to be a relatively common occurrence at one time but health and safety regulations now ensure that the spaces between bars on items such as cots and railings are too narrow for this to happen.

Flooring

Should be non-slip and where surfaces change there ought to be a change in colour to ensure easier identification.

Fit for purpose

All aspects of a care and education setting should be fit for purpose. This means that whatever is used should be sturdy enough and safe for the purpose for which it was designed. If a water trough leaks then it is not fit for purpose and should be returned to the manufacturer. This is one of the reasons why it is important to ensure that equipment and resources are purchased from reputable outlets, and that they conform to some safety standard.

Safety features

Safety in the design and layout of an environment should always feature highly in the minds of those involved. Below are some features which might be incorporated in a typical setting.

Design feature	Purpose
Textured pavement areas	To ensure partially-sighted are aware of access points
Carpet strips	To ensure edges of carpets are not raised or curled up
Change of colour – floors	To heighten awareness of surface change
Curved corners	To reduce risk of injury from sharp corners of furniture
Temperature guards	Designed to ensure that water or radiators do not exceed the set temperature and this reduces the risk of burns or scalds
Window locks	To ensure safe and secure opening of windows and to restrict degree to which windows can be opened
Safety locks	To prevent unsafe areas from being accessed by children
Non-slip surfaces	To prevent accidents in areas where the likelihood for slips is high, e.g. bathroom areas, sand and water play areas
Camera access	To ensure awareness of visitors to setting and increase vigilance regarding intruder awareness
Swipe card access	Can be used instead of safety locks for rooms and large cupboards and for access to the building as a safety feature

Which setting would you choose?

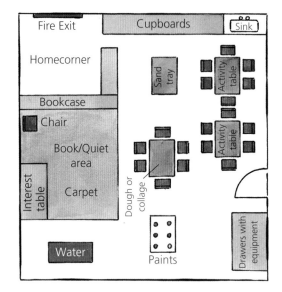
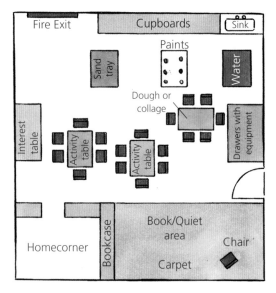

Figure 8.27 *Which one to choose?*

Consider the two layouts:

1 Explain which is the better layout. Give reasons for your choice.

2 Would you make any additions? State which additions you would make and give reasons to support the answers given.

3 What is ergonomics?

4 What are the important points when considering the ergonomics of a playgroup setting?

What are the different play activities to consider when designing a setting?

Once the physical layout of a setting has been designed, it is necessary to consider the various types of activities that are to be provided for the overall development of the children. These activities can be divided into:

- physical
- creative
- structural
- discovery
- intellectual.

It must be noted that many activities overlap. For example, because an activity is 'creative' does not mean that it cannot also be intellectual or a discovery activity.

Physical activities

Activities which cater for physical development are wide-ranging and diverse. They include those which help with the development of large and small muscle groups. Both outdoor and indoor activities are included as can be seen from Figures 8.28 and 8.29 on page 269.

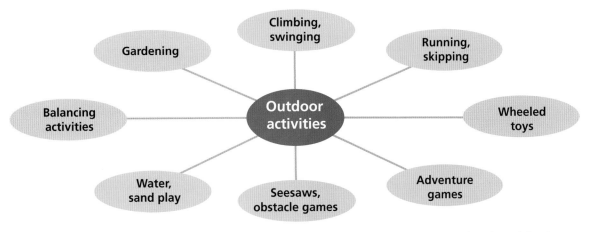

Figure 8.28 *Outdoor activities for physical development*

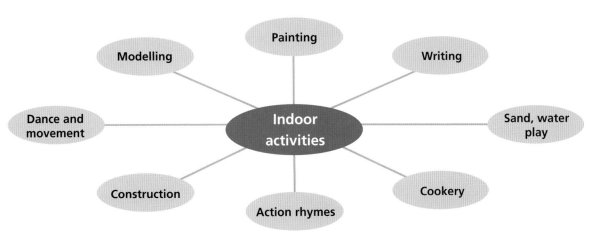

Figure 8.29 *Indoor activities for physical development*

Creative

Children can be creative in many ways and this imaginative aspect of their development must be encouraged. It is the responsibility of early years workers to provide outlets for creative activities. Some ideas are listed below.

Painting	Collage	Playdough
Clay	Construction	Drawing
Making up stories	Sand play	Water play
Pretend play	Imaginative play	Dance and movement

Structures

Children need to be able to build and construct, whether on a small or large scale. There are various toys and activities that enable this to

happen. Table-top activities such as Lego and stickle bricks enable children to create structures that provide opportunity for free and unrestricted thinking and encourage problem-solving development. Larger building and construction materials can be used in a carpeted area where wooden blocks and ramps provide the materials for building design. Building structures often provide further opportunity for **collaboration** and co-operative play and it is through this type of play that mathematical concepts become **embedded** and **consolidated**. Safety is particularly important and early years workers must be aware that small items might be put into the mouth and swallowed or that large items may fall if structures become too high. It is important that the creative flow is not inhibited by the need for safety, however.

Discovery

This is interesting

Discovery play is one of the most important aspects of child development. It is much better to have first-hand experience of something and so develop an understanding, rather than to be told about someone else's experience. Children must be allowed to handle objects and become familiar with their properties. When cooking with children, for example, allow them to break the eggs and to measure the ingredients. Involvement and discovery is far better than just watching, even if it is a bit messy first time round! Children need to experience first hand the science involved in cooking, such as how adding the ingredients changes the texture and how heat changes a liquid to a solid.

Second-hand experiences cannot replace direct and first-hand involvement. It is far better for children to see sheep in a field than just to see pictures or be told about them. Early years workers should always be looking for ways to provide meaningful experiences for children and in this way they will learn to appreciate the world around them.

Intellectual

Intellectual development is experienced in all activities that children engage in, as in so doing they develop mathematical, language, communication, reasoning skills and logical thought processes. Activities to promote and develop these skills can be provided in the setting but may and will be incorporated into other activities. For example, sorting and grading could be developed by the use of puzzles and table-top activities, but may be equally achieved in a domestic play setting when sets of cutlery and crockery are used to set the table, or when different sized dolls require the appropriate sized clothing.

Below are some other suggestions for promoting intellectual development in a care and education setting.

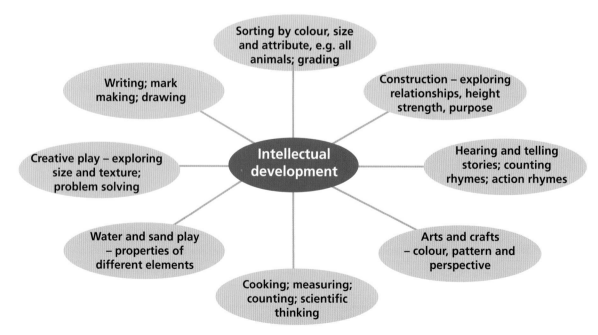

Figure 8.30 *Activities to promote intellectual development*

Key skills ICT 2.3, C 2.3

Layout for a care setting

You have been asked to produce a suitable layout for an early years setting and to discuss the different types of activities that could be carried out in the setting.

The materials you produce are to be used by Mrs Brooker and other trainees to help them understand how to design suitable layouts and what points to consider when doing so.

1 Design a suitable layout for one care and education environment. Focus on play activities.

2 Explain why the layout is suitable for the different play activities. You should make sure that you discuss:

- ergonomics
- safety
- access
- fit for purpose
- safety features.

3 Provide a detailed account why the different play activities have been included. You should consider different play activities such as:

- physical
- creative
- structures
- discovery
- intellectual.

4 Optional Activity

Invite a play leader to the centre to set up a play experience (such as finger painting, water play, dough-making, problem solving activities, building/construction etc.). Role-play being a child who is using the materials. What words would they use when participating in each activity? How does it feel to finger paint? How does it feel to pour water from one container to another?

Remember! Doing is better than watching. You will now have some experience of how a child feels when using the materials.

One of the main tasks for early years workers is to plan activities, and this should be carried out in a logical way. They should concentrate on how the activities will contribute to the development of the child. Good planning will ensure successful outcomes.

How should an activity for young children be planned?

It is useful to sit down and plan out an activity as a paper exercise. Careful planning should ensure that activities cover all areas of development, and should cover the aims, objectives, outcomes required, resources needed and the cost.

Aim

The aim of an activity is what an early years worker intends to introduce a child to. It is an 'umbrella' statement that **encompasses** what is to be carried out during the activity. For example, 'to introduce the child to a simple science activity involving melting snow'.

The detail of what it is to be achieved is given in the objectives. The aim sets the scene and limits the activity to a specific type of activity.

Objectives

The objectives are what a child will be able to achieve. In order to plan the objectives it is quite useful to start with the words, 'By the end of the activity the child will...', and then carry on the sentence such as:

- understand that heat causes snow to melt
- be aware that snow is cold
- demonstrate that snow reduces in volume as it melts.

The objectives break an activity down into small units, each of which are measurable.

For example, if the activity is a cookery session, the objectives may be that the child will be able to:

- measure out the ingredients
- count the cake cases
- fill the cake cases with mixture
- understand that heat changes the properties of a mixture
- show an awareness of health and safety issues.

It is worth considering how to measure the objectives to find out if they have been achieved. This may be through simple questioning or by actually observing a child carrying out parts of the activity.

Resources

When planning activities it is necessary to decide how many children will be involved in the activity and which resources will be required. It is good practice for early years workers to gather all the resources together before an activity starts so that they are not tempted to move away to find another piece of equipment. It is useful to itemise all materials required and to include what will be used to cover tables etc. In this way early years workers can tick off the resources as they are gathered. If there are four children involved in an activity then the list might look like this:

- 4 paint pots each with a different colour paint
- 4 paint brushes
- 4 pieces of A4 card creased down the middle
- plastic covers for table
- seating for 4 children
- 4 aprons
- drying space for finished items.

Time

It is useful to work out roughly how long an activity will take. It may be difficult to judge initially but this will improve with time. However, it is necessary to plan a whole day's activities, and if timing is not very good the activities might not be finished when parents come to collect the children, and this in turn could lead to upset and distress.

Cost

Costing an activity so that **budgets** set are realistic is important. It may be that in the case of private provision the cost of activities needs to be included in the fees that the parents pay. Most activity costs are **minimal** but parents may need to pay extra when the activities are costly or include outings or parties. If consumables are used then they need to be replaced in order to provide for further activities in the future.

What needs of young children must be considered when planning an activity?

When considering activities for young children it is necessary to look at all the areas of development, including physical, intellectual, emotional and social (P.I.E.S.), so that one aspect of children's needs is not addressed to the exclusion of the others.

> **Remember!** Safety and level of supervision must be included when planning activities.

All activities provide for at least one if not more areas of development.

Physical

Activities that meet children's physical needs include those shown in Figure 8.31.

Intellectual

Activities that meet children's intellectual needs are so wide-ranging that it would be impossible to mention them all here. Any activity that involves problem-solving or reasoning skills promotes intellectual development. Examples are:

Activity	Detail
Sorting	By colour By size By category
Jigsaws and puzzles	Pattern Counting Grading Object recognition Matching
Cooking	Early science Counting Measuring
Painting	Pattern Colour recognition Counting
Sand and water	Measuring Counting Weight Volume
Modelling	Shape Size Mass
Role-play	Spatial awareness Sets Matching Grading Problem solving
Construction	Spatial awareness Problem solving Properties of materials

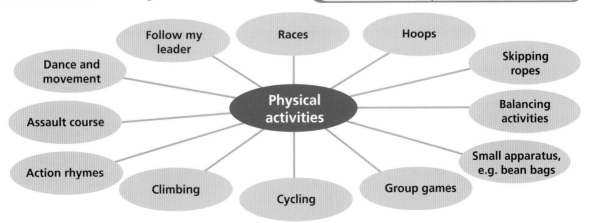

Figure 8.31 *Activities that meet children's physical needs*

Emotional

Although some activities are designed specifically to promote emotional development or allow children to deal with difficult emotions, this is something that could result from any activity in which children participate. One activity, which can lead to meaningful discussion and interaction with children, uses a floor jigsaw of a teddy bear. There are a number of different heads with varying expressions and emotions displayed on the bear's face. These include happiness, sadness, anger, surprise and worry. The child can add the body and limbs and dress the bear in appropriate clothing. The expression chosen gives the opportunity for meaningful discussion on the various reasons for differing emotions.

Social

Activities to promote social development are varied, the only requirement is that more than one child is involved. Obviously, some activities are designed for children to indulge in co-operative play whereas others may just involve children working at an activity in a solitary manner but in the company of other children. Activities whereby children can share and use discussion as part of the activity are the ones which allow for social interaction.

Activity 11
Key skills [N] 2.1

Planning and meeting needs

You have been asked to plan a short intellectual activity for Margo, Chris, Jeremy and Fion, who are three years of age. The purpose is to help them learn about colours.

1 Give the aim of the activity.
2 List at least **three** objectives.
3 List the resources needed and estimate the cost.
4 Explain which needs will be met through participating in the activity.

What health and safety issues need to be considered when planning an activity?

All health and safety issues must be considered when organising and preparing activities (see Unit 8.3). If the activity involves leaving the premises then there are added factors such as travelling arrangements, road safety and the safety of the environment to be visited. The policies of the early years setting must be followed.

Self

It is important for early years care workers to think of safety for themselves because if they are injured then there is the problem of who will look after the children. They should not take any unnecessary risks and should always look out for any hazards. Keeping alert and focused on the task in hand is good advice, for it is when people become distracted that accidents happen. When planning and preparing activities, early years workers should consider what could go wrong and then put safeguards in place to prevent that from happening.

Child

Supervision is one of the main factors preventing harm coming to a child whatever the activity. It is essential that in a care and education setting there are enough members of staff to adequately supervise all the children present. If an activity involves the use of tools, such as a workbench, then one member of staff should be allocated that area and must remain there with a small number of children whilst the equipment is in use. Distractions could result in serious injury to any of the participants.

Equipment

Equipment must be made to British Standards and when purchasing resources for use in the care and education setting it is good policy to look for Kitemarks. The equipment should be fit for purpose and **robust** enough for use by many young children. It is the responsibility of early years workers to ensure that equipment is safe, has not been damaged and that it is not worn enough to constitute a danger if used. Equipment should be checked prior to use.

Materials

The materials used should not constitute a danger. Try to think of the worst use a child could attempt and then try to think of ways to prevent it happening.

Remember: young children will try to drink the most unlikely substances and so there should not be anything present that will do harm. Glue and paint should be in spill proof containers. There should be enough equipment so that children will not squabble over its use. It is good policy to have more resources than you may need. If a cookery activity has been planned and four eggs are required then it would be better to have six in case breakages prevent the activity from progressing satisfactorily.

What is the range of suitable activities that could be considered for children?

The range of activities that children can be engaged in is enormous. A few are given below which are common to most care and education settings.

Jigsaws

Will it all fit together?

Children love to do jigsaws but they should be within their capability. Start with simple large jigsaws and as a child gains confidence and skills then introduce more difficult ones. Vary the type of jigsaw and the theme so that conversation skills can be developed and vocabulary increased. Children need to develop manipulative skills in order to increase manual dexterity.

Board games

These can vary greatly, from matching games where each child has a board to play alone with, to games where children take turns and share ideas. Early years workers should aim to eventually involve children in games that involve sharing with other children as well as catering for intellectual development. Variations to games such as picture lotto can extend learning by introducing such games as sound lotto where the children listen to a sound and then match it to picture, for example an aeroplane taking off.

Storytelling

This is one of the most common activities in a care and education setting and one which gives many children a great deal of pleasure. From very early in a child's life they quickly realise that the marks on the pages in a book convey a message and it is through the world of books that we learn about others and about fantasies. It is important to choose the right kind of book at certain times of day. An adventure story or one that fires the imagination should be told when the child is alert and bright whereas a quiet story is one that can be told at the end or the day or to calm children.

Figure 8.32 Are you sitting comfortably?

Quizzes

Quizzes can be used to stimulate the imagination and can take various forms. They can even be incorporated into other games, such as odd one out. Often quizzes are verbal and children enjoy talking through various answers and solutions.

Lego

Future genius?

Lego and other construction toys provide a great outlet for problem-solving and for logical reasoning. Additionally, they help develop fine motor skills, mathematical thought processes and language development. They are a valuable resource within any early years setting and can virtually grow with a child. Young children can create more complex figures as they develop their skills and knowledge.

Painting

Painting is a great outlet for creative expression and it is often through this medium that children come to terms with events in their life. They may feel very much at home with painting activities and it may be one of the things a new child indulges in readily. Early years workers should provide a variety of colours and brushes and should be aware that paint can be used in different ways. Painting at an easel is only one of the many ways that paint can be used. Butterfly prints, marbling, vegetable/fruit prints, hand/foot prints, adding sand as texture are just a few variations.

Collage

Children love to create pictures using varying textures and glue. This can help with colour recognition and other mathematical thinking. Providing children with the resources and allowing them to experiment is probably the most common way of using collage, but encouraging children to create something linked to a theme can develop the idea further.

How can the success of an activity be evaluated?

Once an activity has been completed, care workers need to evaluate what has taken place. They should think about the activity and consider how effective it was.

Own performance

When considering own performance, early years workers should examine their role in the whole of an activity. Questions they should ask themselves include:

- did I allow the children to investigate and develop their own learning?
- was I sensitive in approach?
- did I interfere?
- did I allow then to make mistakes?
- did I encourage discussion?
- did I draw their attention to relevant points?

Early years workers should look back at the aim of their activity and decide if that was what the activity was really about or should the aim have been altered. Was the aim achieved, and if it was, how successfully? If the aim was not achieved, then the question must be asked, why not, and what could be altered for a more positive outcome?

Objectives

If the objectives of an activity were correctly stated at the outset, then it should be relatively easy to check whether they have been achieved. If they have, then early years workers would know that learning has taken place. It may be that they have had to ask questions to check that a child has understood what was meant. If the correct answers have been given then obviously some understanding has taken place and the objective has been achieved. It is always good practice to go back and consider the objectives which were set initially, and check that they have been met. If they have not, then it may be that the activity was more complex than at first anticipated and needs to be revised.

Outcomes achieved

It is then possible to look at the whole of an activity and decide if the main outcomes have been achieved. Did the children produce what they set out to produce or did they do what they set out to do? If they did, then the outcomes have been achieved. If they did not then there should be a reason, and that must be addressed if the activity is to be repeated.

Improvements

When considering what improvements could be made to an activity, it is necessary to look at the whole event and decide what could be improved for the benefit of the children. With that in mind, it is useful to make a note of changes so that, should that activity be repeated in the future, these alterations could be put into practice. It may be that the activity would have worked better if fewer children were involved at any given time. This could be changed for many indoor activities but may be much more difficult for outings and outdoor events. It may be that improved planning and preparation could address an issue or that the activity was requiring too much from the children at any given time. The activity may be more appropriate after a few months when skills and knowledge have increased.

If an activity has been a total success, then it is obviously well worth repeating, but early years workers should be aware that repeating an activity too often might be problematic and may reduce the motivation levels of the child.

> **Remember!** If a child enjoys an activity they will wish to repeat it and experience a second enjoyable session.

Assessment activity 8.6

Key skills C 2.2

Planning and carrying out an intellectual activity

You are working in an early years setting and have been asked to plan and carry out an intellectually stimulating activity for either one or a small group of children who can be from three to five years old. The activity should last for 10–15 minutes.

1 Plan the activity, remembering to include:

- aim
- objectives
- resources needed
- time scales
- cost.

2 Explain how the activity will meet the needs of the children to include:

- physical needs
- intellectual needs
- emotional needs
- social needs.

3 Describe the health and safety issues associated with the activity, explaining how risks will be reduced. You should consider health and safety from the perspective of:

- self
- child
- equipment
- materials.

4 Carry out the activity with the child or children. Try to be confident in your approach.

5 Evaluate the activity making sure you:

- reflect
- analyse
- draw conclusions
- plan how to improve.

When evaluating you will need to think about:

- own performance
- aim
- objective
- outcome achieved
- improvements.

Glossary

Adept: skilled, accomplished

Advantageous conditions: right for the purpose

Allergies: abnormal reaction to any substances which might not affect others

Attribute: to give

Bonding: developing strong relationships

Budget: the amount of money needed or available

Challenges: tasks, tests

Collaboration: working together to solve problems

Consumables: those items which are used upon a regular basis e.g. paint, paper etc.

Co-operatively: together, jointly

Consolidated: brought together

Control measures: techniques to prevent problems happening

Criminal Records Bureau (CRB): organisation used to screen individuals for police/criminal records

Curriculum: the activities being taught

Destructive: unhelpful, negative

Determine: decide, settle on

Detrimental: disadvantageous, harmful

Economic: making something work without wasting money

Effective: working well

Egocentric: seeing things only from their own point of view

Embedded: rooted in

Emotional: linked to feelings

Empathise: understand, identify with

Encompasses: includes, surrounds

Evacuation: safe practices in leaving a building

Exclusive: restricted, limited

Formal: official, proper

Funding: how a service is financed

Hazards: something which may cause harm

Holistic: treating the whole person rather than just the disease

Hypotheses: theories or ideas to be tested

Independent: able to do things for themselves

Indiscriminate: haphazard

Inferior: second rate

Informal: casual, relaxed and friendly

Initiate: begin, set going

Innate: inborn, inherent

Intervention: involvement, interference

Legislation: relating to legal aspects

Manipulative play: play that involves using the hands to achieve a goal

Minimal: smallest

Nausea: feeling sick

Norms or patterns: level of development appropriate to age

Pallor: paleness

Paramount: supreme, over-riding

Personal: relating to an individual

Prior: earlier, previous

Primary: main, first

Private: not in the public sector i.e. owned by an individual or group of people

Proforma: form giving particular information

Prohibited: banned, forbidden

Psychological: relating to the emotions

Qualified: having the correct qualification or certificates for the job

Reputation: what people believe about a person's/thing's character

Refine: make something clearer

Robust: strong, durable, tough

Scrutinising: looking at things carefully

Safety features: practical measures to prevent harm

Socialise: mixing with and communicating with others

Spacial awareness: noticing what is happening in the space around you

Spectator: watcher, observer

Stability: steadiness, consistency

Staff/child ratio: the number of adults in relation to the number of children

Subsidised: partly paid for from another source

Stereotype: when people are grouped together and thought to have the same traits rather than being looked on as individuals, e.g. all teenagers are cheeky

Substitute: use one item in the place of another

Unattainable: unachievable, beyond reach

Venues: buildings, settings

Verbally inarticulate: unable to speak fluently

Older service users make a positive contribution to society

Who are older people? The age at which a person receives their state pension is currently classed as the 'older' life stage or late adulthood. At the time of print this is aged 60 years for women and 65 years for men, but the government have recently discussed making the age when state pensions are introduced as being the same for both sexes. During recent years medical care and technology has improved, as have living conditions, so people are living longer. It must be remembered that not all older people are dependent on others. Some are able to make very positive contributions, for example, in the form of being on committees, being volunteer workers for charities and fund-raising for different causes.

A wide range of health and social care provision for older people is available, ranging from providing support for people who wish to receive care in their own home to full-time residential care. There are also day care centres as well as respite care facilities.

Older people have a variety of needs which include:

- mental health needs, e.g. an older person could have **Alzeimer's disease** or be confused
- physical illnesses or conditions, e.g. heart conditions, stroke, diabetes

- disabilities, e.g. arthritis, loss of limbs
- personal care and support, e.g. as a result of a stoke or hip replacement.

Whatever the needs of older service users, those who are providing care have a responsibility to make sure that accidents are less likely to happen and that service users have a safe environment in which to live. They are also responsible for ensuring that older service users are protected from abuse.

Being able to communicate effectively with older service users is a very important part of every care worker's role. It is essential if meaningful relationships are to be established between care workers and service users.

Those who have ever visited an older person who is living in a residential or nursing home, or who is in hospital or living alone in their own home, know that they are very pleased to see people. Meeting people gives them the opportunity to hear of things that are going on outside their world and brings interest to their lives. Older people enjoy being mentally stimulated through conversation or through participating in intellectual or creative activities. They also have a lot to offer in the way of experience to those who are younger!

9.1 Describe the different types of provision for older service users and their purpose

What will we learn in this unit?

Learning outcomes

You will learn to:

- Describe the different types of provision for older people and their purpose
- Recognise the different needs of older service users
- Promote and maintain a safe environment for older service users
- Demonstrate effective communication skills when responding to requests for support from older service users and assess own performance
- Carry out practical tasks for older service users and assess own performance
- Carry out a recreational activity with older service users and assess own performance

What provision exists for older service users?

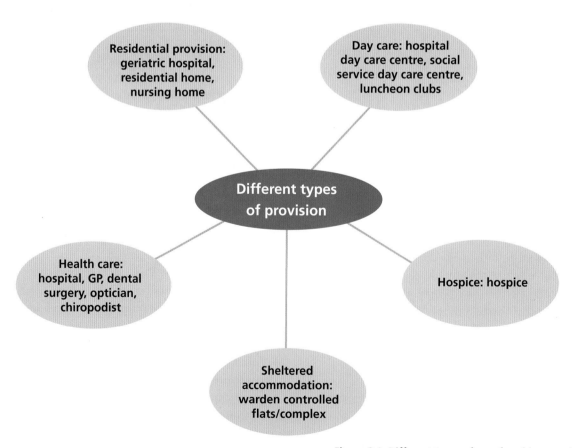

Figure 9.1 *Different types of care for older people*

Residential provision

Residential provision means that the setting in which a service user is staying is entirely responsible for their care, 24 hours of every day. When an older person agrees to have residential care it usually means that they have to give up their own home because they can no longer look after themselves. This could be because:

- they may not have any family to help with their care
- their family may live some distance from them
- their family may have commitments which prevent them from providing the care needed
- the older person may need specialist care which the family cannot provide.

Residential care settings are an older person's 'home', and should provide for their physical, intellectual, emotional and social needs.

Did you know?

Most people living in nursing and residential homes are women! This is because women live longer than men.

Geriatric hospitals

'**Geriatric**' hospitals provide health and access to social care support for older service users who need medical specialist treatment and support. Sometimes a trust hospital has a 'geriatric' section as one of their departments which will provide the same type of treatment and care. 'Geriatric' hospitals are part of the NHS.

Nursing homes

Nursing homes are privately-run settings that care for service users who have health problems, for example, are partially paralysed because they have had a stroke, or have a severe heart condition. Such homes are equipped with specialised equipment for moving and handling service users who cannot move by themselves. They also provide specialist equipment for service users who have conditions such as serious renal or digestive disorders. Nursing homes employ '**direct care**' workers, for example:

- registered general nurses (RGNs)
- health care assistants
- care assistants.

They also make sure that professional care workers visit the nursing home on a regular basis. Examples of such professionals are:

- GPs who care for service users' medical needs
- physiotherapists who provide exercise and massage to help restore movement
- chiropodists who care for service users who have physical needs for their feet
- speech therapists who try to improve speech for service users who have had a stroke
- activities organisers who provide mental and creative stimulation for service users.

Residential homes

Service users who do not have serious medical conditions, but who are unable to care for themselves may choose to live in a residential home. Service users are usually provided with their own room (some have to share), and sometimes can take with them some small items of their own furniture. Residential homes are run by private or charitable organisations, but local authority social service departments may contribute to the cost of the care. This depends on service users' incomes. Residential homes are likely to employ:

- care assistants who help with dressing, washing, going out, enabling people to eat and drink and who give social and emotional support
- RGNs, as many of their residents are on medication and may have minor medical conditions.

Older service users also have the services of GPs. These could be the GPs they had before moving into the home or, if they have moved some distance from their previous location, a GP who sees several people who live in the residential home. They have the right to have a GP of their choice.

Other types of support, such as physiotherapy or chiropody are made available to service users. Many residential homes employ a part-time activities organiser who arranges painting, quizzes and community activities.

Did you know?

By 2011 there are likely to be over 1.2 million people over the age of 85!

Activity 1

Key skills ICT 2.1, C 2.3

Lucinda and Jack

Lucinda is 81 and has recently had several falls. After discussion between Lucinda, her family and her GP, Lucinda decides that she can no longer live in her own home and that she would benefit from 24-hour care and support.

Jack is 72, but has recently had a stroke which has paralysed him down the right side of his body. He is ready to leave hospital but is unable to look after himself. He needs 24-hour care and support.

1 Which type of residential provision would suit Lucinda best? Give reasons to support your choice.

2 Which type of residential provision would suit Jack best? Give reasons to support your choice.

3 Working in pairs carry out research to find out about the care provided by either a local residential home or a local nursing home. (You could arrange to visit or for a care worker to come and talk to the group about the care they provide.)

4 Produce a handout or a leaflet or written report that could be given to either Lucinda or Jack to give them information about the setting chosen.

Day care

Service users who attend day care centres often live in their own homes, although they can also come from residential care homes. Attending a day care centre is one way in which support can be provided. Many older people who live in their own homes also have additional help such as support from care assistants who help with daily living tasks and from GPs, district nurses, and chiropodists.

Hospital day care centre

The main emphasis of the care provided for those service users who attend hospital day care centres is on their medical conditions and monitoring their medical needs. They may be recovering from a medical condition such as a stroke or suffering from an ongoing condition such as rheumatoid arthritis. Service users can attend for a half-day session but others stay for a full day. While at the centre:

- a meal is provided for those who stay for a full day
- group exercises are given to promote health and well-being
- appointments are made for individual service users to see consultants if this is required
- health monitoring is carried out, e.g. blood pressure, temperature
- advice and guidance is given about how to maintain health
- dietary advice is provided
- the opportunity is provided for service users to meet and talk with others
- activities to stimulate intellect are provided
- liasing with other agencies may result when care plans are reviewed and changes are required.

Some socialising is also built into hospital day care programmes, because health involves the 'whole' person, that is, their physical, intellectual, emotional and social needs.

Social service/charitable day care centre

These are attended by service users who live in their own homes and who do not have major medical needs, but who may be socially isolated. They usually attend for a full day, during which time the emphasis is on meeting and talking with others to help meet social and emotional needs. While at the centre:

- a meal is provided at midday which ensures that those attending have a well-balanced meal
- newspapers and journals are provided so that service users can have the opportunity to keep up-to-date with current events. Items of interest often make 'talking points'
- activities are played in small groups, such as cards, scrabble and dominoes, by those who choose to do so
- whole group activities are organised, such as community singing, charades and quizzes

- social workers and care assistants help service users with any personal support required such as reading official letters and giving advice
- some service users take the opportunity to have a bath as health care assistants will provide assistance
- in some day care centres a chiropodist is available.

Luncheon clubs

Luncheon clubs are often provided by faith groups and voluntary organisations. Some meet on a daily basis, while others provide a meal once each week. Service users attending pay a small charge for their meal. The organisers are not intending to make a profit, only the cost of the ingredients need to be met by the charge, as those that prepare and serve the meals give their services free.

Luncheon clubs meet the physical and social needs of service users. The meal provides for service users' physical needs but there is also an opportunity to make friends and to talk about topics with people who have similar interests. Many luncheon clubs provide activities after the meal to intellectually stimulate those attending.

Hospice

A hospice is a place where service users who are dying can choose to stay to enhance the last weeks or months of their lives. Some service users may prefer to die in their own homes, surrounded by family, friends and caring professionals. Over 90 per cent of hospice care is provided in service users' own homes, by professionals who give support for the **terminally ill**.

Other service users choose to stay in a specially equipped hospice where the providers have the skills and resources to enable service users to live as pain-free and as full a life as possible.

> ### Did you know?
> Hospices originated in medieval times and were places where travellers, pilgrims, the sick, wounded and dying could find rest and comfort.

A hospice offers **palliative care** rather than curative treatment. The emphasis is on quality rather than quantity of life. The dying are comforted, professional medical care is given and relief for symptoms is provided. The patient and the family are included in the care plan and emotional, spiritual and practical support is given. This support is based on service users' wishes and the needs of their families. Trained volunteers offer **respite care** for family members as well as for the service users.

The goal of a hospice team is to be sensitive and responsive to the special requirements of each service user and their family.

Some service users who use a hospice do so as 'day patients' when they are first diagnosed as having a terminal illness. Visits can help to prepare service users to know what to expect when they move into the hospice for the final weeks of their lives. They can get to know the staff and the routines and will find it more comfortable when they move in for residential provision.

A chance to talk at the luncheon club

Sheltered accommodation

Figure 9.2 *A warden checks the safety and well-being of service users*

Sheltered accommodation enables service users to maintain their independence by having their own flat or bungalow, but they also have the support of a **warden** who either lives on site or who can be called by using an emergency alarm system. Sheltered accommodation is often a mixture of flats, bungalows or small houses that are built in a small complex. Besides the accommodation there is a:

- community room where the warden organises events such as bingo, faith services and concerts. Residents can choose whether they attend or not
- community kitchen so that refreshments can be served during or after an event
- communal laundry room for residents who do not wish to go to the expense of buying a washing machine.

Each service user has their own front door, and own furniture. 'Meals on Wheels' deliver hot meals if service users are unable to cook their own. The service users are responsible for their own shopping and washing, but have the security of knowing that a carer is on hand if they need support.

The warden visits each flat and bungalow to check that the residents are safe and well. The residents can call the warden if they are feeling unwell, or have a fall, or if they are worried about something. Service users living in sheltered accommodation usually **bond** to form a very close community, looking after one another and being protective of one another.

Healthcare

The healthcare available for older people is the same as is available to all. Older people may use health services more than younger adults because they are more likely, because of the aging process, to develop physical illness and conditions.

Examples of health services available to older people are shown in the table on page 285.

Health services	Examples of services provided for older people
GP	• monitors health • writes prescriptions • diagnoses illnesses • liaises with other agencies • may offer counselling services • may offer chiropody service • offers advice about health issues
Dental practice	• checks teeth and gums • extracts and fills teeth • cleans teeth • takes impressions for and fits dentures
Chiropody	• cares for feet • removes corns and attends to bunions • trims nails
Optician	• eye tests • diagnoses diseases related to the eyes • arranges for the correct lens for glasses • helps service users to choose frames
Physiotherapy (community and hospital)	• designs exercise programmes • provides exercise and massage to restore movement • provides advice
Trust hospital	• provides a wide range of services including: x-rays, dietician, dialysis, physiotherapy, 'geriatric' wards, health checks for the over 70s, e.g. mammography

The services that older people use depends upon their individual needs. Many will not use any services, others may, because of their condition through the ageing process, need to use several services.

Activity 2

Key skills [C] 2.2, 2.3, [ICT] 2.1, 2.2

Service provision

Madge has recently been burgled and does not feel safe living alone in her house in the country. She is able to look after herself and enjoys cooking for friends when they call to see her. She feels she would like to live where there is some support.

Grant has been diagnosed with stomach cancer. He has been told that he only has a few weeks to live. His wife and family are afraid that they will not be able to cope.

Peggy, who is 90 years old, is feeling the affects of the ageing process. She cannot see to read, has problems with her dentures and has high blood pressure.

1 Identify the type of service provision would best suit Madge and explain why it would be suitable.

2 Identify the type of service provision that would best suit Grant. Produce a leaflet or handout to show Grant how the service would help him.

3 Identify three health services that would help Peggy with her health needs. For each service produce a 'Directory' that would show the services they would provide.

4 Carry out research to find out about one local health service in more detail. Produce information for the directory to show the different services provided, availability and location details.

What are the purposes of and differences between the different types of provision?

As we have seen, different types of care provision have different purposes, which can be summarised as:

- personal care and support
- nursing care
- help to live independently
- care for the dying.

These different types of care are compared in the following table.

Type of care	Purpose	Focus of care
Personal care and support	• to maintain independence • to improve quality of life • to maintain dignity	• focus is on service users' social, emotional and intellectual well-being, although some physical help is given with daily living tasks • does not provide health or medical care or treatment for the service user
Nursing care	• to provide medical treatment and • to provide specialist equipment • to maintain health • to monitor health	• Service users need health/medical treatment as a priority • service users' social, emotional and intellectual well-being is also taken into account
Help to live independently	• to provide personal care and support • to improve quality of life • to supporting service users in their own home (e.g. through help of a warden)	• some physical tasks are undertaken to provide support for service users • service users are not likely to have a major medical need • service users' social, emotional needs are taken into account
Care for the dying	• to providing support (wherever a service user wants it)	• to help service users to maintain dignity while dying while there is no cure, the health/medical needs of the service users are provided for • emphasis is on quality of life, not quantity

Assessment activity 9.1

Key skills ICT 2.1, C 2.1a

Care provision for older service users

You have been asked to prepare materials for trainees who think they would like to work with older service users.

They will need to know about a wide range of services that are available including the type of care they provide and the different needs of service users met by the provision.

When preparing the materials, use primary and secondary sources of evidence.

1 Conduct a survey/ carry out research, to find out which services are available for older people. Make sure you include information about:
- residential services
- day care
- hospice
- sheltered accommodation
- care for the dying.

You could produce this evidence in the form of a 'Directory of Services for Older People', but make sure there is sufficient detail about the type of care provided, availability, explaining how the care meets service users' needs.

2 Divide into groups of four or six. Arrange to visit **one** care setting to make notes about the type of care provided and how it meets the needs of service users.

3 Present your findings to the whole group.

4 Make any additions necessary from collecting the primary evidence to the 'Directory of Services' that will be used to inform the trainees.

What are the needs of older service users in care settings?

Everybody has basic needs and older people are no exception to this, whether they live in their own home or in formal care settings. The basic needs of older service users are:

- physical, e.g. food warmth, shelter
- intellectual, e.g. mental **stimulation**
- emotional, e.g. love, affection, being wanted
- social, e.g. friendships, relationships.

Those who work with older service users, particularly if the service user is living in residential care, need to ensure that all their basic needs are met. Care workers should not think that just because an older service user can no longer carry out particular physical tasks or movements their mind is not alert. Such assumptions are far from true as many older service users are very quick and mentally active. Care workers have a responsibility to make sure that service users are responded to as individuals, whether they are living in residential care, receiving day care or living in their own homes with support.

Mental health needs

All older service users have mental health needs even if they are mentally fit. They need mental stimulation in order to keep their minds active and to give them an interest. Mental stimulation can be provided by recreational activities such as:

Activity	Needs met
Painting	Creative and intellectually stimulating
Quiz	Intellectually stimulating
Reading	Intellectually stimulating and could be emotionally stimulating
Jigsaw puzzles	Intellectually and physically stimulating
Making items	Intellectually and physically stimulating

Recreational activities are any activities that are done as a leisure pursuit. A hobby is a recreational activity as is playing snooker and doing a crossword. Older service users usually enjoy taking part in activities and so emotional needs are met as their choice of activity gives pleasure. Recreational activities can relieve stress. Some older service users have specific mental health needs. Conditions and diseases that are common among older service users are:

- Alzheimer's disease
- **dementia**
- depression
- anxiety
- confusion.

Caring for older people with any of these conditions or diseases can be challenging for care workers. However, such service users are entitled to the same respect and dignity as all other service users.

Alzheimer's disease

The cause of Alzheimer's disease is unknown but the number of older service users who experience this disease is increasing. Alzheimer's disease is the slow **deterioration** of mental ability of which loss of memory is one of the first signs. Service users who have Alzheimer's disease have good long-term memory, but do not remember recent occurrences. For example, they could remember all about a book they have read or a play they have seen some time in the past, but they may not remember a visit they made recently to the cinema or the name of a relative who recently visited them.

Did you know?

25 per cent of all people over the age of 85 suffer from Alzheimer's disease.

Dementia

Dementia is another condition where care workers are required to meet older service users' specific mental health needs. When service users have this condition they may become forgetful, for example, forgetting what they have ordered for their meal, or buying things that they already have.

As the condition gets worse, service users may be unable to attend to their own personal needs, being unable to wash or feed themselves without the help of care workers.

Establishing a routine can help when caring for service users who are in the early stages of dementia, because they become accustomed to doing things in the same order and in the same way each day.

Case study

Key skills [C] 2.1a

Grace

Grace, who is 74, is an older service user who lives in a residential home. Grace does not have any relatives living near. Her two sons live a long distance away and seldom visit. Grace is physically fit but she has dementia.

Much of Grace's day is spent wandering around the residential home. She is always asking the care workers, 'Is it time to go home now?' Or she says, 'I must pack as I must get home and get my son's tea, they will wonder where I am'. These questions and statements are said over and over again by Grace during the course of a day.

On other occasions Grace thinks she is at home and lays the dining room table for a meal (usually with the wrong cutlery and equipment), and tries to make things in the kitchen (where she is not allowed to go as she is a danger to herself).

Most of the care workers in the residential home are very patient with Grace. At the weekend, however, different staff are on duty who are not so patient. One shouts constantly at Grace and tells her, 'I'm going to tie you to a chair if you don't stay out of this kitchen'. Or 'I'll wash your mouth out with soap if you ask me that again'.

1 In what ways are Grace's mental health needs not being met?

2 How should the weekend workers be reacting to Grace's behaviour? Think of examples of what they could do in practice.

Depression

Depression is another condition that affects mental health as it is a 'mood disorder'. Service users who are depressed have a feeling of sadness, which can be a sign of major depression, or are constantly excited or **elevated**, which is a **bipolar** disorder. When a service user is depressed they may have **insomnia**, decreased appetite and be very **apathetic**. Medication is often needed to help service users who have this condition and who need help to deal with the symptoms.

Anxiety

All people experience anxiety at some stage of their lives but many older service users find themselves in a permanent state of anxiety. Anxiety can take the form of intense fear or dread, trembling or restlessness, rapid heart rate and excessive perspiration. Sometimes counselling is needed to help a service user to think and talk about the things that have **triggered** the anxiety. These could be past history, a dream or nightmare, or a current traumatic event.

Confusion

Service users who are confused are often challenging to look after. Confusion is not a disease, it is a **symptom**. The cause of the confusion needs to be identified. This can be done with the help of a GP or a nurse. Some examples of causes of confusion are:

- chest infections
- urine infection
- diabetes
- **dehydration**.

When the cause of the confusion has been diagnosed and treated, the confusion often disappears.

Confused service users may wander away from their place of residence, and therefore care workers need to make sure that doors and windows are secure. They may get up in the middle of the night and wander into another residents bedroom. They may take their medication at the wrong time. Confused service users need a lot of supervision, but it should be remembered that they should where possible be encouraged to make choices and should be treated with dignity and respect.

Physical illness or conditions

Ageing usually brings several physical changes. As people get older, changes become more noticeable. Physical changes can include:

Physical changes in old age	How they are shown in old age
Hair	• loses colour and becomes grey • hair becomes thinner hair loss
Skin	• becomes dry • wrinkles appear • loss of elasticity
Hearing	• some hearing loss
Eyesight	• cataracts can develop • harder to distinguish between colours • long-sightedness can develop
Urinary system	• bladder control becomes difficult • possible urinary infections as the kidneys do not function so well
The skeletal system	• possible loss of height
Circulatory system	• increased blood pressure likely • likelihood of heart problems increases
Respiratory system	• muscles function less well • proneness to chest infections
Nervous system	• poor memory • parkinson's disease

The five main food groups

medical conditions is maintaining hygiene routines. Care workers often have to 'coax' or encourage older service users to have a bath or to have their hair washed as they may find it 'too much trouble'. Providing support with personal hygiene when it is required, is a most necessary task of the care worker. If service users feel good about themselves, they are more likely to take an interest in what is going on around them. If they smell, other service users will want to avoid them. Service users can gradually lose interest in their appearance if they are not encouraged to take an interest in how they look.

A wide variety of physical conditions can affect older service users. Some of the most common conditions are shown below.

The physical needs of service users who are in the 'older service user' group can be provided for through the provision of well-balanced meals. That is, making sure that foods from each of the five main food groups are provided in the right proportions each day.

Service users' physical needs are also met if their personal hygiene standards are maintained. Good standards of hygiene can promote good health. One of the first things that older service users tend to neglect when suffering from illnesses or

Common physical difficulties	Examples of types of disease or condition
Mobility difficulties	• arthritis • osteo-arthritis • rheumatoid-arthritis
Paralyses	• stroke • tumours
Heart conditions/disease	• heart attack • angina
Respiratory difficulties	• emphysema • bronchitis • asthma

Gentle exercise can contribute to physical health and well-being

Older people who have physical diseases or conditions still need to keep as physically active as possible. Physical exercise can:

- increase strength, i.e. strengthen muscles
- increase stamina, i.e. help person not become tired too quickly
- improve suppleness, i.e. keep joints flexible
- improve heart and lung efficiency, i.e. help circulation
- stimulates mental activity, i.e. help person be more alert.

The amount of physical exercise taken by older service users depends on their age and their condition. Some **therapeutic** exercises can be done sitting in a chair. Walking and swimming are activities that are beneficial to older service users if their condition allows them to participate.

Care workers should encourage older service users to get out of bed at some point during each day. This is because sitting out in a chair not only means a change of position for the service user, but also enables the heart to pump blood around the body more effectively, aiding circulation.

Case study

Edna

Edna, who is 87 years old, is living in a nursing home. She is in the early stages of dementia and also suffers from rheumatoid arthritis.

1 Give two key symptoms of dementia.

2 Write a short definition of dementia.

3 How could each of Edna's following needs be met?
   a Intellectual needs.
   b Physical needs.
   c Social needs.
   d Emotional needs.

4 Describe the actions care workers should take to maintain Edna's dignity and rights.

5 What is Alzheimer's disease?

6 What are the symptoms of an anxiety attack?

7 What is a service user who is confused is likely to do?

Disabilities/learning impairment

Some older service users who have disabilities or a learning impairment may be reluctant to ask for help. Care workers need to very aware of body language and other signs such as neglect of diet, exercise and appearance so that they can effectively respond to a service user's need. Observation of specific actions when service users are trying to do tasks, for example, dressing, can help a care worker know exactly what a service user can or cannot do. For example, the care worker could, through observation, tell whether a service user is able to wash themselves, fasten their clothes, or whether they are in pain. Carers can ask service users if they need help and should find out the type of help that is needed. The physical assistance required by each service user is likely to be different, because of the different types of disability or impairment. For example, service users could have a:

- physical disability – which is related to carrying out activities that involve moving or activating the body, e.g. walking or having restricted motor skills
- sensory impairment – this involves the five senses which are hearing, touch, sight, taste and smell, e.g. hearing or sight impairment
- mental health needs – which involves the brain and which could affect the commands the brain gives to other parts of the body, e.g. speech, where the service user is unable to communicate
- learning impairment – this involves the ability of a service user to understand, or the speed at which they can process information, e.g. communication can be very slow, and they may need to be taught how to do routine tasks.

It should be remembered, however, that even though two service users may appear to have the same needs, they may require a different type of help.

A wide variety of aids are available to help meet the needs of service users with disabilities. Look back to Unit 3 where aids were discussed in detail.

The table at the top right of this page gives a summary of the aids and equipment that could be used for service users with various disabilities.

Disability	Aids and equipment
Physical needs	• walking aids, e.g. sticks, Zimmer frame, tripod, wheelchair, motorised aids • climbing aids, stair lifts • aids to help with hygiene and bathing, e.g. grip rails, hoist
Restricted motor skills	• aids to help with dressing, e.g. Velcro fasters, stocking aids, sock aids • feeding aids, e.g. adapted cutlery, feeding cups • lifting aids, e.g. hoist, slide boards • walking aids, e.g. wheelchair, motorised aids
Sensory needs	• aids to help with communication, e.g. adapted computer, adapted telephone • aids to help with hearing, e.g. hearing aid, adapted telephone, flashing door bell • aids to help with sight impairment, e.g. talking computer, glasses, audiotapes • aids for mobility, e.g. guide dog, white stick

Some older service users who have disabilities may, if they live in their own home or in sheltered accommodation, need to have their homes **adapted**. This means that an occupational therapist would assess their needs and could arrange for adaptations such as:

- ramps – to aid access into the home and within the home
- doors widened – to allow a wheelchair to easily pass through
- lowered surfaces in the kitchen and bathroom – to help service users be able to do things for themselves
- stair lifts – to enable service users to access both floors independently.

Aids and adaptations can improve the quality of life for service users with disabilities and learning impairment. They encourage independence, help to promote safety and encourage service users to live their lives in a similar manner to those who are able-bodied. They also promote confidence as service users can rely on aids or adaptations as a form of support.

Personal care and support

Personal care and support is provided for all older service users in care settings. It can take the form of providing assistance with washing, dressing, bathing and help with daily living routines. Service users who live in their own homes benefit enormously from receiving personal care and support as part of 'care in the community'. Care is provided through NHS practitioners and local authority social services working together to provide individual care plans for service users. The voluntary sector can also be involved.

A service user's needs are assessed by a social worker, a GP or an occupational specialist. The service user is involved in these discussions and the plan is drawn up taking the service user's wishes into consideration. A plan could involve several practitioners working together to meet the service user's needs. This is known as a **'multi-disciplinary approach'**. An example of a care plan could be:

Care Plan: Mrs...		
10.00 a.m.	Medication	Give with food
10.30 a.m.	Physiotherapy	Maximum 15 minutes
11.30 a.m.	Return to bed	

Figure 9.3 *A care assistant can enable a service user to continue to live in their own home*

Service users who wish to remain in their own home, but who need care and support in order to do so, require different professionals at different times, depending on their individual needs. Care in the community enables this to be provided. Some service users may have to pay for some services, depending on their income. For example, some service users may be asked to contribute towards the cost of a care assistant if they have an income above a certain level.

The advantage of care in the community is that the services provided can be tailored to meet each individual's needs and the service user can stay in surroundings with which they are familiar, and have their own furnishings and personal items around them.

> **Discussion point**
>
> *What is meant by the term 'multi-disciplinary team'? Give an example of who could be in a multi-disciplinary team and what tasks each would do.*

Assessment activity 9.2

Recognising the needs of older service users

Bryony Pace is 92 years old and is confined to a wheelchair. She is dependent on others to feed, dress and wash her. She is living in a nursing home.

Vince Makepeace is 73 years old and has mobility problems. He can move around with the use of a walking stick in own home but uses a Zimmer frame when he goes out. He can look after himself but needs help with daily tasks such as cleaning, washing clothes and cooking.

Rhona Peters who is 65 years old is recovering from a stroke. She has no movement in her right arm but is able to walk with help. Rhona is in residential care.

1 For each of the service users in the case studies describe in detail their physical, intellectual, emotional and social needs explaining how these could be met by professional care workers and how the care values would be applied.

2 Prepare questions that could be used to find out about the physical, intellectual, emotional and social needs of an older service user who is living in their own home. Use the questions to collect primary evidence about one older service user.

3 Use the information collected from both the case studies and the primary evidence to explain the needs of a range of service users and to show how professional care workers can apply the care values when meeting these needs.

What responsibilities do care workers have in protecting service users from harm?

Identification and reporting of hazards

Good standards of health and safety do not happen on their own, safe working systems have to be designed and implemented in care settings. The Health and Safety at Work Regulations 1999 require employers to assess risks to employees, service users and others who are associated with the setting.

- A hazard means anything that can cause harm, for example chemicals, electricity, lifting service users.
- A risk is the chance that somebody will be harmed by the hazard, for example, getting an electric shock from a damaged cable.

A risk assessment involves carrying out a careful exploration of what could cause harm to people and how to put in place control mechanisms that will prevent anyone from becoming ill or hurt. For example, look at Figure 9.4 below which shows the bedroom of an older service user.

To identify hazards in all health and social care settings, a named person is made responsible to walk around all areas of the setting, for example, hallways, sitting rooms, bedrooms, toilets, bathrooms, corridors to look at things that can cause serious harm. Harm can be caused by environmental conditions, for example a wet floor, frayed carpets, cables running across the floor. Danger can also come in the form of equipment that is faulty or from people who are not observing health and safety procedures. An example from a care setting for older people could be leaving a confused older service user alone in a bath while fetching towels. This could lead to a serious incident, and could be avoided by collecting all the necessary equipment first.

Under RIDDOR (Reporting of Injuries, Diseases and Dangerous Occurrences Regulations 1995) the following must be reported:

- accidents that result in an employee's death or major injury or being unable to do their work for more than three days
- accidents that result in a person who is not at work (service user, visitor) being taken to hospital
- an employee suffering one of the specified work-related diseases

Figure 9.4 *Hazards that need reporting*

- dangerous occurrences that do not result in injury but which could have the potential to do significant harm.

The responsibility for reporting rests with the identified 'responsible person' for the care setting.

Case study

Peter

Peter, who is in residential care, falls out of bed. He is taken to hospital. His care plan is examined carefully by the identified person responsible for reporting accidents in the home. There is evidence of a detailed assessment being carried out within the care plan. It is stated quite clearly in the care plan that bed rails are not needed.

1 Does this accident have to be reported? Give reasons for your answer.

2 What else should be done as a result of this accident?

It is important that when a hazard is identified the care worker does not ignore it. If they are going off-shift they could think, 'I'll do it tomorrow' or 'somebody else will report it'. This is very poor professional practice because the time gap that is then created could lead to people injuring themselves. By not reporting a hazard immediately the situation can worsen.

Safety features

Within any care organisation there are a variety of safety features that help keep service users and care workers safe. Such features can include the examples shown in the table below.

Additional information about safety features can be found in Unit 4.

Risk assessment

There is no such thing as a risk-free workplace, but risk can be minimised. Risk assessment is the key to a safe working environment and service user safety, and is a legal requirement.

A risk assessment involves a careful examination of the working activities that could cause harm to people. Doing a risk assessment doesn't have to be over complicated but should consider:

- service users in the care setting
- visitors and members of the public who might be affected by work within the setting
- workers who are young, inexperienced, new to aparticular job, trainees or doing work experience
- workers who have a disability.

All care organisations have a duty under health and safety law to carry out risk assessments. The five steps to a risk assessment are covered in Unit 4.4 (see page 170).

The information that is gained as the result of a risk assessment should be:

- understood by everyone that it affects
- be provided in a form which takes account of any language difficulties or disabilities.

Once a hazard has been identified then a written record needs to be made. The appropriate person should be made aware of the hazard so that it can be dealt with as soon as possible. Different organisations identify who is in charge of this type of problem, and it can anyone from a manager to a caretaker.

Safety feature	How they reduce the risks
Policies for health and safety, e.g. moving and handling, fire	• provides guidelines for care workers about the way specific tasks are to be carried out, e.g. moving and handling • promotes health and safety practices and sets standards
Smoke alarms	• gives a warning of danger from smoke • helps to alert people to evacuate the building • prevents damage through inhalation of smoke
Firefighting equipment, e.g. alarms, fire extinguishers, blankets, sprinklers	• alerts people to evacuate the building • helps to prevent the spread of fire • could reduce death and injury from fire as people can escape the building
Equipment for moving and handling, e.g. hoist, slide boards	• prevents injury to staff and service users
To prevent the spread of infection, e.g. gloves, masks, aprons	• prevents both the service user and care workers from cross contamination

Carrying out a risk assessment in an environment for older service users

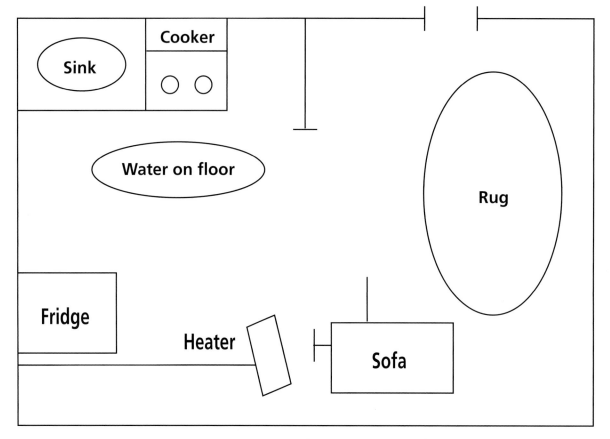

Figure 9.5 *An example of an environment for risk assessment*

The diagram above is an example of an area used by older service users and care staff that contains a variety of hazards. By identifying what the hazards are it is possible to think about how to reduce the risks that they cause.

Hazard 1: there is a large pool of water on the floor in a kitchen area.

Risks: an older person is particularly vulnerable to slipping and falling. Also, as the water is near electrical equipment it might cause the equipment to fuse or lead to a person getting an electric shock.

Risk reduction: mop up the water and dry the floor.

Hazard 2: there is a heater that is very close to a sofa.

Risks: an older service user might burn themselves whilst sitting on the sofa. Also, if the

heater has electric elements the sofa might get hot enough to burn if the heater is left on and left unattended.

Risk reduction: move the heater further away from the sofa.

Hazard 3: there is a heater cable trailing across a room.

Risks: an older service user might trip on the cable and fall. By tripping on the cable the heater could fall on top of the person and possibly burn them.

Risk reduction: move heater closer to the wall so that the cable does not trail. Cover the cable with a protective rubber strip that stops trips.

From three simple hazards there is a list of at least six risks to safety. Once the risk is identified then the way to prevent potential accidents is also identified. Once the hazard is removed the safety problem is solved.

Risk assessment

Jo has been asked to conduct a risk assessment of a bedroom of an older service user who is in a nursing home.

1 Prepare a checklist of the things you would look for when conducting the risk assessment. For each possible risk identified make a suggestion of how the risk could be controlled. You may wish to present your evidence in the form of a table. An example is given below but you should aim to have a list of at least **ten** possible risks:

Possible risk	Control method
Not knowing what to do in the event of a fire	Make sure instructions are placed on the inside of the bedroom door
Window catches	Make sure they are in working order and prevent the window from being opened too far
Lighting	

2 Explain the difference between a hazard and a risk.

3 Explain why carrying out a risk assessment at regular intervals is important.

Attitudes

Did you know!

Health care is one of Britain's biggest employers with approximately 1.2 million employed by the NHS and approximately 0.7 million in the private sector.

All health care staff have a 'duty of care'. To ignore safety issues is unprofessional and dangerous. The main cause of injury resulting in over three-day absences continues to be:

- manual handling/musculo-skeletal injury
- slips and trips
- assault/violence
- struck by something, e.g. sharp knives or falling objects.

Many injuries could be prevented by an improvement in the attitude of staff and employers. For this reason most organisations take a very serious view of staff who do not take an active part in keeping the work environment safe. In most organisations breaches of health and safety are a disciplinable offence and in serious cases can lead to dismissal. Care workers' prime responsibility is the safety of service users and work colleagues.

Legal requirements

The basis of British health and safety law is the Health and Safety at Work Act 1974. The act sets out general duties that all employers have towards employees and members of the public. It also sets out the duties that employees have to themselves and each other.

The employer must attempt to reduce risks and hazards providing it is reasonably practicable to do so. This means that the degree of risk in a particular workplace or work activity needs to be balanced against the time, difficulty and cost of taking measures to avoid or reduce the risk.

The Management of Health and Safety at Work Regulations 1999 state exactly what all employers are required to do under the Health and Safety at Work Act 1974. Like the act, they apply to all work activities. The main requirements are to:

- carry out a risk assessment
- make arrangements for implementing the health and safety measures as identified in the risk assessment
- appoint competent people to implement the arrangements
- set up emergency procedures
- provide information and training to employees
- co-operate with other employers sharing the same workplace.

The principle of risk assessment forms the basis for most modern health and safety law in this country.

Below is a list of some regulations which apply generally to all work areas including health and social care settings for older service users:

Legislation	Provisions
Workplace (Health, Safety and Welfare) Regulations 1992	The premises should not create a risk to the workforce and covers four main areas, e.g. working environment, safety, facilities, housekeeping
Personal Protective Equipment (PPE) Regulations 1992	Designed to protect against risks to health and safety
Manual Handling Operations Regulations 1992	The employer must assess moving and handling tasks and avoid moving and lifting in so far as is reasonably practicable, mechanizing the task where possible
Health and Safety (First Aid) Regulations 1981	Employers must make adequate first aid provision for employees if they become injured or ill at work
Reporting of Injuries, Diseases and Dangerous Occurrences Regulations 1995	Certain accidents and ill-health must be reported
Control of Substances Hazardous to Health Regulations 2002	Storage and use of substances must be safe

The Health and Safety Executive provide guidance to care organizations to help them understand the rules and regulations. It is not compulsory to follow the guidance exactly and employers are free to take other appropriate action. The Health and Safety Executive can also offer practical examples of good practice and give advice on how to comply with the law.

Care workers who work with older people should aim to provide an environment that is as safe as possible.

Assessment activity 9.3

Key skills ICT 2.1, 2.3 C 2.3

Health and safety for older people

You have been asked to prepare a Resource Pack that can be used with new trainees to demonstrate how to promote and maintain a safe environment for older people. You must include information about the responsibilities of care workers.

Case studies should be included to help illustrate the points being made.

1 Try to arrange to visit a care setting for older people or invite a care worker from a setting to the centre to find out how the setting promotes and maintains a safe environment for older service users. Make notes from the information given.

2 Carry out a risk assessment of one area of a setting for older people. Record what you did and the results of the risk assessment. Draw conclusions from the results.

3 Using both the primary and the secondary information gathered, prepare the resource pack. Make sure you cover:
- how hazards can be identified and reported
- what safety features should be in place to promote and maintain a safe environment for older service users. (Give examples and/or case studies to illustrate the points being made.)
- how to carry out a risk assessment and the importance of risk assessments
- how the attitude of care workers can affect health and safety
- legislation that applies to a care setting for older people and its purpose, and how it affects practice in a care setting.

How should care workers respond to the needs of older service users?

Effective communication is essential when responding to the needs of service users. Service users have different needs. The way in which care workers communicate with service users needs to take these individual needs into account. Some older service users are physically frail but mentally alert. Some are mentally confused but physically able, and others are both physically and mentally frail. Taking time to get to know a service user and to talk to them is an important aspect of a care worker's role. Sometimes a service user will relate better to one care worker than to another and this needs to be taken into account.

In some health and social care settings 'key workers' have been introduced. This means that although service users are looked after by a small number of people, one of the group is identified as taking responsibility for a particular service user. Key workers help to make the care provided 'personal' and this improves the quality of care provided. Key worker schemes do, however, depend on effective communication. If communication is poor, the quality of care suffers.

Communication with older people can be affected as a result of them:

- having a physical disability, e.g. **Parkinson's disease**
- having a stroke, e.g. mild **dysphasia**
- having a sensory impairment, e.g. deafness or sight impairment
- being confused, e.g. as a result of a chest infection or mental illness
- not having the ability to speak, e.g. being dumb or having a speech impairment
- not understanding the language, e.g. English not being their first or preferred language.

When responding to older service users who are confused, or who have a hearing impairment or who may have had a stroke, care workers should remember to:

- remove any distractions
- take time to communicate, e.g. sit down and talk in a relaxed way so that the service user does not feel any tension
- only use one idea in each sentence
- use simple vocabulary
- if it is necessary to repeat the information use different words
- use short sentences.

If a service user has a physical disability such as Parkinson's disease, they often find speaking difficult and their words can become slurred. Such diseases can affect the ability to move the muscles in the mouth and tongue that are used to form words. Service users with speech impairment may also have difficulty in communicating with others. Speech therapists often work with service users who find oral communication difficult, to try and improve the quality of their speech. Care workers should, when communicating:

- speak slowly and clearly
- give the individual time to speak and to respond
- be patient
- check that they have understood what has been said
- encourage the service user to speak
- make sure there is no background noise or distractions.

Some older people come to this country from abroad and have not had the opportunity to learn to speak the language. Others may have a **neurological condition** which has lost them the ability to communicate. Family members can be a great help in aiding communication. One method that could be used is to divide a piece of paper in half.

The English word could be listed down the left side and the family member could write the word in the service use's language in the right hand column. For example:

English	Hindi
Comb	
Towel	
Bath	

Beware of using gestures within communication. In some cultures a gesture can mean something entirely different from that in a western society. Care workers should always check with a service user's family if gestures are the same. If they have a slightly different meaning a note should be made of this.

To respond to any service user who does not speak the language or who has a neurological condition or hearing impairment or who is confused, care workers could:

- use a scrapbook with words and pictures
- use communication cards

- use sign language
- provide aids such as computers
- provide hearing aids.

What skills can be used to communicate effectively with older service users?

In Unit 2.2, the oral skills used when communicating were discussed. Look back at that section before reading on.

When caring for older service users the 'spoken word' is the main focus of any communication. Verbal communication can be divided into two main parts:

- what is said
- what is heard.

The speed or pace at which a person speaks when talking to an older person is very important. For example:

- fast speaking can be an indicator of anger, anxiety or excitement

banana

apple

orange

grapes

Figure 9.6 *An example of communication cards*

- slow speech can indicate low spirit, tiredness or depression
- fast speech is difficult to follow, particularly for service users who have a hearing impairment or who are not hearing their first language
- slow speech can be boring and the service user could lose interest.

The tone of voice used is also an indication of a persons emotional state, as it shows how the speaker is feeling. For example, tone can reflect anger, joy, sorrow and disappointment.

Listening is an 'active process' as it involves not only hearing what has been said but also showing the other person that they have been heard. Listening also involves giving time and cannot be done in a hurry, particularly if care workers want to show service users that they value what is being said.

When communicating with older service users a wide range of skills should be used depending on the type of conversation and the **context**.

All of the skills given on the communication tree can be used to promote effective communication. Different skills need to be used to meet the differing needs of service users. The trunk of the tree represents the effective joining together of all the skills. When a tree is growing the roots grow downwards and become firm and the leaves flourish. Similarly, when care workers use all the available skills effectively, the result is likely to be firmly-established trusting relationships between service users and care workers.

Effective communication enables care workers to give messages, to receive messages and is part of the process of making relationships.

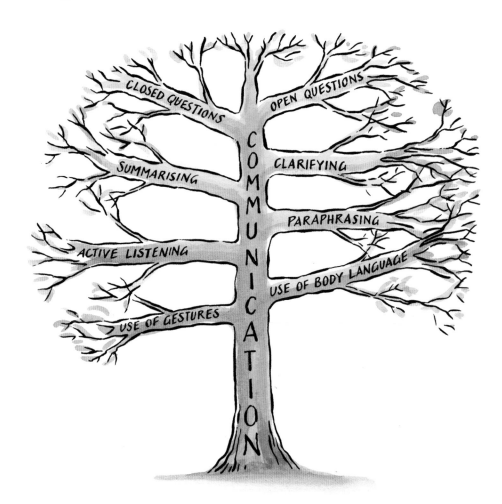

Figure 9.7 *The communication tree*

The table below shows how care workers can use skills to help meet older service users' needs:

Service users need	Skill	Example of use and purpose
Wanting to talk about something that is worrying them	Open question	What's on your mind Doris? Purpose: encouragement to give more than a 'yes' or 'no' answer
Being afraid their afternoon walk will be missed	Closed question	At what time would you like to go for a walk Doris? Purpose: giving a definite time when the event will take place to prevent worry
Wanting the care worker to change where she sits at meal times	Clarifying	So, you are unhappy with where you sit in the dinning room Doris. Purpose: the care worker is seeking understanding of the service users words
Wanting to be sure they have been understood	Summarising	If I have understood correctly you would like to sit next to Len at mealtimes because you have a lot to talk about. Is that correct, Doris? Purpose: shortening what has been said and stating it in a slightly different way
Needing to share (often feelings) and to talk at length about them	Paraphrasing	So all of this has made you feel very upset. Purpose: summarising in a few words what the service user has said in many words
Needing encouragement to say more	Active listening	Go on Doris, tell me a bit more about what happened next. Purpose: giving reassurance that the care worker is listening and that their mind in not on other things
Feeling a little anxious	Use of body language	Smiling when talking. Purpose: showing friendliness and giving reassurance
Needing to be given an aid to help understanding	Use of gestures	If you look over there (arm outstretched and finger pointing), you will see the house I'm talking about. Purpose: adds meaning to what is being said

Activity 3

Key skills  C 2.1a, ICT 2.3

Park Residential Home

Activities organiser Hello, Theo. Are you feeling better this morning?

Theo Yes, I am.

Activities organiser We need to decide which activity you would like to do today, Theo. Would you prefer to paint or to work with wood?

Theo I don't want to paint. It never looks like anything when it's finished.

Activities organiser OK. Talk me through your ideas for working with wood.

Theo Well, I was brought up on a farm and I always fancied doing some carvings of ducks. I like ducks. Some people don't because they chase you, but I liked them. I liked the different colours on their feathers.

Activities organiser You would like to carve some wood to make a duck and then paint it in different colours?

Theo Yes, I'll have a go at that.

Activities organiser (smiling) I think you have chosen quite a hard task, but I'll give you all the help I can. The wood is over there (pointing). Perhaps you would like to sort out which piece you would like to use.

Discuss the following questions about the transcript above.

1 Which is an example of an open question?

2 Give **two** examples of closed questions.

3 Give an example of clarifying.

4 Give **two** examples where body language has been used.

5 What is the purpose of paraphrasing?

6 How can gestures contribute to effective communication?

7 What advice would you give a new care worker about practical ways to respond to older service users.

8 Make a simple aid that could be used to help communicate with a client.

What factors motivate people to communicate?

Environmental

The surroundings or environment can be used to enhance the communication between older service users and care workers, preventing messages from becoming blocked. Environmental factors that can affect communication are shown in Figure 9.8.

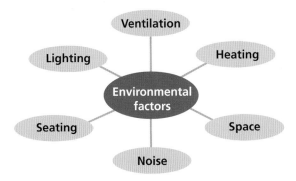

Figure 9.8 *Environmental factors that can effect communication*

Lighting

Making sure there is enough light so that those communicating can see one another clearly is important, especially if some older people use lip reading as a way of understanding what is being said.

Noise

If there is too much noise, those involved in a communication with older people are unable to hear what is being said. However, sometimes some soft music in the background can help service users to talk as it makes them less self-conscious.

Ventilation

Making sure there is enough air circulating and that the room does not become too 'stuffy' prevents people from feeling tired, as older people easily drop off to sleep.

Seating

Older people can communicate more easily in small groups rather than in a large group. In a small group they are often more willing to contribute as they can hear and see what is going on.

Space

Older service users require their own space. If another service user or a care worker is sitting too close, they may 'clam up' because their personal space has been invaded.

Heating

Older people can get cold very quickly. Equally they can soon become too hot. Both extremes of temperature do not motivate older service users to communicate. The room temperature needs to be comfortable for people who are sitting down for long periods. The best temperature considered to be suitable for older people is 21°C (70°F), whereas the room temperature for a younger adult would be set at 18°C (65°F).

Physical

Older service users communicate more freely if they are feeling physically well. Pain can act as a distracter and prevent concentration, as can poor sight and poor hearing. Not having aids such as hearing aids can also prevent service users from communicating. Sometimes service users forget to switch on their hearing aids and then wonder why they cannot hear! Care workers need to be aware of such situations, particularly if they notice that a service user is misunderstanding a conversation or not participating. Having the right aids can help promote communication. Ill-fitting dentures can be a physical factor that prevents communication. It could be that a service user thinks there is a danger of losing their dentures if they speak or their dentures may be rubbing against the gum, causing so much discomfort that the service user cannot concentrate on joining in a conversation. Communication is enhanced if older service users can see those to whom they are speaking without having to twist their neck or body in order to do so. Service users who have physical disabilities should be on the same level as the person or group with whom they are communicating. It is important that care workers and other service users do not tower over a person who is in a wheelchair, otherwise the service user has to strain to look upwards during a conversation. Talking over a wheelchair user's head is not good practice! **Inclusiveness** is important if communication is to be effective.

Social skills to enhance communication

Care workers must take care not to dominate communication between themselves and older service users. This can be boring for service users as well as causing the real issues not to be addressed. It is easily done if care workers attempt to tell service users about a similar situation of their own, or if care workers try to work out solutions to service users' problems.

Care workers can 'block' conversations by:

- yawning
- fidgeting
- smiling at the wrong time
- frowning to show disapproval
- looking bored.

To enhance a conversation care workers should not:

- try to change the subject
- joke at the service user's expense
- criticise the service user
- belittle the service user by making them look small.

Socially supportive skills that can be used by care workers to enhance communication are shown in Figure 9.9 at the bottom of the page.

What are the main barriers to communication and relationships?

Lack of respect

Older service users can become very depressed, anxious, aggressive or withdrawn if they feel that they are not being given respect, and this acts as a barrier to communication. Care workers need to

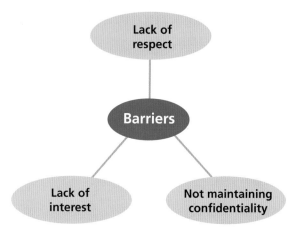

Figure 9.10 *Main barriers to communication*

make sure that they are not creating barriers to communication by the way in which they behave towards older service users. For example, by:

- not listening to the service user
- not allowing enough time to communicate properly
- not understanding the persons culture
- stereotyping service users.

The development of an acceptable sense of 'self' is necessary for a service user to make effective relationships and to cope with complex situations such as communicating with others. If they do not feel that they are respected, service users are likely to develop a poor self-concept and self-confidence, which can lead to withdrawal and isolation.

The way that care workers communicate with service users is a way of showing them that they are valued for themselves, that they are respected and that what they say is important.

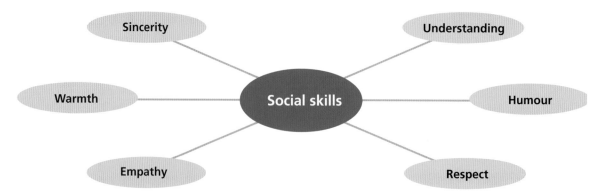

Figure 9.9 *Social skills to enhance communication*

Lack of interest

Older service users who try to talk to care workers but who find nobody takes any notice and they show a complete lack of interest, are likely to feel hurt and angry. They may feel **deflated** which could lead to feelings of sadness and loneliness. They may choose not to communicate with the care workers in the future, keeping important facts to themselves. Therefore a lack of interest shown by not actively listening and communicating could lead to a lack of trust, poor relationships and an older service user's needs not being met.

Not maintaining confidentiality

Older service users have the right to confidentiality of personal information. This means that care workers should not:

- gossip about service users' personal business
- leave personal written records where others can read them
- allow access to unauthorised personnel to service users' computer records
- talk about service users in public places so that they can be identified.

When confidentiality is broken it is likely that communication and relationships between older service users and care workers will be poor. Whatever care workers are told by older service users, they must not pass it on to others unless the service user is in danger or is a danger to others. Confidentiality means keeping information private and secure.

Case study

Liam

Liam arrives back at a residential home having had an afternoon out. He hurries to the lounge as he is anxious to tell someone about his trip. In the lounge is a care assistant and two other residents.

Liam I've have had a wonderful afternoon playing bowls.

Care worker Did you!

Liam Yes, we had a full team, it was beautifully warm and I played well.

Care worker How are you doing with that crossword, Paul? How many have you completed?

Liam We were given tea and some cream scones that Jan had made for us.

Care worker What about four down Paul, do you think…

1 What has gone wrong in this exchange? How has it made Liam feel?

2 Role-play another scenario where Liam is treated properly and the communication goes well

Case study

Xentia

Care worker Good morning Xentia. I see you have already had your post. Are you ready to get up?

Xentia Can I have another ten minutes, I'm really upset by this letter from my niece.

Care worker Would you like to tell me about it?

Xentia She says she is not going to visit me any more as she thinks I smell and that I have nothing to say to her.

Care worker Well, that sounds a bit harsh. You certainly do not smell as we help you to shower every day. Why don't you write back to her later today? We could help you with the letter if you like. I'll go and see to the dining room and give you another ten minutes.
(*In the dining room.*)

Care worker Morning Pat. Xentia is going to be a little while yet. She has this awful letter from her niece that says she smells and that she is boring.

Pat Poor Xentia. I hope she won't get too upset.

(*Later, Xentia has entered the dining room.*)

Pat I am so sorry to hear what has happened Xentia. Fancy your niece saying you smell and that you are boring!

1 How has confidentiality been breached in this exchange?

2 How should the care worker have reacted to Xentia's letter?

How should care workers assess their performance when communicating with older people?

Communicating with older service users can be a very rewarding experience. Service users may:

- ask for support, e.g. help with a small task
- ask for information, e.g. how to get to a place
- want to exchange ideas, e.g. discuss the present with the past
- obtain information, e.g. how to obtain benefits.

When communicating care workers need to remember all the points already mentioned in this unit and in Unit 2. They should consider:

- the skills they will use
- the environmental, physical and social factors that can enhance communication
- how to prevent barriers to the communication.

Examples of ways care workers can provide communication support for older service users include:

- help to read a menu
- help with an activity while talking with the service user

- help to choose a snack
- help to decide where to take a short walk.

It is good practice for care workers to draw up a plan for a communication that they are going to have with a service user. Unit 2 has details about how to draw up a plan, but care workers should consider, for example, to plan:

- what they are going to say in the introduction
- what the main content of the communication will involve
- how they will wind up the conversation

Tips to remember when talking with an older service user are:

- arrange the seating in a suitable way, e.g. so that the service user can be seen and heard and so that direct eye contact is possible
- smile when greeting the service user to help make them feel welcome
- speak at an appropriate pace, i.e. not too quickly
- give the service user time to think about their reply
- use the skills that enhance communication as given earlier in this unit.

Assessing own performance means care workers assessing a communication they have had in the following term.

Assess in terms of	Questions to answer
Strengths	• what was done well, e.g. which skills were used best, was the aim acheived? Why? • Was the content of the communication a strength? Why?
Developmental needs	• What could have been improved? Were there any skills that could have been better used or additional ones that could have been included? • Was the content of the communication managed to achieve the best possible outcome?
Benefits to the service user	• How did the service user benefit? • What were the service user's views about the benefits of the communication?
Methods used to empower the service user	• How was the service user empowered? • Could anything additional have been done to empower them?

Assessing performance is an important aspect of any practical activity that is undertaken. If care workers do not think or reflect on what has been done there is likely to be little improvement. Without improvement they cannot develop their skills to their full **potential**.

When care workers are assessing own performance, the opinions of others are a very valuable way of adding to the assessment. For example, the opinions of:

- a tutor or supervisor
- a service user
- others in a group, e.g. peers
- theorists, e.g. the views of others who have researched the subject.

Assessing means:

- reflecting on what has been done
- making judgements about how well it was done
- drawing conclusions
- planning for improvements.

How can service users be empowered and why is it important to empower them?

In Unit 2 'empowerment' has been discussed in some detail. For older service users it is particularly important that they should be allowed to take control over the main decisions in their lives, because they often feel that they are at a stage in their lives when they are fragile and have less options. Care workers need also to be aware that trying to do everything for service users or trying to solve all their difficulties for them is not a way of helping. Such an attitude is likely to cause service users to become dependent and unable to do things for themselves.

Service users can be empowered by following the signs shown in Figure 9.11.

Empowerment means respecting an individual's right to control their lives and not trying to control it for them.

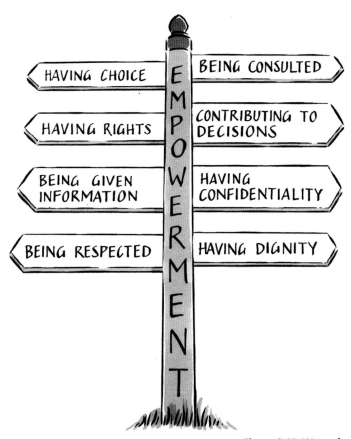

Figure 9.11 *Ways of empowering service users*

Assessment activity 9.4

Key skills C 2.2, 2.3

Effective communication with older service users

Lynda is attending a day care centre. She has difficulty with hand and eye co-ordination and she has asked you for some support to help her complete a collage she is making which is going to be framed.

Erin is attending a nursery school and is making a toy engine using cardboard and other materials. He has asked you for help as he does not know what to do next.

1 Choose **one** of the case studies. Describe in detail the factors that would help to motivate communication for either Lynda or Erin.

2 Explain how you would try to prevent barriers from occurring during the communication.

3 Make a plan for a conversation that you will have with either Lynda or Erin to show:
   • how you will provide communication support
   • the aims, objectives and time scales for the support.

4 Write a transcript of the conversation, which should take approximately ten minutes, showing the different skills you will use and giving reasons why you will use them.

5 Have a conversation (real or simulated) with one of the service users. Remember to arrange for your tutor to assess your performance

6 Assess your performance during the communication. Make reference in detail to:
   • the strengths of your contribution
   • the benefits to the service user of the communication
   • the skills used during the communication
   • the methods used to empower the service user
   • improvements that could be made

7 Explain why it is important to empower service users, giving examples to illustrate the points made.

9.5 Carry out practical tasks for older service users and assess own performance

How should practical tasks for older service users be carried out?

Care workers are asked to carry out a variety of practical tasks for older service users. Some of the most common tasks, whatever the care setting, are:

- making tea
- serving a snack
- taking a service user for a short walk either indoors or outdoors to help maintain mobility.

Care workers may also have to provide instruction for trainee care workers on how to carry out these tasks and, therefore, they need to be very clear about how each task should be done.

Making tea

This is a task that people do every day and care workers may think that everyone knows the steps to take when making tea, but often steps are missed out!

> **Try it!**
>
> Individually and without talking to anyone else, write down the steps for making a pot of tea.
>
> Now follow the steps you have written down. You cannot do anything which is not written down on your piece of paper!
>
> You will probably find that you have missed out quite a few steps! For example:
>
> - did you remember to turn on the tap?
> - did you remember to turn off the tap?
> - did you remember to put the lid of the kettle back on when it was filled?

Figure 9.12 *Service users enjoy having a cup of tea*

A list for making a cup of tea should look similar to this one:

- detach the kettle from the lead if there is one
- lift the kettle and take it to the tap
- remove or lift the lid
- turn on the tap
- fill the kettle to the correct point
- turn off the tap
- put the lid back on the kettle
- take the kettle back to the plug/lead and plug in
- switch on at the socket
- collect the tea and the teapot
- when the water has boiled, lift the lid of the teapot and pour a little water into it
- gently move/swish the water around the teapot and empty down the sink
- put in the correct number of tea bags into the teapot
- switch on the kettle and bring it back to the boil
- when it switches off, immediately pour the boiling water onto the tea bags
- put the lid on the teapot
- wait three minutes
- remove the teapot lid and stir the tea with a teaspoon
- replace the lid
- wait one minute and then pour the tea.

This may seem rather a long list, but these are the steps that people follow every time they make a pot of tea.

Serve a snack

A snack is a small meal. It is having something to eat which is not a full meal. A snack can be made up of one item or several items. For example:

- a packet of raisins
- a sandwich
- a cheese and bean jacket potato, and yoghurt
- cheese and biscuits and an apple
- soup and toast with sardines.

What to serve?

Older people often do not eat as much as an **adolescent** or young adult. They often have their main meal in the middle of the day and perhaps have a snack for their tea. Whatever an older person eats should provide the nutrients required for health. A recent government report, 'The Diet and Nutritional Survey of People Aged 65 Years and Over' showed that 60 per cent of service users living in residential homes were likely to be underweight (one in every six), have a deficiency in vitamin B or be **anaemic**.

Energy requirements decline with age, particularly if an older person does less physical activity. However, it is still important that an older person has the requirements for protein, vitamins and minerals.

When providing a choice of snacks, care workers need to know that they are meeting an older service user's needs. The table on page 311 is a guide to what foods deliver what nutrients.

Older people also need to drink sufficient amounts of fluids, for example, at least six to eight glasses or cups every day.

Any special requirements that service users have should be taken into consideration. For example:

- cultural considerations, e.g. Muslim, Jewish
- Dietary requirements, e.g. gluten intolerance, vegetarian
- portion size, e.g. if on a diet
- likes and dislikes.

How to serve

Older people will eat if the snack that is being served looks attractive and appetising. Therefore, the way in which a snack is served is very important, whether it is served at a table or brought to a service user on a tray. How food should be served to a service user has already been covered in depth in Unit 3.5. Look back at this information before reading on.

Points to remember when serving a snack:
- choose table line, e.g. table cloth and napkin, that **complements** the colour of the food
- make sure the place settings (knives, forks, spoons) are laid neatly and correctly (see Unit 3.5)
- if the service user needs adapted cutlery, remember to place these on the table as for any other place setting

Nutrient	Function	Sources
Fat	To provide warmth and energy, but should be restricted in older people between the ages of 65 and 75 years of age. For those over 75 fats can be used to help those who have suffered weight loss	Animal fats, e.g. butter; vegetablefats, e.g. margarine; fat on meat
Fibre	Helps with bowel problems such as constipation. To enable fibre to work properly it is recommended that plenty of water is drunk	Cereals; fruit; vegetables
Sugar	Provides energy but too much can be harmful	Chocolate; cakes
Iron	Anaemia can result in tiredness and loss of energy if there is little or no iron intake	Red meat; liver; oily fish; beans and pulses
Zinc	Helps the **immune** system and with wound healing such as pressure sores and ulcers	Meat; pulses; wholemeal bread; shellfish
Calcium	Helps to slow down the loss of calcium from the bones	Milk; dairy foods
Vitamin D	Used to help absorb calcium. Deficiency can lead to bone softening and distortion	From sunlight, therefore older people may need to take a vitamin D supplement during winter months
B vitamins	Helps the nervous system	Marmite; red meat; wholemeal bread; green vegetables
Protein	Builds bones and tissues	Meat; fish; cheese; eggs; milk; peas; beans and lentils
Carbohydrates	Provides energy	Bread; potatoes; rice; pasta; scones etc.

- flowers, whether fresh or dried, always help to make a table look attractive so try to place some appropriately on the table, e.g. not blocking the service users view of one another
- make sure there is a jug of water and glasses on the table.
- include napkins. There are several presentation options
- condiments should be placed on the table, e.g. salt, pepper and sauces
- check that the seating arrangement is suitable, so there is enough room for service users to sit comfortably. If a wheelchair user is to be seated make sure there is sufficient room for the wheelchair to be manoeuvred into place and enough space for other service users to eat in comfort
- before bringing service users to the table, ensure they have been able to go to the toilet and wash their hands
- serve the food correctly (see Unit 3.5)
- care should be taken not to spill food over service users
- serve hot food at 63°C to ensure food safety.

Take a service user for a short walk

It is very important that older people remain as mobile as possible because then they are less dependent on others. By providing the opportunity for older people to move around several times during a day care workers help to prevent joints from seizing up and stiffness developing in the limbs. Walking also helps to stimulate the mind and aids breathing. Walks do not need to be lengthy. They can be taken inside or outside of the building depending on the weather and the mobility of the service user. Moving also provides a change of environment for service users which will also add some interest to their day through meeting different people and seeing different things.

Figure 9.13 *Remaining mobile*

Older service users may need encouragement to be mobile and may need support when preparing to be mobile. Providing support does not mean 'taking over' and insisting on doing things for service users. It does mean enquiring how and what help is required.

If service users go outside for their walk they need, depending on the time of the year, to put on outside clothing, such as coats and shoes. Look back to Unit 3 to check the details of how to help with these tasks.

Service users need to be consulted about:
- when they take their walk
- where they would like to go
- who, if there is a choice and a need, will accompany them.

In order to do this, care workers need to use effective communication skills in order to find out service users' thoughts and needs. A good way of beginning such a conversation would be:

Now Charlotte, when did you think you would take your walk today?

This is using a closed question to obtain information that needs to be specific in order to make sure the appropriate help is available. Such a question could be followed up by an open question that explores a little more what the service user's wishes for the walk are. For example, the care worker could ask an open question such as:

What route had you in mind for today's walk Charlotte?

In this way, the service user is deciding for themselves where they would like to walk. Having decided when a walk is to be, where it is to go and what route will be followed, and when the service user is prepared for the walk, a care worker needs to establish what support the service user requires. The care worker will probably know the service user quite well as they will be part of a 'key worker' scheme within a care setting and so will be aware of whether an aid for mobility needs to be used or whether holding onto a care worker's arm is sufficient.

Talking to service users during the preparation for a walk and the walk itself is an essential part of providing support.

While on a walk care workers need to be aware of:

- any frayed carpets in a building that could cause service users to trip over if the whole or part of the walk is inside the building
- any uneven pavements or holes in the surface that could cause service users to twist an ankle
- any dangers from moving vehicles
- the need to allow service users to pause from time to time in order to look around or to gain their breath
- sitting down on a park bench, for example, that the bench is dry and that service users can get up again!

Care workers need to make sure that walks are an enjoyable experience for service users so that they will be motivated to want to be mobile as much as is possible.

How should care workers assess own performance – practical tasks?

Look back to Unit 9.4 which discusses assessing own performance. Remember that assessing own performance means making judgements and drawing conclusions about specific actions taken for tasks. Assessing own performance involves:

- thinking about what has been done or 'reflecting'
- measuring own performance against certain criteria, e.g. has the need been met against the aims, objectives and outcomes required
- considering other people's views and opinions
- drawing conclusions
- gathering together points for improvement.

In this section we will think about assessing performance by looking at an example of a care worker who carried out the practical tasks of:

- making tea
- serving a snack
- taking a service user for a short walk.

Assessing own performance – strengths

The example given below shows how care worker Yussef has assessed his own strengths when making a cup of tea for older service user Amir. He has looked for the things he has done well and thought back to what he did (reflecting), exploring how well (analysing) he did them.

By doing this he has also started to think about areas where he could have done things better.

> **Yussef M**
>
> ### Assessing own performance for tea making
>
> I used a range of practical skills when making a pot of tea for Amir. These included organising skills and measuring water and the amount of tea required correctly. For example, I remembered to fill the kettle to the required level and to put the lid back on. I also 'warmed the pot' by swishing the boiling water round and emptying it away before putting in the tea bags. This means that I remembered the theory that stated that by taking this action a better flavour was achieved.
>
>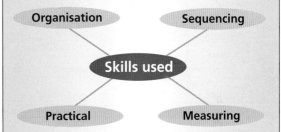
>
> I think I was successful in making a good pot of tea because Amir remarked 'that was a nice cup of tea, I really enjoyed it, it wasn't too strong or too weak'.
>
> For improvement I think I should in future fill the kettle first before getting out the tea and the teapot, as I had nothing to do while waiting for the water to boil. If I had first put the kettle on I could have collected the teapot, tea and cups and saucers while the kettle was boiling and this would have saved time.
>
> My tutor stated that…

When considering this part of Yussef's assessment we can see that he has:

- thought of specific practical skills he has shown as strengths such as
- organising and remembering theory
- used the opinions of another (Amir) to confirm
- that the aim had been achieved and that he was satisfied with the outcome

- considered an area that could be improved, e.g. putting on the kettle before collecting the teapot and the tea.

Assessing own performance – developmental needs

Yussef has started to consider his developmental needs, considering his strengths when reflecting on his performance. Developmental needs are those things care workers need to do to improve. There is always room for improvement. Here is another extract from Yussef's evaluation which concentrates on his developmental needs.

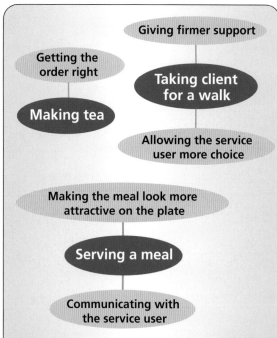

I think I need more practice in doing things in the right order, which is sequencing. Thinking things through more clearly in my mind and getting a clearer picture of what has to be done may help. I could also practice writing things down in the order that they should be done.

When communicating with Amir I needed to speak more clearly so that he didn't have to ask me to repeat what I had said. I also needed to make my questions clearer, for example when I asked if he needed anything, perhaps I should have said 'Can I get you anything else for your snack?'

I tipped the plate as I was bringing the snack to the table. This meant that the salad items got muddled up and looked a bit messy. My practical skills need further practice. I didn't really think about colours when I served the snack as I put the same colours together.

When taking the client for a walk I needed to practice the skill of providing physical support...

Yussef is thinking back on the tasks he has carried out and is analysing how he could have improved the skills used. He is also drawing conclusions as he is making suggestions about what he could do to improve those tasks that were not so successful.

Assessing own performance – the benefits to the service user

Care workers need to consider the actions that they have taken when carrying out tasks, making judgements about how service users have benefited from them. For example, Yussef could ask himself:

- Did the service user enjoy the walk? Why? What made it enjoyable?
- What were the physical benefits of the walk to the service user?
- Were there any intellectual, emotional and social benefits to the service user? What were these?
- Did I achieve my aim? How?
- What is the view of the service user as to how well I provided support?
- Could I have done anything differently?
- How could I improve?

Assessing own performance – methods used to empower the service users

The subject of how care workers can empower service users has been explored in Unit 9.4. As an example in practice, there are various methods that Yussef would have used to empower Amir while carrying out the practical tasks for him. He would have used:

Method	How applied
Effective communication	Talking with the service user and listening to his needs
Practical support	Holding an arm firmly when walking, helping on with outer clothing
Maintaining the service user's rights	Allowing him to make decisions and to choose
Providing choice	Allowing the service user to make decisions

When assessing own performance, care workers need to consider which methods they used, whether there were any additional methods that could have been used and how successful they were in empowering the service user.

Assessment activity 9.5

Carrying out practical tasks for older service users

Havier, who is living in a residential home for older people, has a visitor. He has asked the care assistant for a pot of tea for two and to serve a snack for himself and his visitor. Havier has chosen for the snack vegetarian quiche and salad, served with a bread roll.

After enjoying the snack Havier wants to walk his visitor part way down the drive. He needs help to do this.

1 Role-play making the pot of tea for Havier and his visitor.

2 Role-play serving the snack to Havier and his visitor.

3 Role-play taking Havier with his visitor for a walk part way down the drive. Remember to arrange for your tutor to assess you when doing these tasks.

4 Assess your own performance for all of the tasks by considering:
- strengths
- developmental needs
- benefits to the service user
- methods used to empower the service user

Note: You may wish to take into consideration the assessment made by your tutor and the views of the service users or others when assessing your own performance.

What steps are involved in carrying out an activity?

When carrying out a recreational activity with an older service user, planning is not just one event, but part of a cycle of events that are all linked and dependent on one another.

These events include **implementation** (carrying out), **monitoring** and **reviewing**. This cycle of events allows activities to be continuously improved.

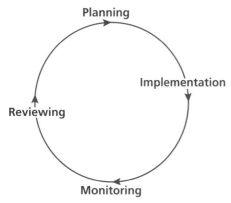

Figure 9.14 *The cycle of events when carrying out an activity*

The more thought and care that goes into planning the better the outcome is likely to be. Planning is essential to the successful outcome of a recreational activity. A successful activity can help make the service user feel valued and can give a great deal of enjoyment.

Planning

Planning involves:

- working out the *aim* – what do you want to achieve?
- setting the *objectives* – the objectives break the activity down into small parts, each of which are measurable. The person planning needs to think about how to measure the objectives to find out if they have been achieved
- identifying the *resources* – when planning activities it is necessary to decide how many service users will be involved in the activity and which resources will be required. It is good practice to gather all the resources together before the activity starts
- setting *timescales* – from when until when and what happens at different times
- *costing* an activity – so that budgets set are realistic is important. If **consumables** are used then they need to be replaced in order to provide for further activities in the future
- considering *health and safety* and how risks can be reduced – health and safety is a basic requirement. The area should be checked for

Figure 9.15 *Examples of recreational activities*

hazards and these should be reduced where possible by putting in place control mechanisms. Hazards could be a torn carpet with the potential to trip or a pair of scissors where there is a danger of the service user cutting themselves.

Consideration must be given to the roles of others who might be helping. It is important that they are briefed correctly so they know exactly what they are expected to do.

Forming aims and objectives

The first thing a care worker considering an activity must do is to form aims and objectives. For example, Karla has been asked to design a practical activity for an older service user. The activity will be creating a picture in the form of a collage of different materials. The service user has requested this activity so Karla is determined to make it a success. The aims and objectives do not have to be complex but they must be appropriate and serve the service user's mental and physical needs.

Karla's aims and objectives for the plan are shown in the table below.

Karla has:

- found an activity that is of interest to the service user
- produced an overall aim
- set the objectives or targets
- set a timescale.

Writing an activity plan

The best way to ensure that an activity works is to create a written plan. This has three main benefits:

- it gives a working record of what is going to take place. This is essential in complex plans where there is opportunity to forget a small point that might ruin the whole event
- it allows others to follow what has been planned and is especially helpful if the person who devised the plan is not present as the work can continue
- it allows the person who has organised the activity to look back at the evidence of what has happened and to create an even better plan for the next event.

For example, Karla could create a plan for her collage picture activity. It could also be used as a checklist as shown at the bottom of the page.

Aim	Objectives
To empower the service user in creating a picture of their choice	• A completed collage picture that the service user is justly proud of • To help maintain physical well-being and mental alertness. Promoting a sense of overall well-being • To keep the service user physically and mentally engaged for thirty minutes

Activity: Collage picture	**Service user:** Doris Watts	
Time and date	14:00 Tuesday 20/4/04	Date suitable
Duration	30 minutes	Time agreed
Place	Day room	Booked
Seating	Day chair and work table	Arranged with caretaker
Materials	Card, glue various cloth, scissors, paper towel	Materials collected
Staff	Self only at present	
Special requirements	1. Foam ring for chair 2. protective apron because of glue 3. Available first aid kit	1. 2. 3.

Activity plans, as they are sometimes called, cover all aspects of an activity in detail from start to finish. They are used to show how the activity is carried out and explain the preparation needed to run the activity. They also indicate the resources that are required. Such detailed planning makes sure there is a level of success because every possible issue is considered before the event. Plans are useful because they take into account the individual needs of service users.

Activities planned in this way can make service users feel valued and give them a sense of individuality.

> **Discussion point**
>
> *Why is planning important?*

Case study

Bridget

Bridget is the activities leader at a local day care centre. She is planning a recreational activity for four of the service users who attend. The service users have told Bridget that they would like to make a picture of some kind. Bridget draws up the plan shown on the right.

Planning for measuring success

When planning it is important to work out a set of 'pre-set criteria' that can be used to measure the success of the activity. Pre-set criteria should be measurable and usable to judge how well an activity achieved its aim. The information could be gathered, for example, through face-to-face questioning of those participating, a questionnaire or a formal interview. Examples of pre-set criteria are:
- was the activity carried out safely?
- did the participant(s) enjoy the activity?
- were the objectives met?
- was the overall aim achieved?
- what were the benefits to the service user(s)

Aim	To encourage the service users to be creative and to provide mental stimulation
Objectives	<ul><li>to understand which materials produce the desired effect for the picture</li><li>to be aware that using different materials produces different effects</li><li>to demonstrate that a picture is a means of expressing feelings</li></ul>
Resources	<ul><li>seating for 4 people</li><li>table space</li><li>4 brushes</li><li>paints</li><li>different materials</li><li>paper</li><li>drying space for finished items</li></ul>
Time	<ul><li>3 x 2 hours</li></ul>
Cost	<ul><li>£4 per person without a frame</li></ul>
Health and safety	<ul><li>make sure there is absorbent paper to mop up spills</li><li>have the activity area near to the sink so water and paints can be cleared up easily</li><li>make sure the cutting equipment, e.g. scissors, is placed away from the edge of the table</li><li>have first aid equipment readily available</li></ul>

Carrying out

Enjoying the activity

Carrying out an activity is also known as 'implementation'. Before an activity can begin, preparation must take place. Good preparation involves thinking ahead and considering the possible problems. Preparation includes looking at the environment in which the activity will take place. Points to consider are:

- seating – correct type, correct height
- tables – are they big enough
- temperature – too hot or too cold
- lighting – too bright, too dark
- overall layout of the room

The activities organiser needs to explain to service users:

- what the activity involves
- how long it will take
- the benefits that they hope the service users will receive from the activity
- the right the service users have to choose whether or not to take part or when they want to stop.

Monitoring

Monitoring is carried out while an activity is taking place. It is a method of checking against the plan that the activity is going according to plan. Monitoring includes:

- checking the environment is safe and making sure service users do not harm themselves
- ensuring there is an adequate supply of materials to use so that choice is provided
- making sure the service users are comfortable and remain comfortable
- checking progress through the activity

If care workers are working in a group they may find that it is not possible to monitor all events on their own. In this situation they should always involve others in monitoring as two sets of eyes are better than one.

Reviewing

Reviewing is also known as evaluating. As part of the process time should be taken to review how well an activity has gone. As this is a cycle of events the information that is gained should be used in the further planning of the next similar event.

To evaluate effectively, a wide range of information has to be gathered from various sources. Both positive and negative feedback is required to help make future events even more successful. Organisers of activities should never be afraid of coping with negative comments. There is an old saying 'the man who never made a mistake, never made anything'. Knowing what went wrong is as important as what was right. **Constructive criticism** is always helpful and allows us to improve activities in the future. When gathering the information consider the following valuable sources:

- the service user who took part in the activity
- other staff who helped
- comments from friends and relatives of the service users, they may be able to give information that the service users could not supply
- the care worker's own personal criticisms.

What are the needs of older service users who are involved in an activity?

Older service users involved in an activity often have a variety of specific needs that must be considered when planning the activity. The table below shows the types of needs that they might have and a variety of ways in which they can be met. It uses the example of the activity Karla was planning for Doris Watts that we used earlier. Karla knows Doris Watts well, but just to make sure that she has all of her needs covered, she has created a written record.

User needs	Ways in which they are accommodated
Access	Doris uses a wheelchair due to her medical condition. The room must be wheelchair friendly with no obstructions. She also requires extra help in transferring her from her chair to a static chair. Foam ring provided to reduce the risk of pressure sores
Dietary	As a **diabetic** everything that Doris consumes during the activity should be suitable by being sugar free
Medical	Doris' disability revolves around being a chronic asthmatic. This stops her from walking due to chronic shortness of breath. She also requires a portable oxygen cylinder and mask with the flow rate set at six litres per minute. In the event of an asthma attack due to over-exertion her **nebuliser** will be set up as a precaution
Care	Doris spends a large amount of time sitting, so it is important that she is stood up at regular intervals to assist her circulation to prevent pressure sores on her buttocks. Particular attention will need to made to her breathing so that any onset of an asthma attack can be predicted and dealt with

By knowing or having access to a service user's clinical history it is possible to make sure that any activity does not cause them harm or distress.

How can service users be empowered to contribute to an activity?

Throughout the whole cycle of events it is important that the service users are empowered and feel that they have control over the activities that affect them. The spider diagram below shows the factors that affect their level of empowerment.

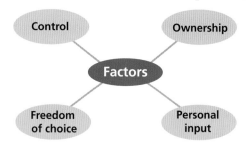

Figure 9.16 *Factors affecting the level of empowerment in an activity*

These factors allow service users to be comfortable with any arrangements that are made on their behalf. They allow service users to feel that they are involved in the processes of their care.

How should care workers assess their own performance – recreational activities

This unit has discussed self-assessment when communicating (Unit 9.4) and when carrying out a practical task (Unit 9.5) for older service users. We know from these that to assess own performance it is necessary to:

- think back and consider what we has been done
- think about *how* the activity was carried out
- analyse against theory how well the task was done
- draw conclusions
- plan for improvements.

Questions that a care worker could ask when evaluating a recreational activity could include:

- was the plan suitable? If not why not?
- did I use the correct skills?
- did I achieve the aims and objectives?
- how could the activity be improved?
- what were the strengths?
- did I manage the time efficiently and effectively?
- what were the benefits to the service user?

Strengths and developmental needs

Now what did I do well when doing the practical tasks? What are my strengths?

Figure 9.17 *What did I do well?*

When considering strengths care workers must look at the positive effects. Was the activity beneficial and if so what did they do that made it so? An example might be that they organised time well. This meant that everything was in place and the whole activity ran **seamlessly** from beginning to completion. Looking at strengths can often result in highlighting weaknesses. By looking in a critical way at what happened it is often possible to see things that would help improve the overall quality of the event. If reflection and analysis takes place and if conclusions are drawn, positive personal development often results. If care workers improve their own performance, then tasks will be carried out to a higher standard if they are repeated.

Benefits to the service user

When considering one particular service user, for example Doris, the benefits of participating can be clearly recognised, as shown in the table on the right.

Type of benefit	Actual benefit to Doris
Physical	Developing her hand-eye co-ordination, using and exercising her hands
Intellectual	Learning about the different visual qualities of certain fabrics, remaining alert, developing a level of skill that can now be improved. Feeling of ownership
Emotional	The satisfaction of creating something beautiful, feeling supported and cared for, feeling of inclusion. Feeling empowered
Social	Pleasure of care worker's company, working together with someone, being part of a team

From one small short activity a whole range of benefits emerge. The activity has benefited Doris in all of the important key developmental areas.

Methods used to empower the service user

Empowerment means enabling service users to feel in control, and encouraging them to participate in the decision-making process.

To establish if a service user has been empowered, care workers should ask:

- was the service user able to control events?
- was the service user given choices?
- was the service user listened to?

Assessment activity 9.6

Key skills 2.3

Carrying out a recreational activity with older service users

You have been asked to plan and carry out a recreational activity with older service users who are either in sheltered accommodation or in a day care centre or who are in a residential home. The activity must be appropriate to the needs of the older service users. You need to explain how the recreational activity meets the service users' needs.

1 Select an appropriate recreational activity and explain in detail how it will meet the needs of the service users

2 Produce a detailed plan for the activity the activity. Remember to include:

- aim
- objectives
- timescales
- pre-set criteria for measuring the success of the activity
- resources required
- health and safety issues.

3 Explain how you will carry out the activity.

4 Explain how and why you will monitor the activity.

5 Carry out the activity, either by arrangement with real service users or as a simulation. Make sure your tutor assesses your performance.

6 Assess your own performance during the activity. You should consider:

- strengths
- your developmental needs
- the benefits to the service user
- the methods used to empower the service user.

Remember to:

- reflect
- think about how you did things
- analyse what you did
- draw conclusions
- plan improvements.

Glossary

Adapted: to alter to fit another purpose or need

Adolescent: a person between the age of 11 and 18

Alzheimer's disease: a disease that affects the brain and results in loss of memory

Anaemic/anaemia: a deficiency of the blood, resulting in paleness and weakness

Apathetic: lacking in interest and energy

Bipolar: depressive state where person is either very excited or very sad

Bond: forming a very strong relationship

Complements: goes together well

Confused: not able to think logically; muddled

Constructive criticism: comments that help make something better

Consumables: items that are used and will need to be replaced

Context: situation; circumstance

Elevated: raised up, high up

Deflated: low in spirit, sad

Dehydration: lacking in fluids

Direct care: having personal contact with the service user when providing care

Diabetic: a person whose body cannot process sugars

Dementia: a condition that means there is loss of memory

Deterioration: getting worse; lowering standards

Dysphasia: lack of speech co-ordination due to brain damage

Enhance: to make look better; to improve

Ensures: to make sure something happens

Geriatric: an elderly person, slightly out of date term but still used in many hospitals

Implement: to carry out; to put into practice

Inclusiveness: to include; to be part of a group

Insomnia: not being able to sleep

Monitoring: to check progress through observation or questioning or measuring

Multi-disciplinary approach: a group of people from different providers/ disciplines, e.g. health and social care, working together to plan and provide care for service users

Nebuliser: a device for turning a liquid drug into a vapour cloud to allow it to be breathed in and absorbed quickly into the body

Neurological condition: a condition affecting the nervous systems, e.g. brain

Ownership: the ability to possess an object or to take control of something

Palliative care: care where the main aim is to stop pain, not to cure

Parkinson's disease: disease of the nervous system leading to tremors etc.

Potential: the best someone can achieve

Respite care: a service that provides care for service users so that informal carers can have a break/ holiday/rest

Reviewing: to think about and to make judgements

Seamlessly: continuous; without a break or interruption

Stimulation: an activity that provides interest, gets the brain and/or body moving

Symptom: a physical or mental change which shows the presence of disease

Terminally ill: dying; will not recover from their condition or illness

Therapeutic: beneficial

Triggered: started off

Warden: a person who keeps a check on older service users safety and well-being when they live in sheltered accommodation

Learning to work together

Understanding how healthcare organisations function is especially important considering the large numbers employed within the health, social care and early years **sector**. However, in order to understand how such organisations function care workers must be aware of the purpose that they fulfil. A variety of important areas such as workplace roles, health and safety procedures and agreed standards must also be understood. This allows care staff to function more efficiently and more immediately.

The information in this unit will also help promote personal behaviour and presentation. It will show how work-based skills are used, emphasising the skills and qualities that employers find desirable.

While you are in the workplace you will need to learn to:

- work on your own while taking some responsibility
- work as a member of a team showing responsibility

Whichever you are involved in you will be contributing skills and knowledge.

In a team there is the opportunity to share knowledge and skills. This can help some people's confidence and there will be others around with whom ideas can be shared and feedback given.

Learning to co-operate with others, ensuring health and safety standards are met, using resources effectively are all important aspects of work experience.

15.1 Describe the structure and purpose of the workplace organisation

What will we learn in this unit?

Learning outcomes

You will learn to:

- Describe the structure and purpose of the workplace organisation
- Review workplace roles within the workplace organisation
- Describe how to work in a healthy and safe way in the workplace organisation
- Illustrate how to comply with agreed standards for personal behaviour and presentation in the workplace organisation
- Plan tasks to be carried out in the workplace
- Undertake tasks in the workplace, using appropriate skills for work
- Evaluate performance of tasks

What is the main purpose and key activities of the organisation?

Workplace organisation

It is important to understand the purpose that services have and where they fit into the health, social care and early years structure. This helps care workers and service users to understand the differences in the workplace environment and the way in which it operates.

Organisations in health and social care are found in many areas and in many forms. They do, however, have one thing in common: the provision of treatment, care and support and care and education for early years. These organisations operate either nationally or at local level and provide a variety of services, many of which are funded by the state, e.g. the National Health Service (NHS) or local authorities. Other services receive their funds from private sources such as insurance schemes and subscriptions. These are in an area known as the independent, or private, sector. In this situation those using the service will probably be asked to pay a contribution towards the cost. Certain organisations run on what is

known as a 'not-for-profit' basis. Although they may charge for their services they do not make any profit as an organisation at the end of the year. All of the money that they earn is used to maintain their services and to pay for their staff and **overhead costs**. Organisations of this type can be charitable or independent depending on their aims and function. Often, company health schemes function in this way to benefit their staff and dependants. Some organisations operate in the voluntary sector, which means that their services are provided free to people by volunteer workforces that are funded by charitable subscriptions from various sources.

Whatever their differences, organisations in health and social care all provide work for healthcare professionals and carers, and this work has many similarities in the skills and qualities that are used.

Care and education
Purposes

A workplace serves three main purposes:

- to provide for its service users
- to provide for its employees
- to provide for the employer.

326 **Unit 15** Work experience in health and social care settings

The purpose of a health, social care and early years organisation is to benefit service users. All such organisations provide some form of treatment, care and education. From an employees perspective the purpose of a workplace is to provide what is known as 'gainful employment'. This means that they will receive some form of benefit from working there.

The purpose of a health and social care workplace for employers is different depending on what sector they are in. If the workplace is in the NHS then the employer works to a set of rules and guidelines laid down by the government, and is in the state sector. These direct the employer as to how the service should be run and the level of service required. The service is not there to make a profit but to efficiently supply quality services to the users.

The independent sector also strives to provide quality services in an efficient manner. The main difference is that most establishments have to make a profit at the end of the year. In this way they are no different to any other private company.

Management of the voluntary sector is different to that of the other providers. These services often have what is known as charitable status. As a registered charity an organisation is not allowed to make a profit. For this reason they must run the service and spend the money efficiently.

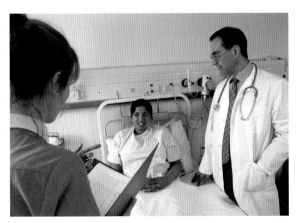

A typical healthcare environment

Discussion point

What are the purposes of:
- *the voluntary sector when providing support?*
- *the independent sector when providing healthcare?*
- *local authorities when providing personal care and support?*

Key activities

The size of an establishment affects the activities that happen within it. Size affects how many staff work there and the level of service that is provided to the users. It also affects the job roles of the staff. For example, in a large hospital a nurse may have one specific role, such as working on a children's ward, whereas in a doctors' surgery there may only be one nurse, who has to help treat all of the patients.

The main or key activities of employees are governed by their job description and their qualifications.

In many organisations treatment is a core part of the work activity. Treatment can be in various forms from the giving of drugs to curing or preventing illness right through to providing operations.

Care is a fundamental function in all of the organisations. It comes in a variety of forms and depends on the age of the service user when its delivery is decided. For example, the care provided to children is different to that provided to older adults.

Rehabilitation usually follows treatment and in some cases can include a level of continuing treatment to help service users recover. For example, a person who has multiple fractures needs time to recover but also needs **physiotherapy** during that period of recovery or rehabilitation.

Care and education organisations vary enormously in the type of management structure in place. For example, in a very large nursery school where there are various departments there could be a hierarchical or a pyramid style of management. In a childminder's home where there is only one key person in charge a flat management structure is more likely to be in place, although it must be remembered that the childminder will have to liaise with a number of other people, for example, inspector panels and other agencies.

Administration

Administration duties appear in every organisation, since all organisations need systems to help them function effectively. These systems have to be carried out efficiently or the organisation will fail in its goal. Administrative duties such as keeping records of treatment and monitoring staff attendance are essential tasks.

All organisations will have policies in place. A policy is intended to help the organisation to implement procedures set out by law, and for the professional care worker to follow the procedures consistently. A number of policies will be in place in organisations. These could include:

- health and safety assessments, audit and surveys
- first aid procedures, e.g. a named person responsible for first aid
- for safety – security that must be followed to protect service users and care workers
- to promote fair employment, e.g. to make sure questions asked at interview are valid, relevant and not encroaching on personal life

- confidentiality – to ensure all care workers know what information must be kept and how to deal with it.

Procedures are made from the policy that has been set. A procedure informs all care staff about how to carry out a particular task. For example, if a service user needs moving from one place to another, the procedure will set out exactly what the care worker must do. Similarly, if a care worker is given some information and told to 'keep it confidential', then if the person is in danger of harming themselves or others, the procedure will show the care worker the exact steps to take.

When a job is offered to a care worker it is their responsibility to find out what policies are in place and what is stated with each procedure set out. A care worker will also be given a job description.

What is a job description?

A job description outlines the tasks and duties of an employee, providing them with a guide as to what they are expected to do in the workplace. Some job descriptions are very specific. For example, a cleaner's duties revolve around making sure the care environment is kept clean and hygienic. Other job descriptions may only have the duties outlined, for example, a nurse's duties could be stated as 'care of the service user'. This could involve a variety of activities, probably too many to list but all of them an important part of the nurse's job.

Activity 1

Key skills **C** 2.3

Carol

Carol wants to work in a health or social care or early years setting. To help her make up her mind she is going to find out about the main purpose of different settings and the key activities carried out by them.

1 Choose one health, one social care and one early years setting. For each describe:
- the main purpose
- the key activities.

2 For one of the chosen care settings describe:
- its aim
- two policies
- two procedures.

3 What is:
a an aim?
b a policy ?

4 Explain the differences between a policy and a procedure.

Job descriptions are usually designed with the worker's qualifications in mind. By using this method everyone knows what to do and what is expected of them. The key activities in the workplace are covered and working efficiency is maintained.

How is management structured in an organisation?

Main features of the management structure

All organisations have to run efficiently. To help them do this they have a management structure. It is not enough just to have job descriptions, there must be levels of responsibility within an organisation. The purpose of this is to define which people make the important decisions, for example how to spend funds and how and when to hire and fire staff. The structure gives everyone '**clearly-defined roles**'.

In any organisation that has more than one person there will be a management structure. Generally, the larger the organisation, the larger the management structure is. With many people working, it is even more important that everyone knows who is in charge and what they are in charge of.

Figure 15.1 shows part of the management structure within a large hospital. It shows the management from the top down. This is a hierarchical structure.

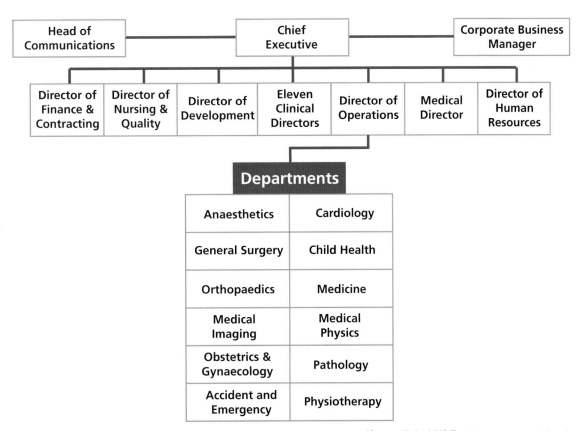

Figure 15.1. *NHS Trust management structure*

Within this overall management structure each department also has its own management structure, for example, Figure 15.2 shows the structure of the Medical Imaging department. (This is often better known as the X-ray department.) The manager of each department reports to the director of operations, who in turn reports to the chief executive.

Different kinds of management structure are used for different health and social care organisations or activities. The three main ones are:

- pyramid management
- flat management
- matrix management.

Pyramid management structure

In the example of pyramid management shown in Figure 15.2 below, the whole structure takes the shape of a pyramid with a senior person at the top and in charge of everyone. It gradually works down to include people at the bottom with less responsibility. The management power of the individual lessens the nearer they are to the bottom of the structure.

Flat management structure

'Flat' management structures in healthcare organisations do not have a lot of management levels within their organisation. They may still have a large workforce but not have many rungs in the ladder between the man on the ground and the top manager. It is claimed that flatter structures assist in saving on managerial costs and also improve communications as there are fewer levels between the top and bottom of the organisation. However, with fewer levels, managers are forced to have a much greater area of control and responsibility. Also, flat management structures reduce the opportunity for progression and promotion and can therefore have a detrimental effect on staff satisfaction and motivation.

In a nursery you often find flat management structures like the one shown in Figure 15.3 at the bottom of the page.

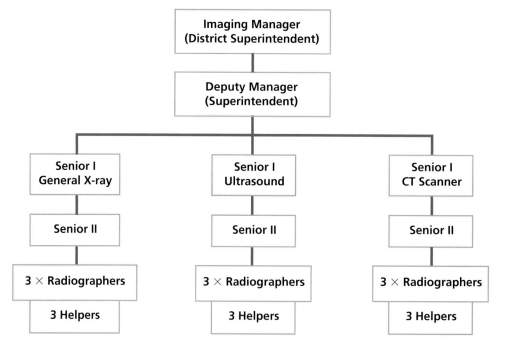

Figure 15.2 *Pyramid management structure in an Imaging department*

Figure 15.3 *Flat management structure in a nursery*

Matrix management structure

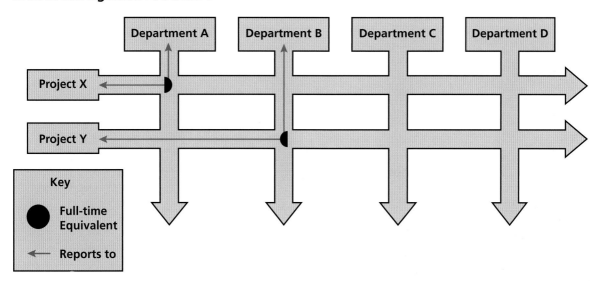

Figure 15.4 *Matrix management structure*

The figure above illustrates the way one member of staff reports to different people with management responsibility. An example of this could be a GP surgery where one nurse works with two doctors. They will find themselves reporting to two different managers who both have some degree of authority over this member of staff.

Matrix management relies on co-operation and communication between everyone involved. Whilst in a GP's surgery the decision-making authority rests with the GP, but by using a matrix environment decisions can also be reached by professional consensus between different managers and departments.

Note that matrix management is often used for one-off projects, in which people or teams of equal expertise from different backgrounds work together.

In some organisations a democratic management system will be in use. By using this method no one person is higher than another and decisions are reached through discussion and majority agreement.

Key personnel

Within the management structure of any organisation there are key personnel who have specific and important positions within the organisation. Starting at the top the following people have key responsibilities.

Chief Executive Officer

The chief executive is normally the head of an organisation. Their purpose is to design a variety of **strategies** that will carry the organisation into the future. They have to plan ahead so that the service which the organisation provides has all of the staff and facilities it needs to continue. Because they have the top job they have ultimate responsibility for the success of the organisation. If the organisation fails then they lose their job. Together with directors, the chief executive designs the mission statement for the organisation. This lets everyone know what the purpose and aims of the organisation are.

Directors

It is not normal for a chief executive to carry all of the responsibility for an organisation, and so they are normally supported by a board of directors. This is a group of experienced individuals with many skills who can help and advise the organisation.

Directors can be senior managers in the organisation or they can be contracted in from other companies or organisations on a part-time basis. They will often have a successful track record in running other organisations.

Service or General Manager

The general day-to-day management of an organisation has to be monitored. This is the job of the General or Service manager. Their function is to put into place any policies or strategies that have been designed and approved by the chief executive and the directors. They convert new policies into working practices and make sure that they actually work. They are the first person to know if the policies do not work and are expected to report back if this happens. They are involved in maintaining the correct staffing levels within the organisation. These managers will also have the overall responsibility for areas such as health and safety of staff and service users.

Personnel Officer (Human Resources)

The human resources officer is concerned with **allocating** staff and servicing their contracts. They are involved in hiring and dismissing staff, grievance procedures, appeals, and union business in line with the organisation's policies and the policies of the government of the day. One of their duties is to check the qualifications and work records of staff that have been recruited.

During this process they will often perform Criminal Record Bureau (CRB) checks to ensure the suitability of the candidates. Part of their job is to make sure that new employees fully understand the terms and conditions of their appointment. They also make sure that the finance or pay office is aware that a new member of staff has started, so that they get paid.

Department or Line Manager

The department manager has specific responsibility for a recognised area of an organisation. Within that area they have responsibility for the following:

- all work that is carried out there
- staff work rotas
- staff holiday rotas
- staff development
- appraisals
- discipline and time keeping
- departmental health and safety
- liaison with higher management and other departments.

The department manager is directed by the general or service manager and usually provides them with information on how well their department is running.

> ### Discussion point
> *Think about working environments that you know, and the management posts within them. What is involved in these jobs?*

The role of management

Management in health and social care can be described as the organisation of labour between several or many people who are the employees of the service. This process is known as the division of labour. It creates different groups of people with different objectives, all of whom have some power to influence the way in which the service works. Division of labour is necessary in any service and there are many ways in which the tasks of management and labour can be split. Normally, managers are given responsibility for particular resources and activities and this is where their management role begins.

Managers aim to make the results of their team's work worthwhile. They have to quickly get to know their team's activities, strengths and weaknesses, ensuring that the team is working together, and not duplicating each other's work. The activities have to be balanced and focused towards the ultimate healthcare goal of the service.

As well as co-ordinating the activities of the team, a manager must act as a **facilitator**, bringing together the skills of the team so that team members can share skills and learn from one another. The manager must also act as facilitator in driving the team's energy, maintaining good **morale** and focusing the team on their goals.

Managers must encourage others to contribute ideas, as all members of a team have their own views on best practice. Positive contributions can help the whole team, providing that credit is given where it is due. If done well this helps increase the pool of shared knowledge and makes employees feel like they are doing something useful.

Managers are responsible for drawing out the best in their team and ensuring that their staff's efforts become more and more effective. One of the ways in which this can be done is through coaching. In this context, coaching means helping others to improve by removing the obstacles in their way. Such obstacles might be:

- lack of confidence
- lack of clarity over personal and professional goals
- confusion over which techniques and approaches to use in a situation.

A manager's coaching role can blur into other areas of management responsibility, such as training and skills development or ensuring that their team has the right resources to do the job. It is important to remember that the coaching support given by a manager is just as important as teaching a new skill or fighting for a share of the resources.

Henri Fayol, a French writer in the early 1900s, identified the functions of management as: Planning, Organising, Commanding, Controlling and Co-ordinating.

> ### Discussion point
> *What is the purpose of the five functions suggested by Henri Fayol?*

What are the main customer and service user groups served by the workplace organisation?

Every health and social care organisation has service users. These are members of the public who receive care services from the organisation.

These groups of people can vary greatly in age, gender and social background. The one thing that links them together is that they all seek a service from the organisation.

Service users could be:

- older people – 65+
- adults – 19–65
- adolescents – 11–18
- children – 4–10
- infants – 0–3

Each group of service users will have different needs, for example, physical, intellectual, emotional and social (P.I.E.S).

Some will have more than one need which the organisation will try to meet by liaising with other organisations. For example, a child in a nursery class will be having care and educational needs met, but if they have an illness or a condition where a health specialist is required, the nursery school will link with that organisation.

Most organisations take particular care in looking after the needs of their service users. There are several reasons for this:

- with no service users the service would not exist
- if service users were not happy with the service then this could cause bad public **perception**
- how much funding an organisation gets is linked to the service users that it serves.

Take, for example, a residential home for older service users. Some of the service users pay for their own place. Others have their place in the care establishment paid for by the local health authority, perhaps because they have no readily disposable income. These two types of service user have some power over the care organisation because they provide the money that is required for it to exist. Both service users expect as high a level of service as possible. The organisation will try to limit the service to what is affordable but will not want to lose the service user. They will both reach an agreement on what is an acceptable level of service for the money available.

Many care organisations in the national framework are funded directly from money provided by the government. This means that many of their service users do not directly pay for the services they receive. They have paid indirectly by being taxed by the government. This does not mean that they have no influence at all over the organisation. In fact, they have as much influence as if they paid directly. This is because the government monitors standards of care on behalf of the service users. They do this by introducing legislation, policies and guidelines that help promote and maintain quality. An example of this is 'Your NHS', a set of guidelines that helps define the level of services that the public can expect from their local healthcare trusts. It also outlines how people can complain about poor and dangerous services. With this level of influence the service user has a great deal of say in how healthcare organisations provide services. This means that they must be listened to.

Assessment activity 15.1

Key skills [C] 2.3, [ICT] 2.3

Organisation of the workplace

You have been asked to provide a training Resource Pack for care workers who are thinking that they would like to work in a health or social care or early years setting.

You need prepare materials that can be used during training sessions. These can be written reports, handouts, leaflets or presentations.

1 Choose **one** setting from either the health or social care or early years sector. For the care setting chosen give an in-depth account of:

- the structure of the organisation
- the purpose of the organisation
- roles within the organisation
- the key activities
- the main features
- key personnel
- roles and responsibilities.

2 Identify the main service user groups served by the care setting, describing how the setting meets their needs.

What is the role of care workers in the workplace?

Own role

It has already been said that jobs are described in a job description, but there is often more to a job than just practical duties.

Our own role within work experience will probably be very different from the role of an employed person, as there will be personal care that is not permitted for us to do.

Having a job means that the person doing the job is paid for the time and effort that they are giving to that particular setting and, therefore, each employed person is expected to contribute to the best of their ability and within the limits of their job description.

During work experience you will be expected to join one or more teams of care workers. It is possible that you will be one of the people that is at the lowest level within that team, but both you and the service user should benefit greatly from your input.

Guidelines will have been given to you by your tutor and/or by your placement supervisor. You must follow those guidelines and carry out your duties with the team in order to deliver the best possible care.

Discussion point

You have been asked to shadow a nursery nurse in a nursery school. What could you expect to do?

Care workers rely on a diverse range of skills when looking after service users, just as a nursery nurse uses a variety of techniques. These are part of their professional skills and are applied to the work after their assessment of the situation.

Case study

Emma

Emma is attending Hill Top Nursery as she is the second nursery nurse there. She has been asked to arrive at 8.00 a.m. Some of her duties are:

- to get out the equipment for the painting and dressing up area
- to make sure there are no hazards within the areas
- to arrange the equipment so that it looks interesting to the children when they arrive
- to make sure the protective clothing is hanged near to the painting area
- to attend a staff meeting at 8.30 p.m. and make notes
- to supervise the children playing in the painting and dressing up areas.
- to help supervise the children at break time etc.

These are some of Emma's own roles. She will be a small part of a team, all of whom are working together to benefit the children in their care.

It is important that whatever 'own role' we are given that we see ourselves as a small cog in the wheel – part of a team that is working together as a whole. We must not see ourselves or our role as being isolated from others within the team.

Care assistants are often the first people that service users turn to for advice. For this reason they must be confident in their own knowledge and abilities. Often the advice that they need to give is based on knowledge gained from training and experience. Occasionally they may find themselves in a position where they are asked to give advice about something that is beyond their knowledge, and should then refer service users to care professionals who can help them. It is very important to give advice that is **factually correct**. Sometimes the best communication skill is just to listen, and may be all that is required.

It is important to ensure the confidentiality of service users at all times

Communicator

As a care worker, communication is a skill that can and should be developed. Care workers need to communicate in different ways with different people. How they communicate with service users should differ from the way that they communicate with their colleagues and the public.

As effective communicators, care workers should try to ensure that all interactions with service users are beneficial. Even passing the time of day can leave a service user feeling better, especially if it is done with caring and feeling. Care workers should seek to appear professional but also sincere in their communications with service users. With each service user, different adaptations should be made to the way in which communication is made. Doing this accommodates their needs and increases the bond; slowly a care worker can build a trusting relationship with a service user.

In contrast, the way in which care workers communicate with fellow professionals may involve a mixture of formality and informality when discussing matters, rather than the informal interactions with service users. For example, care workers may address other professionals by the use of titles such as Dr or Mr, as opposed to using first names which may be the case with service users.

Role of supervisors

The function of supervision is critical to a care organisation's success. It ensures the smooth running of care processes, and that decisive action is taken when service goals are not being met. The supervisor is there not just as a link between management and care workers, but is the first line of management and actually manages the service at the care level. Thus, the role of the supervisor is essential and uses effective delegation to control work activities in the care environment.

Supervisors also have to deal with people, as well as the processes that involve them. Indeed, they are the first point of contact for virtually all care matters. Being able to effectively deal with people, and not just the processes, is critical to the success of the supervisor's job and to the success of the care organisation.

Supervisory skills

Good supervisors are highly skilled people, often having many years of experience in the area of care that they look after. The process of supervision ensures that everyone working knows exactly:

- what task they are doing
- where they are to carry out the task
- why they are doing the task
- when they are supposed to do the task
- who is involved
- how it should be carried out.

All of the skills that make good care professionals are magnified in the supervisor. They reflect all of the best qualities that are required in any job.

A supervisor directs another member of staff in a care setting

A supervisors' prime focus is to help other members of staff practice their duties with professionalism and safety. They also help members of staff focus on their role in the care process, giving them an understanding of what they are doing. A good supervisor is a problem solver, not only of their own problems but the problems of others. On a day-to-day basis they must motivate others by their own example and give real meaning to what is going on around them. With experience comes the ability to be inventive in difficult situations, which is another aspect of their problem solving skills. In order to supervise other workers it is essential that people are excellent communicators and quick thinkers.

It is difficult for any one person to possess all of these skills all of the time and that is what makes being a good supervisor a very demanding job.

The 'supervisor' title is not used in all care areas. The following table identifies the titles used instead of supervisor in some typical care areas.

Profession	Name or title
Nursing	Staff Nurse
Medicine (Hospital Doctors)	Registrar
Radiography	Senior Radiographer
Physiotherapy	Senior Physiotherapist
Care	Senior Care Assistant

How do care worker roles contribute to the overall aims of the organisation?

Support

Care workers play an important role in the overall aims of a care organisation. Their support can mean success or failure depending on how they carry out their work, whether they are the newest employee or the chief executive. Care workers should always have a level of independence so that they are able to make decisions quickly and effectively when required. For example, if a nursery nurse was to find a child choking, they should not need permission

Activity 2

Key skills C 2.1a, 2.3

Carol

Carol has decided that she would like to find out more about one particular setting.
To do this she is arranging to visit a care setting to gather information in preparation for taking part in work experience.

1 Arrange to visit either a health or social care or early years care setting. Produce questions to find out about the role of supervisors in the setting.

2 Visit the setting to find out the role of a job that you could do and the role of the supervisors in the setting.

3 Give a definition of a supervisor.

4 Write a report on the role of supervisors in the setting you visited.

5 Share your findings with others in the group to find out if the role of a supervisor varies in different care settings.

6 Compare the differences and draw conclusions.

to treat the child before reacting to the situation. They should be able to instinctively act to resolve the problem in an independent and professional way. In this way personal independence supports the provision of quality care.

Physical care

Physical care must always be applied to the highest standards. It is the expectation of every service user that they receive the highest standard of care. Understanding what is acceptable in working practice can sometimes be unclear as many care workers work independently. This is why the health and social care sector has professional codes and rules and regulations.

By applying the various codes of practice care workers can make sure that they always provide quality care. This of course benefits service users and makes them more confident in their carers. It also increases positive public view of the care provided. The organisation then benefits from the positive attitude of the public, who make fewer complaints about care, and staff feel valued by the public, service users and the management. From this everyone becomes more confident, which allows further improvements to the service that they provide.

On the negative side, if staff do not observe safety regulations, then this leads to a variety of problems. For instance, there may be injuries to service users and staff. This would then attract criticism from others such as relatives and the general public. Outside agencies such as the Health and Safety Executive (HSE) could get involved and the organisation could be prosecuted. From one small careless action a whole variety of problems can emerge that cause difficulty to all concerned and a reduction in the quality of physical care.

Build confidence

It is very important that care workers always work in a safe and conscientious manner for the good of service users, the organisation and themselves. This helps build confidence in their abilities, and this in turn leads to improvements in the quality of care. Confident staff are usually happy and efficient in what they do and this helps build and maintain quality care. Without confidence there is always a level of uncertainty which can often lead to delays and errors being made in service users' treatment.

Assessment activity 15.2

Key skills C 2.3, ICT 2.3

Roles within the workplace

You have been asked to add to your Resource Pack (see previous Assessment Activity) information about the role of supervisors and a care workers own role while working at a care setting.

1 Explain the role of a supervisor for **one** setting.

2 Produce a case study and explain how the supervisor would help a particular care worker in the workplace organisation for **two** different situations.

3 Arrange to carry out work experience at the setting (with your tutor's agreement).

4 Prepare questions to find out about your role while working at the setting and the ways in which your own role fits into the overall aims of the setting.

5 Visit the setting and use the questions to find out about your own role and the ways in which your role fits into the overall aims.

6 Produce materials for the Resource Pack to show would-be care workers:

- own role while at the setting
- the way in which own role fits into the overall aims of the setting
- the role of the supervisors in the setting.

What are the major issues for maintaining health and safety in the workplace?

The Management of Health and Safety at Work Regulations 1999 sets out standards which all employers, and therefore employees, must follow. They have been set out to protect service users as well as employees, so following them is of the utmost importance. Companies have a responsibility to point out any relevant safety issues to a person before they start working there. Some of the major issues are outlined below.

Safety hazards and precautions

Being aware of safety hazards in the workplace is of the utmost importance to everyone. Care workers must be responsible at all times for the health and safety of themselves and others. They must always be on the lookout for hazards and should make sure that they practice in a manner that does not create hazards. As part of their job care workers should observe and report any significant hazards that could be expected to cause serious harm. This is known as risk assessment, and is dealt with in more detail in Unit 4. It is impossible to eliminate all hazards in the workplace, but the aim should be to reduce risk as far as possible by taking precautions, to meet the requirements of the law, and to monitor and keep on top of the health and safety situation.

The type of hazards that could be seen in a nursery are:

- a slide not being put up properly
- paint that could cause poisoning if it is not the right type
- carpets curled at the edges or with holes in
- poor lighting
- blocked fire exits.

Safety equipment

All care organisations are equipped with a wide variety of safety equipment. There are three fundamental reasons for having safety equipment:

- to protect the service user.
- to help and protect the employee in their daily work.
- to protect the employer from **litigation** or **prosecution**.

For these reasons it is vitally important that care professionals should always use the safety equipment available when they are working with service users. This way they can protect themselves and all around them. For example, there are many types of equipment and devices designed to make lifting or moving service users easier. Care workers must remember that it is important to use proper work practices and body mechanics in combination with equipment and devices. A selection of safety equipment that is used by care professionals for manual handling follows.

Hoist

Mechanical hoists help reduce injury by avoiding unnecessary manual transfers, awkward postures, forceful exertions and repetitive motions. Although these devices may appear to take longer to perform the lift or move, they can save staff time by reducing the number of employees needed to transfer service users. Based on care professionals' evaluations, hoists should be used for all potentially dangerous lifting or moving tasks. This helps **compliance** with lifting regulations.

Slide boards

These are large plastic boards which reduce friction. Some slide boards have hand-holds. Service users are slid or rolled onto the board and the board is then pushed or pulled to accomplish the transfer. In another common practice, the board goes under the service user who is pulled over the board by use of a draw sheet or **incontinence** pad.

Roller boards or mats

These are boards or mats with vinyl coverings and rollers. They are placed between the transfer points. The patient or resident is placed on the board or mat and rolled to the new position.

Low-friction mattress covers

These can be used under draw sheets or incontinence pads to reduce friction during lateral transfers. Slippery sheets or plastic bags can also be used instead of draw sheets or incontinence pads.

Transfer mats

Two low-friction mats can be placed under and strapped onto a service user, one under the head, one under the hips. The mats are then pulled to accomplish the transfer.

Transfer slings

These are slings with cut-outs or rings for handholds. The slings are tucked securely around the patient or resident and help move them between various surfaces. When using these slings, remember that they may dig into or slip off the service user.

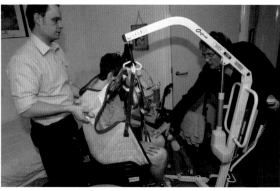

A hoist in use

Other safety equipment

Safety equipment is not just used in manual handling; masks, gloves and aprons also fall into this category and should be used where personal safety and hygiene is an issue (see Unit 4). Also, care professionals should be trained in the use of fire extinguishers and all other related safety equipment. This is also covered in Unit 4.

Reporting procedures

Reporting accidents and ill health at work is a legal requirement under the Reporting of Injuries, Diseases and Dangerous Occurrences Regulations 1995 (RIDDOR). All accidents should be recorded in an accident book. The information gathered in this book helps the local authority and the HSE to identify where and how risks arise and to prevent reoccurrence or further pain and suffering to employees.

RIDDOR requires the following specific types of accidents to be reported to the enforcing authority as quickly as possible and then confirmed in writing using the appropriate notification form (F2508) within 10 days:

- a death or major injury to an employee
- a dangerous occurrence
- an injury to a member of the public resulting in that person being taken to hospital
- an accident at work resulting in a person being off work for more than 3 days
- a specified **occupational** disease certified by a doctor, resulting from work (Notification using F2508A form).

It is important that all relevant accidents are reported. There are three agencies that the organisation must contact, they are:

1 The local Environmental Health Department.
2 The Health and Safety Executive (HSE).
3 The Incident Contact Centre.

They expect accidents that fall into the following categories to be reported to them.

Examples of major injuries

The following is a list of the major injuries that have to be reported by law:

- fracture other than to fingers, thumbs or toes
- **amputation**
- dislocation of the shoulder, hip, knee or spine
- loss of sight (temporary or permanent)
- chemical or hot metal burn to the eye or any penetrating injury to the eye
- injury resulting from electric shock or electrical burn leading to loss of **consciousness**, requiring resuscitation, or admittance to hospital for more than 24 hours
- any other injury leading to **hypothermia**, heat-induced illness or unconsciousness; requiring resuscitation, or requiring admittance to hospital for more than 24 hours

- unconsciousness caused by **asphyxia** or exposure to a harmful substance or biological agent
- acute illness requiring medical treatment, or loss of consciousness arising from absorption of any substance by inhalation, ingestion or through the skin
- acute illness requiring medical treatment where there is reason to believe that this resulted from exposure to a biological agent or its toxin or infected material.

A victim of a workplace accident is attended to by the ambulance service

Examples of work-related diseases

The following is a list of work-related diseases that also have to be reported if they occur:

- some types of poisoning
- some skin diseases such as occupational **dermatitis,** skin cancer, chrome ulcer, oil **folliculitis** and acne
- lung diseases including occupational asthma, farmers lung, **pneumoconiosis, asbestosis, mesothelioma**
- infections such as **leptospirosis, hepatitis, tuberculosis, anthrax, legionellosis** and **tetanus**
- other conditions such as occupation cancer, certain **musculo-skeletal** disorders, decompressions illness and hand-arm vibration syndrome.

Examples of dangerous occurrences

The following is a list of examples of dangerous occurrences that also have to be reported if they occur:

- collapse, overturning or failure of load-bearing parts of lifts and lifting equipment
- explosion, collapse or bursting of any closed vessel or associated pipe work
- plant or equipment coming into contact with overhead power lines
- electrical short circuit or overload causing fire or explosion
- accidental release of a biological agent likely to cause severe human illness
- explosion or fire causing suspension of normal work for over 24 hours
- unintended collapse of any building or structure under construction alteration or demolition where over 5 tonnes of material falls, a wall or floor in a place of work
- accidental release of any substance which may damage health.

First aid at work

People at work can suffer injury or illness. Whether or not this is caused by their work, what is important is that the care environment has made arrangements to ensure their employees receive immediate attention if they are injured or taken ill at work. The initial management of injuries and illness, until expert medical attention is received, can make a difference between life and death.

The Health and Safety (First Aid) Regulations 1981 require employers to provide adequate and appropriate equipment, facilities and personnel to enable first aid to be given to employees if they are injured or become ill at work. These regulations apply to all workplaces including those with five or fewer employees and to the self-employed. Employers are required to carry out an assessment of first aid needs. In other words they need to identify the level of risk to their employees in carrying out their work duties and consider what first aid equipment, personnel and facilities they need to make available.

First aiders

Any member of staff can become a first aider at work. All first aiders that are needed in your workplace must gain a certificate of competence from a training organisation that has been approved by the HSE. Courses involve at least 24 hours of training and are usually held over four days. Other courses are designed to be spread over several weeks. First aid at work certificates are usually valid for three years and re-qualification courses normally take 12 hours held over two days.

Health and safety representatives

Did you know?

Independent research has shown that where trade union safety representatives have been appointed, employees are 50 per cent less likely to have an accident than those who are employed in a workplace where they do not have trade union protection.

Care organisations who consult their employees over health and safety issues promote good health and safety practice. In human and financial terms, this benefits everyone. In legal terms, this consultation is now compulsory. The Safety Representatives and Safety Committees Regulations 1977 (SRSCR) gave trade unions the legal right to appoint workplace safety representatives. In 1996, the Health and Safety (Consultation with Employees) Regulations 1996 (HSCER) came into force. The only exceptions to this are domestic servants and the masters and crews of sea-going ships. These regulations make it compulsory for all employers to consult with all those employees not represented by union safety representatives.

This means all healthcare workers in Britain today have the right to be consulted about safety, through their representatives. This includes being consulted about:

- any proposed new measures that may substantially affect their health and safety
- the appointment of people competent to advise employers under the Management of Health and Safety at Work Regulations 1999
- required health and safety information
- health and safety training arrangements
- health and safety consequences of introducing new technology.

Trade union safety representatives have a wide range of rights and functions. These include rights to:

- make representations on behalf of their members to the employer on any health, safety and welfare matter
- represent their members in **consultations** with HSE inspectors or other enforcing authorities
- make their employer set up a safety committee within three months of the request.

Health and safety representatives also have the right to make inspections. They can inspect designated workplace areas at least every three months. They can also make additional inspections if work practices change or new information arises.

In doing this they can investigate:

- potential hazards
- complaints by employees
- the causes of accidents, dangerous occurrences and diseases.

They should also be provided with assistance, information and training and should receive:

- help and facilities from the employer to enable them to carry out inspections
- legal and technical information from inspectors
- information from the employer to enable them to carry out their functions
- time off with pay to carry out their job as safety reps, including time off for any training they may require.

Who appoints safety representatives?

Independent trade unions recognised by employers have the right to appoint safety representatives. Each union has to decide on their own arrangements for appointment. It is not a matter for employers to decide. In most cases, safety representatives are elected by the members they are to represent. The employer must also be told in writing which group or groups of employees the appointed safety representative represents.

Who can be a safety representative?

In most unions that represent healthcare workers any member can become a safety representative if they are trained and become knowledgeable in health and safety procedure. They work closely with their trade union colleagues and ensure that they do not take decisions without the support of the members they represent.

Employers have no role in this, although they are always informed of any changes. If a care worker has been elected or appointed as a health and safety representative, they should always notify their regional official.

Activity 3

Key skills C 2.3

Greg

Greg is the named health and safety representative at a setting. He carries out surveys to locate hazards and to check that safety features and precautions are in place. Greg also deals with reporting procedures at the setting.

1 **a** What is a hazard?
   b What is a safety feature/precaution?

2 Make a list of **ten** checks that Greg could make if conducting a safety survey/ audit of a communal kitchen in a setting.

3 List **three** safety precautions/ features that could be put in place in any care setting. Explain how each would help.

4 Explain what is meant by the term 'reporting procedures'.

5 What is meant by the term 'first aider?

6 Explain an employer's and an employee's responsibility for first aid at work.

What are the procedures for emergencies and certain accidents?

During a care worker's daily duties they are likely to come across a variety of situations where, because of an accident, they will have to help somebody. To do this they should follow recognised procedures to give help and first aid.

Cuts

For example, a service user may cut themselves on a broken drinking glass. The care worker would need to deal with the emergency in the following way:

1 Cleanse cut area thoroughly with warm water, carefully washing away any small fragments of glass.

2 Apply direct pressure to wound until bleeding stops or slows.

3 Put sterile bandage on wound.

4 If the cut is deep, get the patient to a doctor as quickly as possible.

If the service user only has an abrasion (graze) then the following action can be taken:

1 Wash thoroughly with soap and warm water.

2 If the graze bleeds or oozes, bandage it to protect it from infection.

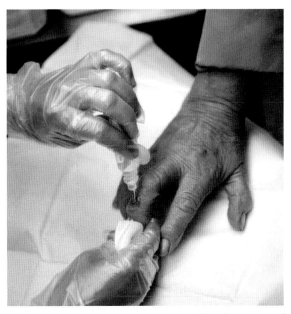

Dressing a wound

If they have to look after the injured person, care workers have to be aware of the signs of a wound becoming infected. These can be:

- swelling
- redness
- pain
- fever
- presence of pus.

Fractures

Often an accident can be more involved than those listed on page 343, for instance, the injured person may have fractured a bone. A simple fracture does not pierce through the skin. If it is not cared for properly, it could become a compound fracture. To support the service user the care workers should use the following procedures to help:

1 Check for swelling around the affected area.
2 Check for discoloration of the skin.
3 Check if the victim complains of tenderness and pain in the area or says that they felt or heard a bone snap.
4 If the above checks indicate a fracture, take the person to see a doctor immediately.

A compound fracture pierces through the skin. Serious bleeding may occur with this kind of wound. Care workers should not apply pressure to a compound fracture to stop the bleeding. For a compound fracture they should:

1 Cover the injured part with a sterile pad.
2 Apply a splint to keep the bone from causing further injury to the surrounding tissues.
3 Wait for medical help.
4 Avoid moving the injured person, but keep them warm, comfortable, and reassured.

Burns and scalds

The body's natural barrier, the skin, is destroyed by burning, leaving it exposed to germs. Burns can be caused by dry heat, corrosive substances and friction. Scalds are caused by wet heat, hot liquids and **vapours**. Burns can also be produced by extreme cold, and by radiation, including the sun's rays.

Assessing a burn

There are a number of factors to consider when assessing the severity of a burn and the method of treatment, including the cause of the burn, whether the airway is involved, the depth of the burn, and its extent.

The extent of a burn indicates whether shock is likely to develop. The greater the extent of the burn, the more severe the shock is likely to be. Burns also carry a serious risk of infection, which increases according to the size and depth of the burn.

Superficial burns

These involve only the outer layer of the skin, and are characterised by redness, swelling and tenderness. Typical examples are mild sunburn, or a scald produced by a splash of hot tea or coffee. Superficial burns usually heal well if prompt first aid is given, and do not require medical treatment unless extensive.

Partial-thickness burns

These damage a 'partial thickness' of the skin, and require medical treatment. The skin looks raw and blisters form. These burns usually heal well, but can be serious, if extensive.

Full-thickness burns

These damage all layers of the skin. Damage may extend beyond the skin to affect nerves, muscle and fat. The skin may look pale, waxy, and sometimes charred. Full-thickness burns of any size always require immediate medical attention, and usually require specialist treatment.

Treatment of burns and scalds

Minor burns and scalds are usually the result of domestic accidents. Prompt first aid generally enables them to heal naturally and well, but the advice of a medical practitioner should be sought if there is doubt as to the severity of the injury.

- DO NOT use adhesive dressings.
- DO NOT break blisters, or interfere with the injured area.
- DO NOT apply lotions, ointments, creams, or fats to the injured area.

1 Cool the injured part with copious amounts of cold water for about 10 minutes to stop the burning and relieve the pain.
2 Gently remove any jewellery, watches, or constricting clothing from the injured area before it starts to swell.

3 Cover the injury with a sterile dressing, or any clean, non-fluffy material to protect from infection. A clean plastic bag or kitchen film may be used. Burns to the face should be cooled with water, not covered.

4 Ensure that the emergency service is on its way. While waiting, treat the casualty for shock. Monitor and record breathing and pulse, and resuscitate, if necessary.

Choking

Choking occurs when the airway is partially or totally blocked by a swallowed object.

The aim of treatment is to clear the blocked passage. Choking victims instinctively clasp their necks, which is now recognised as the universal choking sign. Act quickly; speed is essential. Brain death can occur in 4–6 minutes if a person cannot breathe.

Treatment of a conscious adult

1 Ask, "Are you choking?" If the victim can speak, cough or breathe, do not interfere – they are not choking.

2 If the victim cannot speak, cough or breathe, give upward abdominal thrusts.
To do this, stand behind victim and wrap your arms round the waist. Grasp one fist with your other hand and place thumb side of your fist in the mid-line between waist and rib cage. Press fist into abdomen with 4 quick upward and inward thrusts.

3 Do not use abdominal thrust when dealing with a pregnant woman or overweight victim. In these cases use chest thrusts – press on breastbone as in **CPR**.

4 Stand behind victim and place your arms under their armpits to encircle the body.

5 Grasp one fist with the other hand, and place thumb side on the middle of the breastbone. Press with quick backward thrusts.

6 Repeat above **sequence**. Be persistent.

7 Send for medical aid, call an ambulance and continue treatment until help arrives.

(Self help: if a person is choking and alone. Lean over a chair or railing as you act to help release obstruction.)

Treatment of an unconscious adult

1 "Call for Help"; dial 999.

2 Open airway and begin A of resuscitation procedure (see Figure 15.5 below).

3 If unsuccessful, deliver five abdominal thrusts.

4 Use finger probe in mouth to dislodge the foreign body.

5 If unsuccessful, repeat the above sequence until help arrives.

Stage 1

Stage 2

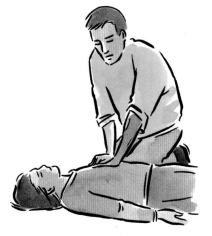

Stage 3

Figure 15.5 *Resuscitation process*

Treatment of children

If a child (1–8 years) is choking, proceed as for adult, depending on whether victim is conscious or unconscious.

If an infant (up to 1 year) is choking, turn the infant face downwards supporting the body along your arm with hand supporting head and neck.

1 Ensure airway is open.

2 Deliver five back blows between the shoulders, then turn over and give five chest thrusts.

3 Remove object if visible.

4 Do not perform blind finger sweeps in infants and children. When obstruction is removed and infant is still not breathing and has no pulse, start CPR.

5 Call help fast.

To prevent further complications, all cases of choking should receive medical inspection even if the first aid measure relieved the obstruction.

What are a care worker's own rights and responsibilities regarding health and safety?

Care workers have the right to be able to work in a safe and hygienic environment. They should always be provided with the correct equipment to carry out their daily tasks. This may include items such as gloves, aprons and masks. Care workers also have the right to training, especially in the area of health and safety. The employer must train members of staff in the fire procedures that have been designed for the building they work in. Care workers must receive lifting and handling training to enable them to protect the service user and themselves.

Care workers also have the right and responsibility to report dangerous situations in their work environment. They should report firstly to management. If this is unsuccessful they can then contact the environmental health department or the HSE to help them.

All care workers have a responsibility to maintain a safe working environment. It is one of the criteria that defines a true care professional.

Assessment activity 15.3

Key skills C 2.1b, 2.3   ICT 2.2, 2.3

Health and safety in the workplace

You have been asked to give a presentation about how to work in a healthy and safe way in a setting.

You will need to prepare overheads or PowerPoint presentations as well as notes and handouts.

1 Arrange to visit **one** care setting to conduct a safety survey/ audit of the communal lounge.

2 Carry out a safety survey/audit of the lounge and describe the safety features/precautions that are in place. Use the information as part of the presentation and handouts.

3 Prepare a handout that could be given out during the presentation to provide information for **one** setting about:
   • First aid at work
   • First aiders
   • Health and safety procedures.

4 Prepare presentation materials and/or handouts to explain reporting procedures for the care setting chosen

5 Demonstrate during the presentation **four** first aid procedures for treating casualties in an emergency.

6 Explain care workers' own rights and responsibilities for health and safety in the workplace.

What are the agreed standards and how are they complied with?

Equal opportunity policy

Every healthcare organisation wants to employ the best people and also wants them to stay. Having to continuously interview staff is an expensive process and does not help maintain good standards of care. Unequal treatment, prejudice or **sexual harassment** discredits organisations, is not acceptable and can be very costly.

It is illegal to discriminate against people on the following grounds:

- sex or sexual orientation
- marital status
- race or colour
- nationality or ethnic origin
- religion or beliefs
- disability
- pregnancy or childbirth
- membership or non-membership of a trade union.

It is also **unlawful** to discriminate against part-time workers, and as of 1 October 2004 the government extended the protection available to disabled people to allow better access to the working and social environment.

Organisation procedures

Most organisations have a procedure to help new employees understand their purpose and to settle in. This is usually started within an employee's induction program. During this program and later, while in training, employees are informed of important information which may include:

- fire safety procedures
- Health and safety issues (lifting and handling)
- staff welfare
- sickness and absence policy
- pay policy
- dress code and personal standards
- information recording and filing.

The type and range of information can and will vary from employer to employer. Many of the areas in the list above are very important and are the same for every employer.

Figure 15.6 *Everyone should have equal chances*

Dress codes

Dress and appearance codes set out the rules by which employees should present themselves at work. What is acceptable depends on the type of business and the role being undertaken by the employee. Any business has an image which it wants to portray to its customers, but at the same time it must comply with any health safety regulations. Dress and appearance rules convey the values and culture of the organisations that people work for. They portray an image to existing employees, prospective employees, suppliers and business competition.

If a specific dress code is required, then employers have justifiable reasons for it. Good employers always involve any affected employees in consultation leading up to a decision to change or implement a new dress code.

An employer should always be able to clarify exactly what is meant by phrases such as 'smart', 'appropriate' and 'business-like', and be able to give examples of their expectations of what the employee should look like.

The employer may decide to have a different dress code for a specific work area or type of worker, for example, for clinical areas and health and safety reasons.

Many employers build clauses into staff contracts that make failure to follow the dress code a disciplinary procedure. Having done this they ensure that any policy is fairly and consistently applied to all workers that are affected by it. It may sound petty but uniforms are vital to good running of a care environment.

Most uniforms are linked to health and safety practices – employees need to wear clean uniforms, aprons and whatever else is required by the job in hand. Also, without uniforms in a care environment, visitors could be mistaken for care workers. Employees may or may not be able to tell what other employees did. Another good reason for wearing them is that care workers will not damage their own clothes.

Time-keeping

Time-keeping is especially important for those who work in care. As a member of a team it is important to remember that a lack of punctuality or absence can cause many problems and a great amount of stress. For example, if a person is a member of a team of four carers on a shift and turns up late, they will affect the lives of their colleagues, not to mention the clients. By being late another member of staff may have had to stay to cover the work, or the remaining carers will have more work to do because they are one person short. This in turn could make them stressed and they may attempt to work in a manner that could lead to accidents. By being late a pre-shift briefing could be missed containing valuable information about the service users. This in turn could lead to a reduction in the quality of care or even an accident.

Good time-keeping is one of the major factors behind being a reliable worker. Reliability is made up of a variety of factors. Consistent quality of work and punctuality are good signs of reliability. If work is substandard then the task or treatment may have to be repeated, which helps no one. Being able to meet deadlines also reflects on a care worker's reliability. If they fail to finish a task on time then the work of others may be affected.

Reliability

Reliability is generally based around a care worker's commitment to their work, the quality of their work and their ability to perform a task within a set time-frame.

Different types of healthcare uniforms

Standards in care settings

Carol is trying to gather information about how care workers in her chosen care setting comply with standards for personal behaviour and presentation. She has asked if she could see the equal opportunities policy and would like to know their procedures for dress and time-keeping.

1 Arrange to visit a care setting to find out how equal opportunities are applied at the setting. You may wish to prepare some questions to take with you.

2 Draw up a table to summarise the procedures for applying equal opportunities at your chosen setting. List the procedures in one column, and then explain what each procedure does in another.

3 Describe the dress code for the setting you have investigated.

4 Explain the procedure the setting has in place for time-keeping.

5 Why is good time-keeping important?

Confidentiality

Confidentiality is a major issue in health and social care. If a service user comes for advice or treatment, they need to know that any information they give goes no further. Otherwise, they might not seek the help they need at all. Patient and client confidentiality is protected by various codes of practice. These identify core values that define how people working in healthcare should conduct themselves.

All healthcare professionals must maintain standards of confidentiality laid down by their professional body, such as the Royal College of Nursing or the General Medical Council. As a rule, such standards have been developed to clarify what the law means in a healthcare setting and to set out any additional principles or ethical standards for that profession. If a healthcare professional ignores these codes of practice or standards they are likely to face disciplinary proceedings, and may even be prevented from working in their healthcare field again.

More information about confidentiality can be found in Unit 1.

Data protection

The Data Protection Acts of 1989 and 1998 gave new rights to protect the public against the problems created by storing personal information in the computer age. They created new obligations for those keeping personal information and means that the public now have the right to:

- be given a copy of any information which is kept about them, and have it clearly explained (this is known as the 'right of access')
- have any inaccurate information corrected or deleted
- have their name removed from a direct marketing list
- complain to the Data Protection Commissioner if they think someone keeping data is not complying with the act
- claim compensation through the courts if they suffer damage through mishandling of information about them
- find out from any person or organisation whether they keep information about them, and if they do, to be told the type of information kept and the purposes for which it is kept.

People keeping personal information must give individuals access to their personal information and correct or delete any found to be inaccurate.

They must:

- obtain personal information fairly and openly
- use it only in ways compatible with the purpose for which it was given in the first place
- secure it against unauthorised access or loss
- ensure that it is kept accurate and up-to-date.

They must not:

- disclose it to others in a manner incompatible with the purpose for which it was given
- retain it for longer than is necessary for the purpose for which it was given.

A service user can write to the company or individual concerned and ask for it. When doing this they should give any details which might be needed to help the person identify them (e.g. hospital number) and to locate all the information that they keep about them.

The information must be given within 40 days of the request being received. The organisation providing the information is allowed to make a small charge for this service. This charge varies from one organisation to another but it is not allowed to be excessive (usually not more than £5). The organisation must also provide someone to explain any information that they do not understand.

Keeping to agreed standards with minimum supervision

It is important that all care workers keep to agreed standards for personal behaviour and presentation in the workplace as this helps to maintain the high level of quality care that service users are entitled to. If care workers act professionally and work to high standards the level of supervision required is lessened. The benefit of this is that care workers feel more comfortable in their work and do not feel as if everything that they do is being watched.

The management of the working environment can therefore be reduced. This also benefits care workers because it may make more money available to provide extra help with care tasks, due to a reduced level of management cost.

Keeping to agreed standards helps maintain everyone's trust. The trust that develops from this benefits everyone and helps support an environment of quality care.

Assessment activity 15.4

Key skills C 2.3, ICT 2.3

Standards of personal behaviour and presentation in the workplace

You have been asked to include materials in your Resource Pack to show would-be care workers how to comply with agreed standards for personal behaviour and presentation in a setting.

1 For one care setting investigate and prepare materials for the agreed standards:

- equal opportunities and how they are applied in the care setting

- organisational procedures for the setting
- dress codes for the setting
- time-keeping and how it applies to the setting
- reliability and how it applies to the setting
- confidentiality and how it applies to the setting
- data protection and how it applies to the setting.

2 Why is it important to keep to the agreed standards set within the setting?

What should be taken into account when planning a task?

Instructions

When planning a task it is important that care workers give clear instructions to those who are doing or helping with it. Sometimes people are reluctant to admit that something is unclear. They may think they can work out a way to do it on their own, rather than ask for help. The following are guidelines for a care worker that will help in the formation of clear and concise instructions.

- Clarify in your own mind and estimate what the finished task should look like so that others will be clear when it is explained to them.
- Write an outline plan of what you want to happen. You will find it helps clarify exactly what you want and it will help you convey this more clearly.
- For the activity planned list all the health and safety situations that could arise and note what could be done to reduce the risk.
- Draw a plan of the room/area which you will be using for the activity.
- Write out instructions to follow when doing the tasks within the activity.
- Give the date and time of the deadline.

By using the guidelines any misunderstanding can be reduced to a minimum.

Steps in tasks

When planning a task the whole series of events should be broken down into individual steps. This allows the task to be planned more accurately. It also allows for the task to be examined to see if there are any hidden problems that might hinder its completion. By using a step-by-step process the task will be easier to follow, especially if the instructions are based around it. The more complex the task the bigger the number of steps needed. However, it is important that care workers do not get too carried away with the number of steps required.

A step-by-step process should include the following:

1. All the items the person needs to complete the task.

2. Every detail the person needs to know in the process.

3. Instructions lain out in the right order.

4. Enough information to help, but not so much that the reader is confused.

5. Reasons for the instructions where they will be helpful.

6. Repeated important points if necessary.

7. Expression that is informal but polite and direct.

> ### Try it!
>
> 1. Pick a task that you do on a regular basis, for example, making cheese on toast or helping a service user to the table, and create a step-by-step guide. Give it to another member of the group and see if they can do the task from your step-by-step instructions.
>
> 2. Listen to their comments and revise your step-by-step instructions.

Using resources

When planning a task it is important for care workers to remember that the correct resources should be available. There is little point in starting a task and finding that they have run out of what they are using. It is also important that they do not over-provide for the task. Waste can be very costly and may even be a danger to the environment. Sometimes a variety of resources are available and there may be a need to choose between them. It is important that the correct items are selected for the task. A poor choice can slow the task down or even cause it to be abandoned.

For example, a care worker may have the choice of washing-up liquid or washing machine soap powder to wash the plates and cutlery with. If they picked the wrong one they could find that they have more soap suds than they bargained for!

Health and safety issues

When planning a task it is important that care workers remember that all activities must be carried out safely. There are a variety of rules and regulations that have to be followed (look back to earlier in this unit and Unit 4).

If the task is to involve moving a service user then lifting and handling regulations have to be observed. Failure to do so could lead to the injury of a service user or a colleague. The knock-on effects of this could be a compensation claim or even a prosecution by the HSE. This is an area where it is essential to take advice if there is any uncertainty about what precautions to take. The rules for health and safety are very explicit and there is always someone to advise if it is required.

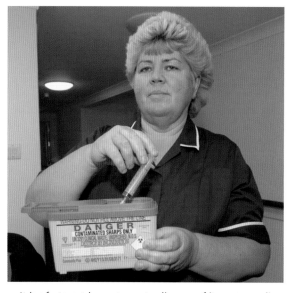

It is of utmost importance to dispose of items according to health and safety rules

> **Discussion point**
>
> *What are the responsibilities of a named health and safety person?*

Activity 5

Key skills C 2.3

In the workplace

Care workers need to work together as a team in the workplace, making sure that each individual follows a plan for their roles and responsibilities. You have been asked to take the role of a care assistant in a residential home. One of your tasks is to make coffee for the residents during the afternoon.

1 Draw up a line diagram to show the steps involved in any tasks set.

2 Make a list of the resources needed for this task.

3 Identify the health and safety issues involved when carrying out this task, explaining how you would reduce the hazards as far as possible.

4 Explain the importance of clarity when giving instructions to care workers for the tasks they must undertake.

5 Visit **either** a residential home **or** a playgroup **or** a nursery **or** a day care centre and observe the tasks undertaken by **one** care worker. List the skills required to carry out some of these tasks.

Estimated time-scales for completion

The time that people set aside for a task is often a mental limitation. That is, if they think that they need three hours to do a particular job, the job often takes three hours to complete. They can affect how long it takes to do a job just by thinking about it. Others may be in charge of what tasks are done, but care workers are in charge of how they manage their time.

One of the best ways of getting used to managing time is to conduct a record of daily activities to see how the time is spent. Carers also have to identify priorities for their activities so that they are performed in the correct order. This then makes best use of their time.

Often a task naturally breaks down into smaller components. These components may not all take the same amount of time. Sometimes a task may follow the 80/20 rule. When it is performed, 80 per cent of the task requires 20 per cent of the time, while 20 per cent of the task requires 80 per cent of the time. Therefore care workers often have to manage the most productive 20 per cent of their time effectively.

It is important that care workers avoid **procrastination**: they should not put off until tomorrow what can be done today. They should also identify activities and interruptions that waste time. This helps to minimise wasted time, although it is not always possible to remove wasted time completely.

It is important that care workers develop effective time management strategies to help them. By trying a variety of strategies they can adopt ones that best suit them. Here is a list of strategies that a care worker could follow.

- Have clear objectives for the tasks that you undertake.
- Break up large tasks into smaller tasks.
- Know when 'good enough' is quite acceptable instead of 'perfect'.
- Set yourself defined periods in which to complete tasks ("I'll finish that job in the next half hour").
- Don't just prepare 'to do' lists; prioritise the elements of your list.
- Do not get distracted by time wasters.
- Be assertive – say "no" or "not for the moment" if you haven't got time to do what someone else asks you to do.
- Know your deadlines.
- Be organised.
- Keep your work area tidy.
- Use a good filing system.
- Make a number of telephone calls together; list the points you want to cover
- Ensure that meetings (e.g. with your supervisor) have clear objectives and an agenda.
- Meetings should produce minutes that list and clearly identify 'agreements' and 'action points'. Having a written record can minimise any subsequent confusion.

Relevant legislation/policies to be followed

There is a lot of legislation and policies that affect how care is managed and provided. Many of them are specific and will only apply to certain areas of care. Others have wider-reaching effects and cover all areas of care. The following is an outline of some of the different legislation and policies that affect care. (Legislation is covered in more detail in Units 1 and 4.)

Disability Discrimination Act 1995

This act is concerned with preventing discrimination against people with disabilities. It covers housing, transport, employment, access to education and obtaining goods and services. This act is constantly in the process of being reviewed and improved, especially in the area of public transportation.

Health and Safety at Work Act 1974 (Health and Safety at Work Order 1978 in Northern Ireland)

This act makes explicit the health and safety responsibilities that employers and employees have at work. It requires risk assessments to take place and a written policy statement in workplaces employing more than five people. Accident books have to be kept to record accidents and injuries. The act makes it compulsory to report accidents that are considered serious, for example broken bones and major injuries.

Sex Discrimination Act 1975 (Sex Discrimination Order, 1976 in Northern Ireland)

This act makes it unlawful to discriminate between men and women or to discriminate on the grounds of whether people are married. It covers employment, and buying and obtaining goods and facilities. The Equal Opportunities Commission monitors, advises and provides information on sex discrimination and reports on a regular basis to the government.

Figure 15.6 *Working together*

Team members and roles of team members

When planning a task particular care must be taken when selecting the team required to do it. Individuals should be selected because of the strengths and abilities that they possess and not because they are friends. In order for a team to work well, it is vital that the individual's role is recognised. Each member must be reliable, trustworthy, and capable of following instructions. It is important that all members of a team are given specific roles in the task.

Members of a team should also be aware of the importance of their roles in the team and be supportive of each other. A team only works if all of its members work together. If the team is to work efficiently there should only be one leader. If everyone starts making their own decisions about what they think should be done it can be a recipe for disaster. All requests and suggestions should go through the team leader, which removes the possibility of others developing their own agenda.

Teams are made up of people who contribute different skills and knowledge. Listening and communicating with others is an important part of being a team member as it can improve the standard of work and can also improve the individual's attitude to the work.

When working in a team knowledge, skills and resources must be shared in order to achieve the objectives. For teamwork to be effective each member must agree to keep to the agreed schedules. There should be regular meetings to check on progress and to agree to any changes proposed.

There must also be a way of keeping the work of the team organised. Each meeting must have an agenda in order to keep the meeting on track and records of the meeting should be kept. Minutes of meetings should always be sent to team members.

The team leader is the person who will need to bring the team together so that everything goes smoothly. The team leader will:

- take control of the situation
- be able to see the objectives clearly
- be a good listener
- have the ability to explore ideas

- be able to motivate the team
- be able to draw out the best from all members
- have respect for team members
- be a good organiser
- be creative
- pay attention to detail
- be accurate in record keeping

Team workers will:

- carry out tasks to the best of their ability
- contribute well to team spirit
- be a good listener
- be loyal
- be supportive
- be willing to contribute skills and ideas
- be willing to work hard.

Assessment activity 15.5

Key skills C 2.3

Planning to carry out tasks in a care setting

You have been asked to carry out tasks in a setting. To do this you must first plan how the tasks are to be carried out, which involves:

- receiving instructions
- dentifying the steps in the tasks
- identifying the resources needed
- making sure health and safety issues are
- addressed
- giving the estimated time-scales
- being aware of relevant legislation and policies
- knowing team members roles and their roles.

1 Describe the importance of listening to instructions carefully.

2 You have been asked to carry out at least **two** tasks in the care setting chosen. For each task identify the steps involved

3 For each task draw up a plan. An example has been given below:

Plan to clean the basin in a toilet outside the communal room

Plan	Requirements	Reasons for the actions
Resources needed		
Health and safety issues		
Time-scales		
Team members		
Roles of team members		

4 Identify any relevant legislation and policies that relate to each task and explain their application.

5 Identify and give information about any procedures and health and safety regulations that must be followed.

What skills should be utilised in undertaking tasks?

Teamwork

Charles Handy once described teamwork by saying "Organising talented people is akin to the proverbial herding of cats – difficult by definition".

An effective team includes a diversity of skills and roles. The former is fairly obvious since the work that is to be done will cover a range of tasks. A healthcare team needs dedicated caring staff, all of whom have an enormous impact on the success of the team.

When trying to create a team there are various ways in which it can be strengthened. A care worker should consider these ideas for building a team:

1 Work together on a short-term challenge. This may be completely unrelated to the job, e.g. undertaking a sponsored walk together, or painting a community building. The process of working together on a task offers a chance for a team to talk to each other, build relationships and to achieve success.

2 It is often an advantage to have a team meeting away from work – either going away for the day, or, even better, an overnight stay. Being away from the workplace helps to generate team spirit.

3 Everyone likes to have fun so have a shared social event. A party or a day out can be a great way of allowing people to get to know one another without the pressure of work.

4 Look together at successful examples of teams, and understand what team members have in common. Look at different types of teams, such as sporting teams and business teams. Think through how their strengths can be reapplied in your team. You might even consider going together to watch a sporting event.

5 Share personal experiences and expectations. Each person can outline why they want to be on the team, what they can bring to the team and what they are hoping to get out of it.

6 As a team, work out the tasks and roles needed to achieve the goal. Open discussion allows the development of what will be done independently and what will be done together.

These suggestions are likely to require a team to invest in a reasonable amount of time to ensure that they are working effectively. It also helps the members of a team to feel comfortable with one another. This is time well invested, as it creates stronger teams.

Problem solving

Sound problem-solving skills are helpful in all areas of a person's working life. As well as being the skills which enable them to deal with the many small decisions in day-to-day work, they are also what enables them to take control and turn situations to their advantage.

Problem solving can involve:

- flexible thinking
- using past experience of the problem at hand
- using available knowledge
- reading and researching
- seeking advice where necessary.

In the workplace, problem-solving skills are relevant in a variety of settings. For example, a care worker might use these skills to produce a report within a deadline, to carry out a project with a team of colleagues, or to deal with a complaint.

When faced with a problem, care workers often think of a solution immediately and then implement it. This may not be the most appropriate or effective solution to the problem. It is possible to develop solutions in three ways.

These are:

- The instant solution which immediately occurs based on experiences of similar situations in the past.
- The logical solution which evolves as all the information is considered.
- The innovative solution where a wider vision of the situation and consideration of different or creative approaches to the problem is taken.

Care workers can develop their approach so that their own decisions improve and support their work, rather than create even more problems. Here are some ideas that might help a care worker solve problems more easily:

- Don't start developing solutions until you've correctly defined the problem. If you feel that you have not got to the cause of a problem simply ask the question "Why?" This allows you to dig deeper and identify the correct problems on which to work.
- Review the information you have gathered.
- Share your ideas with someone who's opinion you value – two minds are usually more productive than one.
- List all the possible solutions and evaluate them all. Consider the good and bad points of the instant solutions, logical solutions and innovative solutions before you decide what to do.

Communication

In a care environment poor communication wastes time and can be dangerous to the service users. As a care professional the purpose of communication is the effective exchange of information. To ensure efficient and effective communication three things must take place:

- the speaker must make the message understood
- the listener must understand the intended message that is received
- you should exert some control over the flow of the communication.

Care workers must learn to listen as well as speak. If they do not explicitly develop the skill of listening, they may not hear the information that allows them to complete a task effectively.

Suppose the manager gives an instruction which contains an ambiguity that neither person notices. This may result in totally the wrong actions being taken.

Ambiguities can arise in communications because:

- some words have multiple meanings (e.g. a 'funny' meeting is either humorous or strange)
- some words are not the ones intended – everybody makes mistakes
- some words may have been misheard in the first place (e.g. simply leaving out 'no' from the sentence 'there is no active infection noted in the left lung' can change the meaning and lead to possibly devastating consequences)
- sometimes a listener may not understand what the speaker meant.

There is an easy way around this problem. In everything that is said, written or heard, it is important for care workers to look out for possible misunderstanding and clarify the ambiguity. This can be done simply by asking for confirmation, such as saying, "let me see if I have understood correctly, you are saying that..." and rephrasing what the speaker has said. If this version is acknowledged as being correct by the original speaker, then there is a greater degree of confidence and understanding. For any viewpoint/message/decision, there should be a clear, concise and verified statement of what was said; without this someone will get it wrong.

If possible, important communications should be written down and sent to everyone involved as a double check. This has several advantages in providing:

- further clarification – is this what was agreed?
- a consistency check – the act of writing may highlight defects/omissions
- a formal stage – a statement of the accepted position provides a point from which to proceed.

When speaking, care workers can cause problems by adding information. This can be avoided if each tries to understand how the other person is thinking, and tries to ensure full understanding so that the meaning does not get added to.

Figure 15.7 *Messages can get confused when passed on*

When communication is difficult and problems are encountered, care workers must be professional. They should not lose self-control, or argue. Instead, they should talk through the issues and listen to what the other person has to say – and then the problem will be solved much more quickly and professionally.

Information giving

The exchange and provision of information is the centre point of an open and honest relationship between healthcare professionals and patients. It is also an essential part of caring for patients.

When service users are well informed and involved they are better able to understand and make their own decisions. They are also able to understand future events and are less likely to complain.

One of the principal ways of empowering patients is to ensure that they have the necessary information that allows them to understand and participate in their care. The ability to assess patients' needs for information requires the ability to listen, combined with a willingness to avoid second-guessing what they want to hear or be able to understand.

Information giving is part of developing trust between care worker and service user. Trust can only be developed by openness. Openness means that information is given freely, honestly and regularly. It is important for care workers to be honest about their concerns and those of service users. Informing patients and, in the case of young children, their parents, must be regarded as a process and not a one-off event. Information should be:

• given in a variety of forms (written, oral, audio-visual), it should be given in stages and be reinforced over time

- tailored to the needs, circumstances and wishes of the service user or carer
- based on the current available information and be in a form that is understandable to patients and their carers
- regularly updated and developed with the help of patients and carers, whether in leaflet, tape, video or CD format
- available when service users and, where appropriate, carers, have been given the opportunity and time to ask questions about what they have been told.

Service users (patients) should be told that they may have another person of their choosing present when receiving information about a diagnosis or a procedure. Before any procedure, patients and, where appropriate, carers should always be given an explanation of what is going to happen. After the procedure they should have the opportunity to review what has happened and ask any questions that have arisen.

Seeking guidance

It is very important that whatever task care workers are doing they understand why it is being done and how they should do it. If for any reason they are unsure about these two factors they should seek guidance and advice. To carry on blindly with a task can often be dangerous to service users and themselves. For example, if a care worker is changing a dressing and it is stuck, they should not just rip it off. If they are uncertain about how it should be removed then they should seek advice.

Care workers should never be afraid of seeking advice. This is because one person cannot know everything. If care workers seek to guide each other then mistakes can be minimised and care services improved.

Following instructions

Once care workers are certain that they have understood the instructions (see 'communication') the task should be carried out as directed. Care workers should not take short cuts when following an agreed set of instructions, nor should they decide that they know better, without first consulting. This is important because failure to follow instruction can be dangerous, especially in events like fire evacuation procedures. In this instance failure to comply could lead to someone's death.

Activity 6

Key skills (C) 2.1a, 2.3

Working in a care setting

Jodi works in a playgroup as a nursery nurse. She is part of a team with other nursery nurses, a play leader and support workers. Jodi does have her own role and responsibilities to carry out. Her work involves communicating with parents and children. She also has to be prepared to solve problems when her plans do not work out as she expected or when the unexpected occurs.

1 Identify **two** other people who are members of the team at the playgroup and explain how they could work together as a team to achieve their targets.

2 Jodi has to use problem solving skills in her work. Give **three** examples of problems Jodi may have to solve, explaining the stages involved when solving problems.

3 Work with another person to produce a quiz to use with others in the group to check their knowledge about 'what makes effective communication'. Look back at Unit 2 for additional information to help you with this task.

4 Give **four** examples of information that Jodie may have to give during her day-to day tasks. For each explain how effective communication could help.

An example of an organisation plan is shown below.

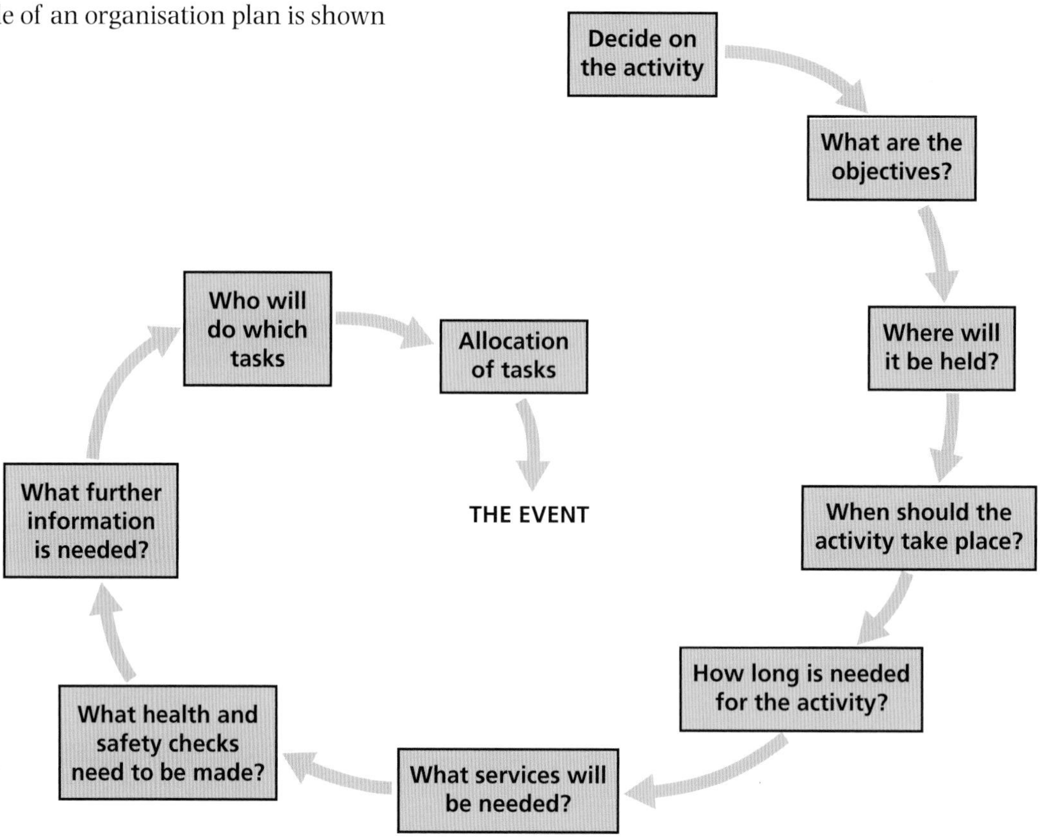

Figure 15.8 *Contributing to ateam activity*

Assessment activity 15.6

Undertaking tasks in the workplace

For your assessment you are to carry out at least **two** tasks in a care setting of your choice. You will need to demonstrate a range of skills in order to carry out the tasks effectively. Skills used could include:

- teamwork
- problem solving
- communication
- information giving
- following instructions.

Sometimes you will need to seek guidance from others within the workplace.

1 Prepare a log that can be used to record the tasks you will carry out in the workplace. The log should record:
- which skills you used for which tasks
- how effectively you used the skills
- time-scales
- whether you met the requirements or outcomes required

- whether you carried out the task independently or with support
- how you would improve the skills used if you had to repeat the tasks.

2 Carry out at least two tasks in the workplace. Try to use as many skills as possible when undertaking the tasks. Remember to arrange for your tutor to assess you when carrying out the tasks. Also remember to complete the log book.

3 Seek guidance in the workplace on a matter where you are unsure about how to do something or what the policy of the setting is. Record in the log book:
- what you sought guidance about
- what support you were given
- what you did as a result of the guidance received.

Note: arrange for your tutor or supervisor to assess you carrying out the tasks selected and to complete a detailed account of what you did, the skills used and the level of competency achieved. This should be signed and dated.

How should care workers evaluate their performance?

The only way that performance can be improved is to look at what has been done and decide if there is any way in which it could be done better. The way to do this is to analyse if what has been done met the requirements of the task and how effective the time management was. Once these areas have been looked at it is possible to see if improvements can be made for the task in the future.

Meeting requirements

In an evaluation care workers have to know exactly:

- what they were expected to do
- what the end product of the task was
- if the task achieved its aim.

If a task is successful then all well and good, but that does not mean that it could not have been done better. The task must therefore be broken down and looked at closely for improvement.

When reflecting on a task for evaluation, care workers should:

- think about what they did and how they did it
- consider the skills that they used and the reasons why they used them
- ask themselves questions about how effective they were when using these skills and whether they achieved the outcomes they wanted. Did they achieve the aims and objectives set and how well were they meet?
- think about any improvements they could have made
- plan how to improve their skills for the future.

Time-scales

Did you know?

An airline pilot flying at 750 kilometres per hour will be over a kilometre adrift for every 10 seconds of miscalculation. Timing is important for all of us!

It is important that care workers look for wasted time in the tasks they perform. By doing this they can avoid waste and become more efficient. Let us consider some of the ways in which a care worker can waste time:

- not having the correct resources available and having to go back and get something
- being interrupted during the task by others needing their help
- social conversations at the wrong time in the wrong place
- being uncertain about what they are doing
- taking the long way around.

By breaking down the task into components care workers can apply the correct amount of time for each part of the task.

Try it!

Work out how long it takes to make cheese on toast by breaking the task into the following parts:

	Task	Time
1	Slice bread (if required)	
2	Cut or grate cheese	
3	Put bread under grill and turn on	
4	When browned turn over	
5	Add cheese	
6	Put back under grill	
7	Serve cheese on toast	

Estimate the time for each task and then attempt it while someone times you. After you have finished evaluate how accurate your time estimates were. Even a simple task like this can require a lot of thought. For example, how much cheese, and how long bread takes to brown, can depend on the type of equipment you use, such as gas grill or electric grill.

This idea can be applied to any task, and time can be saved by running more than one task together. For example, you could brown the toast under the grill and cut the cheese at the same time.

Improvements and recommendations for future tasks

Having drawn conclusions, it is good practice for care workers to think about the ways they could improve their skills and actions. For example, they could consider:

- could the methods used be improved?
- what other methods could have been used/what else was available?
- was the order in which they did things appropriate?
- could any of the skills used be improved?
- should other skills have been used?
- could the service user have received more benefits if something had done differently?

If care workers do not think about how they can improve the things they do, they cannot get any better in the tasks they are carrying out. Care workers should always be thinking about their own professional development.

Activity 6

Key skills 2.3

Evaluating

Jodi has completed her tasks for the day at the nursery school. She is now thinking about how well the activities went and whether they met the needs of the children. Did the activities meet all of the children's needs – their physical, intellectual, emotional and social needs? She wonders whether she could have done anything differently.

1 What does it the term 'evaluate mean'?

2 Think of **four** questions Jodi could think about to help her decide whether the activities she was responsible met the requirements of the children. Write down the questions.

3 Write down **four** questions that Jodi could think about to assess the skills she used and how well she used them.

4 What question could Jodi ask herself about the time-scales for activities?

5 Think about questions Jodie could ask herself about improvements that could be required.

6 Collate the questions into one list that you can use to help you evaluate the tasks you have completed.

What should care workers use to evaluate their own performance?

Own evaluation

In the first instance, care workers evaluate their own performance, asking themselves the questions already mentioned. They should not be afraid of self-criticism.

When doing this, the evaluating skills used are:

- reflection
- analysis
- drawing conclusions
- planning.

The use of these skills helps improve the way in which activities are performed in the future.

Feedback from supervisor

To help evaluate their tasks, care workers should always consider constructive criticism and guidance from:

- their assessor/tutor
- their peers, e.g. those people who are in our group or class can make suggestions
- service users may give us some indication of how effective we have been.

The feedback advice and guidance received from others can help us to think about any improvements that can be made for the future. This helps improve the quality of care that is provided to service users.

Contribution of tasks to workplace goals

As mentioned earlier, each workplace has a set of agreed goals that it aims to work towards. For example, these could be improved patient care, treatment of more patients, and increased staff retention. Whatever the task is, it must be effective and contribute positively to at least one of the overall goals of the workplace. Activities that have a negative effect on the environment are of little value and are not considered to be consistent with professional behavior. It must be remembered that if a job is worth doing it is worth doing well.

Assessment activity 15.7

Evaluating performance of tasks

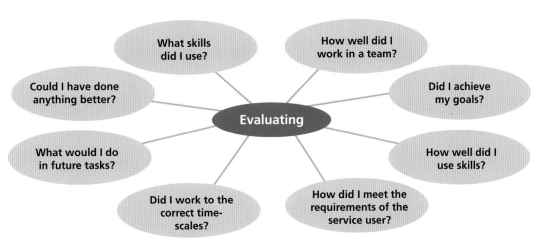

1 Think about the tasks you have undertaken. Reflect on how well you did them in terms of the questions in the figure above. Make a spider diagram or notes to record your thoughts.

2 Think about each task you have undertaken and analyse:
- what did you do?
- how well did you do it?
Make detailed notes to record your thinking.

3 Draw some conclusions about what you did and how well you did it.

4 How could you improve the tasks you did? Make suggestions based on:
- your own thoughts
- feedback comments made by your tutor
- feedback comments made by a supervisor.

5 What was your contribution to workplace goals through carrying out the tasks?

Glossary

Allocating: giving an area of responsibility to someone

Ambiguity: a comment that is very unclear

Amputation: to remove or cut off, e.g. a leg, arm or finger

Anthrax: a dangerous disease caused by the spores (types of seed) of a fungus

Asbestosis: a serious disease of the chest caused by asbestos dust

Asphyxia: to suffocate

Clearly-defined roles: specified jobs for certain people

Compliance: obeying a requirement

Consciousness: the state of being awake

Consultations: to talk to and advise

CPR: Cardiopulmonary Resuscitation; a method for restarting heart and lung operation in an unconscious person

Demoralising: the removal of morale giving a low feeling

Dermatitis: inflammatory disease of the skin

Facilitator: somebody who makes a task more easy to achieve

Factually correct: all evidence being accurate

Folliculitis: inflammation of the base of hair strands

Hepatitis: inflammatory disease of the liver

Hypothermia: dangerous loss of body heat due to cold conditions

Incontinence: to be unable to control your urine and faeces

Legionellosis: a pneumonia-type infection of the chest and lungs

Leptospirosis: a parasitic disease that is contracted from certain animal's faeces, e.g. rat

Litigation: to take someone to court over an issue

Mesothelioma: a very active cancer made up of unusually small cells

Morale: a state of happiness and being in control and on top of everything

Musculo-skeletal: anything related to the muscles and skeleton

Occupational: what one does for work, type of job

Overhead costs: general running expenses for a business such as heating, lighting, rent etc.

Perception: what you think might be happening or going to happen

Physiotherapy: treatment using physical manipulation and movement

Pneumoconiosis: lung disease caused by dust which is eventually fatal

Procrastination: to keep putting off doing something because you do not like it, e.g. your homework

Prosecution: using the court and law to prove a person guilty

Radiography: the production of x-rays

Sanctity of the confessional: confidential information given to a catholic priest at confession that can be told to no-one, not even the police.

Second-guessing: trying to guess what a person might say without them saying it

Sector: a part of an organisation

Sequence: the way that one event should follow another

Sexual harassment: to pester a person for sexual favours

Strategies: different ways of doing things

Tetanus: a disease obtained from bacteria due to a cut that can make the whole body go rigid

Tuberculosis: infectious disease that mainly affects the lungs

Trade union: an organisation that supports workers

Unlawful: an activity that is outside of the law

Vapours: a liquid and gas mixture

Index

childminders 234, 244
Children Act 1989 36–7, 250, 258
chiropodists 285
choice 101, 102–3
    for dressing 116–17, 121–2
    for meals 131–3
    for outings 312
    providing information for 3, 9, 102–3, 131–3
    rights to 3, 101
choking 136, 345–6
Citizens' Advice Bureau 21
clarity of communication 10–11, 32, 58, 74, 357
cleaning procedures 156–9, 161–2
clostridium 145
clothing
    for care work 150–2, 155, 157, 163
    during pregnancy 187
    for early years 222–4, 236
    see also dressing
coaching 333
coeliac disease 236
collage 276
communication 53–5, 55–7, 88–92
    accuracy and clarity 10–11, 32, 58, 357
    barriers 66–7
    effects of the environment 62–6, 87–8, 303
    with older people 299–308, 312
    planning 87–8
    purposes 58–62, 70–1, 87, 90, 303–4, 307
    skills 10, 55, 72–8, 88–92, 300–2, 336
        for conversation 74–5, 80–1, 90–4, 243
        development 200–5, 240–1, 260–1
        evaluation 93–6
        practice 204
    see also information
community rooms 169
complaints procedures 13–14, 20, 38
confidentiality
    legislation 28–30
    of personal information 4, 28–30, 305
    policies and procedures 30–4
    responsibilities for 33, 34, 86, 105, 250
    rights to 4–5, 43, 85
    in the workplace 349
confusion 288
consultation, rights to 9, 342
conversation skills 74–5, 80–1, 90–4, 243
cooking food 148, 163–4
co-operative play 213, 263

co-ordination development 193, 196
copying 201, 202, 203
COSSH Regulations 2002 168
cots 224
crawling 192, 194, 195
creative play 261, 269–70
Criminal Records Bureau checks 252
cross-contamination of food 164, 165
cultures, diverse 23, 25, 82, 105, 249
    and communication 69–70, 83, 204, 300
cuts 343

D
dairy products in the diet 185
data protection 4–5, 21, 28–9, 31, 85, 349–50
day care centres 282–3
day nurseries 233
dementia 287–8
dentists 285
department (line) managers 19, 34, 332
dependency of service users 100, 123–4, 307
depression 288
detergents 161
development areas (P.I.E.S) 183
diet
    and choice 132
    for early years 235–6
    for eating difficulties 131, 132, 236
    for newborn babies 217–18
    for older people 289, 310
    before and during pregnancy 184–5
digestive route of infection 148–9
directors 331
disabilities
    and communication 70, 204, 299
    of older people 291
    post-natal tests for 215
    see also sensory impairment
Disability Discrimination Act 1995 353
discipline, and self-esteem 211
disclosure of information 34
discovery play 261, 270
discrimination profiles 39
discriminatory behaviour 8, 26–8, 82, 83–4, 347
    anti-discrimination policies 25, 26, 37–8, 39
    challenging 14–15, 82
    legislation 353
    racial 37
    recognition 82, 83
    sexual 37–8, 347

teamwork 247–8, 332, 354, 356
temperature
    of cooking 163
    for early years environments 229, 236, 266
    effects on communication 64, 303
    of food storage 163–4, 165
    of sterilisation 157
tests, post-natal 215
theft 17–18
thyroid function test 215
time management 352–3, 361
time-keeping 348
tinea 147
tone of voice 10, 74, 201, 301
trade unions 341–2
training
    on care of older people 309
    on early years care 251
    for fire drills 180
    managers' role in 333
    policies 20
    to reduce risks 170
transfer mats and slings 340
tripods 125
trust hospitals 285
typhoid fever 143, 154

U
unconsciousness
    reporting 340, 341
    treatment 136, 345, 346

V
Velcro 120
ventilation 64, 266, 303
viruses 142, 143–4, 146–7
visits, and intellectual development 203
vocabulary 10
    development 202, 241, 260–1
voluntary care sector 42, 326, 327
vomiting 136

W
walking
    aids 124–5, 129, 291
    development 193, 194, 195
walks, with older people 311–13
wardens 284
washing
    babies 221–2
    baby clothes 223–4
    hands 152, 163
    nappies 220
    see also cleaning procedures; hygiene
waste disposal 158, 165
wheelchairs 126–8, 167
work experience 335
workplace organisation 42, 325, 326–34

Z
Zimmer frames 125, 129